Conducting
Choral
Music

sixth edition

Conducting Choral Music

Robert L. Garretson
Colorado State University
Fort Collins

PRENTICE HALL, *Englewood Cliffs, New Jersey 07632*

Library of Congress Cataloging-in-Publication Data

GARRETSON, ROBERT L.
   Conducting choral music.

   Includes bibliographies and index.
   1. Conducting, Choral.   I. Title.
MT85.G175C6   1988   784.9'63   87-32857
ISBN   0-13-167362-9

Editorial/production supervision: Carole Crouse
Interior design: Joan Stone
Cover design: Ben Santora
Manufacturing buyer: Ray Keating

 © 1988, 1981, 1975, 1970, 1965, 1961 by Prentice-Hall, Inc.
A Division of Simon & Schuster
Englewood Cliffs, New Jersey 07632

Printed in the United States of America

10   9   8   7   6   5   4   3   2

ISBN 0-13-167362-9

PRENTICE-HALL INTERNATIONAL (UK) LIMITED, *London*
PRENTICE-HALL OF AUSTRALIA PTY. LIMITED, *Sydney*
PRENTICE-HALL CANADA, INC., *Toronto*
PRENTICE-HALL HISPANOAMERICANA, S.A., *Mexico*
PRENTICE-HALL OF INDIA PRIVATE LIMITED, *New Delhi*
PRENTICE-HALL OF JAPAN, INC., *Tokyo*
SIMON & SCHUSTER ASIA PTE. LTD., *Singapore*
EDITORA PRENTICE-HALL DO BRASIL, LTDA., *Rio de Janeiro*

Contents

2

Tone and Diction,   59

3

Style and Interpretation,   109

4

Rehearsal Techniques, 153

5

The Jazz/Show Choir,   190

6

Programs and Concerts,   212

7

Planning and Organization,   231

Appendix: Source Information,   270

Index,   343

Preface

This sixth edition of *Conducting Choral Music* begins with the aspiring conductor's most immediate concerns dealing with conducting techniques, progresses through specific and practical matters dealing with the rehearsal of choirs and choruses, and ends with topics pertaining to various planning and managerial procedures.

Portions of all chapters have been revised and elaborated upon and illustrated with additional examples. In particular, information has been added on conducting septuple meter (at fast tempi), developing conducting skills, stretching exercises (prevocalizing warm-ups), maintaining vocal health, Renaissance tone quality, the singers' responsibilities, improving music reading, mental attitudes (of singers), conducting choral/orchestral works, musical terms for the orchestral player/conductor, selecting accompanists, and selecting choir apparel. The list of references at the end of each chapter has been updated; however, a number of older publications that are out of print, but available in libraries, have been retained for the reader who wishes to make some comparative analysis of the ideas presented in choral music texts over the decades. If these books are not available in a nearby library, inquire about obtaining them through their interlibrary loan service. The source information in the Appendix has also been revised and updated, with special attention being given to the chronological list of choral composers, the inclusion of new choral octavo publications and extended choral works, current addresses of music publishers/distributors, sources for obtaining choir apparel and various types of musical equipment, and hand signals for television.

This book is addressed to conductors of school choirs and choruses, to church choir directors, to leaders of community choral groups, and to students who wish to improve their understanding of the art of choral singing. It may also be of interest and help to administrators and other individuals seeking a knowledge of the aims and problems of the choral conductor. Its design and content are intended to deal with the principles and techniques studied in college and university courses in choral conducting, choral methods and materials, and secondary school music.

Results of a study by the author focus attention upon the fact that many choral conductors regard their professional training as inadequate. It was the consensus of a large group of conductors, whose views were sought, that their training should have been of a more practical nature. With this guiding thought in mind, the author has endeavored to present an approach to the solution of particular problems that the conductor is likely to meet, especially during his first few years of conducting experience. Specific practices and techniques have been presented to give the reader the utmost assistance. Since few teaching situations are identical, the inclusion of basic principles will be helpful in increasing the conductor's insight and in providing a general approach for meeting and solving problems as they arise.

Areas of particular concern to the choral conductor and necessary in his professional training are conducting techniques, tone and diction, style and interpretation, rehearsal techniques, the jazz/show choir, programs and concerts, and planning and organization. A chapter, therefore, is devoted to each of these areas. It is hoped that this book, based upon the teaching needs of numerous choral conductors, will contribute to the betterment of choral singing.

The author is well aware that many women are active today as choral conductors, and their contributions to choral music education in schools, churches, and community groups are well known. Throughout the book, however, the reader will note the use of the words *he, his,* and *him* when reference is made to "the director." No denigration of women is meant; the style was adopted because the words appear so frequently that use of *he and she* or *him and her* throughout would have resulted in awkward writing and difficult reading.

Many persons have contributed to the author's concepts as presented in this book. Some of the ideas have been formulated through observation and discussion with choral conductors throughout the country. The techniques suggested have crystallized during the author's application of them while working with various groups: with school choirs and choruses, church choirs, and choral groups on the university level. To all concerned—conductors and singers—I express my gratitude.

For permission to use excerpts from their choral publications, I am indebted to the following music publishers: Art Masters Studios, Inc., Augsburg Publishing House, Belwin Mills Publishing Corp., Boosey & Hawkes, Inc., Broude Brothers, Ltd., Galaxy Music Corp., Hinshaw Music, Inc., Neil A. Kjos Music Co., Edward B. Marks Music Corp., MCA Music, Inc., Otto Heinrich Noetzel Verlag (Wilhelmshaven BRD), Plymouth Music Co., Theodore Presser Co., G. Ricordi & Co., E. C. Schirmer Music Co., G. Schirmer, Inc., Shawnee Press, Inc., Walton Music Corp., and World Library Publications.

For permission to quote from their publications, I express appreciation to Oxford University Press, W. W. Norton & Co., Inc., *The NATS Bulletin,* Harcourt Brace Jovanovich, Inc., and Macmillan (London and Basingstoke).

To friends and colleagues Lon Lee, Robert Conlon, M.D., Eph Ehly, John Lueck, James McCray, Willfred Schwartz, Robert Molison, Ron Revier, and Herb Goodrich for their helpful suggestions I am especially indebted, and to my wife, Aretha, who typed the manuscript and has offered continual encouragement, I am particularly grateful.

R.L.G.

Introduction

During the twentieth century, particularly since World War I, choral singing has assumed a position of increasing importance and popularity in our society. School and college choirs and choruses, church choirs, community choruses, and choruses sponsored by industrial and commercial firms have increased in size and in quality. Individuals are quite naturally drawn to activities that they enjoy. Let us, however, examine some of the underlying reasons for this increase and development of choral singing.

Considerable credit should be given schools and colleges for this phenomenal growth. In the past several decades choral music has progressed from a largely extracurricular activity to an integral part of the school curriculum. This would not have occurred without at least some degree of recognition of the values of music participation. Without attempting an exhaustive consideration of these values, for our purpose they may be summarized as follows.

Although the benefits of choral singing are many, the *aesthetic* and *expressive* values of music are considered to be the most important. All persons need to develop a sensitivity to beauty in music and other art forms, because understanding and appreciation of them may serve to refine and humanize their entire existence. As music is a significant and an integral part of man's culture, it is the school's responsibility to help students become more intelligent consumers of music. Participation in musical activities can serve as a means through which individual musical taste may be improved. Through a study of the vast wealth of music literature, students may learn to discriminate between the musically trite and the rich musical heritage that is the right and the privilege of every individual. All people have a need for individual self-expression in as many varied ways as possible. Although many concepts and ideas may be expressed through language, other aspects of one's experience can be best expressed through various other art forms. The aesthetic and expressive values of music are, therefore, the principal justifications for its inclusion in the school curriculum.

The *personal-social* values of choral singing also deserve consideration. All individuals need opportunity to engage in activities that promote physical development and that feeling of well-being which is characteristic of good mental health. Music participation can contribute to these ends. Correct posture and proper breathing techniques are emphasized as an adjunct of choral singing and are a necessary attainment of the well-trained choral group. Music also serves as a wholesome outlet for and expression of individual emotions. Through music, individuals not only can express themselves, but also can release pent-up feelings of frustration so common in our present-day society.

By contributing time and talent to various social organizations, and through being accepted by other members of such groups, people fulfill their need "to belong": Their social beings find expression. A characteristic of the adolescent, as he or she strives to become a social being, is the strong desire to belong to the "gang," inasmuch as membership in various groups usually results in satisfaction and acceptance by members of the peer group. Through cooperative group endeavor, the chorus or choir provides additional opportunity for the development of democratic attitudes and a wholesome channeling of interests toward members of the opposite sex. Students in music activities develop pride in being identified with a fine musical organization and make many social adjustments through the close association with their peers. Certain critics of present-day society say that it has become too individually oriented and that what we need are activities necessitating more group effort. Choral singing certainly fulfills this need.

Finally, and not to be overlooked, are the *avocational* and *vocational* values that accrue from music participation. Changes in the attitudes of our society, coupled with many modern living improvements, have resulted in a greater amount of leisure time for most individuals. These changes are highly desirable and offer increased opportunity for individuals to explore many possible areas. As a result of improved educational programs, many people have discovered music to be an area from which they may derive great personal enjoyment and satisfaction. If continuing programs of music instruction are to be maintained in our society, vocational needs must also be met. In addition to a teaching career, opportunities exist in the area of professional music. If one is to be eminently successful in these areas of endeavor, knowledge and skills must be developed at a reasonably early age.

Many institutions other than schools have contributed to influencing the status of choral music. Increasing awareness of the importance of music as a force in religious worship has resulted in a resurgence of emphasis upon church music programs. An increasing number of churches employ people full-time people to assume responsibility for the development of the music program. Often these individuals carry the title of Minister of Music, and in effect their duties reflect this title. Choirs for children of elementary school age, for junior and senior high school youth, and for adults are maintained to meet the musical and social needs of all age groups.

Industry's increasing awareness of the importance of rapport in a cohesive, closely knit organization has prompted the establishment of numerous company choruses and other related music activities. Under capable leadership, these organizations have improved employees' morale, developed a feeling of belonging, improved labor and management relationships, and through periodic concerts have strengthened community ties.

The media of radio, television, motion pictures, and recordings have considerably influenced the tastes of the listening public in recent years. Radio has promoted greater understanding and has brought various sections of the country closer together. Remote and isolated areas have reaped a particular benefit. Music of many types has been made available to interested listeners at a minimum cost. Many FM stations, in particular, continue to present music of a high quality.

The impact of television has been overwhelming, but its cumulative effects have not been fully evaluated. Although an increase in the quality and the quantity of musical programs seems desirable, a limited number of excellent programs are being presented. Forward-looking teachers have brought these programs to their students' attention and have used them as a valuable educational tool.

Some choirs and choruses have been fortunate enough to make periodic appearances on television. Such experiences, by motivating a choral organization toward maximum group effort, can contribute substantially to the attainment of higher musical standards. The increased use of videotape for such programs also provides a choral group with opportunities to observe and to evaluate the visual as well as the musical aspects of their performance. Educational television especially has utilized the talents of amateur choral groups, and has presented a number of other programs designed to promote musical understanding and appreciation. Since choral music programs may be televised with a minimum of staging and production costs, further possibilities will undoubtedly be explored in the future.

Music serves effectively to heighten the intensity of dramatic situations in motion pictures; and the public is currently experiencing a barrage of tonal sounds and effects associated with theatrical and television productions and the modern dance. Although choral music per se has been too infrequently featured, this background music has perhaps to some extent developed a general awareness of a variety of vocal tone qualities and instrumental tone colors.

Recorded music, especially since the advent of the long-playing record, has made available to the listening public more music of a high quality than ever before. Numerous recordings of college and university choirs, church choirs, and professional choruses from the United States and Europe are presently available. Previously produced recordings of choral organizations number in the hundreds, and new recordings are being released periodically. Especially strong interest was developed with the advent of high-fidelity and stereophonic recordings. Although some of this interest may stem from mechanical or engineering factors, rather than musical aspects, this development has been generally beneficial to the improvement of musical tastes. Inherent in choral recordings are tremendous educational possibilities that, if effectively utilized in educational programs, may further improve the quality of choral singing in America.

Choral music has grown considerably and is still growing in America. However, the previously discussed influences are bound to reap a desirable cumulative harvest. Capable and inspired leadership—emphasizing wide participation and high musical standards—will ultimately place choral music in its proper sphere as a social and an aesthetic art.

1

Conducting Techniques

The basic function of the conductor is to interpret the music for the singers. Through varied means he* endeavors to instill life and vitality into the music—the result of which can be a truly thrilling and genuinely aesthetic experience for both the participants and the listening audience.

The conductor must be more than a mere time beater. His musical knowledge and interpretative wishes should be conveyed through his conducting technique. Of course, the importance of demonstrations and verbal explanations should not be minimized, but during rehearsals, lengthy verbal explanations should be kept to a minimum. It is through his *technique*[1] that the experienced conductor can more quickly help the group achieve the desired interpretation.

FUNDAMENTAL CONDUCTING PATTERNS

Each conductor is likely to have his own methods, but the fundamental patterns are the same. The student conductor should practice the basic

---

*To avoid clumsy and awkward language, the generic masculine is used throughout the book, without prejudice, when referring to "the conductor."

[1]*Technique* in this context refers to the multitude of devices used by a conductor to convey the intent of the music and to achieve musical and artistic results. Fundamental conducting patterns, important as they are, are really subservient to the bodily and facial expressions that reflect the mood of the music. Nevertheless, they provide a necessary basis from which to start.

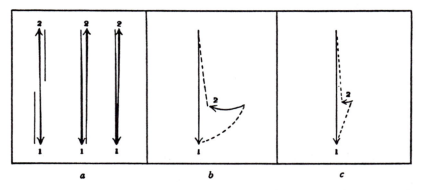

FIGURE 1 Duple meter (2/4, 2/2, 2/8): (a) the general direction of the pattern (i.e., down, up), (b) the pattern for slower tempi, and (c) the pattern for faster tempi.

movements until they become automatic. For the purpose of clarification, each of the basic meter patterns, as illustrated in Figures 1–5, is presented in at least two ways. The first diagram in each figure indicates the basic direction of the beats within the pattern. The subsequent patterns illustrate the manner in which the conductor may apply them in the interpretation of music. The dotted lines in these conducting diagrams are called *rebounds* or *afterstrokes*. Although they should be considered subordinate to the basic movements within the pattern, they serve as connecting motions between the various beats and as preparatory motions to each subsequent beat. A degree of tension should occur toward the end, or point, of each beat, which is followed by a degree of relaxation during the rebound. Combined, these factors serve to give the conducting movements definition, clarity, and smoothness or flow—all of which are essential to artistic conducting.

In conducting fast tempi in triple meter (Figure 2c), the second and third beats are negated or omitted, and only the first or primary beat is utilized. In such instances, a slight pause generally occurs at the bottom of this beat; however, the faster the tempo, the less opportunity for pause.

The pattern for conducting quadruple meter is illustrated in Figure 3. Diagram *a* illustrates only the general directions of the beats (down, left, right, up), whereas *b* illustrates how the pattern may be utilized with music of a moderate tempo in a legato style. Note that, following the downbeat and the initial rebound, beats two, three, and four are conducted on a horizontal plane, with the rebound of the fourth beat returning to one. A pitfall into which the young conductor often falls is using a beat that is too "rounded" in style, with the third beat sometimes rebounding too high, so as to appear as an additional

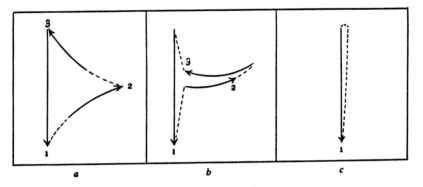

FIGURE 2 Triple meter (3/4, 3/8, 3/2: (a) the basic directions of the pattern, (b) application of the pattern for moderately slow and medium tempi, and (c) pattern for fast 3/4 or 3/8 tempi.

downbeat in the measure. Thus the conducting pattern is often unclear and confusing to the singers. In summary, keep beats two, three, and four on a horizontal plane.

Three different patterns for conducting sextuple meter are presented in Figures 4–6. In Figure 4, diagram *a* illustrates the general directions of the pattern, and diagram *b* illustrates how the pattern may be applied in the conducting of actual music. Many conductors prefer such a pattern because the fourth beat is clearly defined with a movement in a direction opposite from the first three beats and from the gradual stepwise return to the next downbeat.

Figure 5, however, illustrates an alternative pattern, with one clear downbeat and the other beats indicated on a somewhat horizontal plane. Pattern *a* illustrates the general directions of the beats, whereas pattern *b*

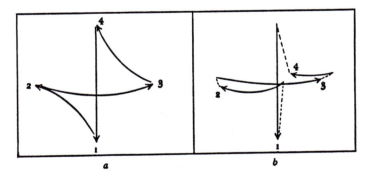

FIGURE 3 Quadruple meter (4/4, 4/2): (a) the basic directions of the pattern, and (b) application of the pattern to music of a moderate tempo.

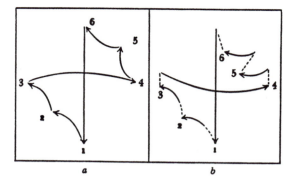

FIGURE 4   Sextuple meter (6/8, 6/4): (*a*) the basic directions of the pattern, and (*b*) application of the pattern to music of a moderate tempo.

illustrates how the movements might be applied in the conducting of actual music. The advantage of this pattern is simply that there can be no doubt that there is only one downbeat in the measure.

Still another alternative is illustrated in Figure 6. The advantage of this pattern is the similarity in the direction of the fourth beat. In pattern *a*, six beats are indicated; in pattern *b*, the secondary beats—that is, two, three, five, and six—are negated or omitted so that the pattern may be adapted for use with faster tempi. Because of the similar direction of the primary beats (one and four), the conductor may more easily alternate between one pattern and the other. This flexibility allows the movements in Figure 6 to be used with music involving irregular or changing tempi.

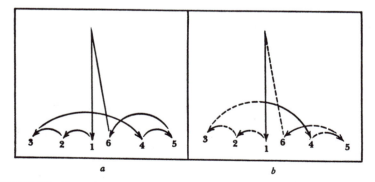

FIGURE 5   Sextuple meter (6/8, 6/4): (*a*) the basic directions of the pattern, and (*b*) application of the pattern to music of a moderate tempo. Note that all beats, with the exception of the downbeat, are on about the same plane, and the pattern may be used as an alternative to Figure 4.

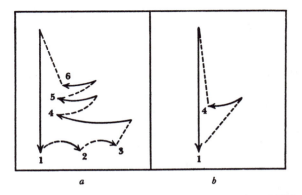

FIGURE 6 Sextuple meter (6/8, 6/4): (*a*) for slower tempi, and (*b*) for faster tempi.

IRREGULAR METER

Music in irregular meter—that is, 5/4, 7/4, and so on—may be analyzed in combinations of two and three, or three and two, and three and four, or four and three, depending on the strong and weak syllables of the text structure. Irregular meter occurs rather infrequently in choral music; when it is encountered, however, it is suggested that the conductor generally utilize combinations of the duple, triple, and quadruple meters previously presented. For example, "Nächtens" ("Nightly") by Johannes Brahms (G. Schirmer, No. 10133), written in 5/4 meter, should be conducted throughout by combining duple- and triple-meter patterns (Figure 7). The second downbeat, however, should be conducted on a slightly lower plane so as not to elicit any undue stress on the third beat of the measure. (Actually, the movement should not even be considered as a downbeat, since the gesture for this beat is very small and implies or evokes no particular stress. In contrast, a real downbeat begins from a higher plane, the movement has greater length, and through supporting facial expressions and body gestures elicits a particular degree of stress and intensity.)

In "To Agni" (from the *Rig Veda*) by Gustav Holst, also written in 5/4 meter, every other measure should be conducted with a triple- and duple-meter pattern, and alternate measures with a duple and a triple pattern.[2]

---

[2]To develop alertness and the flexibility to move from one meter pattern to another, practice conducting the following sequence of changing meters:

2/4, 3/4, 4/4, 5/4, 6/4, 7/4

Devise various other combinations of patterns to conduct, and write them on the chalkboard. Another alternative is for one person, through various hand signals, to indicate a changing and varying sequence of patterns.

FIGURE 7   Excerpt from "Nächtens" by Johannes Brahms (Op. 112, No. 2) in 5/4 meter, which may be conducted by combining duple- and triple-meter patterns. Copyright G. Schirmer, Inc., 1953. Used by permission.

Occasional exceptions, however, to the use of such patterns may be encountered. For example, in measure 19 of "Walking on the Green Grass" by Michael Hennagin (Boosey & Hawkes, No. 5443), the rhythmic notation is $\frac{5}{4}$ ♪ ♪ ♩. ♪ | and should be analyzed not as 2 + 3, or 3 + 2, but as 1 + 4. This becomes apparent in examining the score, and one should be guided by the dictates of the music. Thus the conductor should employ a downbeat, followed by another downbeat on a lower plane and a regular 4/4 pattern.

MUSIC IN FREE RHYTHM

Occasionally the conductor will encounter music without a time signature and measure bars, and seemingly without any regular or systematic rhythmic accent or pulsation. In such instances it is desirable to conduct all the beats downward, with the exception of the last beat in the phrase, which generally should be upward. The beginning of the phrase should receive a regular precise downbeat; the subsequent words should be treated with a slight downward movement, varying in length according to the relative importance of the words. In determining the frequency and the appropriate size of the downward movements, the conductor should carefully analyze the text of the music. The final measures of "Our Father" by Alexander Gretchaninov (Presser, No. 332-13000) necessitate this type of conducting treatment (Figure 8).[3] The downward movements are indicated under the music.

SUBDIVIDED BEATS

In conducting music of a moderate tempo, the conductor may utilize effectively the patterns previously illustrated. However, as these patterns are applied to slower tempi, there comes a point where the precision of the beat may become lost and the pattern becomes relatively ineffective. The solution to this problem, therefore, is not simply to slow the beat down further, but to subdivide the beats within the pattern so that in effect they *consume more time by moving through more space.* Through this means, the rhythmic pulsations of the conductor's patterns become more marked and are distinguished by greater clarity; as a result, he is able to obtain a higher degree of precision from the group. When the music is of an exceptionally slow tempo, often indicated by the musical markings *largo* and *grave,* the conductor generally should employ the divided beat to clarify his intentions.

Two well-known examples of choral music that necessitate use of the subdivided beat, as illustrated in Figure 9, are "Crucifixus" (from the B Minor Mass) by Johann S. Bach (E. C. Schirmer, No. 1174) and "Surely He Hath Borne Our Griefs" (from *Messiah*) by George F. Handel (G. Schirmer, No. 6598). Excerpts from these selections are shown in Figures 10 and 11.

A subdivision of the conducting beat may also be desirable when the rhythmic movement of a particular passage needs to be emphasized or brought out, and during a ritardando, when the rhythmic precision

---

[3]Other examples of music in free rhythm are "Glory Be to God" by Rachmaninoff (Kjos; H. W. Gray), "Gladsome Radiance" by Gretchaninov (H. W. Gray), and "To Thee We Sing," Russian liturgy, arr. Tkach (Kjos).

FIGURE 8 The final measures of Gretchaninov's "Our Father," with all but the last beat in the phrase conducted downward. Copyright 1916, Oliver Ditson Company. Used by permission.

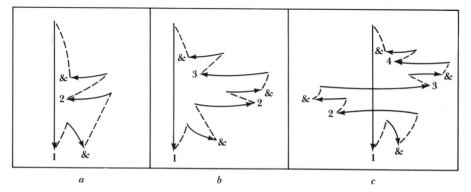

a   *b*   *c*

FIGURE 9 (*a*) Subdivided duple meter, (*b*) subdivided triple meter, and (*c*) subdivided quadruple meter.

FIGURE 10 Excerpt from "Crucifixus" (from the B Minor Mass) by J. S. Bach, which should be conducted with a subdivided triple-meter pattern.

of the group needs to be stabilized. Such instances are likely to occur at the ends of phrases and in the final few measures of a composition. However, any of the beats within a given measure may be subdivided if the tempo of the selection allows sufficient time for the additional movements. The subdivided beat should not be utilized unless there is adequate time for the rebound of the subdivided or second half of the beat, as well as for the rebound for the principal beat strokes. Figure 12 offers a case in point, and the correct treatment depends upon the tempo being utilized. Thus, if the tempo were approximately M.M. $\quad = 54$, the use of the subdivided beat as illustrated in Figure 12*a* would be most appropri-

FIGURE 11 From the introduction to "Surely He Hath Borne Our Griefs" (from *Messiah*) by G. F. Handel, in which the subdivided quadruple-meter pattern should be used.

Near - er   come we _   now — Let   your mus   cles   bend.

FIGURE 12 "Volga Boatmen" (folk song). In conducting the final measure, shown here, pattern *a* is utilized with very slow tempi, pattern *b* with moderate tempi.

ate. On the other hand, if the music were being conducted at approximately M.M. $\quad$ = 70, the added motion of the divided beat would undoubtedly detract from the clarity of the conductor's movements. In this and similar cases involving moderate tempi, it is suggested that the conductor avoid the subdivided beat pattern and simply accentuate the rebound of beats one and two, as illustrated in Figure 12*b*. In this treatment a slight pause should occur at the end of each rebound prior to the stroke of the subsequent beat. This serves to accentuate the rhythmic movement of the divided beat.

Where he has a choice of the preceding alternatives, the conductor should thoughtfully consider the tempo of the music and the conducting pattern appropriate to the music's most effective interpretation.[4]

ATTACKS AND RELEASES

To be effective, attacks and releases must be executed by the entire ensemble at precisely the same time. To achieve this precision, the group must be alert, it must respond to the rhythmic pulsation of the music, and the conductor must give a clear and precise preparatory beat or movement for each attack or release.

[4]For further discussion of tempo, see section titled "Determining the Tempo" later in this chapter.

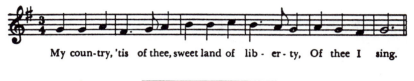

My coun-try,'tis of thee,sweet land of lib - er- ty, Of thee I   sing.

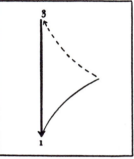

FIGURE 13   "America" by Henry Carey. The preparatory beat for the attack is indicated by the dotted line preceding the first beat.

The preparatory beat should always be given at the same rate of
speed as that desired in the subsequent measures. Prior to beginning a
selection, the conductor should thoughtfully consider his desired tempo
and the appropriate preparatory movement. This is especially important
to the beginning conductor; later, as one gains experience, this process
becomes somewhat automatic in nature. In general, the preparatory
beat should approximate the direction of the movement preceding the
beat upon which the music begins. For example, if the music begins on
the first beat of a measure in quadruple meter, the preparatory movement should occur in the fourth beat preceding and should be made in
the same general direction of the beat utilized for the standard conducting pattern for quadruple meter. Of course, when the music begins on
the first beat of a measure in triple meter, the preparatory movement
will occur on the third beat preceding the downbeat or actual attack
(Figure 13).

Effective and precise attacks depend not only on adequate preparatory movements executed by the hand and arm, but also on an alert
physical stance of the body and appropriate facial expressions. The attack is facilitated if the conductor is alert to the readiness of the singers,
breathes with the group during the preparatory movement, and mouths
the words in the first measure or so of the text.

One must also prepare adequately for releases if any degree of
precision is to be achieved. A slight upward movement is usually sufficient as a preparatory motion to the actual release, which is generally a

precise downward or sideways movement. The size of these movements (the preparation and the actual release) should coincide with the mood of the music and the general size of the conducting pattern being utilized. That is, the preparation and the release of music of a soft, subdued nature will demand a shorter upward preparation and downstroke, whereas the release of a dramatic *fortissimo* passage will necessitate a larger upward movement and a longer, deeper downstroke for an effective and a precise release.

The preceding general rules are particularly appropriate for a release at the end of a selection, for phrases with some degree of finality, or for those followed by a slight pause. The conductor should use a modified technique, however, for many of the phrases within the "heart" of a choral selection—particularly when the last note or chord in a phrase needs to be extended to its maximum value and quickly released, with the group "grabbing" a quick catchbreath before the attack of the subsequent phrase. A suggested movement to utilize in such cases is to simply turn the palm of the hand over and close it. This movement has been likened to "turning off a water faucet." In certain musical selections one or more of the parts may need to be "cut off" while the others are sustained. When these voice parts are to the conductor's right, this subtle release may be done with the right hand; when they are to the conductor's left, the left hand may be used for the release, while the basic conducting pattern is continued with the right hand.

Attacks on Incomplete Measures

Problems in achieving precise, accurate attacks most frequently occur when dealing with *incomplete measures*. Following are several variants and suggested techniques for dealing with each.

1. When a composition begins on a full or complete beat, the conductor should prepare the group by conducting the preceding beat as a preparatory movement. For example, when in quadruple meter the music begins on the fourth beat, the conductor should utilize the third beat as the preparatory movement (Figure 14).
2. When a composition begins on the second half of the beat, the first half of the beat is given as the preparation (Figure 15).
3. When a composition begins after the second half of the beat and is closer to the following than to the preceding beat, then use a full or complete beat as the preparatory movement according to rule 1 (Figure 16).

It will be noted that no special treatment is utilized in Figure 16 for the sixteenth note preceding the fourth beat. Since this note falls more closely to the following (fourth) beat than to the preceding (third) beat, the same preparatory movement is utilized as that for any music begin-

Oh beau - ti- ful for spa- cious skies for am- ber waves of grain,

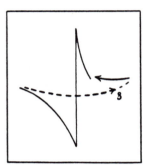

FIGURE 14 "America, the Beautiful" by Samuel A. Ward. The preparatory beat is indicated by the dotted line preceding the fourth beat.

ning on a full or complete beat (compare the diagram in Figure 16 with that suggested for use with "America, the Beautiful" [Figure 14]).

An exception to the treatment of a sixteenth note occurs with the note following the fermata in Figure 17.

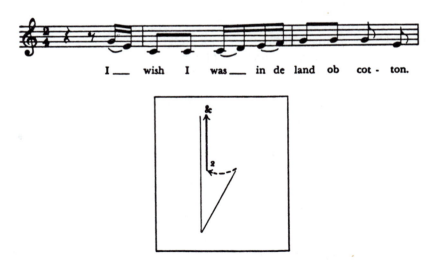

I __ wish I was __ in de land ob cot - ton.

FIGURE 15 "Dixie" by Daniel Emmett. The preparatory beat is indicated by the dotted line.

Ye   sons   of   France, a -   wake   to   glo -   ry!

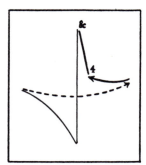

FIGURE 16   "La Marseillaise" (French national anthem) by Rouget de Lisle. The preparatory beat is indicated by the dotted line preceding the fourth beat.

De __ sun so   hot I   froze to death, Su- san-na don't you   cry.

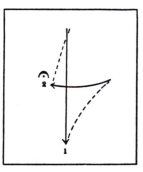

FIGURE 17   Excerpt from "Oh! Susanna" by Stephen Foster. The preparatory movement (following the fermata) is the upward motion that precedes the first beat of the following measure.

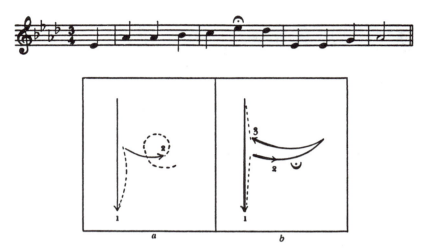

FIGURE 18   "Flow Gently, Sweet Afton." Two procedures for releasing the fermata: (*a*) complete release, and (*b*) carryover.

FERMATAS

One should prepare for all *fermatas,* or holds, if precision in performance is to be expected; that is, the movements preceding the fermata should be especially clear, concise, and definite. When a slight ritardando precedes the fermata, as is often the case, the conductor should slightly enlarge the pattern of his beat as a means of gaining attention and preparing the group for the fermata. Raising the plane or height of the beat on which the fermata occurs is often helpful when the group is sustaining a *forte* passage. This is not always necessary, however, when the group is singing *piano.*[5]

During the hold, the conductor should continue a slow, steady movement of the beat and avoid a stationary position in midair. Musical tone is continuing—not static—and this suggested slight movement will assist the singers in maintaining an even, steady flow of breath necessary for adequate tonal support.

The release of the fermata, or hold, is as important as the preparation, and either of two procedures may be utilized, depending upon the interpretative effect desired. One procedure is to cut off completely the tone following the hold; the alternative is to carry over the tone to the succeeding phrase without a break in the flow of the breath. The conducting patterns for these two procedures are illustrated in Figure 18.

[5]When singing softly there is a tendency for singers to lessen the breath support, thus causing intonation problems. To avoid this difficulty, singers should have the illusion of using more and not less energy when singing softly.

UNIFYING THE TECHNIQUE

As soon as the beginning conductor has a knowledge of the basic patterns, he must begin to apply them in ways that are meaningfully related to the music and at the same time endeavor to integrate them into his total conducting technique. Various factors need to be carefully considered at this point, including correct posture, surety of beat patterns, facial expressions that reflect the mood of the music, coordination of the movements of the wrist, elbow, and hand, and even whether or not to use a baton.

Body Attitudes

The correct posture of a choral conductor can be described as "a body position that enables the conductor to most effectively achieve his task." In this sense, the posture resembles somewhat the "correct" posture of the singer (see Figure 40 in Chapter 2): One foot is placed several inches ahead of the other and the feet are spread apart to provide a solid foundation; this position allows the conductor to remain alert and responsive to the musical situation.[6] Conducting gestures or movements should occur only in the upper body. From the waistline down, the body should generally be stationary. This does not preclude occasionally moving closer to the group during rehearsals or moving from one side of the room to the other to assist various sections. But, for the most part, and certainly during a concert, the conductor should *stand still*. On the podium the conductor should assert a necessary degree of forcefulness, based on a knowledge and surety of the music, and should endeavor to communicate the composer's intentions to the singers. Shyness, coyness, and the like are characteristics that must be masked and that should give way to clarity and definition.

One pitfall to which beginning conductors often succumb is the tendency to merely "draw" the patterns in the air in a somewhat mechanical way. To minimize this tendency, conductors should study the music carefully, identifying the various tensions created through rhythmic and harmonic movement and letting them be reflected in their conducting. Conducting thus becomes a real means of communicating musical ideas to a group of singers and not merely a mechanical exercise.

Facial expressions should reflect the mood or character of the music. In short, the best advice that could be given is to endeavor to "look like the music." Regular practice before a full-length mirror will reap dividends for conductors desirous of improving this aspect of conducting technique.

---

[6]When the feet are in this position, the conductor should be careful not to rock back and forth, or to bend the upper body too far forward. Should either of these situations occur, it may be helpful to place the feet in a more parallel position.

Self-Analysis

It is essential that undesirable traits be eliminated in the beginning stages and not be allowed to become reinforced and habitual. Following are some specific points of which young conductors should take careful note.

1. The wrist should be held firm, because any looseness or floppiness is distracting and lessens the clarity of the point of each beat.
2. The elbows should be flexible and not held too closely to the body, since freedom of movement is inhibited. They should at least be high enough to allow the palms of the hands to face the floor. Conversely, the elbows should not be extended too far outward because that also is distracting.
3. The fingers should be held close together. With young conductors there may be a tendency to spread them somewhat apart, and this is not only distracting, but sometimes even humorous to the singers. Spread fingers have been referred to as "Dracula" hands, and an extended little finger has been referred to as the "teacup hand position."
4. Most of the time, one should conduct primarily in front of the body so that the singers can perceive the conductor's beat patterns or gestures as related to his facial expressions and thus integrate them into a whole. Extended movements to one side of the body may be utilized for a special purpose only, but they should be the exception rather than the rule.
5. The conductor should maintain eye contact with the singers to the greatest extent possible and should never "bury his nose" in the music. It is essential to maintain eye contact at the beginning and ending of phrases, at fermatas, and during any change of tempo. The conductor should be familiar enough with the music that he needs to use it only as an occasional reference point.

If a conductor could view himself as others see him, many problems would be eliminated or at least minimized. This is possible, of course, on a videotape recording: The various points just mentioned become not only more meaningful, but sometimes also shockingly real. It is essential for the young conductor striving for proficiency to practice on specific aspects of technique on a daily basis. Practicing in front of a mirror is helpful, but it is of even greater benefit for two persons to pair off, to practice conducting each other alternately, and then to provide immediate "feedback" or reaction to the other's conducting.

Use of a Baton

Whether or not to use a baton is largely a matter of personal taste; however, for the beginning conductor use of a baton has a distinct advantage in that it helps to delineate the point of each beat to a greater extent, thus providing a degree of necessary and desirable discipline. The baton serves as an extension of the hand and arm and is helpful in working with larger groups, particularly with a large chorus or orchestra, or both.

The advantage of using the hands only—rather than a baton—is that the conductor is able to achieve a somewhat more fluid and flexible beat. This is particularly advantageous in legato sections of a piece. Some conductors, however, have been known to use both techniques with a particular choral work—a baton when conducting the larger choral and orchestral forces and the hands only during a more subdued, legato choral section of a work. A choral conductor who anticipates working with combined choral and instrumental organizations would be well advised to develop an adequate baton technique.

DETERMINING THE TEMPO

Performing a musical work in the proper tempo is an important aspect of artistic interpretation. In the process of determining a tempo, the conductor should consider a number of factors.

Style and Historical Period

Any consideration of tempo should begin with an analysis of the musical style and the characteristics of the historical period from which the music was an outgrowth. Artistic forms of expression are shaped by various social, economic, and political forces that influence a composer during his life. Tempo, therefore, as well as other interpretative considerations, should reflect the basic spirit of the times. (For a discussion of tempo during the various historical periods, see Chapter 3.)

Changes between historical periods were not abrupt, but evolved slowly. Within a given period, one may find unique differences among the styles of individual composers. With a concept of the general characteristics of particular periods as a starting point, the conductor should carefully analyze the style of the composer whose music he is preparing to perform. Although such a procedure may seem like a never-ending task, all efforts in this direction will contribute to a clearer understanding of the essential factors influencing interpretation.

Metronome Markings

Some music will contain metronome markings indicating the desired tempo of the composer or the arranger. The metronome marking indicates the number of beats occurring within the duration of a minute, and the type of note that receives this basic pulsation. For example, the abbreviation M.M. ♩ = 60 indicates that 60 quarter notes may be sounded in the duration of one minute, or 1 quarter note each second.[7] If the metronome marking were M.M. $\quarternote$ = 120, the tempo would be double that of the previous tempo, and 120 quarter notes would be sounded in the duration of one minute, or 2 quarter notes each second. Prior to introducing a new selection to the group, it is desirable for the conductor to check his own tempo concept with that indicated by the metronome marking. Although such markings need not be slavishly followed, they can be helpful in providing the conductor with a basis for determining his ultimately desired tempo.

Tempo Markings

Although not all composers include metronome markings on their music, many will indicate the approximate desired tempo through the use of appropriate words, sometimes in English, but usually in Italian. Following is a basic group of Italian terms that the conductor is most likely to encounter.

Very slow:	*Largo*—large, broad, stately
	Grave—heavy, slow, ponderous
Slow:	*Larghetto*—slow (the diminutive of *largo*)
	Lento—slow
	Adagio—slow, leisurely
Moderate:	*Andante*—moderately slow, at a walking pace
	Moderato—moderate (tempo)
Moderately fast:	*Allegretto*—quite lively, moderately fast
Fast:	*Allegro*—lively, brisk, fast
	Vivace—brisk, spirited
Very fast:	*Presto*—very fast, rapid
	Prestissimo—as fast as possible

Although these Italian terms are only relative indications of tempo, they do provide the conductor with a general basis for determining the approximate tempo suggested by the composer or the editor. Equally important, however, are those terms indicating a change in the basic tempo. Some of the more common terms are

Accelerando—gradually increasing in tempo

Ritardando—gradually decreasing in tempo

Rallentando—gradually decreasing in tempo

Allargando—gradual broadening of tempo, with slight increase in volume

Calando—gradual decrease in tempo and volume

---

[7]The metronome, a mechanical device used to indicate a particular desired tempo, was invented in 1916 by Maelzel, hence the name Maelzel Metronome, or the abbreviation M.M.

Stringendo—gradually increasing in tempo and excitement
A poco a poco—little by little, gradually
Poco meno mosso—a little slower
Poco più mosso—a little faster
A tempo—return to the original tempo

In addition to the preceding terms, the conductor will encounter many others, particularly those pertaining to musical expression. Until the conductor becomes thoroughly acquainted with all such markings, it is suggested that he maintain, for quick and easy reference, a standard dictionary of musical terms.

Mood of the Text

A thorough study of the mood of the text will provide additional insight in determining the most desirable tempo. An excerpt from the Christmas spiritual "Go Tell It on the Mountain" (Galaxy, No. 1532) is included for illustrative purposes (Figure 19).

The author has heard this spiritual performed at various tempi, ranging from approximately M.M. ♩ = 60 to M.M. ♩ = 130. With such a wide variance in tempi, just what should be the conductor's guiding criterion? Although the mood of some spirituals is somber and serious, the text of this particular one describes the joyous, happy news that "Jesus Christ is born!" With this prevailing thought in mind, the author is inclined to select a beginning tempo of approximately M.M. ♩ = 100. The tempo of contrasting sections within the music, however, should be considered separately in light of the prevailing mood of the text.

FIGURE 19   "Go Tell It on the Mountain" (Christmas spiritual). Copyright © 1945, 1973 by Galaxy Music Corporation. Used by permission.

Ability of the Singers

The complexity of various vocal lines and the harmonic aspects of the music are highly important factors in determining the correct tempo. Certainly the skill with which the singers can execute a difficult florid passage must be considered. For singers with limited technique, it is a far better practice to perform a selection at a slightly slower tempo than the metronome markings might indicate or than one might wish, and to sing it *well,* rather than in a slovenly, unmusical manner. Folk-song arrangements that are straightforward in nature can often be sung at a more rapid tempo, without sacrificing tonal stability, than can music with an unusual harmonic treatment.

Acoustics of the Performance Room

The acoustical properties of the rehearsal room or the auditorium have a telling influence upon the total musical effectiveness of a selection. In comparison with instruments, the human voice—especially that of an inexperienced singer—has less sustaining quality. In rooms with little reverberation, a lifeless tonal quality, with an insufficient connection between various tones within the musical phrase, will often result. In such instances music may sound best at a slightly faster tempo than one would normally use in an auditorium or a room with reasonably good acoustics. Conversely, the conductor will find it desirable to employ restraint when rehearsing or performing in rooms with exceptionally live acoustical properties.

ACHIEVING EXPRESSIVE CONDUCTING

In developing one's conducting technique, the fundamental patterns merely provide a necessary basis from which to begin. The conductor must also consider such matters as the conducting plane or height of the beat, the size of the beat in relationship to tempo and dynamics, clarifying the beat, the style of the beat in relationship to the manner of articulation, preparing for changes in tempo and dynamics, the length of the musical phrase, the use of the left hand, and the cueing of entrances.

The Conducting Plane

The level of the conducting beat is determined by the size of the musical organization and the eye level of the singers. If the size of the organization is reasonably small and if the group is seated on risers, the plane of the conductor's beat, for the most part, should be from the shoulder level down to the waist. If the musical organization is exceptionally large, the conductor will find it desirable to raise the conducting plane slightly so that all singers may clearly see his beat.

The conducting plane may be raised or lowered to effectively indicate the shape of a phrase or an increase and decrease of phrasewise tension within the musical phrase. The choral selection "A Thought like Music" by Brahms (Plymouth, No. A.S. 103) is an excellent example of music requiring this treatment (Figure 20). The phrase should be begun with a beat about chest high and gradually raised to the peak of the phrase in the second measure. After the peak of the phrase is reached, the conducting plane is gradually lowered. Another example of this treatment occurs in "How Lovely Is Thy Dwelling Place" by Brahms (Carl Fischer, No. 632).

FIGURE 20 Excerpt from "A Thought like Music" by Johannes Brahms, in which the conducting plane may be raised and lowered to indicate the rise and fall or increase and decrease of tension within the phrase. Copyright © 1958 by Plymouth Music Company, Inc. Used by permission.

Size of the Beat

The size of the conductor's beat should be determined by the dynamic level, the tempo and rhythm of the music, and the style of articulation (discussed in a following section), as well as by the general mood or character of the music. The conductor should determine the appropriate dynamics of the music and adapt the size of his beat accordingly. Music of a high dynamic level generally necessitates a larger, broader beat, whereas music of a low dynamic level requires a relatively smaller movement. Particularly with music of a subdued nature, some conductors are inclined to use movements that are too large, and often, therefore, imprecise and unclear.[8] For example, in the choral selection "Since All Is Passing" by Paul Hindemith (Schott, No. AP37), the size of the conducting pattern that is appropriate to the first phrase—marked *piano* (*p*)—need not be more than six inches in height; for the second phrase— marked *pianissimo* (*pp*)—the pattern should necessarily be reduced slightly in height; the third phrase—marked *forte* (*f*)—should be prepared for vigorously and should be approximately fourteen to sixteen inches in height. The dynamic level of the final phrase is identical to the second and should be conducted accordingly.

In the motet "Create in Me, O God, a Pure Heart" by Brahms (G. Schirmer, No. 7504), an extremely quiet beginning is necessary and the conductor must strive for an appropriate dynamic level (Figure 21). To help achieve the desired effect, the conductor's initial preparatory movement should be extremely small—only a precise movement of several inches is necessary, since a larger movement may elicit too loud a response.

Dynamic contrast is a problem of considerable concern to many directors, some of whom have often stated—somewhat in jest—that their choral groups seem to know only two dynamic levels—loud and louder. In view of this seeming dilemma, it behooves conductors to give careful consideration to the appropriate size of their conducting movements as they relate to the dynamic level of the music. This is essential if their groups are ever to sing in an expressive manner.

The tempo of the music is also an important factor influencing the size of the beat. Because of physical limitations, it is necessary for the conductor to limit the scope of his beat with music of a relatively fast tempo if any degree of precision is to be achieved. For example, in the well-known Ukrainian carol "Carol of the Bells" by Leontovich (Carl Fischer, No. CM 4604), the tempo necessitates a relatively small beat. Although some parts of the music may be conducted one beat to a measure, the introductory section in particular requires a small, crisp

---

[8]The conducting movements for music of a low dynamic level should, for the most part, be immediately in front of the body; thus a more coordinated effort between the hand and arm movements and the facial expressions may be achieved.

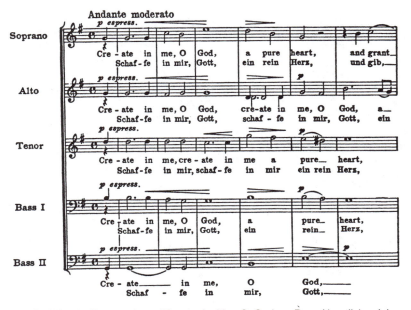

FIGURE 21 Excerpt from "Create in Me, O God, a Pure Heart" by Johannes Brahms, in which the conductor must use an exceptionally small beat in the beginning to achieve the desired dynamic level. Copyright G. Schirmer, Inc., 1931. Used by permission.

three-beat pattern. And, to reiterate, if the pattern is to be clear and precise, it must be relatively small.

In conducting certain figures or patterns containing notes of unequal duration, it is often desirable, particularly in legato music, to reduce the size or scope of the beat on unaccented pulses (Figure 22). For example, in conducting the Negro spiritual "My Lord, What a Mornin'" (Ricordi, No. 412), it is desirable to minimize the movements for the second and third beats in measures 1, 3, and 4 (Figure 22a) and to minimize the movements for all beats except the first in measure 2 (Figure 22b). This modification is more expressive of the music, it serves to lessen the singers' physical response on unaccented pulses, and it facilitates a more legato effect. Although this example is but one, the principle is basic and may be applied in numerous rhythmic patterns as a means of eliciting a more musical response.[9]

[9]It will be helpful to practice conducting various rhythm patterns with the objective of negating, or reducing the size of, beats where there are rests or little rhythmic movement. For example:

Devise various other rhythmic patterns to conduct.

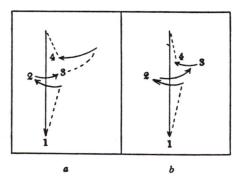

a   b

FIGURE 22   Excerpt from "My Lord, What a Mornin'" (Negro spiritual), arr. H. T. Burleigh (© 1924 by G. Ricordi & Co., New York; used by permission of Franco Colombo Publications, a division of Belwin Mills Publishing Corp.), in which the conducting patterns are modified (*a*) for the rhythmic pattern ♩ ♩ ♩♪ , and (*b*) for the rhythmic pattern ♩ ♩ ♩. Note the rebound of the first beat and the relatively short strokes of the following beats. Compare these patterns with Figure 3.

Clarifying the Beat

With fast tempi there may not be adequate time to conduct each beat in the pattern in a clear, distinct manner. Although decreasing the size of the beat pattern will help (so that the hand does not have to move through so much space), the only solution is sometimes to eliminate or leave out certain beats in a measure. This is often referred to as *negation*. For example, in the "Neighbors' Chorus" by Jacques Offenbach (Broude Brothers, No. 130), the meter is 3/8 and the tempo marking is $\downarrow$. = 69 (Figure 23). Therefore, the most effective gesture is simply to conduct

FIGURE 23 Excerpt from "Neighbors' Chorus" from *La Jolie Parfumeuse* by Jacques Offenbach, in which beats two and three are either negated or reduced in size to clarify the conductor's gestures. Copyright Broude Brothers, 1954. Used by permission.

FIGURE 24   Excerpt from "All Breathing Life, Sing and Praise Ye the Lord," from the motet *Sing Ye to the Lord* by J. S. Bach, in which a small, precise three-beat pattern is used to set the tempo and indicate the rhythmic movement of the sixteenth-note pattern.

the music with one strong beat to a measure, thus negating, or at least minimizing the size of, beats two and three in each measure. Occasionally, however, three small beats per measure may be conducted to indicate the restraint necessary at the end of a phrase, such as in measures 11 and 12. Measure 13, of course, returns to the original tempo.

The reverse of this situation occurs in "All Breathing Life, Sing and Praise Ye the Lord" by J. S. Bach (G. Schirmer, No. 7470) (Figure 24). In contrast, the conductor will want to utilize a small three-beat pattern to set the tempo and to indicate the rhythmic movement of the sixteenth-note figure. Then, two or three measures of this pattern may be followed by a "one-to-a-measure" pattern (with beats two and three being negated) for the remainder of the phrase. At the beginning of most phrases, however, the conductor will generally revert to the small three-beat pattern.

Style of the Beat

It is highly important that the conductor's beat reflect the manner or style of articulation of the music—that is, legato, staccato, or marcato.[10] In conducting music in a legato style, the director should maintain a continuous movement to his beat, for when it stops, the natural tendency is for the singers to stop also, or at least to lessen the flow of the breath. One of the difficulties involved, especially in slow, sustained passages, is maintaining control of the arm movement. When the arm moves too quickly and the end of the beat is reached too soon, the conducting will appear jerky and the smooth, legato effect will be lost. To eliminate this fault, the conductor should imagine a definite resistance to his movements. Pretending to move one's hand through a pool of water will often produce the desired feeling.

Music in a staccato style must be conducted in a crisp, detached manner to indicate the desired articulation of the music. To do so effectively, however, the conductor should use a relatively small beat. Because singing in a marcato style necessitates a sharp inward movement of the abdominal muscles on each note marked $>$, this action should be reflected in the conductor's motions. Thus music in a marcato style demands a vigorous movement, with a precise and definite point to each beat. Whereas there are many compositions that are in either legato or staccato styles throughout, few, if any, compositions are in marcato style throughout.[11] Phrases indicating marcato are so marked for special effect and, to be effective, should be in contrast to other sections. Figure 25 includes an excerpt from "The Last Words of David" by Randall Thompson (E. C. Schirmer, No. 2294) that illustrates a considerable use of marcato. Note the relationship of the marcato markings to the text of the music. "Glory to God" by J. S. Bach (Ricordi, No. NY 1397) is an excellent example for analysis and performance that alternates between marcato and legato styles. An example combining all three styles— legato, staccato, and marcato—is "When Love Is Kind" (English folk song), arr. Salli Terri (Lawson-Gould, No. 843).[12]

Controlling Tempo and Dynamics

A conductor must retain absolute control of the tempo of a choral group. Under certain circumstances singers may be inclined either to rush or to drag the tempo—neither of which helps to achieve a musical performance. At the very least they may not be as responsive to the conductor as is necessary. When a conductor is in control, he has the

---

[10]For a discussion of the relationship of diction to these basic styles of articulation, see section titled "Styles of Diction" in Chapter 2.

[11]For examples of music in legato, staccato, and marcato styles, see section titled "Styles of Diction" in Chapter 2.

[12]Another style of articulation is *portato*—a style or manner of performance halfway between legato and staccato. The music notation will be marked as ♩ or ♩ .

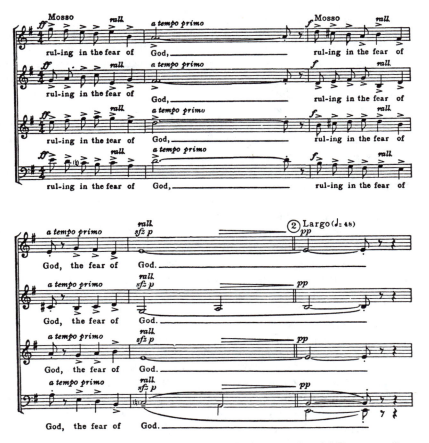

FIGURE 25   Excerpt from "The Last Words of David" by Randall Thompson, illustrating a marcato style, which necessitates vigorous and marked conducting gestures. Copyright E. C. Schirmer Music Co., 1950. Used by permission.

feeling that the singers will respond to his gestures for the most subtle of nuances (almost like one being in command of a "mighty"organ). First of all, the group must be trained to watch the conductor carefully, and the conductor should not always necessarily conduct a piece at the same exact tempo (sometimes due to the varying acoustics of the performance halls). Also, the treatment of phrase endings may be handled slightly differently. The conductor, in this respect, should not always be predictable; if he is and the group feels that they can second-guess him, so to speak, they are not likely to be as attentive as necessary.

Additionally, for the conductor to control the tempo of an ensemble, two conditions are essential: the precision of the initial beat and the clarity of the afterstroke, or "rebound." There should be a definite point to each beat followed by a clear rebound to the next beat. It is the preciseness of the point of each beat that enables a choir to maintain a steadiness of the pulse, and it is the nature of the rebound that enables the conductor to change the tempo—either faster or slower.[13] Effective changes in tempo are not achieved by merely slowing down or speeding up the conducting pattern. Rather, the pattern must be modified in a way that will both attract the attention of the singers and signal the intentions of the conductor.

For the conductor to express his desire for accelerando, the size of the overall conducting pattern should be lessened in size, but with particular attention being given to a gradual quickening of the rebound of each beat. For a ritardando, the first half of each beat should be gradually lengthened, but the rebound in particular should consume slightly more time by moving through more space; that is, the point of each subsequent beat is not reached quite as soon.

If the choir determines their own ritardandos (which they are sometimes inclined to do), there will be too many versions of tempi, inaccuracy, and overexaggeration of the ritard. To alleviate this problem, the conductor should insist that the group maintain a steady tempo—like a team of horses pulling a heavy load (or use any other apt analogy), and he should "pull on the reins" ever so slightly when he feels it is necessary. Such an approach helps to maintain the intensity and the drive of the pulse and places the conductor more in command of the choir.

As to dynamic changes, the size of the beat is paramount. An almost ludicrous situation exists when the conductor asks for a *pianissimo* verbally and through his facial expressions, but continues to flail away with a relatively large conducting pattern. Soft passages necessitate a small, precise conducting pattern, which may be increased in size according to the relative level of dynamics. For one to become more sensitive to what is being asked of the choir, some periodical practice in front of a mirror can be most helpful. The key question to be asked by the conductor is: "Do I like what I see and how would I as a singer respond to the conducting gestures observed?"

[13]To test the clarity of one's conducting gestures, ask the choir or the members of your conducting class to respond by clapping their hands together on each beat. Try different tempi, moving from slow to fast and utilizing various pauses between beats (in a somewhat erratic manner). Can the group follow you? The test of the conductor's clarity is whether all the clapping sounds occur precisely together, with *no* sounds occurring before or after the intended beat.

Extending the Musical Phrase

Some singers are inclined to take unnecessary breaths between short phrases or in the middle of phrases. The conductor can eliminate some of this difficulty by making a circular movement toward the group—indicating that a breath is not to be taken and that the musical phrase is to be extended. This circular movement should commence at least one beat, and in faster tempi, two beats, prior to the end of the phrase that is to be carried over.

The Left Hand

Conductors, as a general rule, are inclined to overuse the left hand. Some fall into the habit of allowing the left hand to follow the pattern of the right. Since overuse of the left hand renders it relatively ineffective for special situations, it should, for the most part, be held near the waistline. Conductors may then more effectively use the left hand for special emphasis, such as sudden accents, abrupt changes in tempo, cueing entrances of certain sections, crescendo and decrescendo, and to assist in effecting clear, precise attacks and releases.

In actual practice many conductors do use both hands simultaneously in conducting the basic patterns. There is nothing terribly wrong with this practice, particularly when it is used, for example, to convey a certain dramatic intensity in the music or to rhythmically solidify a chorus of considerable size. It does become unnecessary, however, when conducting music of a restrained nature and a low dynamic level. In this instance, too much arm movement is inimical to the best artistic performance of the music and simply might best be described as "overkill."

Cueing

Effective cueing should provide a sense of security to the singers and facilitate the precision of attacks and an improved musical interpretation. It also allows the singers to become more aware (if they watch) of important entering solo voices or sections that are generally of musical importance to the listeners. This concept should be communicated to the singers so that they understand the necessity for some voices to occasionally predominate and others to be subservient to the melodic line.

Cueing has been referred to as "effective phrasing with a timely look in the proper direction." Several methods of cueing are currently utilized. The conductor may employ any of the following approaches, depending upon the tempo of the music, the style of the music, and the frequency of the entering parts.

1. Use of the *hands,* providing there is adequate time to execute the movements.
2. Use of the *head,* when a multiplicity of entrances occur in the music.
3. Use of *facial expressions,* appropriate in dealing with more subtle and delicate entrances.
4. A *combination* of two or more of the preceding methods.

Some subtle cues may be indicated by a very slight hand movement combined with appropriate facial expressions, such as a nod of the head, or perhaps by mouthing the vowels in the first word or so. Other entrances may necessitate a more vigorous motion, sometimes with both hands being used. The appropriate gesture depends, of course, upon the dynamic level of the music, the tempo, and the number of entrances required.

A good many cues that involve the entrance of only one part may be best accomplished by simply pointing the beat or hand and arm in the direction of the group or section whose entrance needs to be assisted. When several sections or the entire choir is cued, it is generally best to reinforce the gesture by the use of both hands.

Cueing entrances of various parts is essential to rhythmic security and should be given the same careful treatment and preparation as the entire ensemble is given at the beginning of a choral selection.

CONDUCTING ACCENT AND CHANGING METER

Basic conducting patterns often need to be modified in a variety of ways to reflect the character of the music and to elicit the proper musical response from the group. Rhythm, meter, and accent account for many of these modifications; therefore, the following procedures are suggested for conducting syncopated figures, offbeat accents, displaced rhythmic accents, and changing meter and shifting accents.

Syncopated Figures

The conducting of certain syncopated figures may be made more effective by utilizing a vigorous rebound from the beat preceding each accented or syncopated note in the figure, and shortening or reducing the size of the following beat. See, for example, the excerpt from "Ching-A-Ring Chaw," adapted by Aaron Copland (Figure 26), and the illustration of the modified conducting pattern for the figure $\frac{2}{4}$ ⅄ ♩ ♪| ♩ ⅄ |.

For a similar example involving the same conducting principle—yet somewhat more complex—see the final three measures of "Now Is the Hour of Darkness Past" by Daniel Pinkham (Figure 27). It will be

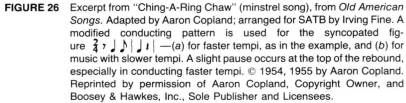

FIGURE 26 Excerpt from "Ching-A-Ring Chaw" (minstrel song), from *Old American Songs*. Adapted by Aaron Copland; arranged for SATB by Irving Fine. A modified conducting pattern is used for the syncopated figure ³⁄₄ ♩ ♪ | ♩ ♪ | —(a) for faster tempi, as in the example, and (b) for music with slower tempi. A slight pause occurs at the top of the rebound, especially in conducting faster tempi. © 1954, 1955 by Aaron Copland. Reprinted by permission of Aaron Copland, Copyright Owner, and Boosey & Hawkes, Inc., Sole Publisher and Licensees.

noted that the accents fall on the second beat, the second half of the third beat, and the second beat of the following measure, and that the music is marked *senza rall*. While a conductor might initially be inclined to simply conduct the rhythm of the words, this creates difficulties in terms of rhythmic accuracy. One is advised to conduct a strict three-beat pattern with an accentuated rebound on the second half of the third beat in measure 3. The size of the first beat in the following measure should

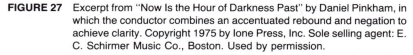

FIGURE 27 Excerpt from "Now Is the Hour of Darkness Past" by Daniel Pinkham, in which the conductor combines an accentuated rebound and negation to achieve clarity. Copyright 1975 by Ione Press, Inc. Sole selling agent: E. C. Schirmer Music Co., Boston. Used by permission.

be negated or minimized to allow for a clearer emphasis on the accented second beat.[14]

Offbeat Accents

A group of offbeat accents—that is, those occurring on the second half of each beat or pulse—may be conducted effectively by utilizing a slight downward movement of the hands and arm on the first half of the beat, followed by a definite and precise upward movement on the second half of the beat. The pattern should be entirely up and down, with the rebound retracing the path of the downbeat (see the excerpt from "Ezekiel Saw the Wheel" and the illustration of the suggested conducting pattern in Figure 28).

Displaced Rhythmic Accents

The accenting of beats other than those expected—that is, the strong beats of a measure—is a rhythmic device used by various contemporary composers. One means is the use of traditional rhythmic patterns in nonsymmetrical forms. For example, in the composition "It Is Good to Be Merry" by Jean Berger (Kjos, No. 5293), the traditional 9/8 pattern of 3 + 3 + 3 is altered to 2 + 2 + 2 + 3 (see Figure 29). In Leonard Bernstein's "America" (from *West Side Story*), the 6/8 pattern of 3 + 3 is altered to 3 + 3 + 2 + 2 + 2 (see Figure 30). In "Ballad of Green Broom" by Benjamin Britten (Boosey & Hawkes, No. 1875), the 6/8 pattern of 3 + 3 is altered to 3 + 1½ + 1½ and 1½ + 1½ + 3 (see Figure 31).

In conducting such patterns, the director must first analyze the music for the shift of accents and then determine the most appropriate

---

[14]In addition to the conductor's gestures, it is helpful, in this instance, to ask the chorus to count aloud together—one, *two*, three *and*, one, *two*, three, one, and so on. In counting, emphasize the accents and repeat as many times as necessary.

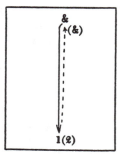

FIGURE 28   Excerpt from "Ezekiel Saw the Wheel" (spiritual), arr. Simeone, in which the modified pattern shown is used for conducting the offbeat accents ⅔ ♩ ♪ ♪ ♩ ♪ |. From the Fred Waring choral arrangement. © Copyright MCML, Shawnee Press, Inc., Delaware Water Gap, PA 18327. Used by permission.

movements to convey clarity and evoke rhythmic precision from the group. The conducting pattern should not be too large if precision is to be achieved. Following the downbeat, it is suggested that the subsequent movements (beats) be made from right to left in a crisp, short, decisive manner (see Figures 29–31).

Changing Meter and Shifting Accents

In preparing to conduct selections with changing meter and shifting accents, the conductor should carefully analyze the music, identify

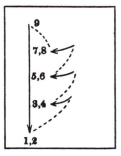

FIGURE 29 Excerpt from "It Is Good to Be Merry" by Jean Berger, together with a conducting pattern for the nonsymmetrical figure $\frac{8}{8}$ ♩ ♪♪ ♩ ♪♪ | (2+2+2+3). Used by permission of Neil A. Kjos Music Co., San Diego, Calif. Copyright 1961.

the significant aspects of the rhythm that need to be clarified or conveyed to the singers, and then determine the most appropriate gestures or patterns to convey musical meaning and the intentions of the composer.

In Randall Thompson's "Glory to God in the Highest" (E. C. Schirmer, No. 2470) (see Figure 32), for example, the first six measures change alternately from 2/4 to 3/8 to 2/4 (two measures) to 5/8 to 2/4.[15]

[15]Other suggested selections for study with changing meter are "It Is Good to Be Merry" by Jean Berger (Kjos, No. 5293) and "Festival Te Deum" by Benjamin Britten (Boosey & Hawkes).

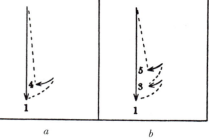

FIGURE 30 Excerpt from "America" from *West Side Story* by Leonard Bernstein, arr. William Stickles, and patterns for conducting the nonsymmetrical figure 🎵🎵🎵🎵🎵🎵 | ♩ ♩ ♩ | (3+3+2+2+2): (a) for measures one and three, and (b) for measures two and four. © 1957, 1959, by Leonard Bernstein and Stephen Sondheim. Used by permission.

A suggested approach to conducting this section of changing meter, as illustrated in Figure 32, is as follows. In measure 1 (in 2/4), a two-beat pattern with a strong full downbeat and a short precise secondary beat should be used. In measure 2 (in 3/8), because the eighth note maintains the same value as in the previous measure (♩ = 120) and since it would be awkward, and not really necessary, to conduct three distinct move-

FIGURE 31 Excerpt from "Ballad of Green Broom" from *Five Flower Songs,* Op. 47, No. 5. Words anonymous; music by Benjamin Britten. Conducting pattern (a) for measure one: ♪ ♪ ♪, pattern (b) for measure two: ♪ ♪ ♪ ♪ ♪ ♪, and pattern (c) for measure three: ♪ ♪ ♪ ♪. © 1951 by Boosey & Co., Ltd. Renewed 1979. Reprinted by permission of Boosey & Hawkes, Inc.

ments, beats two and three should be negated and only one strong beat conducted in the measure. (Actually, there is a pause on the second beat, and the rebound from the downbeat occurs on the third beat.) Measures 3 and 4 should be conducted in two, as in measure 1. In measure 5 (in 5/8), the first eighth note is conducted with a downbeat, on the second eighth note the beat is negated, and the third eighth note is indicated by the rebound, which is restricted with the hand and arm returning only part way. The conductor will thus be in a position for the secondary beat of a two-beat pattern, with the last two eighth notes in the measure being conducted as in measure 1. The principal reasons for using this pattern, and particularly for negating the second beat in the measure, are the moderately rapid tempo (♩ = 120) and the need for clarity in the conducting pattern. Each of the five eighth notes should be equal in dura-

FIGURE 32   Excerpt from "Glory to God in the Highest" by Randall Thompson. Suggested conducting patterns for (*a*) measures 1 and 4, (*b*) measures 2 and 11, (*c*) measure 5, and (*d*) measure 12. Copyright E. C. Schirmer Music Co., 1958. Used by permission.

FIGURE 32 *(continued)*

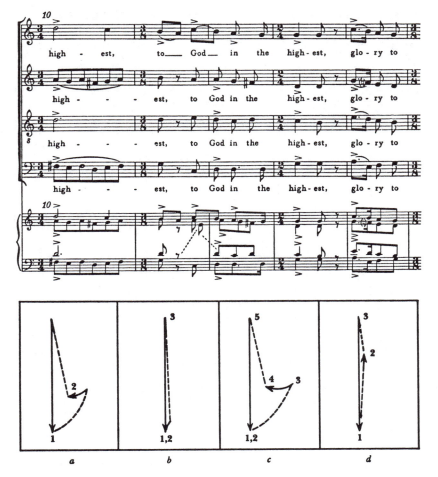

tion, and if the conductor executes the pattern as described, no problem of unevenness should occur. Measure 6 (in 2/4) should be conducted with a strong downbeat, but with a short movement on the secondary beat to indicate the duration of an eighth note followed by the eighth-note rest.

In measures 11–13, the accents shift from the third beat, to the second, to the first. In measure 11 (in 3/8), the first beat should be conducted with a vigorous downbeat—but short and precise; the second beat should be negated (with a slight pause); and the third-beat accent should be indicated by a precise, directly upward, movement or rebound. In measure 12, the downbeat on beat one should be followed by

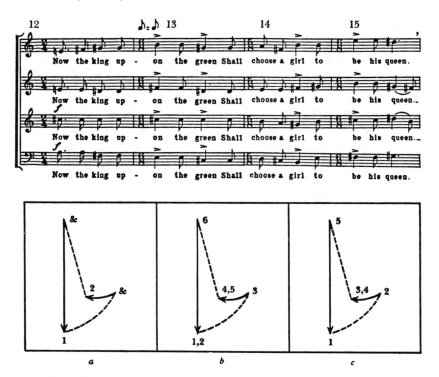

FIGURE 33   Excerpt from "Walking on the Green Grass" by Michael Hennagin, with suggested conducting patterns for measures 12–15: (*a*) for measure 12, (*b*) for measures 13 and 15, and (*c*) for measure 14. Note that the conducting pattern for measure 14 (in 5/8) uses the first half of the pattern for measure 12 (in 2/4) and the last half of the pattern for measure 13 (in 6/8). © 1962 by Boosey & Hawkes, Inc. Reprinted by permission.

a precise upward rebound on beat two and the third beat should be negated. In measure 13, the first beat is accented with a precise downbeat.

Another interesting example involving changing meter (see Figure 33) may be found in "Walking on the Green Grass" by Michael Hennagin (Boosey & Hawkes, No. 5443). Measure 12 (in 2/4) and measure 13 (in 6/8) are both conducted with a two-beat pattern; however, the tempo of the eighth note remains constant ($\flat = \flat$), with the rebound to the downbeat occurring on the second eighth note in the 2/4 meter and on the third and sixth eighth notes in the 6/8 meter. Measure 14 (in 5/8 meter) may be considered a composite of the two previous measures: The conducting pattern for the first two eighth notes is the same as that used for measure 12, and the pattern for the remaining quarter note and eighth note is the same as that used in the last half of measure 13. In other words, the rebound of the beat pattern used for 2/4 meter occurs on the second half of the beat, whereas the rebound for the 6/8 meter occurs on the third and sixth eighth notes in each measure.

It must be remembered that the conducting pattern used depends on the rhythm. For example, in measure 14 of "Walking on the Green Grass" the basic rhythm is 2 + 3, whereas in measure 5 of "Glory to God in the Highest" the basic rhythm is 3 + 2. Compare the suggested patterns for conducting each of these rhythms and practice each alternately as follows:

Alternate the practice of 5/8 patterns with 2/4 and 6/8 patterns until you can move from one to another with *security*.

Conducting 7/8 meter at a moderate-to-fast tempo also necessitates the use of a pattern different from that used for slow tempi. Although the precise technique used will vary according to the rhythm within each measure, a practical approach is to conduct a basic 4/4 pattern with an accentuated rebound on each beat except the last, which is negated with the rebound returning, on the seventh pulse (if felt or conducted in 8/8) in the measure, to the next downbeat (Figure 34). Benjamin Britten's "Festival Te Deum," Opus 32 (Boosey & Hawkes), contains several examples of 7/8 meter that may be conducted in the manner just described.

Another alternative is to conduct the 7/8 measures with the first two movements or beats of a triple-meter pattern (with the rebounds accentuated) and the last half of a 6/8 pattern, as illustrated in Figure 35. (This pattern is preferable for conducting the first three measures of the excerpt.)

The principle in the selection of beat patterns, then, is to analyze and break down the rhythmic patterns into their basic components, usually units of two or three (duple- or triple-meter patterns), and identify patterns or movements that are the simplest to coordinate, particularly during moderate-to-fast tempi. Economy of movement is necessary if rhythmic clarity and precision are to be achieved. Gestures that are too large and too numerous can impede rhythmic drive and lessen the intensity and effectiveness of the interpretation. In measures with irregular meter, one should look not only to the rhythm but also to the text to determine the most appropriate conducting patterns.[16]

In conducting septuple meter at quick or fast tempi (allegro), the conductor must use gestures that are very deft, precise, and eco-

[16]For further suggestions on conducting music in multimeter and nonsymmetrical patterns, see page 137.

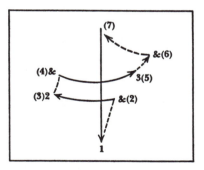

FIGURE 34   Excerpt from "Festival Te Deum," Op. 32, words liturgical; music by Benjamin Britten, in which the measures in 7/8 may be conducted with the pattern indicated. © 1945 by Boosey & Co., Ltd.; renewed, 1972. Reprinted by permission of Boosey & Hawkes, Inc.

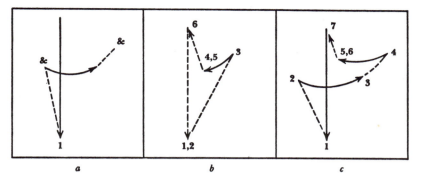

FIGURE 35 (a) First two movements of a triple-meter pattern (with accentuated rebounds), (b) last half of a 6/8 pattern, and (c) combination of a and b into a 7/8 pattern for conducting selected measures in Benjamin Britten's "Festival Te Deum."

nomical—that is, limited in size or movement. The faster the tempo, the shorter the downbeat, the less space the gestures will take up, and the closer together they will be. Movements will become more vertical and less horizontal. In fact, they consume less time by moving through less space.[17] Figure 36 illustrates conducting patterns appropriate for use in the 7/8 portions of "Hosanna" by Knut Nystedt (Hinshaw Music, No. HMC-518), with a tempo marking of $\quad$ = 120. The music necessitates the use of patterns appropriate for both 2 + 2 + 3 and 3 + 2 + 2 rhythms. Figure 36b (2 + 2 + 3) is also appropriate for use in conducting the 7/4 portion of *Chichester Psalms* (Part I) by Leonard Bernstein (G. Schirmer, No. ED 2656), marked *Allegro Molto,* ♪ = ♩ = 120 (¢ + 3/4).

Following is a list of other examples of choral music containing changing meters, in many but not all instances, from measure to measure. These are all excellent study, as well as performance, pieces for the conductor. Each should be thoroughly analyzed as regards the most appropriate and effective conducting patterns to be used, and practiced until one's technique becomes stable and secure. The sequence of meter changes is indicated following each selection.

Hindsight—Brent Pierce.   Walton Music Corp. No. 2964. (6/8, 5/8, 6/8, 5/8, etc.)
A Fancy—Emma Lou Diemer.   Carl Fischer No. CM8011. (2/2, 3/2, 2/2, 3/2, etc.)
Who Hath a Right to Sing?—Lloyd Pfautsch.   Lawson-Gould No. 52048. (6/8, 5/8, 6/8, 5/8, etc.)
Shout the Glad Tidings—Larry Willcoxen.   Harold Flammer No. A-5583. (3/8, 5/8, 9/8, 5/8, etc.)
The Ninth of January—Dmitri Shostakovitch.   G. Schirmer No. 12123. (6/8, 5/8, 3/8, 3/4, 4/4, 7/8, 5/8, 3/8, 2/4, etc.)

[17]Compare this principle with that of conducting subdivided beats.

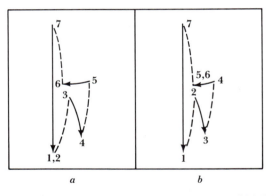

a   b

FIGURE 36 Excerpts from "Hosanna" (for treble voices, SSAA) by Knut Nystedt, with suggested patterns for conducting 7/8 meter at fast tempi (♩ = 120): (a) for 3 + 2 + 2, and (b) for 2 + 2 + 3. Copyright Hinshaw Music, Inc., 1981. Used by permission.

Praise Ye the Lord—John Rutter. Oxford University Press No. 42.357. (3/4, 4/4, 3/8, 5/8, 3/8, 4/4, 7/8, 4/4, 6/8, 4/4, etc.)

Mary Hynes (from *Reincarnations*)—Samuel Barber. G. Schirmer No. 8908. (4/4, 3/2, 3/8, 4/4, 3/8, 5/8, 3/4, etc.)

Festival Te Deum—Benjamin Britten. Boosey & Hawkes. (3/4, 5/8, 7/8, 4/4, 3/4, 3/8, 5/8, 2/4 . . . ; 2/4, 7/8, 3/4, 11/8, 7/8, 5/8, 2/4, . . . ; 6/8, 18/8, 4/8, 5/4, 4/4, 7/8, 3/4, 5/8, 3/4, etc.)

Symphony of Psalms—Igor Stravinsky. Boosey & Hawkes. (Part I: 2/4, 4/4, 1/4, 3/2, 4/4, 3/2, etc.; Part II: 4/8, 3/8, 2/8, 4/8, etc.; Part III: 4/4, 3/2, 4/4, 3/2, 2/2, 3/2, etc.)

Chichester Psalms—Leonard Bernstein.   G. Schirmer, Inc. (Part I: 6/4, 3/4, 3/8, 5/4, 2/4,
5/8, 6/4, 2/4, 5/4, 7/4, etc.; Part II: 3/4, 2/4, 3/4, ¢ 3/2, 3/4, **C** , ¢ ; Part III: 9/4,
10/4, 5/2, 9/2, 12/2.)

STUDYING THE SCORE

In preparing for a rehearsal, the conductor should first thoroughly
study the score (singers generally resent the conductor who learns the
music along with the choir). Before introducing a new choral selection,
he should first peruse and analyze the text to determine the overall
mood and then play the music on the piano to acquaint himself with the
musical means that the composer used to express his creative thoughts.
Rhythm, tempo, dynamics, harmony, and the texture of the music—all
have a bearing upon the conductor's choice of gestures, which should
grow out of his understanding and desire to effectively interpret the
music.

After careful study, the conductor should mark his score by either
underlining, encircling, or drawing over portions of the music. For example, tempo and dynamic indications might be underlined or encircled; accents, phrasing lines, changing meter signs, and moving parts
that need to be emphasized or brought out may be encircled. (Some
conductors prefer to highlight their markings by using a red- or blue-
colored pencil). These markings may effectively serve as a reminder for
the use of appropriate conducting gestures during either subsequent
study or actual rehearsals.

In studying the score, the conductor should read through the music and try to conceptualize his interpretation. He should give specific
consideration to each measure and leave nothing to guesswork. To illustrate this point, guidelines for preparing the first twelve measures of
"Create in Me, O God, a Pure Heart" by Brahms (G. Schirmer, No.
7504) are given in Figure 37.

After the score has been carefully studied and prepared, it is also
helpful to employ the use of mental imagery. Without actually conducting, follow the score and mentally imagine the gestures that would be
most appropriate and that would best convey to the singers the intent of
the music. Freedom from unnecessary muscular tension and more refined conducting skills may result. While such an approach should obviously be interspersed between the actual practice of conducting gestures, its importance should not be overlooked! One's ultimate goal
should be to make the technique automatic, so that it will flow naturally,
emanate from, and express the intent of the music.[18]

---

[18]Studies have shown that the use of mental imagery is conducive to the development of various skills outside of music. See, for example, Maxwell Maltz, *Psycho-Cybernetics*
(New York: Pocket Books, 1969), pp. 35–36.

MEASURE	SUGGESTED CONDUCTING GESTURES
Incomplete	Use extremely small movement, because a large gesture will elicit too loud a response.
1	Use small beat pattern; negate beats two and three.
2	Raise plane of beat slightly; place slight stress on third beat.
3	Negate beats two and three; support tone with left hand.
4	Lower plane of beat; indicate decrescendo with left hand.
5	Negate beats two and four; make precise sideways movement (from left to right) to indicate the release of the second and the beginning of the third beat in measure.
6	Negate first beat; cue soprano line on second beat.
7	Conduct quarter-note movement in baritone line.
8	Restrain volume with left hand; raise plane of beat gradually.
9	Continue to restrain volume on first beat; gradual crescendo beginning with second beat may be indicated by raising slightly the conducting plane.
10	Lower conducting plane gradually; indicate decrescendo by lowering the left hand.
11	Negate second beat; cue and stress entrance of bass line on third beat.
12	Indicate decrescendo of tenor line by lowering left hand and conducting plane.

FIGURE 37   Guidelines for conducting the first twelve measures of "Create in Me, O God, a Pure Heart" by Johannes Brahms.

In summary, and perhaps to overstate the obvious, conducting should never be simply a matter of establishing the tempo, conducting a meter pattern, and then "watching the notes go by." Young conductors, in particular, should know their scores, develop some specific musical expectancies, and then express them to the choir both verbally and through their conducting. Try preparing a number of selections in detail, as previously indicated, and then note the development of your conducting technique!

SUMMARY: DEVELOPING CONDUCTING SKILLS

Choral conducting involves the development of skills and specific techniques not entirely dissimilar to the development of techniques in voice or on an instrument. For example, the playing of long tones and the practice of scales and arpeggios in all keys are essential to developing technique on woodwind instruments. Similarly, all instrumentalists have felt compelled to "woodshed" certain passages in music with which they were having difficulty. Likewise, conducting involves certain basic skills and techniques that need to be isolated, practiced, and refined to the extent that they become automatic, so the conductor can concentrate on the interpretation of the music rather than on the technique per se.

Aspiring conductors should practice these specific techniques daily in front of a mirror or with a conducting partner who can provide helpful suggestions, but preferably before a video camera so they may evaluate their own conducting gestures. Following is a summary of the techniques, presented previously in this chapter, that the conductor must master. Once each technique has been perfected, or improved upon, it should again be applied to the conducting of specific choral selections. Below each particular technique is a listing of selected octavo music (most of which is available in college and university libraries) that is particularly suitable for practice of that technique. Gradually expand this list by seeking other appropriate music to which the techniques may be applied. If you or others are critical of your conducting at any point, then periodically return to practicing the specific techniques in isolation without the music.

1. Duple, triple, and quadruple meters   Practice conducting patterns in 2/4, 3/4, and 4/4, concentrating on the cleanness of the downbeat and the horizontal movement of the other beats in the pattern, particularly in 3/4 and 4/4 meters.

2/4: "Oh! Susanna"—Stephen Foster, arr. Mark Hayes.   Shawnee Press, No. A-1745.
3/4: "Kyrie" (from Mass in G)—Franz Schubert.   Kjos, No. 5989.
4/4: "Gloria in Excelsis"—Franz Joseph Haydn.   Hal Leonard, No. 08679600.

2. Timing and flow   Practice moving your conducting hand back and forth in a tubful of water (or in a swimming pool). The natural resistance of the water enables a conductor to develop a feel for the proper timing and the flow of the beat.

"Sure on This Shining Night"—Samuel Barber.   G. Schirmer, No. 10864.

3. Sextuple meter   Practice the three patterns for sextuple meter (pp. 8–9), and consider the advantages of each as applied to specific pieces.

"She's like the Swallow" (Newfoundland folk song)—arr. E. Chapman.   Oxford, No. X64.
"Zamba for You"—Ariel Ramirez, arr. Eduardo Gomez.   Lawson-Gould, No. 52242.
"Silent Night"—Franz Gruber, arr. Malcolm Sargent.   Oxford, No. OCS 876.

4. Irregular meter   Practice conducting patterns in 5/4 and 7/4 in combinations of 2's and 3's, and 3's and 4's, and vice versa. Minimize the size of the second downbeat in each pattern.

"Nächtens" ("Nightly")—Johannes Brahms.   G. Schirmer, No. 10123.

5. Subdivided beats   Practice the suggested patterns (p. 12) in both 3/4 and 4/4 meter, making certain that your beat is precise and clear and that you "consume more time by moving through more space."

3/4: "Crucifixus" (from B Minor Mass)—J. S. Bach. E. C. Schirmer, No. 1174.
4/4: "Surely He Hath Borne Our Griefs" (from *Messiah*)—G. F. Handel. G. Schirmer, No. 6598.
4/4: "Crucifixus"—W. A. Mozart. National Music Publishers, No. WHC-141.

6. Attacks Practice the three types of preparatory movements for beginning music on incomplete measures (pp. 18–19).

4/4: ♩ | ♩ "A Sigh Goes Stirring through the Wood"—Johannes Brahms. Associated, No. A-379.

2/4: ♩ ♪ ♫ | ♫ "The Girl I Left Behind Me" (Irish folk song; in *Five Traditional Songs*)—arr. John Rutter. Oxford University Press.

4/4: ♪♫ ♩ | ♩ "La Marseillaise" (French national anthem)—Rouget de Lisle; in *357 Songs We Love to Sing*. Schmitt, Hall & McCreary, No. 9015.

7. Releases Practice releases with both the right hand and the left hand and at various tempi ranging from slow to fast (releases should be in the tempo of the music being performed).

Practice releases on all selections listed.

8. Fermatas Practice the two types of fermatas—the complete release and the carryover technique.

"Chorales from *The Passion According to St. John*"—J. S. Bach. Lawson-Gould, No. 51145.

9. The conducting plane Practice a pattern appropriate for a particular size of choral ensemble; for example, a chamber choir of 20 voices and a large choir of 120 voices. Following this, practice a pattern to reflect the line of various musical phrases.

"A Thought like Music"—Johannes Brahms. Plymouth, No. AS 103.

10. Dynamics Practice conducting patterns appropriate for *p, mf,* and *f* passages by varying the size of your beat.

"Since All Is Passing"—Paul Hindemith. Schott, No. AP 37.
"Locus iste a Deo factus est"—Anton Bruckner. C. F. Peters, No. 6314.
"Create in Me, O God, a Pure Heart"—Johannes Brahms. G. Schirmer, No. 7504.

11. Crescendo and decrescendo Practice conducting a four-measure phrase (in 4/4 meter), starting from *pianissimo* with a gradual crescendo to *forte,* and after two measures followed by a gradual decrescendo to *pianissimo.*

"Ave Maria"—Sergei Rachmaninoff. Lawson-Gould, No. 52344.

12. Negation Practice conducting various rhythmic patterns in which the size of the beats in different measures is minimized to reflect the notation of the music. For example:

$$\frac{4}{4} \; \mathrm{d.} \quad \mathrm{J} \; | \; \mathrm{d.} \quad \mathrm{J}\mathrm{J} \; \mathrm{J} \; | \; \mathrm{d} \quad \mathrm{d} \; | \; \mathrm{o} \quad \|$$

"My Lord, What a Mornin'" (spiritual)—arr. H. T. Burleigh. Ricordi, No. 412.
"Gloria in Excelsis"—W. A. Mozart. Frederick Harris Music Co., No. HC 4034.

13. Clarifying the beat Practice moving from three beats (3/4 or 3/8) to one beat per measure, and then back, to maximize your assistance to the choral group and to assist them in singing in a precise and an articulate manner.

"Neighbors' Chorus" (from *La Jolie Parfumeuse*)—Jacques Offenbach. Broude Bros., No. 130.
"All Breathing Life, Sing and Praise Ye the Lord"—J. S. Bach. G. Schirmer, No. 7470.

14. Style of the beat Conduct a pattern in 4/4 meter to coincide with different styles: *legato* (smooth and connected), *staccato* (short and detached), *portato* (a style halfway between legato and staccato), and *marcato* (accented beats or notes). Then, try combining two styles—for example, two beats legato, followed by two beats in marcato style: | ♩ ♩ ♩ ♩ | and so on. Devise and practice all possible combinations.

"When Love Is Kind" (English folk song)—arr. Salli Terri. Lawson-Gould, No. 843.
"Glory to God"—J. S. Bach. Ricordi, No. NY1397.
"The Last Words of David"—Randall Thompson. E. C. Schirmer, No. 2294.

15. Changing and controlling tempo The clarity of the *rebound* of each beat is the cue to control of the tempo. Practice this procedure (in 4/4 meter) with a friend and ask him to clap his hands on each beat of your changes to see how clear your gestures are. If possible, try this procedure with your entire class.

16. Cueing Practice cueing imaginary sections of the choir with the right hand by directing your beat toward that section. Know where your sections are located and devise exercises with entrances on various beats of a measure, to help develop maximum flexibility. Also utilize head movements and facial expressions as either alternatives or reinforcements to the primary cueing gestures. Watch yourself in a mirror and evaluate the clarity of your gestures. Can you follow yourself?

"Sing a New Song"—Michael Haydn. Flammer, No. A-5970.
"Dona Nobis Pacem"—Ludwig van Beethoven. National Music Publishers, No. WHC-143.
"Hallelujah"—G. F. Handel. Music 70 Publishers, No. M70-330.
"Zigeunerleben" ("Gypsy Life")—Robert Schumann. Walton, No. 2706.

17. Syncopation and offbeat accents Modify your conducting pattern by accentuating the rebound of your beat(s) to emphasize the rhythmic stress in the music. For example: $\frac{2}{4}$ ♩ ♪| ♩ ♪ | ♩ ♪| ♩ ♪ | (see pp. 37–39).

"Ching-A-Ring Chaw" (minstrel song)—adapted by Aaron Copland and arr. Irving Fine. Boosey & Hawkes, No. 5024.
"Ezekiel Saw the Wheel" (spiritual)—arr. H. Simeone. Shawnee Press, No. A-0130.

18. Displaced rhythmic accents Analyze the following choral selections to determine the alteration of rhythmic stress, mark your score accordingly, and practice appropriate conducting patterns (see pp. 39–43).

"It Is Good to Be Merry"—Jean Berger. Kjos, No. 5293.
"America" (from *West Side Story*—choral selections)—Leonard Bernstein. G. Schirmer, No. 10703.
"Ballad of Green Broom"—Benjamin Britten. Boosey & Hawkes, No. 1875.

19. 5/8 (quintuple) meter Is the rhythm 2 + 3 or 3 + 2? Conduct the first half of a 2/4 pattern and the last half of a 6/8 pattern, then vice versa. Practice both of these patterns in alternating measures so that moving from one to the other becomes automatic: $\frac{5}{8}$ ♫ ♫♫ | ♫♫ ♫ | and so on.

20. 7/8 (septuple) meter Is the rhythm 2 + 2 + 3 or 3 + 2 + 2? Practice conducting the first two beats of a 3/4 meter pattern (with accentuated rebounds) and the last half of a 6/8 pattern (for 2 + 2 + 3). Then, conduct the first half of a 6/8 pattern followed by the second and third beats of a 3/4 pattern (with accentuated rebounds; for 3 + 2 + 2). Apply these patterns to the appropriate measures in the following music.

"Festival Te Deum"—Benjamin Britten. Boosey & Hawkes, No. H.15656.
"Hosanna"—Knut Nystedt. Hinshaw Music, Inc., No. HMC-518.

21. Changing meter and shifting accents Practice conducting the patterns suggested on pages 40–46, for the changing meters of 2/4, 3/8, 2/4, 5/8, 2/4, 3/4, 3/8, and 2/4. Adjust your rebounds to fit the music!

"Glory to God in the Highest"—Randall Thompson. E. C. Schirmer, No. 2470.
"Walking on the Green Grass"—Michael Hennagin. Boosey & Hawkes, No. 5443.

(See also the listing of music with changing meters on pp. 49–51.)

In addition to the choral octavo music previously suggested, one may find collections of choral music of various types and styles to be particularly helpful in furthering the aims of the conducting class. The following publications are recommended.

The Conductor's Manual of Choral Music Literature, by Lee Kjelson and James McCray. Belwin
   Mills Publishing Corp.
Choral Perspective, compiled by Don Malin. Edward B. Marks Music Corp.
Five Centuries of Choral Music, compiled by a committee of teachers in the Los Angeles
   Public Schools, William C. Hartshorn, Supervisor. G. Schirmer.

For additional choral collections, see the listing in the Appendix, pages 320–21. For a source of easy song material for beginning conductors, see the list of "Community Song Books" on page 269.

TOPICS FOR DISCUSSION

1. Recall and identify the personality attributes of successful conductors you have known. With this information as a basis, discuss the factors that you believe are important to conducting success.
2. Recall and identify the facets of effective conducting technique that you have observed in various conductors.
3. Describe in class some of the conducting problems not usually encountered. Discuss the most appropriate means of handling these problems.
4. Discuss the differences in interpretation of a choral composition as illustrated in two or more recordings. Which interpretation do you believe is most effective, and why?
5. What effect do tempo, dynamics, accent, rhythm, phrasing, style, and mood of the music have upon the basic conducting patterns?

SELECTED READINGS

BUSCH, BRIAN R., *The Complete Choral Conductor.* New York: Schirmer Books, 1984.
CAIN, NOBLE, *Choral Music and Its Practice,* chap. 14. New York: M. Witmark & Sons, 1942.
CHRISTY, VAN A., *Glee Club and Chorus,* chap. 1. New York: G. Schirmer, Inc., 1940.
DAVISON, ARCHIBALD T., *Choral Conducting,* chaps. 1, 2. Cambridge, Mass.: Harvard
   University Press, 1945.
DECKER, HAROLD A., AND JULIUS HERFORD, *Choral Conducting Symposium* (2nd ed.), chap.
   5. Englewood Cliffs, N.J.: Prentice-Hall, 1988.
FINN, WILLIAM J., *The Conductor Raises His Baton.* New York: Harper & Row, Pub., 1944.
JONES, ARCHIE N., *Techniques in Choral Conducting.* New York: Carl Fischer, Inc., 1948.
KAPLAN, ABRAHAM, *Choral Conducting.* New York: W. W. Norton & Co., Inc., 1985.
KJELSON, LEE, AND JAMES McCRAY, *The Conductor's Manual of Choral Music Literature.*
   Miami: Belwin Mills Publishing Corp., 1973.
KRONE, MAX T., *Expressive Conducting.* San Diego: Neil A. Kjos Music Co., 1949.
LABUTA, JOSEPH, *Basic Conducting Techniques.* Englewood Cliffs, N.J.: Prentice-Hall, 1973.
McELHERAN, BROCK, *Conducting Techniques: For Beginners and Professionals.* New York:
   Oxford University Press, Inc., 1966.
MOE, DANIEL, *Problems in Conducting.* Minneapolis: Augsburg Publishing House, 1968.

POOLER, FRANK, AND BRENT PIERCE, *New Choral Notation.* New York: Walton Music Corporation, 1971.

ROE, PAUL, *Choral Music Education* (2nd ed.), chap. 8. Englewood Cliffs, N.J.: Prentice-Hall, 1983.

RUDOLF, MAX, *The Grammar of Conducting* (2nd ed.). New York: Schirmer Books, 1980.

SATEREN, LELAND B., *Mixed Meter Music and Line in Choral Music.* Minneapolis: Augsburg Publishing House, 1968.

SIMONS, HARRIET, *Choral Conducting: A Leadership Teaching Approach.* Champaign, Ill.: Mark Foster Music Co., 1983.

STANTON, ROYAL, *The Dynamic Choral Conductor,* chaps. 2, 3. Delaware Water Gap, Pa.: Shawnee Press, Inc., 1971.

2

Tone and Diction

Tone quality is the very substance of choral singing. Without properly produced tones, coupled with correct diction, effective choral singing is impossible to attain. Dynamic contrasts, proper blend and balance, accurate pitch and intonation, and effective phrasing are all dependent upon correct vocal production. Furthermore, projection of the mood or spirit of the music is dependent upon correct diction, as well as on proper tone quality. Since good tone quality and correct diction are fundamental considerations in the training of choral groups, the conductor should develop a well-defined concept of all factors influencing tone and diction. Because choral groups react in varying ways, he should also develop a wide variety of techniques for achieving his objectives.

THE VOCAL INSTRUMENT

The human vocal instrument possesses the three components that are essential to the functioning of all musical instruments: an *actuator,* a *vibrator,* and a *resonator.* In addition, it has a component unique to the human voice: an *articulator.* Generally, the components of the vocal instrument (see Figure 38) may be identified as follows:

1. The respiratory, or breathing, muscles serve as the actuator.

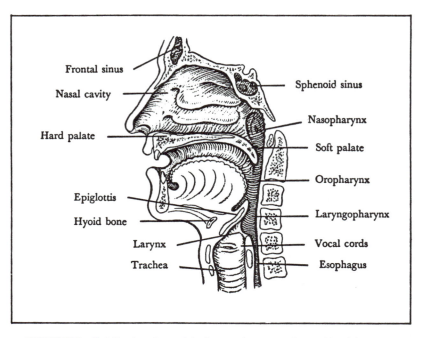

FIGURE 38   Relative locations of the larynx, the resonating cavities (pharynx, mouth, and nasal cavity), and the articulating organs (tongue, lips, teeth, palate, and lower jaw). Note the divisions of the palate (hard palate and velum, or soft palate), and the pharynx (laryngopharynx, oropharynx, and nasopharynx).

2. The vocal cords (sometimes referred to as vocal folds) serve as the vibrator and are the source of the sound.
3. The pharynx, mouth, and nasal cavity serve as the resonator, which amplifies the sound.[1]
4. The tongue, lips, teeth, palate, and lower jaw serve as the articulator.

The principal muscles used in normal breathing are the diaphragm, the abdominal muscles, and the intercostal muscles. Although

[1]Some authorities also consider the paranasal sinuses, the trachea, the bronchi, and the chest cavity to be part of the resonating system. The concept of the nasal and sinus cavities as resonating chambers appears to be rather widely accepted among voice teachers. There is a contrary opinion, however, that rejects the concept of both the nasal and the sinus cavities as resonating chambers, and scientific evidence is cited against the latter. For statements of these opinions, see Richard Luchsinger and Godfrey Arnold, *Voice-Speech Language* (Belmont, Calif.: Wadsworth, 1965), p. 458, and John Carroll Burgin, *Teaching Singing* (Metuchen, N.J.: Scarecrow, 1973), pp. 84–87. Whatever the opinion held by various persons, perhaps greater agreement might exist on at least the "sensation" of head resonance. This is not to say that it occurs physiologically but that it is at the very least a pedagogical device for achieving voice placement.

there is still some difference of opinion concerning the action of these muscles, the following is generally accepted. During inspiration, the diaphragm contracts and pushes downward, while the contraction of the intercostal muscles lifts or raises the ribs. The combined action of these muscles enlarges the thorax, which allows the lungs to fill with air. During normal expiration, there is supposedly no muscle contraction necessary; the chest is decreased in size by the elastic recoil of the thoracic wall. In prolonged expiration, such as in singing a sustained note, the abdominal muscles gradually contract while the diaphragm slowly relaxes, and the intercostal muscles maintain enough tension to prevent bulging of the intercostal spaces. During the act of singing, breath control is of the essence; therefore, a delicate interplay or balance must exist between these opposing sets of muscles. When one set contracts, the other set should relax—but not completely—since their mutual activity provides for the best utilization of the air in the lungs.

The larynx functions somewhat like a valve—when open, it allows the singer to inhale and exhale air to and from the lungs. The vocal cords or folds are the vibrating edge of the thyroarytenoid muscles, the posterior ends of which are attached to the arytenoid cartilages. The anterior, or front, ends of the vocal cords are attached to the thyroid cartilage, commonly known as the "Adam's Apple." The vocal cords are tensed by the contraction of the cricothyroid muscles. The tension of the vocal cords is decreased by the contraction of the thyroarytenoid muscles, of which they are a part. The vocal cords are approximated or brought together by muscles controlling the position of the arytenoid cartilages, and are set into vibration by the flow or the pressure of the breath during exhalation. The fissure or opening between the vocal cords is referred to as the glottis. During deep inspiration, the glottis assumes a somewhat round shape, but during quiet or normal breathing, it assumes a V-shaped position. When one sings a high pitch, the vocal cords come very close together and the glottis becomes a thin, narrow slit or opening (see Figure 39).

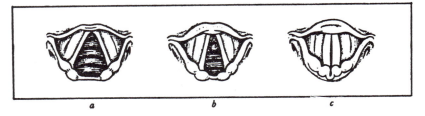

    a   *b*   *c*

FIGURE 39   The larynx as observed through a laryngoscope, illustrating differences in the size of the glottis (*a*) while taking a deep breath, (*b*) during quiet or normal breathing, and (*c*) during phonation.

The pitch of the tone is determined by the tension of the vocal cords and the pressure of the breath against the vocal cords. If this pressure or breath support is inadequate, the laryngeal muscles often function incorrectly in their effort to obtain the correct pitch. This induces fatigue and undue strain on the voice.

In general, the resonating cavities may be divided into two types—fixed and adjustable. The nasal cavity is fixed, whereas the pharynx and the mouth are capable of special utilization. On each side of and above the vocal cords are cavities that amplify the vibrations produced by the vocal cords and increase their intensity as they are projected from the larynx. These cavities are fully utilized as resonance chambers only when the throat is relaxed and kept open. Similarly, the mouth is best used as a resonance chamber when all the muscles, including the tongue, are relaxed and the cavity of the mouth is enlarged, thus allowing for an increased resonance chamber. The nasopharynx and the nasal cavity are most effectively utilized as resonance chambers when a slight opening between the oropharynx is maintained, thus allowing for an extension of the vibrating column of air emanating from the larynx.

Flexibility of the articulating organs—the tongue, the lips, the velum (soft palate), and the lower jaw—is highly important if the vocal mechanism is to function at optimum efficiency. Procedures for coordinating the various components of the vocal instrument are discussed in the following sections.

DEVELOPING CHORAL TONE

In the process of developing the tonal quality of a choral group, the conductor should take into consideration a number of factors: correct singing posture, proper breath control, the function and the value of particular vocalises, and the development of deep-set vowels and high-forward resonance. Development of the high range, particularly in male voices, and the achievement of vocal flexibility are also areas of special importance and concern.

Achieving Correct Posture

Correct posture is necessary to the development of good tone production. Since vocal tone is affected by all the muscles of the body, the individual must maintain an alert body position while singing, whether standing or sitting (Figure 40).

When in a standing position, one should place the feet approximately six inches apart, with one foot several inches in front of the other. This stance affords the singer better balance and lays the founda-

FIGURE 40   Correct posture for standing and sitting.

tion for the proper use of the breathing muscles. The weight of the body should rest to a great extent on the balls of the feet—not on the heels. The knees should be slightly flexed; they should never be in a locked position, because this only contributes to unnecessary body rigidity and tension.[2] The abdomen should be drawn in, and the spine should be kept as straight as possible. The singer's upper back should feel as wide as possible and the chest should be held relatively high, but without strain or excess tension. Since the throat functions as an organ pipe, the head must be kept perpendicular to the shoulders in order that this "pipe" be kept clear and open. The singers must hold their music in such a position that they may easily see the director without lowering or raising their heads, since any deviation in the position of the head is likely to affect the tone quality.

When the singer is seated, the correct posture from the waist up

[2]Excessive tension in the body, such as occurs when locking the knees, can constrict venous return of the blood from the legs, thus contributing to dizziness and fainting. Other relevant factors include overly warm room temperatures, decreased circulation, and singers being "packed" too tightly and unable to move. Attention to proper posture, room temperature, and adequate ventilation, using an adequate number of choir risers to accommodate the choir, and moving singers into different standing arrangements between sets of music can help to minimize the aforementioned problems.

will be almost identical with the standing posture. The only basic difference is that the legs assume a bent position. While in a sitting position, the singer must keep both feet on the floor and lean slightly forward, away from the back of the chair, in order to maintain adequate breath support. Some of the body weight must be distributed to the lower limbs and the feet. The proper coordination between the breathing muscles and the vocal apparatus will result only if this correct posture is maintained while singing.[3]

Improving Breath Control

The next consideration in developing good choral tone is the establishment of correct breathing habits. This is necessary to ensure the steady flow of the breath to the vocal cords and is fundamental to both tone quality and tone control.

Clavicular, or collarbone, breathing does not fill the lungs to capacity and the resultant tension in the upper chest and shoulder muscles affects the muscles around the larynx and inhibits the proper action of the vocal cords.[4] Improper breathing habits that have developed over a period of years are not always easily corrected. First, the singer must thoroughly understand the effect of poor breathing habits upon his or her own tone production and upon the tone quality and blend of the choir. He or she must achieve a conception of the correct method of breathing.

In singing, it is necessary to use the muscles around the entire midsection of the body, not just the diaphragm. The muscles of the upper chest and shoulders should be relaxed, with the greater amount of work being done by the intercostal muscles, the diaphragm, and the abdominal muscles. These are the muscles used in correct breathing technique (see section titled "The Vocal Instrument" earlier in this chapter).

---

[3]To augment the ideas presented on posture, the reader may wish to explore and study the Alexander Technique, which is a process or procedure for increasing individual awareness of movement and posture habits that create tension and inefficient use of the body mechanism. It is used by musicians (both vocal and instrumental), by actors, and by dancers, as well as by others, to help reduce unnecessary effort and tension and to achieve greater efficiency in body movements, thus contributing to their improved performance.

The Alexander Technique is best learned through individual instruction by a competent person trained in this technique. Information about qualified teachers in the United States is available via the American Center for the Alexander Technique, 129 W. 67th St., New York, NY 10023. Also, the National Association of Teachers of Singing and various other professional organizations offer workshops on the Alexander Technique. For dates, locations, and other information, see *The Alexander Review: The Independent Journal of the F. M. Alexander Technique* (available from Centerline Press, 2005 Palo Verde Avenue, Suite 325, Long Beach, CA 90815). For references on this subject, see the listing at the end of this chapter.

[4]This type of incorrect breathing is exemplified in the inspiration movements used by a child in preparation for blowing out a candle.

The director should continually emphasize the formula *Breathe deeply, expand around the entire midsection—in the back and around the sides, as well as in front.* Have the choir members bend over, from a standing position, until the upper part of the body is parallel to the floor. In this posture clavicular breathing is difficult and somewhat unnatural. By pressing the hands against the waist, with thumbs to the back, one can get the "feel" of correct breathing. Try it! Another procedure, which is more easily managed in a crowded rehearsal room, is to have the group lean forward in their chairs, placing one elbow on the knee. Proper breath action may then be checked by pressing the other hand against the waist. After the singers learn how the muscles are utilized in correct breathing, they must strive toward the attainment of proper breath control until it becomes automatic. Proper breath support and control will improve only through continual emphasis.

Stretching Exercises (Prevocalizing Warm-ups)

The current popularity of physical fitness programs, including jogging, walking, swimming, and dance aerobics classes, has had an influence on choral music programs. Each of these activities emphasizes the importance of preparing for aerobic exercise through appropriate stretching and warm-up exercises to avoid any unnecessary muscle strain.

Similarly, choral directors have utilized some of these exercises, not necessarily to avoid muscle strain, but to increase blood circulation and to help singers to get "in tune" with their own bodies. The exercises may be done as a group at the beginning of rehearsal or undertaken on an individual basis prior to rehearsals. A suggested sequence upon which to focus is as follows: face, neck, shoulders, arms, and torso.

1. Facial muscle relaxation Rubbing the facial muscles with both hands to release any excess or unnecessary tension is a good place to begin. Concentrate first on the forehead, then on the cheeks, and last on the lips and jaw.

The following exercises should be done from the *pelvic tilt* position. That is, stand with the feet approximately shoulder-width apart and the knees slightly bent. Tuck in the pelvis by tightening the lower abdominal muscles and contracting the muscles of the buttocks. This position helps prevent back strain and avoids "swayback" and undesirable shortening of the muscles of the lower back.

2. Neck stretches Slowly lower the head frontward and then backward. Then dip the left ear to the left shoulder, and the right ear to the right shoulder. Repeat several times. Following this, drop the head and slowly roll it to the left and then to the right (180 degrees). Do these movements slowly and avoid doing them too vigorously. Do not rotate the head in a 360-degree movement, because this may injure the spinal column.

Another variation of the side-to-side neck stretch is to reach behind and hold the left arm with the right hand before dipping the right ear to the shoulder. Then, before dipping the left ear to the shoulder, reach behind and hold the right arm with the left hand. Such use of the arms helps to keep the shoulders more level. Hold each stretch at least five or six seconds.

3. Shoulder shrugs Raise the shoulders upward toward the neck and ears, and then depress the shoulders by stretching downward; push hands toward the floor.

4. Shoulder stretch Place the left forearm above the head (with bent elbow). Place right hand on left elbow and pull easily but steadily to the right. Bend to the right from the waist. Repeat procedure by pulling right elbow with the left hand and bending from the waist to the left.

5. Arm and shoulder stretch Place left arm in front of body. Place right hand on left elbow and pull easily but steadily to the right. Repeat procedure by pulling the right arm with the left hand.

6. Arm circles Extend the arms to both sides of the body and slowly move them in circles—first frontward and then backward. Start with small movements and gradually increase their size. To provide adequate room for arm movements, the singers should turn 45 degrees to the left (or right). As an alternative, stretch the arms in front of the body before moving them in circles.

7. Upward arm and torso stretches Raise the arms over the head and attempt to reach toward the ceiling with first the right arm and then the left arm. Alternate reaching slowly right and then left—four or more times each side.

8. Torso stretch Reach left across the body with the right arm, and then reach to the right with the left arm. Repeat four or more times each side.

9. Lower back stretch Standing on the left leg, with the left knee slightly bent, bring the right knee toward the chest, feeling a gentle stretch in the lower back and posterior hip. Then repeat the stretch with the left knee. The "buddy system" (with persons next to each other in a back-to-back position) is useful in maintaining balance. Hold each stretch for ten to fifteen seconds.

Directors will likely find it best not to follow a rigid sequence of exercises, but to vary the selection, the order, and the time devoted to specific exercises, just as they would with vocalises. To achieve effective results, singers must totally understand and appreciate the purpose of the stretching exercises and must approach them with seriousness and in silence. Any single student or small group of students who makes light of a situation will lessen the benefit to the whole group. To minimize any problems, the director should lead the group through the exercises, thus being able to control not only the selection but also the pace of the routine.

After singers have focused upon getting "in tune" with their bodies, then proceed to a series of vocalises from which they may now receive greater benefit than they would have without doing the stretching exercises. Stretching exercises should segue naturally into the vocalization period.[5]

Use of Vocalises

Choral conductors generally employ vocalises as a part of the vocal training of their choir members. They are used specifically for the improvement of choral tone and blend. Some conductors use vocal exercises only as a part of the warm-up period, as athletes use mild exercise to prepare themselves for the more strenuous rigors of competition. Other conductors feel that exercises employed for such purposes are largely a waste of time, since they are not directly connected with the immediate problem of improving the performance of the choral music. This latter group will often take a troublesome portion of the music out of context and use it as a vocal exercise.

Although some conductors may feel that only one of the previously mentioned procedures should be followed, it seems reasonable to assume that both practices have considerable merit and that each approach should be employed to some extent. To be effective, vocal exercises must be varied periodically. Continued concentration on particular devices or exercises will eventually lead to boredom, lack of concentration, and less than maximum physical effort. As a result, more harm than good may occur. Therefore, *variety* is the watchword—variety in vowel sounds, in the types of exercises, and in the time of the rehearsal period during which they are utilized.

Vocal exercises should be employed discriminately, since each exercise, if performed correctly, will produce a different type of color or tone quality. It is important to realize, then, that the overuse of one

[5]Exercise enthusiasts in the choir may mention other exercises, such as leg stretches, sit-ups, push-ups, and jumping jacks, which, although beneficial, are obviously inappropriate for class use. Suggest that they do them individually prior to rehearsals. Jogging in place for ten to fifteen seconds is one activity, however, that can be done in the rehearsal room.

exercise to the neglect of another will not always produce the best or the desired results. For example, if the choir sings with an overly dark tone, the conductor should avoid too much vocalization on the darker vowels, such as **aw** and **oh.** It might be well for the choir director or the voice teacher to think of various vocal exercises as a physician might think of a prescription or a form of therapy—that is, as a remedy or a treatment for a specific individual or group need. For choral blend, a uniformity of vowel production must be achieved. Although the conductor is definitely concerned with individual voices and needs, the problem in practice is, for the most part, one of dealing with the tone problems of a large group.

Let us first of all examine the type of tone quality desired for high school, college, and community choral groups. There are several schools of thought concerning the "ideal" quality, and in addition, certain choral selections require subtle changes in voice quality. Nevertheless, it is essential that the conductor develop his concept of tone through private voice study and by listening to numerous choruses and choral recordings, and then strive toward that goal. A word of caution, however! Sometimes the inexperienced high school conductor is overzealous in his attempts to achieve the mature quality found only in adult choirs, and in his eagerness develops a tenseness and a rigidity in the youthful voices. High school choirs have characteristic qualities common to that age level. Those qualities should be carefully nurtured and allowed to develop slowly. Only in this way will the ultimate in high school choral singing be achieved.

Individuals participating for the first time in a choir generally display an abundance of technical faults. Some may sing with a throaty tone, others with white, nasal, or colorless tones. Without uniformity in tone production, blend is practically unattainable.

Just what type of voices are we endeavoring to develop? There are two characteristics that the conductor should strive to develop in voices at the outset: (1) a deep-set vowel and (2) a high-forward resonance. When these two characteristics are present, the tone quality is rich and beautiful and capable of lending itself to the wide gamut of emotions found in choral literature. Various exercises contribute to the development of these qualities and will be presented on the following pages.

Achieving Deep-set Vowels

The deep-set vowel is usually associated with maturity and roundness of tone and with naturalness of production. It is achieved through minimizing unnecessary tension in the vocal apparatus and by correctly utilizing the resonance cavities of the mouth and throat. As has been previously discussed, correct posture and breath control are essential conditions. Clavicular breathing should be avoided, since the resultant tension in the shoulder muscles and the upper regions of the chest is often reflected in the muscles surrounding the larynx, thus inhibiting the proper functioning of the vocal mechanism.[6]

The writer has observed high school and adult choral groups in various sections of the country. One of the most objectionable faults is that many teenagers, as well as adults, sing with a tight, rigid jaw. Some individuals believe that this condition is a reflection of environmental tensions. More likely, the condition results from lack of proper vocal training and individual awareness of the problem. Whatever the exact cause, the effect is disastrous upon choral singing. Tenseness in the jaw and facial muscles results in strident, pinched, and colorless tones. Depth of tone and subsequent choral blend are impossible to attain until the condition is alleviated. Following are suggested devices, techniques, and exercises to help eliminate this problem.

1. Singers should be instructed to concentrate upon relaxing their facial muscles. Gently stroking the face with the fingertips is one means of eliminating excessive tension that may be utilized in rehearsals. To develop further the singers' understanding of the importance of this relaxation, choir members should be asked to observe the facial expressions of a recognized concert singer on television. In addition, they should compare their mental conception of this singer with their own facial expressions by checking in a mirror. (Enlargements of close-up group photographs taken during rehearsals provide a further objective means for the singers to analyze their difficulties.)

2. In addition to relaxing the lips and facial muscles, singers must relax their jaws and open their mouths wide if they are to achieve deep-set vowels. The darker vowels, such as **oh, aw,** and **ah,** should have a great deal of depth and should be formed low in the throat. In order to make them round and full, one should think of singing the vowels up and down rather than across. The jaw should be free from any rigidity. Exercise 1 is an excellent device for loosening the jaw and "rounding out" the tone.

EXERCISE 1

Yah, yah, yah, yah, yah,   Yah, yah, yah, yah, yah, *etc.*

1. Vocalize from low B♭ (below the staff) to E♭ (fourth space, treble clef). Much of the value of the exercise is lost if it is sung in the extreme high range of the voice.

[6]This is a particularly troublesome problem with high school boys, since large chest expansion seems to be associated with manliness. The problem here can be lessened somewhat by means of a frank and open discussion concerning athletes who employ deep abdominal breathing in order to increase their own breath control.

2. In this exercise use lots of jaw action. A helpful physical device is for the singer to place the tips of each index finger on the approximate hinge position of the jaw. This procedure serves to increase one's awareness of the jaw movement.

3. In singing this exercise, there is an unconscious tendency for some singers to pull the upper lip downward over the upper front teeth. This practice should be discouraged since it is likely to darken the tone quality too much. Singers should be instructed to hold the upper lip stationary, with just a portion of the upper teeth remaining visible. A useful device is to have the singers check this position with a hand mirror. It should prove enlightening to them.

4. It has been found profitable for the singers to check one another's jaw movements on this exercise. This procedure seems to provide the proper motivation for those persons who have difficulty with the exercise.

When the vowel **ah** is used, Exercise 2 is also helpful in developing the deep-set vowel. It has an added ear-training value, in that it provides an opportunity for the singers to hear their parts more clearly in relationship to the other tones in the chord.

EXERCISE 2

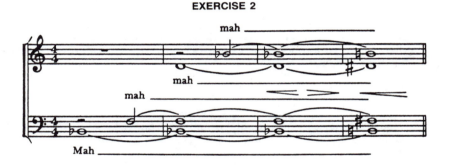

1. Director should cue each entrance.
2. Singers should hold back the breath, explode the attack, and drop the jaw.
3. Crescendo, then decrescendo, on final chord.
4. Proceed upward or downward by half steps.
5. For the purpose of developing uniformity of vowel production, the exercise should also be sung on the various other vowels. Each vowel should be preceded by the consonant **m.**

Developing High-Forward Resonance

The preceding exercises, if used consistently, develop depth in the voices and transform the thin, shallow voices of inexperienced singers into rounder and deeper voices. If used to the total exclusion of other exercises, however, they will make the voices dark and throaty; as a result flatting sometimes occurs. To be most effective, these devices and exercises must be coupled with exercises designed to develop focus or high-forward resonance in the voices.

When sound is produced by vibration of the vocal cords, it moves in many directions and is resonated and amplified in the various cavities of the body—that is, the chest, the pharynx, the mouth, and the nasal cavity. A sound, unrestricted by muscular tension, will seek and utilize *all* these resonating areas. Muscular tension and interference, however, often limit the maximum use of these resonating chambers. Tension in the throat muscles prevents the most effective use of the pharynx as a resonator, and, as previously mentioned, a tight, rigid jaw and an unruly tongue reduce the size of the oral cavity and lessen its effectiveness as a resonator.

Of particular concern to the choral conductor is the development of focus or high-forward resonance in the voice. By this is meant simply the maximum utilization of the resonating cavities or chambers above the oropharynx and the mouth, specifically the nasopharynx and the nasal cavity. The key to the most effective use of these resonating areas is to maintain a sensation of an opening between the oropharynx and the nasopharynx. The organ that regulates the size of the opening is the velum, or soft palate (see Figure 41). When food is swallowed the velum

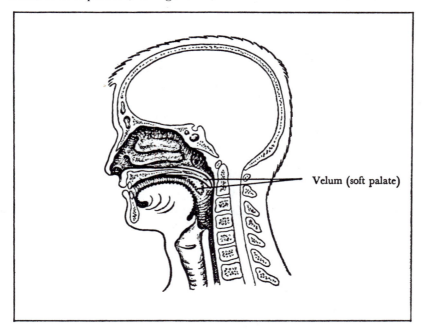

Velum (soft palate)

FIGURE 41 The velum, or soft palate—a controlling factor in the utilization of the nasopharyngeal cavity and the nasal cavity as resonance chambers. The dotted lines indicate the velum in its lowered or relaxed position.

moves posterosuperiorly and maintains contact with the posterior wall of the pharynx. This muscular adjustment also occurs in the articulation of certain consonants. If this adjustment did not occur, air would escape through the nose, and the precise articulation of these consonants could not be achieved. As the nasal consonants **m, n,** and **ng** are produced, the velum is in its relaxed, or lowered, position, the nasal port is widely open, and the nasopharynx and the nasal cavity serve as a more predominant center of tonal resonance. The velar opening, or nasal port, may be maintained, however, by a means other than relaxing or lowering the soft palate. It also may be opened by an upward and forward tension of the velum—as experienced in a deep yawn.[7] This suggested movement of the velum is contrary to the velopharyngeal contact utilized in articulating certain consonants.[8]

According to a survey by Burgin, there appears among voice teachers to be a general acceptance of the concept of a raised soft palate in singing. Yawning serves the purpose of raising the soft palate, as well as opening the throat. Also, according to Burgin, "this device [the yawn] appears to be among the most popularly accepted in the broad scope of training the singing voice."[9]

Singers should strive to develop a high-forward arch to the velum, or soft palate, so that the nasal port may remain slightly open, thus allowing for an extension of the vibrating column of air emanating from the larynx and a more effective use of the upper resonating cavities.[10]

Thus singers should think of the nasopharynx as an extension of the oropharynx and should concentrate on drawing the breath "inward and upward." Many choral conductors recommend yawning as a means of developing a sensation of the high-forward arch of the velum. Other directors simply suggest singing with a sensation of a high arch in the back of the mouth. Both devices, however, achieve the same desired purpose and can be utilized to facilitate this necessary physical adjustment.

Muscles work in pairs throughout the body. When one set is in tension to effect a specific movement or action, the opposing set of muscles should be relaxed. When the opposing set of muscles is not relaxed, unnecessary tension occurs, resulting in wasted energy. The

[7]Cf. G. Oscar Russell, *Speech and Voice* (New York: Macmillan, 1931), p. 18.

[8]Cf. Robert F. Hagerty and others, "Soft Palate Movement in Normals," *Journal of Speech and Hearing Research,* 1, no. 4 (December 1958), 325–30.

[9]John Carroll Burgin, *Teaching Singing* (Metuchen, N.J.: Scarecrow, 1973), p. 77.

[10]There is not complete agreement on the extent of the opening between the oropharynx and the nasopharynx. X-ray studies during phonation indicate a changing size, depending on the vowel produced, and variations on the same vowel among different singers. However, regardless of the size of the opening, the imagery of directing the tone through this space is helpful in achieving high-forward resonance.

singer, therefore, must endeavor to relax the opposing muscles, so that the others may function at optimum efficiency. This is the singer's goal. However, until the correct vocal adjustment becomes automatic in nature, the singer must apply a degree of conscious effort toward arching the velum and opening the passage between the oropharynx and the nasopharynx.

Sagging facial muscles are also detrimental to the development of high-forward resonance. The feeling of a short upper lip and a lifting of the facial muscles directly above the upper lip will aid in the development of this resonance. When the correct singing sensation is achieved and the process becomes automatic, then the singer will be able to produce fully resonated tones with a minimum of effort. Exercises 3–5, and the specific suggestions pertaining to their use, will be helpful in developing high-forward resonance in the voice.

EXERCISE 3

Hah,   hah,   hah,   hah,   hah,   hah,   hah,   hah.

1. Vocalize on the descending major scales C, D♭ (C♯), D, and E♭. Sing each scale slowly, taking a "catchbreath" between each scale step.
2. Sing with the tips of two fingers between the teeth. This ensures an open mouth and a freer emission of the tone.
3. The feeling of the high arched roof of the mouth, as in yawning, is necessary for the proper adjustment of the velum, or soft palate, and the correct focus of the tone or voice. Strive to develop this sensation.
4. When yawning, notice the position of the lips. In their most relaxed position, they are extended away from the teeth; the upper lip is raised slightly and a portion of the upper teeth is visible.
5. Concentrate on the sensation of drawing the breath inward in a relatively narrow stream and focusing the tone in the resonating cavities behind the bridge of the nose. (Using various physical devices will assist the singer in achieving the correct tonal focus. Drawing the hand inward toward the body facilitates the singer's concept of the correct direction of the flow of the breath.[11] Placing the fingertips on the bridge of the nose is also a reminder of the correct point of tonal focus.)
6. Vocalize all voices to their lowest tones. Avoid forcing the voices in the lower register.
7. Avoid distorting and altering the vowel sound. A common pitfall is to change the vowel **ah** to **uh** when vocalizing in the lower register of the voice.

[11]The flow of the breath is actually from the lungs, through the larynx, and into the resonating chambers or cavities. The sensation of drawing the breath inward simply assists in directing the tone into the cavities above the pharynx and the oral cavity.

After a sufficient degree of progress has been made toward achieving correct resonance, Exercises 4 and 5 may be alternated with Exercise 3.

EXERCISE 4

Hah, _____   hah, _____

hah, _____   hah. _____

1. Sing each scale (C, D♭, D, E♭) slowly, taking a full breath between each descending scale.
2. Sing with the tips of two fingers between the teeth.
3. Vocalize all voices to their lowest tones. Avoid forcing the voices and distorting the vowel sounds in the lower register.
4. Concentrate on achieving correct tonal focus (see suggestions 3, 4, and 5 in Exercise 3).

EXERCISE 5

Hah, _____   hah, _____ *etc.*

1. Start on middle C and vocalize upward by half steps an octave or more.
2. Vocalize with the tips of two fingers between the teeth. A freer emission of the tone is thus assured.
3. Raise the upper lip and extend away from the teeth.
4. The feeling of the high arched roof of the mouth, as in yawning, is necessary for the proper adjustment of the velum. Strive to attain the sensation.

When practicing Exercise 5, male singers quite often become easily discouraged when their voices crack or break in the upper range. Considerable benefit can accrue to the singers if they are encouraged to continue the exercise upward in a light, head-voice or falsetto quality.

One of the obstacles to achieving the proper placement of voices relates to many singers' misconception that the darker vowels, such as **ah** and **oh,** are to be placed far back in the mouth or throat. In baritones and basses, in particular, this idea often results in an overly dark sound that is difficult to blend and too heavy to be properly supported by the breath, thus resulting in pitch and intonation problems for the choir. Exercises 6 and 7, therefore, have the same basic objectives as Exercises 3, 4, and 5, but they may be used as alternatives and will be particularly helpful for lightening and focusing the tone.

EXERCISE 6

Ee __ ah _____ , ee __ ah _____ *etc.*

1. Vocalize upward by half steps, but stay primarily in the middle range of the voices.
2. Drop the relaxed jaw on the **ah** vowel, endeavoring to keep the placement forward. Strive for a bright **ah** vowel, and avoid the darker sound that occurs if it is placed farther back in the mouth.

EXERCISE 7

Ee ay ah_____ , ee ay ah_____

1. Vocalize upward by half steps, but stay primarily in the middle range of the voices.
2. Maintain a frontal placement on all vowels; that is, strive for a bright sound.

To afford further variety, Exercises 8, 9, and 10 also may be utilized periodically as warm-up exercises.

Exercise 8 may be notated on the chalkboard or introduced by means of syllables (all voices sing the interval of the octave—*do* to *do;* sopranos sustain *do,* altos descend to *mi,* tenors descend to *sol,* and basses descend to *do*).

EXERCISE 8

Ee - ah _____

1. Singers should endeavor to maintain the forward placement of the **ee** vowel throughout the exercise; however, as the sound changes to **ah** the jaw should drop and be kept relaxed.

2. Singers should maintain adequate breath support and should crescendo toward the end of the exercise.

3. The exercise may be repeated upward by half steps (not to exceed four or five half steps, depending on the maturity of the voices).

To afford variety, Exercises 9 and 10 may be alternated on subsequent days with Exercise 8.

EXERCISE 9

Ee ah _____ ee ah _____ oo (or ee)

1. Sing the exercise in unison.
2. Combine two parts—**SA, TB, ST, AB.**
3. Sing in four parts.
4. Repeat upward or downward by half steps.

EXERCISE 10

Ee ay ah oh ee ay__ ah__ oh__ ee ay__ ah__ oh__ ee

The use of the nasal consonants (**m, n,** and **ng**) as a means of establishing a sensation for and a feeling of correct resonance is a somewhat controversial subject. One position states that "humming is not singing" and that the two acts require a different adjustment of the velum. In the broadest sense, this statement is true; that is, in humming, the velum is in its relaxed, or lowered, position, whereas in singing, this is seldom, if ever, the case.

The use of humming prior to singing, the use of the consonants **m, n,** and **ng** as a prefix to the vocalization of various vowels, and the vocalization of such words as *sing* and *hung* (immediately moving to and sustaining the **ng** sound) have become common practices. Proponents of the value of humming maintain that it provides the best muscular setting for the attainment of resonance. In this respect, the use of the nasal consonants has value, because during this act the vocal mechanism is well coordinated. Excessive tension in any aspect of the vocal mechanism will prevent the attainment of a fully resonated tone. Therefore, humming and the use of the other nasal consonants have value in that they facilitate the beginning of phonation without excessive muscular tension. Because of this "relaxing effect," choir members should endeavor to retain the humming sensation while singing.

EXERCISE 11

Hm

The humming exercise shown in Exercise 11 may be used for the purpose just described. In addition, it has a certain ear-training value, if the group is instructed to listen carefully and to hold the chord until it is perfectly in tune. Instruct the singers to avoid gasping for breath; when a breath is needed they should drop out of the ensemble, take a full breath, and then reenter as unobtrusively as possible. Some persons may hum incorrectly. To check, ask the group to open their mouths, while humming, at a given signal. If the tone changes into the vowel **ah,** the group is humming incorrectly. When the mouth is opened, the correctly produced tone should change from **hm** to **ng.** It is wise to use this checking device frequently. The **ng** sound has greater intensity than the **hm** sound, and may be preferable for use with certain selections calling for a humming background. Some high school directors have even found this exercise to be a profitable time-saver—when the students in the chorus enter the rehearsal room, they immediately take their seats and commence humming their respective tones. After all the choir members have arrived, the director may immediately begin the rehearsal, since the group is in a more receptive frame of mind and less inclined toward verbal outbursts.

In striving for the development of deep-set vowels and a high-forward resonance, one could mistakenly get the idea that one vocal characteristic should purposely be developed prior to the other. In practice, the two should be developed simultaneously.

If the utmost is to be gained from the previously mentioned exercises, they should be sung with a free, open throat. Excess tension in the muscles around the larynx should be eliminated insofar as possible. Vocalization on the vowel **oo** has been found to be helpful in opening the throat. When vocalizing on this vowel, it is suggested that the tips of two fingers be placed between the front teeth. This procedure assists in opening the throat and aids in a freer emission of the tone, substantially assisting in the development of the higher range of the voice.

Developing the Vocal Range

Voices with a limited vocal range make the performance of a considerable amount of choral literature prohibitive. If music with an extreme tessitura is used, the voices are likely to sound harsh, strained, and unmusical. Under such circumstances, blend, balance, and good intonation are impossible to attain. Therefore, developing the singers' vocal range is an important and essential task of the choral conductor.

The singing of correctly produced high tones is dependent upon an open throat (achieved through vocalization of the **oo** vowel) and a high-forward resonance (see Exercises 3 and 4). The heavy chest quality of the middle range is not easily produced in the upper limits of the voice, and any attempt to do so will often result in unmusical sounds and breaks in the flow of the tone; therefore, the singers should try to lighten their voice quality in vocalizing Exercise 12, which is suggested for helping to develop the upper range.

EXERCISE 12

1. Vocalize, in the beginning, on the vowel **oo.** This vowel opens the throat and facilitates a freer production of tone. As progress is made, however, it is desirable periodically to alternate the **oo** with the **ah** vowel. The latter vowel will give greater brilliance and "ring" to the voice.

2. Vocalize with the tips of two fingers between the teeth. This device facilitates the dropping of the jaw, which is an absolutely essential condition in singing the high tones.

3. When singing *high,* think *low,* and vice versa. This thought facilitates the necessary muscular adjustment.

4. Vocalize all voices up to the extreme limits of their range. Sopranos and tenors should vocalize up to high C, and altos and basses at least up to high A♭.

Female voices will find Exercise 12 comparatively easy—that is, much easier than will the male voices. Female voices are able to sing the higher pitches without the unique muscular adjustment problem that occurs with male voices. With female voices, the range simply needs strengthening and developing. The problem is not quite the same with the male voice. In vocalizing Exercise 12, male voices will quite naturally and normally change into a "falsetto" quality at a certain point. At first there may be some embarrassment on the part of the younger singers, but this should be expected. They should be told of the many fine singers who have extended their ranges by first learning how to use their falsetto voice correctly. Indeed, there may even be places in the literature where such a quality will be desired by the tenor voices.

There will exist, however, many other instances where it will be necessary and desirable for the male singers to sing with a full resonant quality in their high range. In order to do so, it will be necessary to develop the so-called covered tone, in which the vowel sound is slightly altered or modified toward one which is more easily produced in the upper register. It is full and resonant and is devoid of any falsetto characteristics. In singing the covered tone, a certain firming of the vocal mechanism occurs and the vowels are slightly modified—generally toward the **uh** sound.[12] Exercise 13 is suggested as a means of obtaining the desired tone quality and placement.

EXERCISE 13

Beginning on first line E (treble clef), slur up an octave, keeping the resonance high and forward. The sounds **ing** and **ay** are generally the best to begin with; however, eventually the other vowels should be used as well. Remember that the jaw must be dropped on all high tones. On the open vowels, sing with the tips of two fingers between the teeth. In singing the closed vowels **ee** and **i,** the back sides of the tongue should be held against the upper back teeth. This device facilitates an easier and freer production of tone. Basses should eventually vocalize up to high A♭ and the tenors to high C.

[12]The covered tone versus the open tone has been a controversial subject for many years. For a historical background, as well as an experimental analysis, see Luchsinger and Arnold, *Voice-Speech Language,* pp. 103–6.

In developing the lower range of the voice, it is suggested that the singers vocalize, using the vowel **ah,** on the descending five-tone scale (see Exercise 19 in Chapter 7). The exercise should be begun on about first space F (treble clef) and should be sung slowly downward. The voices should not be forced, but should be produced with a naturally resonant quality. The greatest deterrent to developing the lower range in both male and female voices is that the singers often fail to drop the jaw. As a result, a considerable portion of the lower range of the voice frequently remains undeveloped. In addition, when the jaw is not dropped, the vowel sound will often change from **ah** to **uh.** Singing the exercise with the tips of two fingers between the teeth will help to alleviate this problem.

Developing Flexibility

A flexible voice is usually a freely produced voice—one that is devoid of excessive strain and tension. A marked degree of flexibility is essential if desired interpretative effects are to be achieved in choral music. Exercises 14a and 14b, shown here, should prove profitable in developing flexibility in voices.

EXERCISE 14

1. Vocalize only in the middle range of the voice. Proceed upward by half steps.
2. Insert the tips of two fingers between the teeth. This assists in a free emission of the tone.
3. Avoid singing too loudly. Excessive tension is sometimes created in this way, thus making the exercise more difficult and thereby decreasing the benefit from it.
4. At first, sing the exercise quite slowly—until the student becomes acquainted with it; then gradually increase the tempo.
5. Practice exercises in both a legato style and a half-staccato style.

ACHIEVING CORRECT DICTION

Correct diction, necessary to the effective communication of the central thought of the text, is the overall manner of vocal utterance as it pertains to the conveying of meanings and ideas. Pronunciation, enunciation, and articulation are all integral aspects of diction; these terms are often used rather loosely, and frequently their precise meanings are misunderstood.

Pronunciation is the manner of uttering the words, as regards the use of appropriate vowel and consonant sounds and the proper accent of words and phrases. "Sing as you speak" is a statement often heard. This advice would be worthwhile, providing everyone spoke correctly and there was a reasonable degree of uniformity in the speech mannerisms and habits of individuals. Careful analysis of words spoken or sung by individuals will reveal a wide variety of similar, yet distinctly different, pronunciations of each vocal sound.

Vocal mannerisms characteristic of particular regional areas should be avoided, and a standardized "general American" approach to pronunciation, as utilized by most radio and television announcers, should be adopted. In an attempt to become "educated," singers should avoid extreme alterations in pronunciation, lest they sound unnatural, affected, and ridiculous to local audiences. An exception to the use of a standardized general American approach to pronunciation in choral singing is readily evident in the performance of certain folk songs requiring a dialectal treatment. Pronunciation problems inherent in these choral selections should be carefully analyzed in regard to vowel and consonant sounds and accent or stress, and then diligently rehearsed. Careful attention must be given to all pronunciation problems if effective communication of the text is to be achieved.

Enunciation pertains to the manner of vocal utterance as regards distinctness and clarity of the various vowel and consonant sounds. Individuals who mumble their words and who slur or omit consonants have fallen into slovenly habits that are not conducive to good communication. The conductor should use every possible means to develop the singers' awareness of this problem. Demonstrating the singers' faults through imitation, and playing back tape recordings of rehearsals and performances, are suggested procedures for improving enunciation.[13] Only when effective enunciation is achieved will the central thought of the music be communicated to the listening audience.

---

[13]Imitation of singers' faults always should be done in a spirit of joviality—never in a ridiculing manner. Imitation should be followed immediately by the conductor's demonstration of correct procedures and the chorus's renewed efforts toward improvement.

Articulation pertains to the physical action of the articulating organs (tongue, lips, teeth, palate, and lower jaw) in forming and altering the channels and in projecting the various vocal sounds necessary to achieve intelligible communication. A further differentiation may be made between articulation and enunciation. When an individual is unable to speak distinctly because of lack of physical control, such as occurs with young children, he may be said to have poor articulation. When an individual's vocal utterance is indistinct because of slovenly diction and lack of concentrated effort, it may be said that his speech or singing is poorly enunciated.

Difference between Vowels and Consonants

The vowels are used for sustaining the singing tone, and the breath flow is continuous. In the sounding or the articulation of the consonants, the flow of breath is momentarily interrupted. This is the basic difference between the vowels and the consonants.

Vowels are the chief vehicle for sustaining the vocal tone, whereas consonants have shorter sustaining qualities and in some instances may detract from the legato flow of the music. The vowels are all voiced sounds—that is, the vocal cords are set into vibration. However, approximately one third of the consonants are voiceless. Intelligibility of the consonants is dependent upon the precise movements of the articulating organs, while the vowels are dependent more upon duration and resonance for their identity.[14] Singing a choral selection on the vowels only is a useful device for achieving uniformity of vowel production and improving tonal blend. Moreover, it demonstrates the fact that vowels have little meaning by themselves, and that intelligibility of the text is dependent primarily on the precise articulation of the consonants.

Vowels

If uniform tone production and tonal blend are to be achieved, the choral conductor must be cognizant of the precise differences of vowel sounds used in speaking and singing, and he must develop a similar awareness on the part of his choristers. Singers as a group are usually familiar with the primary vowels (**ee, ay, ah, oh, oo**), since these are used extensively as a beginning point in vocalization. However, they are less familiar with the precise differences among the other vowel sounds. The vowel chart in Figure 42 illustrates the variety of vowel sounds that occur in the texts of choral literature. The International Phonetic Alphabet,

---

[14]The formation of intelligible vowel sounds is, of course, dependent upon the adjustment of the articulating organs; however, the vowels are not so dependent upon such a rapid and precise adjustment as are the consonants.

PHONETIC SYMBOLS	DIACRITICAL MARKINGS	ILLUSTRATIVE SYMBOLS	EXAMPLES
i (long e)	ē	ee	see, each, tree, Easter, free, glee, feet, sleep, deep, sheep, wheel
ɪ (short i)	ĭ	ĭ	sing, is, will, him, thing, ship, wish, April, similar, crib, been, king
e (long a)	ā	ay	say, faith, age, angel, rain, same, maiden, away, day, way, great
ɛ (short e)	ĕ	eh	yet, end, enter, help, never, every, let, men, said, then
æ (short a)	ă	ă	at, rang, mantle, ashes, agony, began, can, cat, that, than
a	ȧ	ȧ	ask, grass, laugh, bath, calf, craft, raft, chance, chaff
ɑ	ä	ah	father, Amen, alms, army, far, heart, calm, palm, psalm
ɒ (short o)	ŏ	ŏ	stop, hot, sorry, olive, God, watch, wander, John, yon
ɔ	ô	aw	law, all, awe, autumn, always, walk, warm, dawn
o (long o)	ō	oh	flow, old, road, hope, low, soul, snow, open, so, boat, home, cold
ʊ	o͝o	o͝o	look, bosom, took, foot, stood, should, would, book, full, brook
u	o͞o	oo	who, too, moon, whose, blue, true, through, flew, soon, tomb
ɝ	ûr	ur	birth, early, earth, world, worth, perfect, burden, were
ɚ	ēr	er	ever, never, another, pleasure, mother, weather, measure
ə	ə, ȧ	uh	about, around, firmament, America, awhile, away, above
ʌ (short u)	ŭ	uh	but, sun, done, creation, other, until, wonder, thunder

FIGURE 42   The single vowels frequently occurring in choral literature, with symbols and examples by which the conductor may illustrate and correct pronunciation difficulties.

with a specific symbol for each sound, was devised by phoneticians for the purpose of providing an accurate means of identifying and differentiating among the various vowel and consonant sounds. In the first column of this chart, the phonetic symbols for the different vowel sounds are listed. The diacritical markings for these vowels, as used in English dictionaries, are listed in the second column. Both the phonetic symbols and the diacritical markings are presented primarily as a reference for the choral conductor. Because their precise meanings would not always be readily evident to a group of amateur singers, various illustrative symbols for each vowel are included in the third column, and

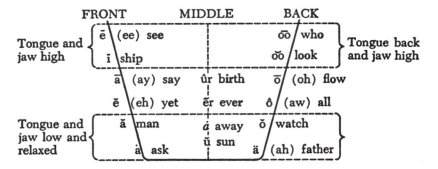

FIGURE 43   Front-to-back vowel formation.

are suggested for use with the choir members. When pronunciation difficulties occur in rehearsals, the conductor should identify and isolate particularly troublesome vowel sounds. These illustrative symbols may be written on the chalkboard, discussed, pronounced, and sung as a means of clarifying in the singers' minds the desired vowel sounds. Numerous examples of specific vowels as they occur in various words are also listed and may be used for illustrative or comparative purposes.

The formation of each vowel in Figure 43 requires distinctly different adjustments of the articulating organs, with the exception of the following. The vowel ɝ (**ûr**) is the counterpart of ɚ (**ēr**) and the adjustment of the articulating organs is quite similar. The vowel ɝ (**ûr**) occurs only on stressed syllables and the sound ɚ (**ēr**) occurs on unstressed syllables. Also, the vowel ʌ (**ŭ**) is the counterpart of ə and the position of the articulating organs is almost identical. The vowel ʌ (**ŭ**) occurs only on stressed syllables, whereas the vowel ə occurs only on unstressed syllables.

The various vowels are determined by the relative size and shape of the mouth and throat cavities. Specific determinants are the position of the tongue, the jaw, and the lips. As indicated in Figure 43, the vowels **ee** and **ĭ** are formed high and forward, while the vowel **oo** is formed lower in the throat. In singing the **ee** and **ĭ** vowels, the tongue is relatively high, whereas in the **oo** vowel the tongue is back. In both cases the position of the jaw is high and the mouth is somewhat closed. Because of this condition, these sounds are often referred to as *closed vowels*. All other vowels are referred to as *open vowels*, even though the position of the tongue, lips, and jaw will vary to some extent. The tongue is most relaxed and the jaw at its lowest position while singing the vowel **ah,** as in the word *father*. Because of the lesser degree of tension, this vowel is the most freely produced and is therefore frequently used as a beginning point in vocalization. (See also Figure 44.)

ee

oo

ay

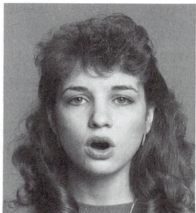

oh

ah

FIGURE 44 Relative positions of the lips and jaw in forming the primary vowels (*ee, ay, ah, oh, oo*). Compare with Figure 43.

In his or her exuberance, the novice chorister may tense the tongue too much and restrict the proper functioning of the vocal mechanism; a thin, shallow tone quality is likely to result. A helpful device is for the conductor to suggest to the singers that when singing the open vowels, the tongue remain in the relaxed position of the **ah** vowel. There is a limit, of course, to the practicality of this suggestion as it affects pronunciation; however, the device does facilitate the reduction of excessive tension in the tongue muscle.

When singing the closed vowels **ee** and **ĭ,** it is suggested that the singers place the back sides of the tongue against the upper back teeth. When the position of the tongue is too high, this device serves to enlarge the oral cavity somewhat and allows for a freer emission of tone. It also prevents one from forming these vowels too low in the throat, which may cause throatiness and flatting, especially in the upper range of the voice.

If a choral group sings with a nasal, white, or colorless tone, then vowels with extreme forward placement, such as **ee** and **ĭ,** should be used sparingly in vocalization, and the vowels formed lower in the throat, such as **aw, oh,** and **oo,** should be used. Conversely, if the group sings with an overly dark tone quality, then greater attention should be given the vowels formed high and forward. All the primary vowels (**ee, ay, ah, oh, oo**), however, should be utilized to some extent in vocalization, and concentration on any one group of vowels to the total exclusion of the others should be avoided.

Diphthongs

The diphthong may be defined as a compound vowel, or a syllable in which the sound changes from one vowel to another. In a simple or single vowel the articulating organs are held in a somewhat fixed position, whereas in a diphthong the articulating organs change position, thus altering the vowel sound. Figure 45 shows the diphthongs as they occur in English.

PHONETIC SYMBOLS	DIACRITICAL MARKINGS	ILLUSTRATIVE SYMBOLS	EXAMPLES
aɪ or ɑɪ	ī (long i)	ah—ī	night, high, light
aʊ or ɑʊ	ou	ah—ŏŏ	our, now, round
ɔɪ	oi	aw—ī	oil, rejoice, joy
eɪ	ā	ay—ī	day, faith, they
oʊ	ō	oh—ŏŏ	old, hope, low
ju or ɪʊ	ū	ī-ōō—	beauty, few, view

FIGURE 45 The diphthongs as they occur in English.

Except for **ju** or **Iu,** the durational stress should be given the primary vowel, and the secondary vowel should be sounded just prior to the release of the diphthong. It is often helpful if the secondary vowels are thought of in terms of the same durational stress as are the consonants. This procedure should be followed whenever the musical notation and the tempo permit the *initial* vowel in the diphthong to be sustained for any reasonable length of time. Thus the word *night* if sustained would be sung as **nah——ĭt,** not **nah-eet,** and the word *round* would be sung **rah——o͞ond,** not **rah-o͞ond.**

The diphthong **ju** is actually a consonant-vowel combination. An example of this sound occurs in the word *beauty*. In this instance it is the secondary rather than the primary vowel that should receive the durational stress. The word should always be pronounced **bĭ-o͞o——ty,** rather than **bē͞e-o͞o-ty.**

In the treatment of all diphthongs, a smoother transition from the primary to the secondary vowel will be achieved if the diphthong is thought of as a single, composite sound, rather than as two separate and distinct vowel sounds.

Classification of Consonants

Generally the consonants may be classified into two types—the voiced and the voiceless (nonvoiced). The voiceless consonants include **k, p, t, f, h, s,** and **sh,** whereas the voiced consonants include **b, d, v, z, zh, l, g, j, w, r, y, m, n,** and **ng.** The consonant **th** is voiced in some words and voiceless in others. In producing the voiced consonants the vocal cords are drawn together and set into vibration, and the consonant is voiced as a result, whereas in the voiceless consonants there is no perceptible movement of the vocal cords. The voiced consonants are softer in character and less explosive than the voiceless (nonvoiced) consonants. Since the voiced consonants have a slight sustaining quality, they may be used effectively to bridge the gap between various vowel sounds, especially in legato singing. Developing the singers' awareness of the essential differences between these consonant sounds will result in improved enunciation.

For a number of consonants, the adjustment of the articulating organs is similar. Only one adjustment is necessary for the following paired consonants: **t-d, p-b, f-v, k-g, s-z,** and **sh-zh.** The first consonant in the pair is voiceless, whereas the second consonant is voiced.[15] The words in Figure 46 serve to illustrate further the similarities between the adjustment of the articulators and the differences in sound duration.

---

[15]Exceptions to the pairing of voiced and voiceless consonants are **h, r, y, w, l, m, n,** and **ng.** All these consonants are voiced except the **h,** which is voiceless.

VOICELESS	VOICED
t—time, turtle, part	d—day, garden, afraid
p—pretty, happy, harp	b—bright, above, crib
f—faith, before, life	v—voices, ever, above
k—kind, because, music	g—garden, finger, flag
s—sing, asleep, peace	z—zenith, music, eyes
sh—sheep, ocean, wish	zh—Jacques, pleasure, rouge

FIGURE 46   Paired consonants, with similar articulator adjustments.

Words are listed that include the use of an initial, a medial, and a final consonant.

Another means of classifying the consonants is by the manner in which the flow of the breath is released. The *explosive* consonants are **p, b, t, d, ch, j (dzh), k,** and **g.** The *continuants are* **w, wh, f, v, th, s, z, sh, zh, r, j (y), h, l, m, n,** and **ng.** In articulating the *explosive* consonants, the flow of the breath is momentarily interrupted by the contact between the articulating organs. An explosive sound is emitted as the articulating organs are separated precisely and the pressure of the breath is released. In producing the *continuants,* the articulating organs assume a relatively fixed position as the sound is emitted.

Still another means of classifying the consonants is by the position or placement of the articulating organs involved in producing the sounds. They are as follows:

Bilabial (p, b, m, w)   Bilabial consonants are formed by the lower and upper lips. In forming the consonants **p** and **b,** the flow of the breath is interrupted momentarily as the lips are drawn together, and the breath is released in an explosive manner as the lips are suddenly opened; **p** is voiceless, and **b** is a voiced consonant. The consonant **m** is voiced and is formed by closing the lips, thus causing the flow of the breath to be emitted through the nasal passages. The consonant **w** is voiced and is referred to as a *bilabial glide.* It is produced by the lips forming a position similar to the **u** vowel and then moving or gliding quickly to the subsequent vowel sound.

Labiodental (f, v)   Labiodental consonants are formed by the lower lips and the upper teeth. The lower lip and the upper teeth are brought together and the breath is forced audibly between the two articulating organs; **f** is a voiceless consonant and **v** is voiced.

Lingua-dental (th)   Lingua-dental consonants are formed by the tip of the tongue touching the back side of the upper front teeth. The breath is forced between these two articulators; **th,** as in the word *thousand,* is voiceless and the sound **th,** as in the word *there,* is voiced.

Lingua-alveolar **(t, d, n, l, s, z)**   Lingua-alveolar consonants are formed by the tip of the tongue and the upper teeth or gum ridge. In forming the consonants **t** and **d,** the flow of the breath is interrupted momentarily by the contact between these two articulating organs. The consonants are sounded and the breath is released in a slightly explosive manner as the contact between these organs is released; **t** is voiceless and **d** is voiced. The **n** is voiced and is formed by placing the tip of the tongue against the gum ridge and directing the sound through the nasal passages. In the consonant **l,** which is also voiced, the tongue is placed against the gum ridge and the sound is emitted over the sides of the tongue. In forming the consonants **s** and **z,** the sides of the tongue are kept in contact with the upper back teeth, and the tip of the tongue rests just behind the upper front teeth, although not touching directly. The flow of the breath is directed over the tongue where it strikes the back edge of the upper front teeth, thus causing the hissing sound descriptive of these two consonants. The **s** is voiceless and the **z** is voiced.

Lingua-palatal **(sh, zh, ch, dzh, j, r)**   Lingua-palatal consonants are formed by the contact between the tongue and the hard palate. In producing the consonants **sh** and **zh,** the sides of the tongue are placed against the upper back teeth, as in the position for the consonant **s,** except that the tongue is drawn slightly back; **sh** is voiceless and **zh** is voiced.

In sounding the consonant combinations **ch** and **dzh,** the tongue contacts the hard palate at a point slightly farther back than for the consonant **t.** The tongue comes in contact with the upper back teeth and the flow of the breath is interrupted momentarily. As the tongue is released, the breath is emitted in an explosive manner. The consonant **ch** is voiceless, but the **dzh** is voiced.

The consonant **j,** as it occurs in certain words, is pronounced **dzh,** as in *judge* and *joy.* In other words, such as *hallelujah,* it assumes a softer, nonexplosive quality as in the consonant **y** in such words as *yet, year,* and *beyond.* The **y** is considered by many authorities to be a voiced consonant; however, some writers classify it as a semivowel.

In pronouncing the consonant **r,** the sides of the tongue contact the upper back teeth. The tip of the tongue is curled or drawn back toward the hard palate and, as the sound is emitted, it glides smoothly to the adjustment necessary for the following vowel sound. This adjustment is common in such words as *run, around,* and *read.* In some words, however, the tongue assumes a much lower position in the mouth, and the glide occurs in reverse order. This action occurs in such words as *heard,* *her,* and *creator,* where the preceding vowel sound is stressed. In this case, the consonant is articulated as the syllable is released. The consonant **r** is a voiced consonant.

*Velar **(k, g, ng)*** Velar consonants are formed by arching the back part of the tongue and pressing it lightly against the soft palate. In the **k** and **g** sounds, the flow of the breath is interrupted momentarily. As the contact is released and the tongue is lowered, the breath is exploded. The consonant **k** is voiceless, but the **g** is voiced. In forming the consonant **ng,** the position of the tongue is similar to that of the **k** and **g** sounds, except that the soft palate, or velum, is lowered slightly and the tongue is more relaxed, thus allowing the sound to be emitted through the nasal passages. The consonant **ng** is voiced.

*Glottal **(h)*** Glottal sounds are formed in the glottis, or the opening between the vocal cords. The vocal cords come together in a position that restricts the flow of the breath slightly, but not enough to set the cords into vibration. The consonant **h** is voiceless and is produced by forcing the breath between the nonvibrating vocal cords. This sound is often referred to as the *aspirate h.*

Styles of Diction

There are three basic styles of choral diction; namely, *legato, staccato,* and *marcato.* Each of these styles is distinctly different and each must be treated in a specific manner if effective interpretation is to be achieved.

Legato diction is smooth and connected. A minimum of emphasis should be given to the rhythmic stress or pulsation of the music in legato style. Legato phrases should be thought of in terms of long soaring and descending musical lines. In addition, the explosive qualities of the consonants should be minimized if they are to be smoothly blended with the vowel sounds.[16] In achieving this effect, the singers should carry over the final consonants of one syllable or word to the following syllable or word. The following examples serve to illustrate this concept: *My Lord, what a mornin'* is sung **mah-ee law—rd hwah-tuh maw—rn-nĭn.** *Lost in the night* is sung **law—stī-n-thuh nah—ĭt.** *My love dwelt in a northern land* is sung **mah-ee luhv dweh-l-tĭn nuh naw-r-thern lă—nd.**

Any exception to this rule occurs as a result of the diction being unintelligible or creating a somewhat ludicrous effect. In the following

---

[16]To achieve a smooth blending between the consonants and the vowels in legato diction, it will be helpful to sometimes ask the singers to sustain the consonants as well as the vowels. This device, although seemingly quite unorthodox, lessens the explosive qualities of the consonants and contributes substantially to the desired legato effect.

examples, it is desirable to separate the sounds, as indicated by the diagonal lines, with a slight break in the flow of the breath.

> *"She's / like the Swallow"* (from "She's like the Swallow," Newfoundland folk song, Oxford, No. X64).
>
> *"Slumbers / not nor sleeps"* (from "He Watching Over Israel"—Felix Mendelssohn, G. Schirmer, No. 2498).
>
> "We Three Kings of Orient / Are" (John H. Hopkins).

When the second syllable occurs on a stressed beat, one may further clarify the sound through careful articulation. That is, in the first example, articulate the word *like* with a "capital L."

Examples of octavo choral selections requiring a legato treatment of diction are included in the following list.[17]

"Ave Verum Corpus"—Wolfgang A. Mozart. G. Schirmer, No. 5471.
"Alleluia"—Randall Thompson. E. C. Schirmer, No. 1786.
"God So Loved the World" (from *The Crucifixion*)—John Stainer. G. Schirmer, No. 3798.
"How Lovely Is Thy Dwelling Place"—Johannes Brahms. G. Schirmer, No. 5124.
"I Wonder As I Wander" (Appalachian carol)—arr. John Jacob Niles and Lewis Henry Horton. G. Schirmer, No. 8708.
"Lost in the Night" (Finnish folk song)—arr. F. Melius Christiansen. Augsburg, No. 119.
"Mary Had a Baby"—William L. Dawson. Kjos, No. T118.
"My Love Dwelt in a Northern Land"—Edward Elgar. G. Schirmer, No. 2366.
"O Divine Redeemer"—Charles Gounod. Schmitt, Hall & McCreary, No. 1602.

In staccato diction, the words should be sung in a detached style as if there were a slight rest between each note. Good staccato diction depends upon distinct and precise articulation of the consonants. The lips should be flexible and devoid of excessive tension, and the lip movements should be exaggerated. The singers should refrain from singing too loudly, since excessive volume is likely to inhibit the precise articulation of the words. (Excessive volume tends to shift the focus from careful articulation to weighty tonal effects.) The vowels should be modified slightly and formed closer to the front of the mouth; words should be thought of as being formed on the lips, since sounds formed too far in the back of the mouth tend to become weighty, cumbersome, and difficult to articulate in a short, detached style. Exercise 15 will be helpful in developing precise lip movements and in improving staccato diction.

EXERCISE 15

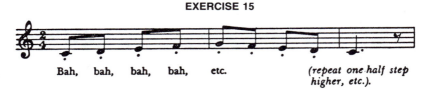

Bah, bah, bah, bah, etc.

(repeat one half step higher, etc.).

[17]For complete names and addresses of the publishers referred to in this and subsequent lists, see Appendix.

1. Use various consonants on this exercise (**b, p, t, f, d,** and so on).
2. Vocalize only in the middle register.
3. Work for clearness and precision of consonants and for flexibility. Flexibility will aid in developing freedom of voice production.

Examples of choral octavo publications requiring a staccato treatment of diction are included in the following list.

"Cicirinella" (Italian folk song)—arr. Max Krone. Witmark, No. 5-W2952.
"Hasten Swiftly, Hasten Softly"—Richard Kountz. Galaxy, No. 1750.
"I Saw Three Ships" (traditional English)—arr. Alice Parker and Robert Shaw. G. Schirmer, No. 10188.
"Rock-a My Soul" (spiritual)—arr. Joseph De Vaux. Bourne, No. B-211128.
"Sleigh, The"—Richard Kountz. G. Schirmer, No. 7459.
"We Wish You a Merry Christmas" (English folk song)—arr. the Krones. Kjos, No. 4006.
"Younger Generation"—Aaron Copland. Boosey & Hawkes, No. 1723.

In marcato diction, each note is sung with an accent, and the rhythm is quite pronounced. Effective marcato diction necessitates correct muscular action, which is precisely a sharp inward movement of the abdominal muscles.[18] Perhaps the most effective means of teaching this concept is to ask the singers to "grunt" each note in the correct musical rhythm. By placing the hand on the abdomen, singers are more likely to "feel" the movement, thus facilitating the achievement of this concept. With attention focused upon this muscular movement, it is helpful to have the group recite the text in correct musical rhythm before attempting further to apply the concept to actual singing. Exercise 16 is also helpful in achieving the correct muscular movement.

EXERCISE 16

Ho, ho, ho,   Hah, hah, hah,   Hee, hee, hee, hee,   hee   *(repeat upward by half steps)*

A marcato treatment of diction is required in sections of the following choral octavo publications, which are included for study and analysis.

"Hallelujah" (from *Mount of Olives*)—Ludwig van Beethoven. G. Schirmer, No. 2215.
"Hallelujah, Amen" (from *Judas Maccabaeus*)—George F. Handel. G. Schirmer, No. 9835.
"Hospodi Pomilui"—Alexis von Lvov, ed. Wilhousky. Carl Fischer, No. CM 6580.
"Let Their Celestial Concerts All Unite" (from *Samson*)—George F. Handel. E. C. Schirmer, No. 312.
"Psalm 150"—Louis Lewandowski, ed. H. R. Wilson. Schmitt, Hall & McCreary, No. 1640.

[18]For a discussion of the function of the abdominal muscles in the respiratory process, see section titled "The Vocal Instrument" earlier in this chapter.

Although many choral compositions require only one specific type of treatment as regards the style of diction, others will contain contrasting sections and phrases, each requiring a different treatment. Prior to introducing a selection to the chorus, the conductor should carefully analyze the text and the music, giving particular attention to the diction requirements. If in doubt about the style of diction, one should always look to the text of the music. The mood and emotional content of the text will reveal many things to the conductor, including various shadings and nuances necessary for the most effective interpretation of the music.

The Sibilant S

Of the sibilants, or hissing sounds, in English (**s, z, sh, zh, ch,** and **j**), the most troublesome, especially in legato singing, is the consonant **s.** Unless handled correctly, the singing of this consonant may remind one of sounds emanating from a snake pit. An example of this may be found in the words "God so loved the world" from the chorus in John Stainer's *The Crucifixion.* Unless careful attention is given to the sibilant **s** in the word **so,** considerable difficulty may occur with amateur choral groups. Amateurs are often likely to sing the phrase as **Gaw—dsssssssoh—luh— vd thuh wuh—rld.** The difficulty here lies primarily in the lack of the singers' accurate response to the rhythmic duration of the first measure. The **s** is anticipated with a resultant hissing sound. Tight, rigid jaws also contribute to the problem. If the jaw is not relaxed and the mouth kept open, the consonants **d** and **s** will inevitably follow too quickly the preceding vowel sound.

A solution to this specific problem, which also will apply to other problems of a similar nature, is first to concentrate upon the development of rhythmic accuracy in the chorus. The fact that the first measure has three beats must be understood and felt by all the singers. Having the group clap or tap the basic pulsation, or even conducting the traditional pattern for triple meter, will be helpful. Next, have the group sing the phrase on a neutral syllable, such as **loo.** After rhythmic accuracy has been achieved, the group should endeavor to prefix the vowel sound **oh** in the second measure with the consonants **ds.** The final result should sound as shown in Figure 47.

Some directors have found it particularly helpful, in dealing with

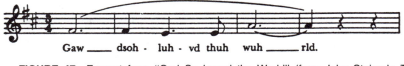

FIGURE 47 Excerpt from "God So Loved the World" (from John Stainer's *The Crucifixion*).

the hissing **s**'s, to assign the singing of them to only a particular portion of the chorus, with the remainder of the group singing only the vowel sound. The use of this approach certainly depends upon the requirements of the musical situation, and its success depends upon a clear understanding on the part of the singers as to their particular assignments.

In certain choral selections it will be helpful to minimize the **s** sound by changing it to the shorter **z** sound. Certainly the obvious advantage of this procedure becomes apparent in singing the words "slumbers not" from Mendelssohn's "He Watching over Israel."

The Troublesome *R*

The consonant **r** is often the source of unmusical sounds in amateur choral groups. The difficulty usually encountered is the overanticipation of the consonant, often caused through the singer's inaccurate response to the rhythmic duration of the music. Words such as *ever* and *world* are particular examples. How often has one heard the sound **eh-vuhrr** or the equally obnoxious sound of **wuhrrrr-ld?** To alleviate the problem, singers must not only be made more conscious of rhythmic duration, but must also be instructed to sustain the vowel preceding the consonant **r** sound, and to add the **r** only briefly upon the release of the syllable. Thus *ever* should be sung as **eh-vuh——r,** and *world* as **wuh——rld.**

The Consonants *M, N,* and *L*

Although most of the consonants have a comparatively short duration, the consonants **m, n,** and **l** are particular exceptions and have a certain degree of sustaining power. As such they may be effectively used, especially in legato singing, to bridge more smoothly the gap between the various vowel sounds. For example, when the group sings the word *amen,* the pronunciation **ah——mehn** contributes little to the smoothness of the legato phrase. A more effective procedure is to sing the word as **ah——m——mehn.** In this manner the consonant **m** serves to bridge the gap between the vowels **ah** and **eh,** thus creating an improved legato effect (Figure 48). To accomplish this successfully, the mouth must be closed

A -   men   Ah - -   m -   mehn.

a   *b*

FIGURE 48   An example of bridging the gap between two vowel sounds. Note (*a*) how the word is written, and (*b*) how it is effectively sung.

momentarily upon the release of the first vowel and opened upon the attack of the second vowel sound. (Obviously, this treatment is appropriate only when dealing with legato diction. Utilizing this approach with a vigorous Handelian chorus would be out of character and highly inappropriate. In most cases the approach used will be dictated by the demands of the musical situation.)

A similar treatment is suggested in dealing with the consonant **n**. In the words *mine eyes,* the tongue should touch the back side of the upper front teeth as the **n** is sounded. The tongue should drop immediately before the first syllable of the word *eyes.* The phrase should be sung as **mah-een-nah-eez.**

In most cases, when dealing with the double consonants, the first of the two should be eliminated. Usually this procedure is dictated by common sense. For example, the word *better* is pronounced **beh—tuhr** and not **beht—tuhr;** the word *torrents* is pronounced **tŏ-rĕnts** and not **tŏr-rĕnts.** An exception to the rule, however, is the treatment of the double consonant **ll.** In the word *allelujah,* for example, both **l**'s should be sounded if legato diction is to be clear and connected. The word *allelujah* should be sung **ahl—lay—loo—jah,** rather than **ah—lay—loo—jah.** The initial **l** should be added upon the release of the first vowel, and the second **l** should prefix the second vowel. Examples of this suggested treatment may be found in the following compositions.

"Alleluia"—Wolfgang A. Mozart. Carl Fischer, No. 541.
"Alleluia"—Randall Thompson. E. C. Schirmer, No. 1786.

The Aspirate *H*

The aspirate **h** is effected by means of a rapid flow of the breath, and when this condition does not prevail, the sound is often strident and ineffective. For example, in the word *hallelujah* in the chorus "Hallelujah, Amen" from the oratorio *Judas Maccabaeus* by Handel, the initial consonant is often slighted, resulting in a poor attack and a tightening of the vocal mechanism. To avoid this pitfall, singers should be instructed to anticipate the attack and precede the initial vowel with a rapid push or flow of the breath. When singing in marcato style, a sharp inward movement of the abdominal muscles will help to activate the flow of the breath. Adequate preparation on the part of both the conductor and the chorus is essential. Singers should be poised, alert, and ready for the attack, and the conductor should provide a clear, precise preparatory beat.

The aspirate **h** will often cause difficulty when combined with another consonant. For example, the word *when* often is pronounced as **wehn** rather than **hwehn.** In addition to activating the flow of the breath, singers must strive for careful, precise lip action to ensure the correct articulation of this consonant combination.

Vowel–Consonant Balance

The concept of "singing on the vowel," important as it is, should not be stressed at the expense of the consonants. Overemphasis upon the vowel sounds to the neglect of the consonants may result in beautiful choral tone, but the singing will generally lack luster and the desirable expressive characteristics.

To achieve correct, understandable diction, a balance must be maintained between the vowels and the consonants. When given only equal stress, the vowel sounds usually predominate over the consonants because of their sustaining characteristics. Therefore, to achieve a desirable balance the consonants should be overexaggerated—not in duration, but in the degree of intensity.[19] Emphasis should be placed upon careful and precise articulation rather than upon excessive duration of the consonants. It should be understood, however, that clear diction will not guarantee good voice production and that any attempt toward precise articulation should not cause unnecessary tension in the vocal mechanism. Articulation should occur away from the throat!

More effective results will be achieved by graphically illustrating on the chalkboard the relative degree of emphasis required in balancing the vowels and the consonants, as in Figure 49.

Final Consonants

Amateur singing groups often do not finish their words, especially at the ends of phrases. The poetic qualities of the text are thereby lost, and projection of the mood or spirit of the song becomes relatively ineffective. The conductor should be careful to provide a clear, precise release to the phrase so that the group may use this movement as a signal to add the final consonants. In addition, the conductor should endeavor to develop in his singers an increased consciousness of the problem. One effective approach is for the director to sing a series of words from which the final consonants are omitted; then ask the singers to identify the words. The variety of guesses will serve to illustrate the importance of including the final consonants of all words.

Tone and diction are the chief means of transmitting the poetic qualities of the music to the audience. Without properly produced and

---

[19] A word of caution! An exception to this treatment occurs in dealing with music in a legato style, as discussed earlier in this chapter under "Styles of Diction." Too much emphasis upon the intensity of the consonants is likely to disturb the legato flow of the music. In this style, emphasis should be placed upon the smooth connection of vowels and consonants.

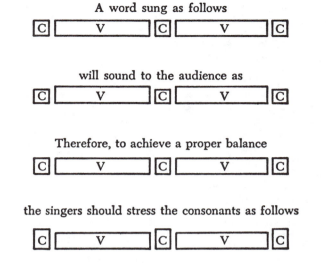

FIGURE 49

appropriate tone quality, the effectiveness of the music is lessened considerably, and without correct diction, choral tone becomes meaningless and little more than instrumental in character. Good tone quality and correct diction are essential to effective interpretation and, to be achieved, must receive the detailed, exacting attention of the choral conductor.

COMMONLY MISPRONOUNCED WORDS

A brief list of some common errors in pronunciation is shown in Figure 50.[20] This list, though incomplete, may serve as a starting point for the conductor who wishes to develop his own list of mispronounced words— or words that are troublesome in his particular locality.

MAINTAINING VOCAL HEALTH

Singers need to know how to adequately take care of their voices; it is important to them as individuals, as well as to the sound of the choir. It is generally understood that a singer's body is his or her instrument, and both its physical condition and one's mental attitude have an effect upon the singing voice. Therefore, it is necessary that directors provide appro-

[20]This list, of course, does not pertain to songs necessitating a dialectal treatment.

WORD	PRONUNCIATION
angel	ayn-je*h*l, not ayn-juhl
beautiful	bī-o͞o-tī-fo͝ol (bū-tī-fo͝ol), not be-o͞o-tee-fuhl
Bethlehem	Bĕth-lē-hĕm, not Bĕth-lē-ham
can	kăn, not kĭn
Christmas	Chrĭs-mȧs, not Chrĭs-muhs
creation	kree-ay-shu*h*n (kre-ā-shŭn), not kree-ay-shĭn
dew	dĭ-oo (dū), not do͞o. (Other words necessitating a similar pronunciation of the diphthong ĭ-o͞o are: new, beauty, few, view, pure, and human.)
for	fôr, not fûr
forget	fŏr-ge*h*t, not fŏr-gĭt
forgiveness	fŏr-gĭv-ne*h*s, not fŏr-gĭv-nuhs
Galilee	gă-lĭ-lē, not gă-luh-lē
get	ge*h*t, not gĭt
glory	glo*h*-ree, not glaw-ree
government	guh-*vern*-mehnt (gŭ-vĕrn-mĕnt), not guh-ver-mehnt
heaven	heh-ve*h*n, not heh-vuhn
judgment	jŭj-mĕnt, not jŭj-muhnt
kindness	kah-īnd-ne*h*s (kīnd-nĕs), not kah-īnd-nuhs
listen	lĭs-e*h*n, not lĭs-uhn
Lord	La*w*rd (Lôrd), not Lahrd, or Lowrd
love	lu*h*v (lŭv), not lahv
manger	mayn-jer (mān-jēr), not mayn-jîr
Mary	Me*h*-ree (Mâ-rē), not May-ree
mountain	moun-te*h*n, not moun-uhn
night	na*h*-ĭt (nīt), not naht, or nah-eet. (Other words containing the long ī [a diphthong] include high, sigh, fly, etc.)
open	oh-pe*h*n, not oh-puhn
poor	po͝or, not pohr
pretty	prĭ-tē, not prĭ-dē
roof	ro͞of, not ruhf
silent	sah-ī-le*h*nt (ŝĭ-lĕnt), not sah-ee-luhnt
spirit	spī-rĭt, not spī-ruht
the	th*ee* before words beginning with a vowel, or the silent *h* (th*ee* everlasting, th*ee* hour); th*uh* before words beginning with a consonant (th*uh* night, th*uh* heavens).
triumphant	trī-ŭm-fănt, not trī-ŭm-funt
virgin	vûr-jĭn, not vûr-juhn
wheel	*h*weel, not weel
when	*h*wĕn, not wĕn (wehn)
worship	wûr-shĭp, not wûr-shup
your	yo͝or, not yuhr

FIGURE 50 Common errors in pronunciation.

priate information on maintaining vocal health and continually stress its importance. Following are some important considerations.

1. Rest and exercise Bodily fatigue and mental stress can have a detrimental effect upon the voice; therefore, adequate rest is important in the prevention of vocal problems. Exercise helps one to sleep better, can reduce one's blood pressure, and is necessary to keep the body "in tune." Exercise may also help a person to achieve his or her desired body weight. Singers should exercise at least every other day for a minimum of twenty minutes. Exercise should be moderate in nature and not overly strenuous. Swimming, walking, and cycling are all recommended; however, the activity must be one that a person enjoys, looks forward to, and achieves satisfaction from doing. While moderate exercise may reduce muscular tension and help a person to sleep better, extremely vigorous exercise may be too fatiguing and detrimental to a singer's voice.

2. Diet   It is important for singers to maintain a balanced diet with at least one daily serving from each of the basic food groups.[21] Good nutrition cannot be overemphasized, since it contributes to overall good health. The old axiom "You are what you eat" might serve as a reminder to watch one's diet. Fatty foods should be avoided or eaten in moderation because they tend to be high in calories and low in nutrients.

The density of the laryngeal mucous is critical to singers because if it becomes too thick, congestion will occur, and coughing and clearing of the throat will usually result. Some mucous-causing foods, which singers should avoid, particularly before a concert, are milk, ice cream, chocolate, coffee, condiments (such as pepper, mustard, and meat sauces), and highly spiced foods. Conversely, drinking water or hot herbal tea with honey and lemon and using throat lozenges will usually increase the flow of laryngeal mucous secretions. While the use of antihistamines to control a postnasal drip has a drying effect, it also results in decreased vocal cord lubrication. Of course, the consumption of alcohol and the use of drugs can be disastrous to the human body and the singing voice. In some people, the chlorine in drinking water may have a drying effect on the mucous secretions around the vocal cords. If such should be the case, then singers may either drink only bottled water or boil their water before drinking it (keep well refrigerated until consumed). In such cases, singers should consult a larnygologist (a physician who specializes in vocal afflictions or difficulties and who is qualified to examine one's vocal cords) or an otolaryngologist (an ear, nose, and throat specialist). The physician can best advise them on their options.

Professional singers often refrain from eating before a singing engagement, and usually wait until after their performance. The reason is that a full stomach may often prevent effective use of the abdominal muscles in breathing, and gases may be emitted that adversely affect the laryngeal mucous. With amateur singers this advice may not always be

---

[21]It might prove beneficial to distribute information on this subject for the chorus to review individually, or have one or more chorus members provide a brief review for the group.

practical; however, they should at least be advised to eat lightly and avoid "stuffing themselves."

3. Body hydration   Individuals should drink an adequate amount of liquids, preferably water, each day to avoid dehydration and subsequent dryness of the vocal mechanism. The vocal cords are covered with a watery, thin mucous, which serves to lubricate the mechanism. During phonation, the vocal cords vibrate and rub against each other approximately 256 times per second on middle C. To avoid irritation and minimize friction, a thin lubricant is necessary. The lubricant required is almost 99.9% water. As an analogy, recall washing your hands with soap and water and then, after drying them, repeating the procedure without soap. Without the lubrication of the soap there is considerably more friction. The amount of water a person drinks each day should be sufficient to keep the urine clear, that is, the color of tap water.[22]

4. The speaking voice   Singers, if they are to protect their delicate vocal mechanisms, should avoid unnecessary loud speaking, and particularly the yelling and screaming that often occurs at school athletic events. While it may sometimes be difficult to control the enthusiasm of high school students, they should understand that such use of the voice is highly detrimental. Ask the singers, "How can you abuse your voice in this manner and expect to contribute to the choir as a singer?"

When singers audition for a choir, the director should note the general pitch levels of both the speaking voice and the singing voice. They should be approximately the same. When a teacher notices a wide difference between the two, then more careful voice testing is in order. Many students are inclined to speak too low, and that is detrimental to the singing voice. It may be noted that people in England often speak in more of a head voice. Suggest to singers that they try mixing the registers as they would in singing, since this can be beneficial to the singing voice.[23] Singers are taught to sing in the mask—that is, focus the tone in the frontal resonance chambers. Likewise, they should learn to speak in the mask, which is contrary to the practice of speaking too low and focusing the sound in the opposite direction.

If some persons appear to be misusing their voices, the director may wish to refer them to a speech pathologist—a specialist who diagnoses and treats misuse of the voice. Speech pathologists work closely with physicians and will not begin treatment until a physician examines the person and determines if the problem is of a nonorganic nature.

[22]Van Lawrence, "Sermon on Hydration" (The Evils of Dry), *The NATS Journal*, 42, no. 4 (March/April, 1986), 22–23.

[23]Cf. Morton Cooper, "Vocal Suicide in Singers," *The NATS Bulletin*, 26, no. 3 (February/March 1970), 7–10.

5. The common cold   The common head cold and sore throat seems to periodically plague singers, particularly when they least expect it. The cold virus is ever-present in the body, and when a person's resistance is lowered through fatigue, stress, poor diet, or exposure to the cold, the thin layer of protective mucous is disturbed and the virus is able to penetrate the nasal and throat cells and reproduce. The body, in turn, begins to fight the infection by stimulating increased blood flow into the areas involved. The blood contains antibodies that attack the virus. Part of the fluid from the additional blood drains out of the capillaries and into the nasopharynx. This fluid mixed with mucous results in the "runny nose" that is so troublesome.[24]

What to do? The best procedure is to get ample rest, keep warm, and drink lots of liquids, preferably warm. Also, don't sing with a sore throat. Warmth and relaxation promote increased blood flow to the surface of the skin, and more antibodies are produced to fight the infection. Drinking warm liquids helps to replace the fluids lost through one's increased temperature (the body's attempt to fight the virus). Acidic liquids, such as orange, lemon, or grapefruit juice, help by acidifying the throat. Cold viruses cannot survive in an acidic environment.[25]

6. The singer's environment   The environment can have an important effect upon one's voice. Is the room dustfree, or does it have drapes that serve as collectors of dust? Are there curtains surrounding the stage where some rehearsals or the final rehearsals are held? Is there adequate ventilation to clear dust particles and stale air from the room? The director should consider the consequences of such an environment for his singers.

People do, however, react differently to substances in their food and environment, and some may be allergic to certain substances that can have a detrimental effect on the delicate balance of laryngeal mucous, causing it to thicken and resulting in coughing and hoarseness. Some of these substances are tobacco smoke, dust, mold, and the pollen from weeds, grasses, and trees. These are among the many substances that one would be tested for at an allergy clinic.

Most singers are particularly sensitive to an air-conditioned environment, because in the cooling process moisture is removed from the air. An extended period of time in an air-conditioned room necessitates that singers drink considerably more water. An extended trip in an airplane, which is air-conditioned, will also have a drying effect on the laryngeal mucous. Also, when heating systems dry out the air, the use of a humidifier to replace the moisture is desirable, particularly in those

---

[24]Tom Ferguson, "Grandmother Knew Best," *The Mother Earth News*, no. 65 (September/October 1980), p. 140.
[25]Ibid.

parts of the country that have a dry climate and where there is relatively little humidity.

Professional singers' vocal health depends on where they live and how they live; that is, their lifestyles and how they take care of themselves. They get ample rest and exercise, they watch what they eat and drink, and they are highly sensitive to their environment. Good singers won't compromise their health!

7. The singer and the laryngologist   Choral directors should thoroughly acquaint themselves with physician-voice specialists in their community. To help identify the physician interested in working with singers, the director may contact a university voice department, a medical society, or a local hospital for recommendations. To discuss one's objectives, the director needs to meet personally with the physician. It is suggested that a time be scheduled immediately after the physician's last appointment for the day so there can be ample time to talk. Through this procedure the director will, it is hoped, find a laryngologist who has a special interest in helping singers and who enjoys this relationship. An invitation may be extended to this person to speak to your choir about maintaining vocal health. Such a physician is generally more than willing to accept such an invitation because he or she fully supports the belief that prevention is the best approach to maintaining optimal vocal health. His or her comments can augment and reinforce the information the director has already provided. After a general presentation, a question-and-answer period is desirable. Such meetings can be highly beneficial to the members of a choir, since singers seem to place more credence in what a physician tells them than in what others tell them.[26] After this meeting, the choir members will know whom to consult when they experience vocal difficulties. When problems occur, singers should arrange for the *last* appointment in the day so the physician will also have time to talk. Singers should introduce themselves and clearly state, "I am a singer and I need your help!" The conscientious physician will take the necessary time to provide guidance and to reassure the patient.

A GLOSSARY OF TERMS ON CHORAL TONE AND DICTION

Actuator: The part of the vocal mechanism that actuates, or begins, the flow of the breath, i.e., the lungs, the diaphragm, the intercostal muscles, and the abdominal muscles.
Articulation: The action of physical adjustment of the articulating organs in the formation of intelligible sounds.
Articulators: The part of the vocal mechanism that forms or shapes the various language

[26]For further information on maintaining vocal health, see the references listed at the end of this chapter.

sounds and that determines their particular distinguishable characteristics. Specific determiners are the tongue, lips, teeth, and lower jaw, the hard palate, and the velum, or soft palate.

Aspirate h: A vocal sound characterized by a slight constriction of the vocal cords; the cords are approximated, but not close enough to be set into vibration.

Bilabial: The consonants formed by the upper and lower lips **(p, b, m, w).**

Breath support: The flow or pressure of the breath against the vocal cords in an amount sufficient to effect the vibration necessary for a given pitch; considered to be adequate when phonation occurs without unnecessary constriction or tension in the laryngeal muscles.

Closed vowels: The vowels **ee, ĭ,** and **oo,** classified as such because of the relatively small oral cavity caused by the high position of the tongue in the mouth.

Consonants: The vocal sounds formed by precise, articulate movements of the lips, tongue, and jaw and characterized by an interruption or restriction of the flow of the breath. Consonants give intelligibility to vocal expression.

Covered tone: A slightly modified or altered vowel sound utilized by male singers in the production of tones in the upper register. The covered tone is full and resonant and lacking in any falsetto characteristics. A firming of the vocal mechanism occurs, and the vowel being sung is modified toward the **uh** vowel.

Deep-set vowels: Vowels characterized by a roundness and a fullness of tone quality, and a naturalness of tone production, creating a sensation of being formed low in the throat. Essential physical conditions are a relaxed tongue and an open throat.

Diaphragm: A broad muscular partition located between the chest cavity and the abdomen. The diaphragm is one of the principal muscles used in inhalation. It is arched and dome-shaped in its relaxed state. As the diaphragm is tensed, it contracts and flattens out, thus pushing downward against the organs in the abdominal region. Coupled with the action of the rib muscles, the diaphragm contributes to the enlargement of the chest cavity, and as a result the air pressure is lowered. The lower air pressure is equalized by air entering the lungs. When the diaphragm relaxes, it returns to its normal state and pressure is made upon the small air sacs in the lungs, thus causing exhalation, and completing the cycle of breathing.

Diphthong: A compound or double vowel, in which the vowel sounds change smoothly from one to the other. For example, the word *round* contains the diphthong **ou (ah** and **oo)** and is pronounced **rah-oond.**

Enunciation: The manner of vocal utterance as regards distinctness and clarity of vowels and consonants.

Falsetto: A light, head voice, lying above the natural or normal range of the male voice. In a falsetto tone, only the inner edges of the vocal cords vibrate.

Final consonant: The last consonant in a word.

Glottal: Relating to or produced in the glottis; the aspirate consonant **h,** formed in the glottis.

Glottis: The fissure or opening between the vocal cords or bands.

Hard palate: The portion of the roof of the mouth between the alveoli and the velum, or soft palate. The hard palate is a structure of bone with a layer or cover of tissue.

High-forward resonance: A focusing of the tone in the "mask," or more specifically in the frontal cavities of the head. Essential physical conditions are an open throat and an arched velum.

Hooty tone: A muffled tone quality lacking in correct tonal focus.

Initial consonant: A consonant situated at the beginning of a word.

Intercostal muscles: The muscles that lie between the ribs and that partially control the process of respiration.

Labiodental: The consonants formed by the lower lip and the upper front teeth **(f, v).**

Laryngeal muscles: The muscles that regulate the size of the glottis, control the degree of tension of the vocal cords, and close off the larynx during swallowing.

Larynx: Sometimes referred to as the voice box; a cartilage that houses the vocal cords, situated at the upper part of the trachea, or windpipe.

Legato diction: A style of diction in which the vowels and the consonants are smoothly connected. The explosive qualities of the consonants are minimized, and the final consonants of most syllables or words are carried over to the prefix of the following syllable. For example, the words *night time* are sung **nah-ĭ taheem.**

Lingua-alveolar: The consonants **t, d, n, l, s,** and **z,** formed by the tip of the tongue touching the alveoli (teeth or gum ridge; portion of the jaw where the sockets for the upper teeth are situated; area between the teeth and the hard palate).

Lingua-dental: The consonants formed by the tip of the tongue touching the upper front teeth (**th** as in *thousand,* and **th** as in *there*).

Lingua-palatal: The consonants formed by the contact between the tongue and the hard palate (**sh, zh, ch, dzh, j,** and **r**).

Marcato diction: A style of diction in which each note in the music receives an accent and the explosive qualities of the consonants are exaggerated.

Medial consonant: A consonant situated within a word.

Nasality: An undesirable, exaggerated nasal quality often arising from some obstruction in the nasal cavity. When the nasal cavity becomes infected and swollen, as with a head cold, this quality usually occurs.

Open throat: An expression used to describe the feeling of a relaxed throat; an essential condition to correct voice production.

Open vowels: All the vowels with the exception of **ee, ĭ,** and **oo.** They are classified as open vowels because of the relaxed tongue position and the relatively low position of the jaw. The basic open vowel is **ah,** as in the word *father.* This vowel is the most naturally produced and is widely used as a beginning point in vocalization.

Palate: The roof of the mouth. (*See also* Hard palate; Velum.)

Pharynx: Cavity extending from the base of the skull to the esophagus.

Phonation: The act of uttering or producing vocal sounds in singing or speaking.

Pronunciation: The manner of pronouncing words as regards the selection of appropriate vowels and consonants, and the proper accent of words.

Registers: The compass or range of the voice in which the singer is able to sing without readjustment of the vocal cords. Principal classifications are the chest and head registers; however, some authorities consider the middle range of the voice as a third register. Certain other authorities emphatically deny the existence of vocal registers.

Resonance: The amplification and enrichment of a fundamental tone emanating from the larynx—by means of supplementary vibrations in the bodily resonance cavities.

Resonator: The part of the vocal mechanism that amplifies or resonates the tone and provides its characteristic timbre—specifically, the pharynx, the mouth, the nasal cavity, and the sinuses. (Some authorities believe that the trachea, the bronchi, and the chest cavity also contribute to vocal resonance.)

Respiration: The process of breathing, involving the alternate inhaling and expelling of the breath; inspiration followed by expiration.

Sibilants: The hissing sounds caused by the raised tongue position and the flow of the breath being directed at the back side of the upper teeth. The sibilants in English are **s, z, sh, zh, ch,** and **j.**

Soft palate: *See* Velum.

Sonorous: A full, richly resonant tone quality.

Staccato diction: A style of diction in which the notes and the words are distinctly separated or detached.

Strident quality: A harsh, grating, unpleasant tonal quality.

Sustained consonants: Consonants with a longer degree of sustaining power, such as **l, m,** and **n.**

Syllable: A single sound or a part of a word, which may be pronounced separately without interruption.

Tessitura: The average range of the melodic line or a voice part.

Throaty quality: An excessively dark tone quality sounded or resonated deep in the throat.

Tonal focus: Direction of the vocal tone to a particular localized area of the frontal resonators.

Tremolo: An excessively wide and slow vibrato that detracts from the expressive qualities of the voice.

Velar: The consonants formed by arching the back part of the tongue and pressing it against the velum, or soft palate (**k, g, ng**).
Velum, or **Soft palate:** A muscular membrane, continuous with and attached to the bone of the hard palate. It serves an important function in phonation in that it may be raised to prevent the breath from entering the nasal passages during the articulation of certain consonants.
Vibrato: A rapid fluctuation of vocal tone alternately above and below a given pitch level—for the purpose of adding beauty and warmth to the tone.
Vibrator: The part of the vocal mechanism in which the sound originates; the vocal cords or membranes that are attached to the inner portion of the larynx and that are set into motion or vibration by the flow of the breath.
Voiced consonant: A consonant phonated with a distinguishable movement of the vocal cords.
Voiceless consonant: A consonant phonated without movement of the vocal cords.
Vowels: The vocal sounds utilized for sustaining the tone and in which the flow of the breath is continuous. The primary vowels are **ee, ay, ah, oh,** and **oo.**

TOPICS FOR DISCUSSION

1. What environmental factors cause a singer to use clavicular or high-chest breathing, when, as a child, one quite naturally employs abdominal breathing?
2. Discuss the tone quality of various choirs and choruses you have heard either in concert or in recordings. What tonal characteristics do you feel are desirable? What characteristics are undesirable?
3. What is the relationship between flexibility and good tonal quality?
4. Differentiate between the terms *pronunciation, enunciation,* and *articulation.*
5. What truths and what fallacies exist in the statement "Sing as you speak"?
6. How may the choral conductor employ the concept of *front-to-back vowel placement* as a device for the improvement of tone quality?
7. Which consonants are likely to cause a choral group the most difficulties? Why? What procedures may be utilized to overcome these difficulties?
8. Why does each varying musical style require a distinct type of treatment in terms of diction? In terms of tone quality?
9. Why is it desirable for the choral conductor to have a *variety* of techniques for achieving good tonal quality and correct diction?

SELECTED READINGS

ADLER, KURT, *Phonetics and Diction in Singing: Italian, French, German, Spanish.* Minneapolis: University of Minnesota Press, 1967.
BURGIN, JOHN CARROLL, *Teaching Singing.* Metuchen, N.J.: Scarecrow, 1973.
CAIN, NOBLE, *Choral Music and Its Practice,* chap. 10. New York: M. Witmark & Sons, 1942.
CHRISTY, VAN A., *Glee Club and Chorus,* chap. 4. New York: G. Schirmer, Inc., 1940.
DARROW, GERALD F., *Four Decades of Choral Training.* Metuchen, N.J.: Scarecrow, 1975.
DEWEY, PHILIP, *Bel Canto in Its Golden Age.* New York: King's Crown Press, Columbia University, 1950.
DYKEMA, PETER W., AND KARL W. GEHRKENS, *The Teaching and Administration of High School Music,* chap. 8, pp. 90–94. Boston: C. C. Birchard & Co., 1941.

FIELDS, VICTOR A., *Training the Singing Voice*. New York: King's Crown Press, Columbia University, 1947.

FINN, WILLIAM J., *The Art of the Choral Conductor*, chaps. 2, 3, 4, 13, 14. Boston: C. C. Birchard & Co., 1939.

FRISELL, ANTHONY, *The Tenor Voice*. Boston: Bruce Humphries, 1964.

HAMMER, RUSSELL, *Singing—An Extension of Speech*. Metuchen, N.J.: Scarecrow, 1978.

HOWERTON, GEORGE, *Technique and Style in Choral Singing*, chaps. 1–4. New York: Carl Fischer, Inc., 1958.

HULS, HELEN STEEN, *The Adolescent Voice: A Study*. New York: Vantage Press, 1957.

JONES, ARCHIE N., *Techniques in Choral Conducting*, chaps. 2, 3. New York: Carl Fischer, Inc., 1948.

KAGEN, SERGIUS, *On Studying Singing*. New York: Holt, Rinehart & Winston, 1950. (Also Dover edition)

KRONE, MAX T., *The Chorus and Its Conductor*, chaps. 4, 5. San Diego: Neil A. Kjos Music Co., 1945.

MARSHALL, MADELINE, *The Singer's Manual of English Diction*. New York: G. Schirmer, Inc., 1953.

MORIARTY, JOHN, *Diction*. Boston: E. C. Schirmer Music Co., 1975.

REID, CORNELIUS L., *The Free Voice*. New York: Colman-Ross Co., Inc., 1965.

ROE, PAUL F., *Choral Music Education* (2nd ed.), chaps. 4, 5. Englewood Cliffs, N.J.: Prentice-Hall, 1983.

SHEWAN, ROBERT, *Voice Training for the High School Chorus*. West Nyack, N.Y.: Parker Publishing Company, 1973.

STANLEY, DOUGLAS, *Your Voice*. New York: Pitman Publishing Corporation, 1945.

STANTON, ROYAL, *The Dynamic Choral Conductor*, chaps. 4, 5. Delaware Water Gap, Pa.: Shawnee Press, Inc., 1971.

SUNDERMAN, LLOYD F., *Some Techniques for Choral Success*, chaps. 2, 3. Rockville Centre, N.Y.: Belwin, Inc., 1952.

VENNARD, WILLIAM, *Developing Voices*. New York: Carl Fischer, Inc., 1973.

WESTERMAN, KENNETH N., *Emergent Voice* (2nd ed.). Ann Arbor, Mich.: Privately published, 1955.

WILSON, HARRY R., *Artistic Choral Singing*, chaps. 6, 7. New York: G. Schirmer, Inc., 1959.

References on the Anatomy and Physiology of the Human Vocal Mechanism

APPELMAN, D. RALPH, *The Science of Vocal Pedagogy*. Bloomington, Ind.: Indiana University Press, 1967.

BERG, JANWILLEM VAN DEN, "Calculations on a Model of the Vocal Tract for Vowel/i/ and on the Larynx," *Journal Acoustical Society of America*, 27 (1955), 332–38.

————, "Myoelastic Aerodynamic Theory of Voice Production," *Journal of Speech and Hearing Research*, 1, no. 3 (September 1958), 224–27.

————, "Transmission of the Vocal Cavities," *Journal Acoustical Society of America*, 27 (1955), 161–68.

————, AND A. SPORR, "Microphonic Effect of the Larynx," *Nature*, 179 (1957), 525–626.

————, J. T. ZANTEMA, AND P. DOORNENBAL, JR., "On the Air Resistance and the Bernoulli Effect of the Human Larynx," *Journal Acoustical Society of America*, 27 (1957) 626–31.

BOONE, DANIEL R., *The Voice and Voice Therapy* (3rd ed.). Englewood Cliffs, N.J.: Prentice-Hall, 1983.

BORCHERS, ORVILLE J., "Practical Implications of Scientific Research for the Teaching of Voice," *Music Teachers National Association, Volume of Proceedings*, 1947, pp. 209–15.

————, "Vocal Timbre in Its Immediate and Successive Aspects," *Music Teachers National Association, Volume of Proceedings*, 1941, pp. 346–58.

BRODY, VIOLA, *An Experimental Study of the Emergence of the Process Involved in the Production of Song*. Unpublished Ph.D. thesis, University of Michigan, 1947.

DENES, PETER B., AND ELLIOT N. PINSON, *The Speech Chain: The Physics and Biology of Spoken Language*. Baltimore: Bell Telephone Laboratories, 1963.

FARNSWORTH, D. W., "High Speed Motion Pictures of the Human Vocal Cords," *Music Teachers National Association, Volume of Proceedings,* 1939, pp. 305–9.

HAGERTY, ROBERT F., AND OTHERS, "Soft Palate Movement in Normals," *Journal of Speech and Hearing Research,* 1, no. 4 (December 1958), 325–30.

HIXON, E., *An X-ray Study Comparing Oral and Pharyngeal Structures of Individuals with Nasal Voices and Individuals with Superior Voices.* Unpublished M.S. thesis, State University of Iowa, 1949.

HUSLER, FREDERICK, AND YVONNE RODD-MARLING, *Singing: The Physical Nature of the Vocal Organ; A Guide to the Unlocking of the Singing Voice.* London: Faber & Faber Ltd., 1965.

JONES, DAVID S., RICHARD J. BEARGIE, AND JOHN E. PAULY, "An Electromyographic Study of Some Muscles of Costal Respiration in Man," *The Anatomical Record,* 117, no. 1 (December 1953), 17–24.

LEWIS, DON, "Vocal Resonance," *Journal Acoustical Society of America,* 8 (1936), 91–99.

LUCHSINGER, RICHARD, AND GODFREY ARNOLD, *Voice-Speech Language.* Belmont, Calif.: Wadsworth, 1965.

NEGUS, V. E., *The Mechanism of the Larynx.* London: William Heinemann Ltd., 1929.

NORRIS, M. A., *X-ray Studies of Vowel Production as It Is Related to Voice.* Unpublished M.A. thesis, State University of Iowa, 1934.

RUSSELL, G. OSCAR, "First Preliminary X-ray Consonant Study," *Journal Acoustical Society of America,* 5 (1934), 247–51.

———, *Speech and Voice.* New York: Macmillan, 1931.

———, *The Vowel.* Columbus: Ohio State University Press, 1928.

———, "X-ray Photographs of the Tongue and Vocal Organ Positions of Madame Bori," *Music Teachers National Association, Volume of Proceedings,* 27 (1932), 137.

SECORD, ARTHUR E., *An X-ray Study of the Hyoid Bone, Thyroid Cartilage and Cricoid Cartilage in Relation to Pitch Change in the Human Larynx.* Unpublished Ph.D. thesis, University of Michigan, 1941.

STRONG, LEON H., "The Mechanism of Laryngeal Pitch," *Anatomical Record,* 63, no. 1 (August 1935), 13–28.

VENNARD, WILLIAM, *Singing: The Mechanism and the Technic* (rev. ed.). New York: Carl Fischer, Inc., 1967.

WESTERMAN, KENNETH N., "Resonation," *Music Teachers National Association, Volume of Proceedings,* 1949, pp. 295–300.

WESTLAKE, HAROLD, *The Mechanics of Phonation, An X-ray Study of the Larynx.* Unpublished Ph.D. thesis, University of Michigan, 1938.

WILLIAMS, R. L., "A Serial Radiographic Study of Velopharyngeal Closure and Tongue Positions in Certain Vowel Sounds," *Northwestern University Bulletin,* 52, no. 17, 9–12.

WOLFE, W. G., *X-ray Study of Certain Structures and Movements Involved in Naso-Pharyngeal Closure.* Unpublished M.A. thesis, State University of Iowa, 1942.

References on the Alexander Technique[27]

ALEXANDER, F. MATTHIAS, *Constructive Conscious Control of the Individual.* Long Beach, Calif.: Centerline Press, 1985.

———, *The Use of the Self.* Long Beach, Calif.: Centerline Press, 1984.

BARLOW, WILFRED, *The Alexander Technique.* New York: Warner Books Edition, 1980.

BEN-OR, NELLY, "The Alexander Technique," in *Tensions in the Performance of Music,* ed. Carola Grindea. London: Kahn & Averill, 1978.

GELB, MICHAEL, *Body Learning: An Introduction to the Alexander Technique.* New York: Delilah Books, 1981; London: Aurum Press, Ltd., 1981.

JONES, FRANK PIERCE, *Body Awareness in Action: A Study of the Alexander Technique.* New York: Schocken Press, 1976.

[27]The references in this section are generally available from Centerline Press, 2005 Palo Alto Ave., Suite 325, Long Beach, CA 90815. A catalog listing these publications, as well as various others, is available upon request.

WESTFELDT, LULIE, *F. Matthias Alexander: The Man and His Work.* Long Beach, Calif.: Centerline Press, 1986.

References on the Maintenance of Vocal Health

BOONE, DANIEL R., *The Voice and Voice Therapy* (3rd ed.). Englewood Cliffs, N.J.: Prentice-Hall, 1983.

BRADLEY, MARK, "Prevention and Correction of Vocal Disorders in Singers," *The NATS Bulletin*, 36, no. 5 (May/June 1980), 38–41, 49.

BRODNITZ, FREDERICK S., *Keep Your Voice Healthy* (2nd ed.). Boston: College-Hill Press. Little, Brown, 1987.

COOPER, MORTON, "Vocal Suicide in Singers," *The NATS Bulletin*, 26, no. 3 (February/March 1970), 7–10.

FERGUSON, TOM, "Grandmother Knew Best," *The Mother Earth News*, no. 65 (September/October 1980), p. 140.

LAWRENCE, VAN, "Sermon on Hydration (The Evils of Dry)," *The NATS Journal*, 42, no. 4 (March/April 1986), 22–23.

SANIGA, RICHARD D., MARGARET F. CARLIN, AND PATRICIA R. HAYS, "The Prediction of Vocal Abuse in Professional Voice Students," *The NATS Journal*, 42, no. 4 (March/April 1986), 8–11.

SATALOFF, ROBERT T., "Professional Singers: The Science and Art of Clinical Care," *American Journal of Otolaryngology*, 2, no. 1 (August 1981), 251–66.

———, "Bodily Injuries and Their Effects on the Voice," *The NATS Journal*, 2, no. 1 (May/June 1987), 23–24.

———, "The Professional Voice: Part I. Anatomy, Function, and General Health," *Journal of Voice*, 1, no. 1 (March 1987), 92–104.

Style
and
Interpretation

The primary function of the conductor is to interpret the music. He must interpret it in such a way that the intentions of the composer are "brought to life" and projected to the audience. To do this properly, the conductor must have, among other qualities, a clear concept of the music's basic style. *Musical style* may be simply defined as the distinctive manner or mode in which musical thought is expressed. It includes those characteristics that make a particular musical work uniquely different from others.

An understanding of the main historical periods, as well as the different styles within each period, is a requisite to the proper interpretation of any composer's music. Basic styles of art expression change periodically as a result of various social, political, and economic forces. Although the characteristics of the music of any one period begin to develop in the previous period and carry over to the next, various points of demarcation may be determined. The main currents of musical expression since the year 1400 may be divided into five periods as follows: *the Renaissance period* (ca. 1400–1600), *the Baroque period* (1600–1750), *the Classic period* (1750–1820), *the Romantic period* (1800–1900), and *the Modern period* (1890 to the present).

Although the characteristics of the music of each period could be presented in a variety of ways, we have chosen the following five factors for discussion: meter and stress, tempo, dynamics, texture, and expressive aspects of the music. These factors have undergone change, were often distinctly different during the various periods, and can be controlled somewhat by the conductor in striving toward his interpretative goals.

THE RENAISSANCE PERIOD

Although we should not forget that cultural change is a slowly moving process and that ascribing particular dates to certain periods is an arbitrary matter, the approximate 200-year period that we call the *Renaissance* (ca. 1400–1600) does have certain salient characteristics. In some circles of European society, the religious orientation declined before rising secular interests. This shift of interest was to culminate in the development of the modern scientific inquiry of the seventeenth century. The Renaissance intellectual began to emphasize his destiny here on earth, rather than considering life only as a prelude to the hereafter. He developed new confidence in his ability to solve his own problems and to determine his own fate. The wisdom of the church usually was not denied, but, in addition, the claims of other sources of truth were staked out.

Considerable discussion has taken place as to the exact beginnings of the Renaissance period in music. There appears to be some uncertainty as to the beginning of the period, but the year 1400 seems to be the most suitable date. Jeppesen concurs with this date and offers the following, well-founded reasons:

> As far as can be discerned at present, there is a marked and very significant boundary line, especially in a musico-technical respect, at about the transition from the 14th to the 15th century. What happened at that time may be characterized as a change in the conception of consonance—the definite, practical recognition of the 3rd and 6th as not only having privileges in musical art equal to the 4th, 5th and 8th, but moreover as main consonants—tonal combinations decidedly preferred above all others, and regarded as fundamental factors in musical composition.[1]

Meter and Stress

Most of the music of the Renaissance period was unmetered, with stress occurring only through the emphasis of particular syllables in important words. The barline, with the resultant stress on the first beat of the measure, generally was not used. Although the barline did come into being during the latter part of the period, it was used only as a

---

[1]Knud Jeppesen, *The Style of Palestrina and the Dissonance*, 2nd ed. (Copenhagen: Ejnar Munksgaard, Publisher, and New York: Oxford University Press, Inc., 1946), p. 222. Used by permission.

"measure" of elapsed time and as a means of keeping the singers to-gether.[2] When metrical stress is used for music of this period, the inher-ent beauties and flow of the vocal lines are destroyed.

In Figure 51*a*, an excerpt from Palestrina's *Missa Papae Marcelli* is shown, illustrating the use of the traditional barlines. The normal syl-labic accents occurring on the words "*Ple*-ni sunt *coe*-li et *ter*-ra" are obscured, and the rhythmic counterpoint so necessary to the music does not occur with this manner of barring. Figure 51*b*, however, is barred according to the natural accent of the text, thus revealing the beauties of the rhythmic complexity of the music.

The conductor should be always alert to the tendency of singers to stress certain figures of rhythmic groupings in a manner that is inimical to the proper interpretation. For example, in the motet *Cantantibus Organis* by Marenzio (Pustet, No. B32), singers often have a tendency to stress, in a somewhat mechanical manner, the first and third of each group of four eighth notes (Figure 52). This practice should be avoided, because stress should occur only through the natural accent of particular syllables in important words. The sacred music of this period, in particu-lar, should be performed in a smooth, flowing manner, and phrases should be thought of in terms of long ascending and descending lines.

The conductor should remind the singers to think always melod-ically and never chordally, except when tuning various intervals, and to avoid the regular recurring accents common to barred music. To help achieve the correct syllabic stress, ask the singers to read the text aloud with accents in the correct place and in accordance with the rise and fall of the various vocal lines. The conductor should use the tactus, or down-ward and upward movement of the hand and arm, to minimize any tendency toward metrical stress and to allow for the interplay of rhyth-mic polyphony.[3]

Tempo

The tempo of Renaissance music is determined largely by the syl-labic setting of the text and the mood of the music. When one syllable is set to a melodic figure (melisma), the tempo should be restrained so that

---

[2]As a convenience to the singers, modern-day publishers employ several means to facilitate the reading of Renaissance music. Some employ the use of regular barlines; others utilize dotted barlines as a means of minimizing the natural stress following the barline. Still other publishers use a short vertical line before certain words at regularly spaced intervals to serve as a guide to the singers.

[3]Each tactus has two beats in opposite directions—up-down or down-up (usually the latter is employed)—each one at a tempo ranging between M.M. = 50–60. This tempo was related to man's normal heartbeat (during quiet respiration) or his leisurely walking stride; thus the tempo of Renaissance music remained relatively steady. Both movements of the tactus were made with equal force whether it was conceived as down-up or up-down. For a further discussion of tactus, see Curt Sachs, *Rhythm and Tempo* (New York: W. W. Norton & Co., Inc., 1953), pp. 202–33.

FIGURE 51   Excerpt from *Missa Papae Marcelli* by Palestrina: (*a*) illustrates the use of traditional barlines; (*b*) is barred according to the natural accent of the text. From *A History of Music and Musical Style* by Homer Ulrich and Paul A. Pisk, © 1963 by Harcourt Brace Jovanovich, Inc.

FIGURE 52 An excerpt from the serie *Cantantibus Organis.* Madrigal by Luca Marenzio, in which mechanical stress should be avoided in the eighth-note groupings in measures 2, 3, and 4, and the music performed in a smooth, flowing manner. Used by permission of Otto Heinrich Noetzel Verlag, Wilhelmshaven BRD.

the inherent beauty of the vocal line may be revealed. On the other hand, when each syllable is set to a different note, of a comparatively longer duration, the tempo may be pushed slightly forward.

The tempo should remain relatively steady throughout the entire composition, or at least throughout a particular section. Any change in tempo should result only through a contrasting change in the mood of the text and a resultant change in the musical texture. Any changes in tempo within a given section should be extremely gradual and subtle, lest the symmetry of the music be destroyed.

Rallentando, as we know it today, did not exist in the music of the Renaissance period. Composers of the period were, however, aware of this effect, and when it was felt desirable they made it a part of the music itself. That is, they achieved the effect by simply broadening or lengthening the musical notation. Therefore, conductors should avoid the deliberate use of rallentando, because this would only distort the musical interpretation.[4]

A somewhat greater freedom, however, may be said to exist in the performance of madrigals and related genre than with the masses and the motets of the Renaissance period. Madrigal composers were captivated by the expressive qualities of the words. The mood of the text, therefore, is an essential determining factor in the selection of the correct tempo (and the proper dynamics). Restraint and avoidance of extremes, however, should always be paramount in the conductor's mind.

Dynamics

The dynamics of the music of this period are related to and are dependent upon any changes of mood in the text. Changes in dynamics would occur only as with changes in tempo—that is, with a contrasting mood between sections of the music. Within the overall framework of the music, however, dynamic levels should be moderate; extremes should seldom occur. Owing to the high degree of consonance, the pervading imitation, the lack of harmonic complexity, and the restraints inherent in the style, a climax seldom occurred and was not even sought by composers of the period.[5]

Through the use of the "seamless" technique, there existed an overlapping or dovetailing of cadences; that is, one phrase ended in two or more of the parts, while another began in the other parts. Through this technique many cadences were minimized, thus lessening the necessity for dynamic changes. It should be added, however, that dynamics, especially in the madrigal, frottola, and canto carnascialesco, may be realized simply through the natural tessitura of the voices, as well as in the intensity of the word symbolism.

Texture

The music of the period was primarily contrapuntal in texture; that is, the various vocal lines were conceived as horizontal in nature. Composers wrote using anywhere from three to six or more parts. When first examining music of the period, one might feel that some composi-

---

[4]Cf. Sachs, *Rhythm and Tempo*, pp. 218–19.

[5]Cf. Robert Stevenson, *Music before the Classic Era* (London: Macmillan & Co. Ltd., 1955), p. 42.

tions or portions of others were conceived harmonically rather than contrapuntally. Upon careful examination, however, one will often discover that, for example, the third in a particular part may be omitted in an effort to achieve the best movement in the various vocal lines.[6]

Imitation as a contrapuntal device was used by composers from Dufay through the remainder of the period. The term *point of imitation* pertains to the introduction of a figure or motive in one part, which is taken up successively in the other parts. These points of imitation should be emphasized slightly. The entrances need to be definite and precise, but vigorous accents are out of place and should be avoided. These entering parts should be brought out slightly, but should never overshadow the other contrapuntal lines. As other parts enter, they should recede into the background.

Expressive Aspects

The sacred music of the Renaissance period sounds remote and restrained, primarily because of the large degree of consonance. There was a wide use of unisons, thirds, fifths, sixths, octaves, and triad sounds. Dissonance of the unprepared variety was used sparingly and was considered something "vehement and violent." Therefore, the objective was to conceal or muffle it insofar as was possible.[7]

Renaissance music possesses very subtle points of harmonic arrival. As previously mentioned, with the "seamless" technique there existed an overlapping or dovetailing of phrases; that is, one phrase ended in two or more parts, while another began in the other parts. Through this technique many cadences were somewhat obscured and the tension of the cadence was minimized. The conductor should search out all the suspensions in Renaissance music, mark them in his score, and have the chorus "lean" on them ever so slightly during performance.

The masses and the motets of the Renaissance are impersonal in nature and should be performed with an atmosphere of quiet reflection and sincerity of feeling—in other words, as a prayer unto God, and not as a concert. The tone quality, therefore, should be kept light and clear, with a minimum of vibrato. Heavy dramatic quality and excessive vibrato in the voices are inimical to the expressive character of the music; both should be eliminated.[8]

[6]See, for example, Jeppesen, *The Style of Palestrina*, p. 92.

[7]Ibid., p. 108.

[8]Singing in the early church was limited to the voices of men and boys. During the early part of the Renaissance period, men singing in their falsetto voices often were used to reinforce the boys' voices. During the sixteenth century, falsettists eventually supplanted the boys and sang the treble, or upper two, voice parts. Today, these voices are called *countertenors*. An excellent example of their use and how these voices might have sounded during the Renaissance is demonstrated by the King's Singers (see the *Schwann Record*

As previously mentioned, Renaissance music, when performed correctly, sounds remote and restrained. The resonance in the church or the hall in which it was originally performed contributed substantially to this effect. The impersonal quality of Renaissance sacred music is comparable to the detachment that may be observed in certain paintings of the period in which the Madonna is not caressing her child, but is maintaining a distance between Him and herself.[9]

A somewhat greater freedom existed with the madrigals and related secular styles of the period. Composers were well aware of the expressive qualities of the text and often employed word painting in their music. That is, they used the music to portray, in a variety of ways, the character of certain words. For example, leaps in the melody were often used to depict joy, while the voices might ascend on such words as *heaven* and descend on words such as *earth*. To depict grief and sadness, a diminished or an augmented triad was often used, and dissonance was employed to represent such words as *sadness* and *pain*.

The conductor should study his score and identify the various word-painting devices employed by the composer and, for an effective performance, must lead the singers to an understanding of those devices. The music must be sung with an emotional expressiveness that can result only through proper understanding of it. Secular music of the period, although light in texture, should never be sung in an insipid manner. The rhythmic interplay among the voices should be emphasized somewhat, and the text articulated in a crisp manner, especially in English secular music. While a firmness of approach is necessary to performance, the inherent emotion in the music should not be allowed to run rampant; rather, the music should be performed with a certain degree of restraint.[10]

THE BAROQUE PERIOD

The Baroque period began toward the end of the sixteenth century and is generally considered to have ended by 1750—the year of the death of

---

Catalog for a listing of their available recordings). Since choral conductors are concerned with authentic performance practices and since today's choirs use women (rather than falsettists) on the treble parts, the tone quality should be light and clear, with a minimum of vibrato—if any is used at all. Perhaps the best model of mixed voices performing Renaissance motets is the Roger Wagner Chorale in their album *Echoes from a 16th-Century Cathedral* (Angel S-36013).

For further information on the use of the falsetto voice during the Renaissance, see Robert L. Garretson, "The Falsettists," *The Choral Journal*, XXIV, no. 1 (September 1983), 5–9.

[9]See, for example, the painting *The Cowper Maiden* by Raphael (1483–1520).

[10]For a further discussion on the interpretation of madrigals, see Charles Kennedy Scott, *Madrigal Singing* (London: Oxford University Press, 1931).

Johann Sebastian Bach. The word *baroque* is said to have originated from *barrôco*, a Portuguese word meaning "a pearl of irregular form." In the nineteenth century, the term *baroque* was used in a pejorative manner, implying that the exceptionally ornate style of the arts of this period was in poor taste and a debasement of the Renaissance style. Today, however, such a connotation of the word has largely disappeared and the Baroque is considered to be one of the greatest periods of dramatic expression.

The art forms of the Baroque period were characterized by expansiveness, grandeur, and impressiveness. Baroque architecture was expansive and monumental; paintings were dynamic, alive with color, and filled with the tension of opposing masses; and the interior decoration of churches was highly ornate and dramatic.

Through the Counter-Reformation, beginning about the middle of the sixteenth century, the papacy, utilizing all its resources, set out to regain the faith of the people previously lost to Protestantism. The Counter-Reformation sought converts by trying to reach the spiritual through the senses. A vigorous program, incorporating the impressive aspects of all the arts, was put into action. As a result, cultural forms were developed that were both grandiose and sublime.

The period of the early Baroque began to take form during the pontificate of Sixtus V (1585–1590), and the new Catholicism was reflected in all the arts.

> The early baroque was, at first, a period of Catholic churchly art, and it was again the Society of Jesus which gave this art its peculiar traits of character. From the sphere of quiet devotion, the faithful were lifted into the world of the triumphant Church whose cult was celebrated by richly decked clergy under the vaults of a mighty architecture, surrounded by statues and pictures, before scintillating altars ornamented with gold and silver, to the accompaniment of the impressive and resonant music of multiple choirs, orchestras, and organs. In elaborate processions with flags, candles, and torches, triumphal carriages, floats, and arches, with the marchers singing, accompanying soldiers' bands blaring forth with their trumpets, the bells tolling and cannon booming, priests and students, guilds and corporations with their emblems, princes and the populace all united to demonstrate their adherence to the regenerated triumphal Church.[11]

Whereas the Counter-Reformation prompted the creation of a vast amount of sacred art, Protestantism showed little interest in pictorial and decorative art, presumably because such churchly ornamentation would be contrary to the evangelical precepts of the church.[12] Protestant piety

[11]Paul Henry Lang, *Music in Western Civilization* (New York: W. W. Norton & Co., Inc., 1941), p. 319. Copyright renewed 1968 by Paul Henry Lang.

[12]Extreme Calvinists sometimes went so far as to destroy stained glass windows and smash religious statues in their rejection of traditional symbolism.

held that the proper reverence to God's word would be weakened if the congregation's attention were diverted by ornaments and decorations. In the main, therefore, the Protestant churches remained relatively simple, their architecture merely imitating that of pre-Reformation times. Although music also suffered as a result of this artistic hostility, it was the one art form that eventually became an integral part of the reformed faiths. After a while, music came to epitomize the highest degree of artistic expression in Protestantism.[13]

Meter and Stress

The barline and metered music came into being during the Baroque period; accentuations, therefore, generally occur at regularly spaced intervals. To evoke these accentuations in the performance of Baroque music, the conductor should use a definite and precise beat. This approach is particularly appropriate for music such as Schütz's "Cantate Domino canticum novum" (Bourne, No. B201889). The conductor, however, should avoid a mechanical, machinelike stress following each barline. For example, in Carissimi's "Plorate filii Israel" (Bourne, No. B210369; E. C. Schirmer, No. 1172), a broad legato style with a minimum of stress is required. The conductor should analyze each selection under consideration, and particularly each phrase, to determine those places requiring greater stress—sometimes those notes at the peak of the phrase.[14]

The frames of Baroque paintings usually did not encompass the entirety of a particular scene, but often cut through various objects, thus giving the illusion of boundless space.[15] Composers achieved a similar effect by often beginning their music on a beat following a rest, thus providing the feeling to the listener that the music was a continuation of something that had already been underway. This delayed entrance effected a tension and rhythmic drive leading to the nearest downbeat.[16]

The practice of lengthening the dotted note and shortening the complementary note is an important consideration in the proper interpretation of Baroque music. For example, the rhythm ¢ 𝄿 ♩· 𝄽 ♪ | should often be performed as ¢ 𝄾 𝄿 ♩·· 𝄽 ♪ | and ⁶⁄₈ ♩·♪ ♩·♪ | as

---

[13]Lang, *Music in Western Civilization*, pp. 320–21.

[14]It should be mentioned that in the Baroque period, two basic stylistic practices existed—the *stilo antico* and the *stilo moderno*. In the *stilo antico*, or old style, which was suitable for the church, the music dominated the text. In the *stilo moderno*, or new style, the text dominated the music. These styles are sometimes referred to as *strict style* and *free style*. Some composers (Eberlin, for example) mixed these styles, rather than keeping them separate.

[15]See, for example, the painting *Landscape with the Chateau of Steen* (1636) by Peter Paul Rubens (1577–1640).

[16]Sachs, *Rhythm and Tempo*, p. 266.

§ ♩♫ ♫♩ | . Why is it that the composers did not indicate what they desired? Simply because it was easier to tell the performers how the music should be performed than to write out the notation. This treatment of the dotted note began during the early part of the seventeenth century and carried through to the beginning of the nineteenth century. The music of Monteverdi, Purcell, Bach, and Handel (as well as the later music of Haydn, Mozart, and Beethoven) all necessitate this treatment.[17] During the latter part of the eighteenth century, however, composers began to indicate more carefully their desired intentions in the music.

The purpose of this practice is the achievement of a crisp, clear manner of articulation, as opposed to a lazy and sluggish treatment. This manner of articulation also minimizes the tendency for performers to rush their parts. Of course, the conductors should use discretion in applying this convention. One criterion for consideration is the general character of the music; that is, the lengthening of the dotted notes would be more appropriate to brilliant and majestic music and somewhat less appropriate to music of a lilting, graceful character.

A different treatment of dotted rhythms, however, should occur with trochaic rhythms in compound triple meter, which are sometimes written as dotted rhythms. For example, the rhythm notated as ¾ ♫ ♫ ♫♫ | should be performed as § ♩♪ ♩♪ ♫♫ | . To determine the proper handling of these rhythms the conductor should analyze the music; when the dominant rhythm is compound triple meter (often determined by the triplet groupings), then the passage should be performed as indicated in the second example in this paragraph.[18]

A somewhat more controversial problem is encountered in the handling of dotted eighth notes against triplets. An example of this occurs in the Bach sacred cantata No. 4, *Christ lag in Todesbanden* ("Christ Lay in Death's Dark Prison"), *Versus VI*.[19] The dotted rhythm ♫ ♫ in the bass line of the orchestral accompaniment (continuo) occurs against the triplet figure ♩♩♩ ♩♩♩ in the parts for soprano and tenor. As a general rule, duplets should yield to triplets.[20] In this case the dotted eighth note should coincide with the first two triplets and the sixteenth note with the last triplet (Figure 53).[21]

[17]Thurston Dart, *The Interpretation of Music*, rev. ed. (London: Hutchinson Publishing Group Ltd., 1960), pp. 81–82.

[18]Ibid., p. 89.

[19]Another example of this problem occurs in Bach's *Jesu, Joy of Man's Desiring* (E. C. Schirmer, No. 317).

[20]For an example of the suggested interpretation, listen to the recording by the Robert Shaw Chorale, RCA Victor LSC-2273.

[21]For a further discussion of dotted rhythms, see Sachs, *Rhythm and Tempo*, pp. 303–6, and Dart, *The Interpretation of Music*, pp. 81–83, 88–89, 111, 125–26, and 171.

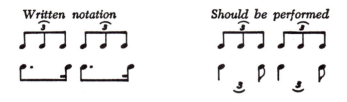

FIGURE 53

Tempo

The tempo of Baroque music should generally be somewhat moderate and deliberate, and extremes should be avoided. Even fast tempi should be performed with some restraint. During the Baroque period Italian terms, such as *allegro* and *largo,* were used to indicate the character of the music, rather than as specific directions as to tempo. As a result some conductors, misunderstanding the meaning of these terms, are inclined to rush the music marked *allegro* and *vivace,* and to conduct too slowly music marked *adagio* and *largo.* Italian markings should be considered as an indication of mood rather than tempo. *Allegro* should be interpreted literally, as merry, lively, brisk, rather than as fast, while *largo* should be considered as simply broad, rather than as very slow.[22]

Handel often wrote the Italian marking *largo* at the end of many of his sacred choruses. The composer's intent in adding this marking at the end of a chorus implies simply that the quarter note for the *allegro* becomes exactly twice as long for the *largo;* for example, if the *allegro* has been conducted at $\quarternote = 120$, then the *largo* will be conducted at $\quarternote = 60$. He also, however, sometimes wrote notes of a larger or greater value as a means of achieving the desired intention of *largo,* that is, simply broad. For the conductor to further slow down the pulse of the music would make the ending too slow and thus distort the desired effect.[23]

In the early Baroque monody, a considerable flexibility existed in the tempo so that the emotions in the text and the music might be fully expressed. In the late 1630s, however, a reversal of this trend occurred and the tempi of music became more strict and restrained.[24] The relative freedom of emotional expression gave way to rhythmical shifts within a stricter tempo.

[22]Richard T. Gore, "The Performance of Baroque Church Music," *Music Teachers National Association, Volume of Proceedings,* 1950 (Pittsburgh: The Association, 1953), pp. 156–57.

[23]Ibid., p. 157.

[24]Sachs, *Rhythm and Tempo,* pp. 265–66.

According to Machlis, one of the most notable characteristics of Baroque music is its steady pulsation or unflagging rhythm.[25]

> The Baroque, with its fondness for energetic movement, demanded a dynamic rhythm based on the regular recurrence of accent. The bass part became the carrier of the new rhythm. Its relentless beat is an arresting trait in many compositions of the Baroque. This steady pulsation, once under way, never slackens or deviates until the goal is reached. It imparts to Baroque music its unflagging drive, producing the same effect of turbulent yet controlled motion as animates Baroque painting, sculpture, and architecture.[26]

Although a steady pulsating drive is important to proper interpretation, this does not mean that the tempo should be completely unyielding. For instance, at cadences immediately prior to subsequent sections, a slight holding back of the tempo is often desirable. The exact treatment of each cadence, however, will vary according to the music itself.[27] In reference to the handling of cadences *Grove's* states,

> Each needs its own natural flexibility, though this may vary according to circumstances from the merest easing scarcely consciously perceptible, at the one extreme, to a majestic broadening at the other. It is for the performer to judge on the merits of each case between sentimental excess and self-conscious rigidity.[28]

Accelerando and ritardando (or rallentando) are inappropriate and out of place in Baroque music, principally because these concepts of gradually increasing or gradually decreasing the tempo did not exist in this period. These concepts grew out of the Mannheim school in the latter part of the eighteenth century. Another concept, often misunderstood, is the treatment of the fermata. A fermata in Baroque music simply indicates the end of a phrase and a point at which the singers may take a breath. The concept of the fermata as an untimed hold developed during the latter part of the eighteenth century, as did also the modern concept of accelerando and ritardando.

[25]Exceptions to this general characteristic of Baroque music are the *recitative*, which is sung in a declamatory style with stress or accent occurring as a result of important words or particular syllables, and the *arioso*, which in style lies somewhere between the recitative and the aria and possesses some of the characteristics of each.

[26]Joseph Machlis, *The Enjoyment of Music*, 5th ed. (New York: W. W. Norton & Co., Inc., 1984), pp. 361–62.

[27]For a discussion of conflicting viewpoints in regard to tempo changes, see Sachs, *Rhythm and Tempo*, pp. 277–80.

[28]Eric Blom, ed., *Grove's Dictionary of Music and Musicians*, Volume II (New York: St. Martin's Press, Macmillan & Co., Ltd., 1954), p. 986. Used by permission of Macmillan, London and Basingstoke.

Dynamics

The concept of crescendo and decrescendo did not widely exist during the Baroque period, principally because the instruments of the period did not have the necessary flexibility to achieve these ends. The organ, for example, did not possess swell shutters, and the piano was not invented until the latter part of the period. Therefore, contrast was sought by other means.[29] Contrast in dynamics was achieved by adding or dropping out various instruments or voice parts. This was referred to as *terraced dynamics,* meaning various levels or plateaus of dynamics. Extremes in dynamics, therefore, should be avoided, because the concept of terraced dynamics would render them undesirable.[30] Usually the music itself will take care of the often slight dynamic changes in terraced dynamics, and one should question editorial markings that seem to place undue emphasis upon these changes. Terraced dynamics are only part of the change, however, the other being the density due to the increase or decrease of the number of voices participating. Composers up through J. S. Bach generally did not include dynamic markings, but in those instances where they did, it was to make clear a change that might not have been recognized in the performance practice of the time or where an absolute insistence of change seemed necessary by the composer. The conductor should utilize a dynamic range only from *piano* to *forte.* Extending the dynamics above or below these levels is inappropriate and should generally be avoided except upon rare occasions.

Texture

The beginning of the Baroque period ushered in a change from a texture of independent but interrelated parts to a single melody or voice part supported by chords or chordal combinations. This change from modal polyphony to a homophonic style necessitated a change in the harmonic system—from the medieval church modes to a system of major and minor tonality. Whereas the polyphony of the Renaissance symbolized the submissiveness of the individual, the new style fulfilled the need for greater individual expression. Secular music gained vastly in importance, and the new style allowed for a greater emotional expression of the text. When polyphony returned, after a brief lapse, it did so within a different harmonic framework—the system of major–minor

[29]According to *Grove's Dictionary of Music and Musicians,* 5th ed., crescendo and decrescendo were not entirely unknown to Baroque composers, since written indications of it are found in the mid-seventeenth-century music of the Italian composer Mazzochi (*Grove's,* Vol. II, p. 988).

[30]Gore, "The Performance of Baroque Church Music," pp. 157–58.

tonality.[31] Even when the new harmonic counterpoint came into vogue, some composers continued to write in the old style polyphony (*stile antico*), sometimes called the Palestrina style. Conductors, therefore, need to recognize and treat each style accordingly.

Because Baroque polyphony functions within a harmonic framework of tonality and generally well-defined chord progressions, cadences are important aspects of arrival but may be different according to the overall texture of the music; that is, some may be lighter and others heavier (see previous section on tempo for a discussion on the treatment of cadences). Also, the complexity of the texture as well as the complexity of the chords, especially when some have been chromatically altered, may have an influence on the tempo of the music. In lighter textures the tempo may be pushed slightly forward, while in denser textures the tempo may be held back somewhat. As to imitations, answering voices should be replicas of the announcing voice's treatment of the subject, including specific rhythmic patterns, trills, and so on.

Expressive Aspects

In contrast to the Renaissance composer, who expressed emotion with considerable restraint, the Baroque composer gave freer vent to his emotions. Nevertheless, his music was still somewhat impersonal, with the emotion stemming not from an individual struggle, as in the Romantic period, but from the tumultuous and dramatic forces affecting all mankind.[32]

Within the new system of major–minor tonality, each chord assumed a definite relationship to the others. Harmonic tension and repose were well understood by composers of the period and were used as devices in composition. There were fewer but stronger cadences, and the drive to the keynote was apparent. There was a considerable increase in the intensity of the music and in the amount of dissonance that was used for the purpose of achieving emotional intensity. Whereas in the Renaissance period, dissonance was permissible only when prepared— that is, when first heard with a consonant interval and introduced through a suspension—the use of unprepared dissonance became accepted and widely used as an expressive device.[33]

Tone painting, or the way in which the music portrayed the words,

[31]While polyphony was rejected by most composers during the early Baroque period, it was never abandoned by the famous three S's: Johann Herman Schein (1586–1630), Samuel Scheidt (1587–1654), and Heinrich Schütz (1585–1672).

[32]George Howerton, *Technique and Style in Choral Singing* (New York: Carl Fischer, Inc., 1957), p. 133.

[33]Claudio Monteverdi (1567–1643) is often credited with the first wide use of unprepared dissonance.

was increasingly given attention by composers of the period. Bach, for example, advised his students to "play the chorale according to the meaning of the words." It must be understood, however, that although the text gave birth to the musical idea, it was the music itself that ultimately reigned supreme.[34]

The Baroque period marked the first time in history that instrumental music assumed an equal position with vocal music. The spirit of the times prompted the development of new instruments and the improvements of the old. The new status of instrumental music has caused certain people to say that some music was conceived instrumentally rather than vocally. The performance of Baroque music, therefore, necessitates a most exacting rhythmic precision. Singers should be as exacting as instrumentalists. They should also maintain a steadiness and a purity of vocal line, devoid of excessive vibrato, since this may adversely affect the intonation and thus blur the polyphonic structure. These qualities are especially important in singing contrapuntal music.

The matter of the proper pitch level at which to perform Baroque music should be given due consideration. Between approximately 1600 and 1820, the standard accepted pitch level—although there were many deviations—was about a semitone lower than the present A-440. The implications of this fact are that, to perform Baroque music in as authentic a manner as possible, one ought to lower the pitch a half step to return it to its original key. Of course, practical considerations such as the difficulty of transposing the orchestral parts, or even the piano or organ accompaniment, often make this practice unfeasible. Another argument against this practice is the additional brilliance that is often achieved through performance in the higher key. On the other hand, when the tessitura of the various parts appears to be too high and thus negatively influences the tone quality, the conductor may consider lowering the pitch. If he elects to do so, he then will have at least two justifications for his decision. By and large, however, the conductor will find his problems minimized if he performs the music in the key in which it is presently written.

THE CLASSIC PERIOD

While Bach and Handel were carrying the Baroque style to its culmination in the first half of the eighteenth century, forces were already at work leading toward the formulation of a new style. The Classic era, generally considered to cover the period from 1750 to 1820, includes such diverse aesthetic trends as the Rococo (*Stile galant*), *empfindsamer Stil*

[34]Machlis, *The Enjoyment of Music*, 5th ed., pp. 360–61.

(literally, "sensitive style"), Enlightenment, and *Sturm und Drang* (storm and stress). The Classic period thus lacked any unifying social and aesthetic philosophy such as shaped artistic expression in the Baroque period. While each of these aesthetic trends had its proponents, it was the master composers of the period—Haydn, Mozart, and Beethoven—who were able to synthesize the elements of each into their music.

The Rococo style (ca. 1720–ca. 1770) repudiated the massive forms of the Baroque. The endless vistas gave way to intimate glimpses; the grandeur of Baroque decoration changed to delicate, often unnecessary, ornamentation; monumental sculpture decreased in size to figurines for the mantle; the center of life moved from the ballroom to the boudoir; and the grandiloquent language of the Baroque changed in manner and tone to witty, tête-à-tête conversations.[35] The expansiveness, grandeur, and impressiveness of Baroque music gave way to an expression of elegance in delicate proportions. The polyphony of the later Baroque was abandoned in favor of a homophonic style, with interest focused on the soprano line that often was adorned with a proliferation of ornamentation.

Whereas the music of Rococo was elegant and ornate and written to please the aristocracy, the *empfindsamer Stil* (or expressive style) was more the music of the middle class. This bourgeois style reflected the attitudes of honesty and goodness and often approached the borders of sentimentality. It is reflected, for example, in the title of a collection of songs by the German composer J. F. Reichardt, "Lullabies for Good German Mothers."[36]

The eighteenth-century Enlightenment, or Age of Reason, began as a reaction against supernatural religions, formalism, and authority. The underlying philosophical belief was that man should be "natural" in all these respects—that is, natural behavior as opposed to formality, and individual freedom as opposed to submission to authority.[37] Denis Diderot's *Encyclopédie*, or *Classified Dictionary of Sciences, Arts, and Trades*, was published serially beginning in 1751 and symbolizes rationalism and the spirit of scientific inquiry. Thomas Paine's book *The Age of Reason* also reflects such rationalism. The Marquis de Condorcet's book, *The Progress of the Human Spirit* (1774), set forth ten stages through which man had progressed from primitive life to near-perfection. This philosophy expressed the belief that man, through the use of his rational and moral powers, could ultimately control his environment. Jean Rameau was an outstanding exponent of rationalism and sought to restore rea-

[35]William Fleming and Abraham Veinus, *Understanding Music: Style, Structure, and History* (New York: Holt, Rinehart & Winston, 1958), pp. 309–10.

[36]Ibid., p. 312.

[37]Donald Jay Grout, *A History of Western Music*, 3rd ed. (New York: W. W. Norton & Co., Inc., 1980), pp. 448–49.

son to musical thought. There is evidence of this philosophy in the optimism expressed in some of the music of Beethoven, who was the movement's most articulate spokesman.[38]

The *Sturm und Drang* (storm and stress) movement in Germany ran counter to the elegance of the Rococo, the optimism of the Enlightenment, and the restricted emotionalism of the *empfindsamer Stil*.[39] These aesthetic trends were rejected in favor of a search for emotional truth and a more flexible use of the imagination. This philosophy may be seen in the literary works of both Goethe and Schiller. The best-known literary example is Goethe's *Faust*. Faust rejects the tenets of the Age of Reason, ceases to search for nature's secrets in books, and seeks the ultimate truth in experiences and emotion. It is felt by some authorities that Haydn, Mozart, and Beethoven were all influenced by this philosophy, as indicated by the pathos and the sometimes violent outbursts in some of their music.[40]

The center of cultural life in the Classic period was the palace. The ruling aristocracy surrounded itself with the arts, which it considered its privileged right. Beauty of expression and elegance of manner became formalized and permeated its existence. The artist of the period created for his patron, who was far above him in social rank. Composers were employed for what they could contribute to the aristocracy's "cultural" surroundings. In general, the patron was interested in the artist's creative products rather than in him as an individual. In other words, a certain degree of reserve existed between employer and employee. In this social setting, where the emphasis was upon courtly manners, the artist avoided becoming too personal in his art, since this would have been considered in poor taste. Objectivity and reserve, therefore, became necessary parts of the artist's creative expression.

Meter and Stress

The art of the Classic era, the Rococo style in particular, strove for elegance and more delicate proportions. These general characteristics were also reflected in the music of the period. Therefore, the pulsation of the music was more delicately marked than in the Baroque period. In order to convey this style clearly to his performers, the conductor should use a lighter beat, yet with a definite or marked precision to delineate the crisp rhythmic patterns of the music.[41]

---

[38]Fleming and Veinus, *Understanding Music,* p. 313.

[39]Some authorities feel that the *empfindsamer Stil* and the *Sturm und Drang* are only different manifestations of an overall Classic-Romantic style.

[40]Fleming and Veinous, *Understanding Music,* p. 314.

[41]Howerton, *Technique and Style,* p. 142.

Tempo

Tempi in the Classic period were generally moderate, and extremes were avoided. Beginning with the Classic period composers indicated to a much greater extent what they desired in their scores. Markings indicating the desired tempo, correct phrasing, and tonal quality were often included. Tempo was often indicated through the use of Italian words (*allegro, adagio,* and so on), and signs indicating dynamic changes were written in.[42] In the waning years of the Classic period, composers, Beethoven in particular, were able to prescribe the desired tempo of their compositions through the use of metronome markings (as noted previously, the metronome was invented by Maelzel in 1816).

Tempo rubato originated from the vocal art and eventually was utilized as a device in the interpretation of instrumental music. It was first discussed in a book on singing by Pier Francesco Tosi, published in 1723. The letters of Mozart reveal that he was well aware of the device and used it in his piano performances. In addition, Karl Philipp Emanuel Bach (1714–1788) discussed tempo rubato in Volume Two of his *Versuch.*[43] It is reasonable to assume that other composers of the period were also aware of this interpretative device. It is suggested, however, in performing music of this period, that tempo rubato be used with discretion and restraint and that its more exaggerated use, as in the subsequent Romantic period, be avoided. In general, the principle of strict time should be followed. The exceptions where tempo rubato seems desirable will usually be dictated by the poetic aspects of the text.[44] The use of ritardando and accelerando became more frequent, especially during the latter part of the period. In accordance with the general characteristics of the music of the period, such alterations in tempi should be slight and performed with restraint.

Dynamics

Although dynamic contrast was an important part of the music of the period, composers did not seek the extremes that occurred during the later periods. One of the most significant developments growing out of the latter part of the eighteenth century was that of *crescendo–decrescendo.* Such a concept was in marked contrast to the terraced dynamics of the earlier Baroque period. While the concept of crescendo–decrescendo was not entirely unknown and had been utilized to some degree

[42]Frederick Dorian, *The History of Music in Performance* (New York: W. W. Norton & Co., Inc., 1942), p. 155.

[43]Ibid., pp. 186–93.

[44]For a further discussion of tempo rubato, see Sachs, *Rhythm and Tempo,* pp. 306–10.

in Italy from the beginning of the century, it had not been widely used elsewhere. Through the efforts of Stamitz, the precision of the orchestra at Mannheim was developed to such a high degree that this carefully controlled crescendo became known as the *Mannheim crescendo*. In choral performances the crescendo–decrescendo should be performed with some restraint, considering the general dynamic level of the passage. The crescendo should not begin from as low a dynamic level, or reach as high a level, as it would during the Romantic period. Generally, in crescendo and decrescendo, the dynamic level should change gradually just one degree higher or lower—for example, from *p* ————— *mp*, and rarely from *p* ————— *f*.

The *forte–piano* contrast was an unwritten law of dynamic execution; that is, repeated phrases or periods should be performed *piano*, as in an echo. Periods performed *piano* the first time should be performed *forte* on the repetition.[45] The harmony itself will provide the conductor with further clues for the treatment of dynamics.

> Philipp Emanuel Bach points out that every tone foreign to the key can very well stand a *forte*, regardless of whether it occurs in dissonance or consonance. . . . Quantz distinguishes clearly three classes of dissonances, to be played *mezzo forte, forte,* and *fortissimo*, respectively. He also explains that the theme of the composition calls for dynamic emphasis. Likewise, all other notes of importance (in a theme, in a contrapuntal passage, or in a harmonic structure) must be stressed by means of dynamics. The notes introducing the theme must be marked; the dissonance must be made stronger than its resolution.[46]

It is also often necessary and desirable to adjust the dynamics to the acoustical conditions of the performance hall. The conductor needs to consider the character of the music, the number and the maturity of the performers, and the size and the acoustical conditions of the performance hall or auditorium. To maintain the classic proportions of the music, it should never become overbearing from the dynamic standpoint. An overly large musical organization, coupled with an auditorium with exceptionally live acoustical properties, can create a dynamic level that is much too high; to be effective, the dynamic level must be reduced in size and scope.

Texture

Composers sought for lightness and simplicity in their music. In place of the heavy Baroque texture, there was a combination of textures in which chordal patterns, running figures, unsupported melodies, and

---

[45]Dorian, *The History of Music in Performance*, p. 166.
[46]Ibid., p. 168.

other devices were used alternately, depending upon the expressive intentions of the composer. Contrapuntal devices were also sometimes used, particularly in the masses; however, polyphony was generally not sought by composers of the period. During the Baroque period, a polarity existed between the melody and the bass parts. The bass supported the melody, while the inner voices sometimes only completed the harmonies. During the Classic period, the inner voices assumed greater importance, and the previous supporting function of the bass part gave way to one of greater flexibility and interplay with the inner voices.[47]

Expressive Aspects

In contrast to the late Baroque period, where the cadences were relatively infrequent and somewhat inconspicuous, and the phrases were "spun-out," the composers of the Classic period used phrases of a regular two- or four-bar length that were shorter and more distinct. There were generally rather strong points of harmonic arrival, and the period structure was well defined. Although the harmonic vocabulary did not differ substantially from that of the late Baroque period, the harmonic progressions were certainly less weighty.[48] Melody reigned supreme; the other parts served to support and enhance it, and were often subordinate to it. Ornamentation developed to its fullest bloom. This embellishment of the melodic line, however, was only reflective of the spirit of the times, where elegance and grace were considered highly important, particularly to the patrons of the arts.

The music of the Classic period was generally abstract in nature and "discreet" in taste and was an integral part of a sophisticated mode of living. It was moderate in style, avoiding the extremes of the later Romantic period. Emotional content was less important, and unity of design became the composer's goal. Form served to eliminate the personal qualities and universalized the style. Symmetry, balance, clarity, and restraint summarized the composer's artistic creations.

THE ROMANTIC PERIOD

The French Revolution, beginning in 1789, resulted in the breakdown of the aristocratic way of life and led to the development of nineteenth-century liberalism. In the world of the arts, it was paralleled by the rise of the Romantic movement, in essence a revolt against formality and authority. Composers had for many centuries worked under the patron-

[47]Homer Ulrich and Paul A. Pisk, *A History of Music and Musical Style* (New York: Harcourt Brace Jovanovich, Inc., 1963), pp. 322–23.
[48]Grout, *A History of Western Music*, p. 417.

age of either the church or the princely courts; under that system, composers generally wrote music to please their patrons and were careful not to let their music become too personal in nature. With the breakdown of the patronage system, composers were free to express themselves individually. They were no longer inhibited or restricted by a patron's demands and were able to please their equals—the general public. With their greater freedom, composers sought out new and unique means of expression. This led to a greater display of emotion, heretofore largely restrained.

Although the composer, no longer bound to his patron, was able to express himself more freely, his financial insecurity often caused him to withdraw from the world about him. He sometimes became preoccupied with his own inner problems and even became pessimistic about the future. Nevertheless, these situations or conditions involving withdrawal, escape, mysticism, religion, as well as the need for self-expression, were often expressed in the composers' music, and they enriched the repertoire as a result.

The term *Romanticism*, as it pertains to the nineteenth century, is inexact and somewhat misleading. The Romantic period contained many diametrical differences, which seemingly run counter to its name. According to Machlis,

> The nineteenth century included many opposites: liberalism and reaction, idealism and the crassest materialism, bourgeois sentimentality and stark realism, mysticism and scientific inquiry, democratic revolution and royalist restoration, romantic optimism and no less romantic despair.[49]

Meter and Stress

Composers in the Romantic period, in their search for freedom from rules, often sought to break the strictness of the rhythm, yet remain within the time-honored rules. A widely used device to achieve this objective was through the use of meter changes without changes in the meter signature.[50] An example of this device may be found in the Brahms Requiem. Such metric alteration results in displaced accents—that is, accents where they are not normally expected—in a relatively short space of time. Whereas Romantic composers achieved these unique rhythmic effects within the boundaries of the accepted rules, the modern-day composer would normally use alternately different meter signatures (see later section "The Modern Period" in this chapter and discussion on meter and stress for examples). Other varied means of

---

[49]Joseph Machlis, *The Enjoyment of Music*, regular rev. ed. (New York: W. W. Norton & Co., Inc., 1963), p. 85.

[50]Sachs, *Rhythm and Tempo*, p. 344.

syncopation also became widely used during this period as an expressive device and as a means of evoking interest. Intricate rhythmic patterns and rhythmic surprise were characteristic of the music of the period. Composers sometimes used a phrase structure that was irregular—that is, of varying lengths. Brahms in particular was noted for his elongated or extended phrases; in some cases they were absorbed into contrapuntal textures so that it is difficult to determine where they actually do end.[51]

Tempo

The restraint typical of the Classic period was abandoned during the Romantic era. It was a period of extremes—fast tempi were often performed exceptionally fast and slow tempi exceptionally slow. Tempo was closely aligned with mood, and since the composer was often expressing varying moods within a composition, extreme, abrupt changes in tempo often occurred. Accelerando and ritardando were more frequently used than in the previous period. As an element of expressiveness, tempo rubato was developed to its ultimate.

During the Romantic period two diametrically opposed schools of interpretative thought existed. One, represented by Mendelssohn, was based on classical principles; the other was the highly romantic, sometimes called the "Neo-German," type of interpretation, which was initiated by Liszt and exemplified by Wagner. The Mendelssohn school sought to preserve the Classical tradition and to eliminate some of the practices that they felt were extreme. Mendelssohn was an exponent of regularity of rhythm and fluency of tempo. Wagner, on the other hand, favored broad, singing melody, and considerable liberty in tempi.[52] He felt that the correct tempo could be determined only through "a proper understanding of the melos."[53]

Although composers may be said to have had tendencies toward one or the other of these positions, and certainly were influenced in one way or another, it would be unwise, as well as impossible, to categorize them all in either group. The music of each composer must be considered individually. Only through a thorough analysis and study of the music will a proper tempo be determined. For example, music with a light texture may be performed in a faster tempo than should music with a heavy, sonorous texture. The latter should be performed somewhat slower if it is to be effective. Relating to this point, the following statement by Robert Schumann is both interesting and revealing.

[51]Ulrich and Pisk, *A History of Music,* p. 485.
[52]Dorian, *The History of Music in Performance,* pp. 230–31.
[53]Ibid., p. 281.

You know how I dislike quarreling about tempo, and how for me only the inner measure of the movement is conclusive. Thus, an allegro of one who is cold by nature always sounds lazier than a slow tempo by one of sanguine temperament. With the orchestra, however, the proportions are decisive. Stronger and denser masses are capable of bringing out the detail as well as the whole with more emphasis and importance; whereas, with smaller and finer units, one must compensate for the lack of resonance by pushing forward in the tempo.[54]

Dynamics

In contrast to the restraint of the Classic period, composers of the Romantic period often used extremes in dynamics ranging from *fff* to *ppp*, but with a slight leaning toward the use of the lower dynamic levels. Some editions of the Verdi Requiem, it may be noted, even contain dynamic markings of *ppppp*.

Crescendo and decrescendo, or the gradual swelling and diminishing of tone, became a widely used expressive device by nineteenth-century composers. In certain compositions it was used to create the illusion of distance—that is, of a group or an object gradually coming closer and then receding into the distance.

Some composers employed a slight accelerando with a crescendo and a slight ritardando with a decrescendo. Rossini, in particular, was noted for combining "a gradual dynamic increase with a great rhythmic momentum."[55]

Composers in the nineteenth century endeavored to indicate more clearly on their scores their intentions through the use of a variety of tempo and dynamic markings. Some of these terms encompassed both tempo and dynamics. For example, *morendo* (dying away) indicates that the music should be both slower and softer, and *andante maestoso* (moderately slow and majestic) implies a moderate tempo, yet with a full sonority.

In addition to crescendo and decrescendo, the use of more sudden climaxes also became a common practice. Grieg, for example, employs this device to a considerable extent in his *Psalms* (C. F. Peters). The use of dynamic accents, such as *sforzando* (*sfz*) and *sforzato* (*sf*), occurred with much greater frequency. See, for example, the Choral Finale to the Ninth Symphony by Beethoven (H. W. Gray; G. Schirmer), *Elijah* by Mendelssohn (G. Schirmer), the Requiem Mass and the *Stabat Mater* by Dvořák (G. Schirmer), and the *29th Psalm* by Elgar (Novello). In contrast to the moderately sized ensembles used in the various princely courts of the Classic era, the combined forces of large orchestras and choirs became the ideal medium for the expression of the dynamic extremes of the Romantic period.

[54]Ibid., p. 227. Cf. Sachs, *Rhythm and Tempo*, p. 379.
[55]Ulrich and Pisk, *A History of Music*, p. 455.

Texture

New harmonic relationships were explored by composers of the Romantic period. Dissonance became more widely used, and an increasing use of melodic and harmonic chromaticism gave the composer a wider range of expressive devices.[56] There was a lessening of harmonic drive, with an increased tendency toward the use of deceptive resolutions and obscured cadences. That is, cadences were sometimes avoided, or resolved deceptively. In contrast to "wandering" chromaticism, composers sometimes used sudden harmonic and enharmonic changes, or shifts of tonal center.

Although a balance between harmony and counterpoint is said to have existed during the late Baroque period, the nineteenth-century Romanticist altered the balance in favor of harmony. The Romantic composer, however, often alternated the texture within a short time span. Counterpoint, when used, focused upon the opposition of masses rather than upon vocal lines. In contrast to the light and clear texture of the Classic period, the texture of music in the Romantic period was often somewhat dense and heavy.

Expressive Aspects

During the Romantic period some composers expressed their opposition to formality, convention, authority, and tradition, while some others expressed a longing for the past—the "golden age"—and made efforts to recapture it in some way. Whereas the Classic composer was highly concerned with expression within a particular form, the Romanticist was not to be restricted by it. He was not to be bound by the previous forms and strove to develop a freer form through which he might better express himself.

Individual expression became the composer's principal goal. To express emotion freely, the composer drew on all the multitude of musical resources at his command. As a means of creating tension and expressing emotion, composers of this period experimented considerably in the field of harmony. Unusual harmonic effects, as well as unusual rhythmic effects, wide contrasts in dynamics, changing moods, and varying textures were all used as expressive devices.

While tone color has always existed as an integral aspect of music, it took on a new importance during the Romantic period. Through tone color, composers sought to express sensuous beauty and tonal enchantment. Musical terms such as *con amore* (with love), *con fuoco* (with fire), *con passione* (with passion), *dolce* (sweetly), *gioioso* (joyous), and *mesto* (sad)

---

[56]The effectiveness of dissonance is certainly related to tempo, since the listener's aural comprehension of a complex and dissonant passage may be blurred by a tempo that is too rapid.

were increasingly used by composers as an indication of their intention to the performers. These terms, in addition, indicate the frame of mind of the composers of the period. Music of this period, both vocal and instrumental, was influenced by the lyricism of the human voice. It is notable that many of the themes of instrumental music of the period have been adapted into popular songs. Their popularity is, in part, affected by their singability.[57]

The center of musical life in the nineteenth century was the concert hall, rather than the palace or the church. Because of the lack of restrictions in regard to size of performance organizations, composers during the latter part of the period increasingly wrote for larger groups and in a more colorful and grandiose style than was characteristic of the earlier part of the period.[58]

THE MODERN PERIOD

Toward the end of the nineteenth century the subjective expression of Romanticism had run its course. Some composers, however, continued to write in a modified Romantic style. Among the more notable of this group of late Romanticists were Sergei Taneyev (1856–1915), Edward Elgar (1857–1934), Gustav Mahler (1860–1911), Richard Strauss (1864–1949), Alexander Gretchaninov (1864–1956), Enrique Granados (1867–1916), Max Reger (1873–1916), and Sergei Rachmaninoff (1873–1943). Most composers, however, began to seek new means of expression. The main currents of musical expression in the Modern period are now described.

Impressionism

Impressionism developed as a reaction against the emotionalism and subjective aspects of Romanticism. It emerged during the last quarter of the nineteenth century and was exemplified in the music of Claude Debussy (1862–1918) and Maurice Ravel (1885–1937). Debussy was highly influenced by the Impressionist painters and the Symbolist poets, who avoided the exact and clear-cut representation of things, but rather sought to create a momentary impression of them. The painters often did not mix their paints, but juxtaposed daubs of pure color on the canvas, with the "mixing" left to the eye of the viewer. Also seeking new paths, the Symbolist poets rejected emotionalism and turned to nebulous suggestion and dreamlike evocation of mood.[59]

---

[57]Machlis, *The Enjoyment of Music*, regular rev. ed., pp. 86–88.

[58]Ibid., p. 88.

[59]Joseph Machlis, *Introduction to Contemporary Music*, 2nd ed. (New York: W. W. Norton & Co., Inc., 1979), pp. 84–86.

Expressionism

Appearing about 1910 as a reaction against the "vagueness" of Impressionism, Expressionism is sometimes referred to as the German answer to French Impressionism. Expressionism also received its impetus from painting and poetry. Artists, perhaps influenced by Sigmund Freud's work in psychology, endeavored to capture on canvas the myriad thoughts from the unconscious. Distorted images, expressing the artist's inner self, took the place of the traditional concepts of beauty. Composers also rejected older aesthetic concepts and sought new means of expression.[60] Expressionistic music is characterized by its continuous intensity, high level of dissonance, angular melodic fragments, complex rhythms, and fluctuating tempi. The expressionist composer utilized all the devices at his command to express the conflicts, fears, and anxieties of man's inner self. The outstanding exponents of Expressionism are Arnold Schoenberg (1874–1951), Alban Berg (1885–1935), Anton von Webern (1883–1945), and Ernst Krenek (b. 1900).

Neo-Classicism

In the phase of musical expression called Neo-Classicism, which appeared after World War I, composers sought to recapture the ideals of the eighteenth century, where the emphasis was on craftsmanship rather than on emotional expression. They sought to restore the proper balance between form and emotion and rejected the excesses of the Romantic period. The return to form was a primary consideration in composition, with emotional expression being a secondary factor. The Neo-Classicists decried the idea of program music and gave more stress to the intellectual aspects of music. Composers who have written in this style include Igor Stravinsky (1882–1971), Paul Hindemith (1885–1963), Darius Milhaud (1892–1974), Francis Poulenc (1899–1963), William Schuman (b. 1910), Benjamin Britten (1913–1976), Irving Fine (1914–1962), Vincent Persichetti (b. 1915), and Lukas Foss (b. 1922).

Some musicologists have applied the labels of Neo-Classicism and Neo-Romanticism to specific composers, most of whom have written in various styles. It is impossible to categorize the works of all composers in this manner. Each student will need to analyze each work under consideration to determine the "tag" that most appropriately applies.

Neo-Romanticism

Twentieth-century composers have not all found the styles of Impressionism, Expressionism, or Neo-Classicism to their liking. Some, therefore, have utilized means of expression more closely aligned with

---

[60]Ibid., p. 335.

the ideas of the Romanticists. This group has been referred to as the Neo-Romanticists. Music in the Neo-Romantic style is usually rich in sonorities, contains frequent climaxes, and is comparatively easy for the nonmusician to listen to. The Neo-Romantic composers utilize many of the tonal and rhythmic devices of the Neo-Classicist, but they convey them in a subjective manner—in such a way as to instill emotion and warmth in their music.

While, during the first part of the twentieth century, the majority of composers had rejected the ideals of the nineteenth century in favor of other modes of expression, the political and economic situation of the second quarter of the century led the way to a more emotional means of expression. World War II, in particular, created an atmosphere more receptive to romantic ideals and a need in some composers for a more personal means of expression, in which greater emphasis is placed upon the poetic and dramatic aspects of music.[61] Some representative composers of this style are Ernst Toch (1887–1964), Carl Orff (1895–1982), Howard Hanson (1896–1981), William Walton (1902–1983), Paul Creston (1906–1985), Samuel Barber (1910–1981), Gian Carlo Menotti (b. 1911), Norman Dello Joio (b. 1913), and William Bergsma (b. 1921).

In addition to the styles of musical expression just discussed, separate consideration must be given to those composers who utilize folk material in their music. This group has often been referred to as the Nationalists. Among the more prominent are Ernest Bloch (1880–1959), Zoltán Kodály (1882–1967), Ralph Vaughan Williams (1872–1958), Charles Ives (1874–1954), Randall Thompson (1899–1984), Aaron Copland (b. 1900), Heitor Villa-Lobos (1887–1959), Carlos Chávez (1899–1978), and Alan Hovhaness (b. 1911).

Whereas the nineteenth-century composer used folk material more for color effects and altered it when it did not fit his compositional scheme, the twentieth-century Nationalist incorporated more of the flavor of the original folk idiom in his music. Modal music and material with asymmetrical rhythms are often used to create fresh, new effects.[62]

Meter and Stress

Impressionistic music possesses less tension and rhythmic drive than does music in the Romantic period. Impressionist music, particularly that of Debussy, gives the impression of being "suspended in space." While Impressionistic music may give the feeling of vagueness, it is quite precise. The conductor should avoid any exaggeration of tempo fluctuations, and the beat should be clear and precise but flexible and responsive to all the subtle nuances in the music.

[61]Ibid., p. 314.
[62]Ibid., p. 257.

In contrast to Impressionism, Expressionistic music possesses considerable rhythmic incisiveness; that is, the rhythm is even more clearcut. The rhythm of the music is generally aligned with the durational values of the text; however, as a means of achieving tension, the Expressionists often distorted the normal accentuations of words. This alteration usually necessitated the use of changing meter to accommodate the resultant rhythm.

A particular characteristic of Neo-Classic music is its rhythm. As a means of avoiding the monotony of the regular stress following the barline, composers employ various devices. One procedure is to alter the meter with each measure (sometimes referred to as *multimeter*).[63] The same effect, however, may be achieved by simply shifting the stresses or accents from point to point within the measure without changing the meter signature. In conducting rhythmic patterns with shifting accents, the conductor should limit the scope of his patterns and utilize a precise rebound to each beat. On accented notes—whether on a downbeat or an upbeat—the stress should be reflected in the tension of the arms and shoulders, whereas limited, yet precise, movements should occur on the unaccented notes.

Still another rhythmic device is the division of traditional meters in nonsymmetrical ways. For example, in 4/4 meter the eighth notes might be grouped as 3 + 3 + 2, or 3 + 2 + 3, rather than 4 + 4. (Another way of stating these rhythmic groupings is 1 2 3 1 2 3 1 2, or 1 2 3 1 2 1 2 3.) In 6/8 meter, a two-measure pattern might be alternately written as 3 + 3 + 2 + 2 + 2. In conducting rhythms in nonsymmetrical forms, the conductor must alter his patterns to conform to the basic rhythm of the music.[64]

Although the Neo-Romantic composer will use many of the rhythmic devices of the Neo-Classicist, he will do so in moderation. He places a greater emphasis on the poetic aspects of music and a means of personal expression that is more universally understood. When modern-day rhythmic devices contribute to this end they are used, and when they do not they are avoided.

Tempo

With Impressionistic music most tempi tend toward the moderate and the slow, with exceptionally fast tempi usually being avoided. A considerable degree of modern music following this period, however,

---

[63]See, for example, various works by Jean Berger: "It Is Good to Be Merry" (Kjos), "The Good of Contentment" (Presser), "Lift Up Your Heads" (Summy-Birchard), and "Seek Ye the Lord" (Augsburg).

[64]For a discussion of this technique, see section titled "Conducting Accent and Changing Meter" in Chapter 1.

exhibits a strong rhythmic drive. Movement and speed are an integral part of our modern-day life, and these characteristics are reflected in much of our modern-day music. The rhythm of Expressionistic music is generally somewhat irregular and rather complex. As a result of the normal accent of words being sometimes deliberately distorted, the tempo often fluctuates with the use of pauses, ritardandos, and accelerandos.

Tempo, of course, is related to both rhythm and mood, and, in determining the proper tempo, the conductor should consider carefully both of these factors. Because clarity of line is essential to the performance of Neo-Classic music, a tempo that is too fast will impede the articulation, whereas a tempo that is too slow will sometimes lessen the intensity and the rhythmic drive. Mood is an important consideration in determining the tempi of Neo-Romantic music. With emotional expression being relatively important, the projection of textual meanings often necessitates a greater flexibility in tempi.

Dynamics

In contrast to music of the Romantic period, Impressionistic music possesses a relatively low level of dynamic intensity. *Fortissimo* occurs rather infrequently, with the medium and the lower dynamic levels, *mezzo forte, piano,* and *pianissimo,* being used primarily. Crescendo and decrescendo, when employed, should be used with considerable care and restraint. In performing music from this period, the conductor should take care to adapt the scope of his beat to the dynamic levels of the music. In conducting a *pianissimo* passage, for example, he should use very slight movements.

Following the Impressionistic period there has gradually developed an increasing use of dynamic extremes. Contrast is often achieved through a rapid change from an extremely low dynamic level to one of great intensity and volume. Modern-day composers are inclined toward using a multiplicity of dynamic effects in their music, including extreme contrast in dynamic levels, rapid crescendos and decrescendos, dynamic accents, and uniform levels of intensity.[65]

Texture

Composers of the Romantic period were highly interested in harmonic experimentation. This interest was intensified by composers of the Modern period. The Impressionists sought to escape the restrictions of the major–minor system of tonality. In the process, Debussy used a variety of devices, including the medieval modes, the whole-tone scale,

---

[65]Howerton, *Technique and Style,* pp. 179–80.

and the pentatonic scale. Parallel fourths, fifths, and octaves were often used above a pedal point, which resulted in unusual effects from the clash between the sustained and the moving harmonies.

Although previous harmonic systems focused upon the relationship of chords and their progression from one to another, the Impressionists utilized individual chords for the sonorous and coloristic effects they created. Thus the tendency for chord resolution was certainly lessened. While triads were sometimes used, seventh, ninth, and eleventh chords were frequently employed either separately or in succession. Composers, furthermore, often utilized these chords on various scale degrees by shifting them up and down without alteration. This "gliding" use of chordal movement, utilizing blocklike chords in parallel motion, was an integral stylistic feature of Impressionism. Escaped chords—that is, those that are not resolved, but seem to "escape" to another key—were also an important characteristic of Impressionistic music. Impressionist composers often achieved a feeling of rest, or point of harmonic arrival, by simply using a less dissonant chord than those preceding it. Tonal color became equated with melody, harmony, and rhythm during this era.

Debussy often deliberately created a vagueness within his music, coupled with an indefiniteness of phrase structures. Ravel, on the other hand, utilized traditional forms and phrases to a much greater extent. The whole-tone scale was not used by Ravel, as it was by Debussy, because he desired a more definite triad outline, clearer phrase structures, and more functional harmony.

Expressionism is generally considered to have begun with Schoenberg, and since twelve-tone music is associated with him, the two terms have become somewhat synonymous. It should be understood, however, that not all Expressionist music is twelve-tone music, because the Expressionistic movement began before this development. In Schoenberg's earlier works (his oratorio *Gurre-Lieder* [Universal], for example) he developed his use of chromaticism to its maximum potential. He then began to seek new means of expression.

Schoenberg's experimentation led to the development of the *twelve-tone method,* or *serial technique,* about 1923. With this method, all compositions are based upon an arbitrary arrangement, or *set,* of the twelve chromatic tones. Each tone row or set is handled in such a manner that no particular tone becomes any more important than the others. No tone is allowed to be repeated until every other tone has been used at least once. This is in marked contrast to the conventional major–minor tonal system. The row or set serves as a unifying factor in the music. After the basic set has been introduced, it may be repeated through a variety of means. It may be inverted—that is, turned upside down—it may be performed backwards (retrograde), or inverted and performed backwards (a retrograde of the inversion). The tone row is a type of variation technique in which great variety is achieved with only a minimum of material.[66] The guiding thought is that no idea should be repeated except in a new form. The older style of repetition and sequence, balanced phrases and cadences, was rejected by the Expressionists.

In the nineteenth century, rhythm, harmony, and tone color were often considered as entities unto themselves, whereas Neo-Classicism considered each of these separate elements as subservient to the whole. The use of counterpoint by the Neo-Classic composers became increasingly important. To differentiate it, however, from the "harmonic" counterpoint of the Romantic era, this new polyphony is often referred to as "linear counterpoint." It is often marked by its transparency of texture and its dissonance and driving rhythm. While striking dissonance often occurs as a result of clashes between vocal lines, each line must maintain its forward drive or thrust.

In the music of the Neo-Romanticists, extreme harmonic complexity is usually avoided. Their music is generally characterized by its sensuous lyricism and its richness of harmony. It is often simply and directly stated, although some music possesses considerable rhythmic drive and intensity. Neo-Romantic music is primarily tonal in nature. Dissonance is used, but generally for comparatively brief periods to highlight the emotional and poetic aspects of the text. Although a considerable portion of Neo-Romantic music is harmonically conceived, some composers utilize contrapuntal devices as well. While their compositional techniques vary considerably, their one common characteristic is a more personal means of expression.

Expressive Aspects

The Impressionistic composer's aim was simply to suggest rather than boldly to state. Music of this period, therefore, should be approached in an objective manner and performed with considerable restraint. The excesses and extremes of the Romantic period should be avoided.

Expressionistic and Neo-Classical music should be approached with an even more objective point of view. Perhaps the most outstanding characteristic of Expressionistic music is its continuous dissonance (and lack of consonance that would allow for a lessening of the tension). Dissonance, along with such other devices as angular melodic fragments, irregular rhythm, and abrupt changes in tempi, is used as a means of expressing the conflicts of man's inner self. The composer's concern is the use of these varied devices to portray these inner feelings, rather than the expression of pure emotion in itself.

[66]Machlis, *Introduction to Contemporary Music,* pp. 340–42.

The Neo-Classicist is concerned largely with craftsmanship and with the statement of his material in an impersonal, objective manner. Emotional expression is minimized. Although it will vary from composer to composer, it is always carefully controlled. The Neo-Classicist endeavors to recapture the classic spirit by striving for symmetry and balance in his music, by utilizing more transparent textures, and by limiting the size of his musical forces.

The Neo-Romanticist, however, seeks a more universalized type of expression. His goal is different from the Neo-Classicist, since he desires his means of communication to be more personal in nature. Although he uses many musical devices similar to those of the Neo-Classical composer, since his purpose is different he uses them in a different way. The conductor should analyze his music and determine the *raison d'être* for each device if he is to employ it for its intended purpose.

In performing music of the Modern period, the conductor should give particular attention to the tone quality and the manner of articulation. With Impressionistic music, the singers need to use a legato style of diction so as not to disturb the smooth flow of the carefully voiced chords often moving in parallel motion.[67]

The melody of Expressionistic music often moves in wide angular leaps, thus creating some serious intonation problems for the performers. Singers, obviously, need to listen carefully. And, because any rigidity in the jaw will inhibit proper articulation, they need to maintain a rather relaxed jaw to facilitate a cleaner articulation of the various interval leaps.

In Neo-Classic music it is usually desirable to lessen the dramatic qualities of the voice so that the clarity of the structure may be brought out. Voices with excessive vibrato or tremolo are particularly detrimental to the interpretation of this style of music. In performing music in a Neo-Romantic style, the voice quality should be warm and expressive so as to convey best the subjective aspects of the music.

MUSIC WITH ELECTRONIC TAPE/ NONCONVENTIONAL NOTATION

The continued search for new means of musical expression brought forth, particularly during the decade of the 1970s, a variety of types of new choral music, including voices combined with electronic tape sounds, choric speech with singing, aleatoric (chance) music, and multimedia presentations. (We are presently in the midst of many new devel-

---

[67]For a discussion of legato diction, see section titled "Styles of Diction" in Chapter 2.

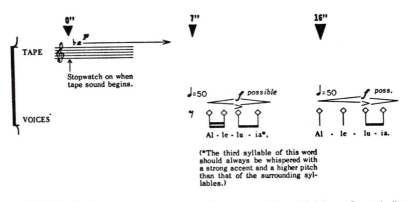

opments and therefore lack the perspective that we have of earlier music. It thus seems appropriate to include this material in a section separate from other twentieth-century music.)

Conventional notation for the vocal parts is usually employed in choral music with electronic tape. In some music, the time for specific cues is indicated in the score, and a stopwatch is necessary to coordinate the two separate sound sources. In other instances, a graphic illustration of the electronic sound is indicated in the score, thus assisting both the conductor and the singers to coordinate their efforts and making the use of a stopwatch unnecessary. Examples of both types are illustrated in Figures 54 and 55.

As composers continue to explore new means of music expression, they find that the conventional means of music notation do not allow them sufficient flexibility, nor do symbols always exist for the expression of their musical ideas. This has resulted in the creation of an entirely new means of notation. Specific notation now has been devised for spoken pitches, raising and lowering the pitch of the voice, shouts, screams, laughter, varying dynamic levels, tone clusters, staccato pronunciations, whispers, various lip sounds, tongue clicks, coughs, hissing sounds, giggles, hand claps, glissandos, vibrato, tempo, duration, accelerando, ritardando, and various other tonal effects.[68] Excerpts from a number of compositions representing this type of notation are illustrated in Figures 56–63.

[68]For a helpful and useful compilation of all these symbols, along with explanations, see Frank Pooler and Brent Pierce, *New Choral Notation* (New York: Walton Music Corporation, 1971).

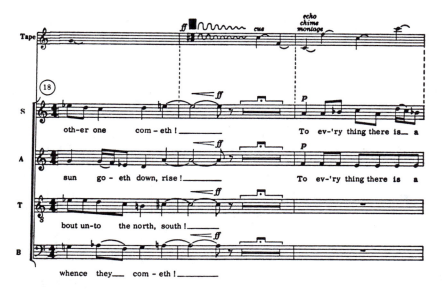

FIGURE 55 Excerpt from *A Time to Every Purpose* by Gilbert Trythall. Graphic illustration of tape sounds for coordination of choral parts with tape. Copyright © 1972, Edward B. Marks Music Corporation. Used by permission.

As part of the total musical diet, avant-garde music has value in that it adds a new dimension to sound as an expressive art, and it can "open singers' ears," so to speak, to new as well as older sounds. Young singers are generally receptive to music of this type, because it is not necessarily far removed from their own popular musical culture. For the conductor who is especially attuned to music of other types and styles, a selective list of choral music with electronic tape and with nonconventional notation will be found in the Appendix. Most of this music will include explanatory information concerning the notational symbols and how to interpret them. Examination and study of these compositions by the conductor, and performance of certain selected works, will balance out the musical diet of the choir or chorus.

SOME CONCLUDING THOUGHTS

Certainly one characteristic of twentieth-century music is the wide diversity of musical styles. It is often difficult to place composers neatly in the previously mentioned categories, since some change their styles during

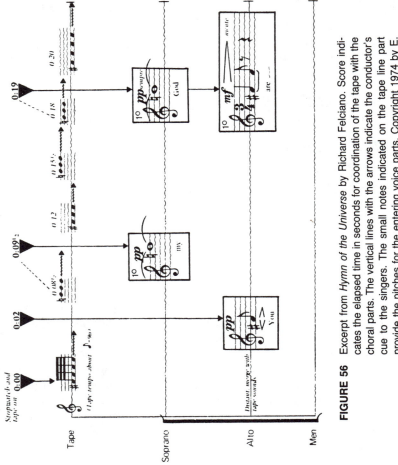

FIGURE 56 Excerpt from *Hymn of the Universe* by Richard Felciano. Score indicates the elapsed time in seconds for coordination of the tape with the choral parts. The vertical lines with the arrows indicate the conductor's cue to the singers. The small notes indicated on the tape line part provide the pitches for the entering voice parts. Copyright 1974 by E. C. Schirmer Company, Boston. Used by permission.

144

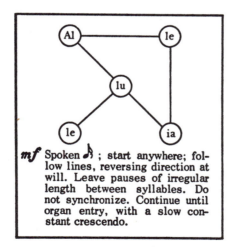

FIGURE 57 Excerpt from *Psalm 27* (Part III) by Robert Karlen. Notation indicates, as closely as possible, the pitch of the spoken sounds. Copyright 1968, A.M.S.I. Used by permission.

their composing years. Other composers might be said to possess an "eclectic" style; that is, they draw from the techniques and devices of various schools, depending upon the musical thought to be expressed. The conductor, therefore, if he is to interpret properly the works of any particular modern-day composer, should study and analyze the music as well as the writings of the composer under consideration. What a composer says about his own music has obvious implications for the conductor seeking the proper interpretation. Whenever such writings do not exist or are unavailable, the conductor may well turn to the vast number of books on twentieth-century composers (as well as those of other periods). What others have written about the lives and the music of particu-

FIGURE 58 Excerpt from *Pentecost Sunday* by Richard Felciano. Chart designed to elicit irregular, nonsynchronized speech sounds. Copyright 1967, World Library Publications, Inc., 3815 N. Willow Rd., Schiller Park, IL 60176. All rights reserved. Used by permission.

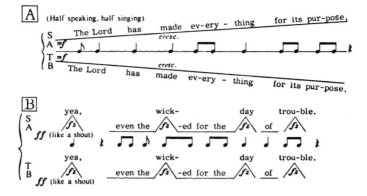

FIGURE 59   Excerpt from *All the Ways of a Man* by Knut Nystedt. Rhythm and text given, but (A) pitch changes indicated by ascending and descending lines and (B) dynamic accents or "shouts" indicated by /fz\. Copyright 1971, Augsburg Publishing House. Used by permission.

lar individuals will often provide the inquiring, analytical reader with fresh insights into the interpretation of music.

The study of style and interpretation is not a subject to be dealt with on a one-time basis —it should be studied throughout one's musical career. The intent of this chapter has been to provide a summary of the most salient points for consideration. To be most meaningful, however, they must be studied in connection with actual music. With this background information, the conductor should carefully study and analyze his scores. Only through reflective thought on the composer's intentions will the proper interpretation be achieved. The choral conductor should also listen critically to the interpretations of various choral organizations—on recordings and in the concert hall. The listener will most likely find that the interpretation of a particular composition will vary somewhat from one conductor to another. "What is stylistically correct and what is incorrect about these performances?" and "What do I like and dislike about the performances?" These questions must be always present on the listener's mind if he or she is to make the proper evaluation essential to further musical growth. The young conductor must give these questions careful consideration if he is ultimately to achieve the correct interpretation for his own choral groups.

Finally, the effective conductor must also be a scholar. He should devote considerable time to further reading in various sources of the main points discussed in this chapter. He should also develop a broad historical understanding of the various periods of artistic achievement. For these purposes, a selected list of publications recommended for further study is included at the end of this chapter.

FIGURE 60 Excerpt from *Pshelley's Psalm* by Richard Felciano. Note combination of designated pitches with other sounds, including hisses, shouts, and hand claps. Copyright 1974, E. C. Schirmer Company, Boston. Used by permission.

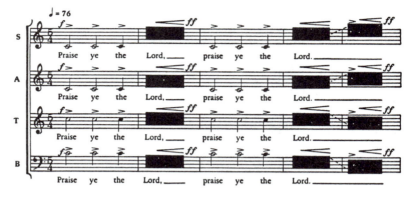

FIGURE 61 Excerpt from *Aleatory Psalm* by Gordon H. Lamb. The box ▬▬ represents a tone cluster within the confines of the symbol (in this instance—a minor seventh in each part). Singers should endeavor to avoid a pitch sung by another person. Copyright 1973, World Library Publications, Inc., 3815 N. Willow Rd., Schiller Park, IL 60176. All rights reserved. Used by permission.

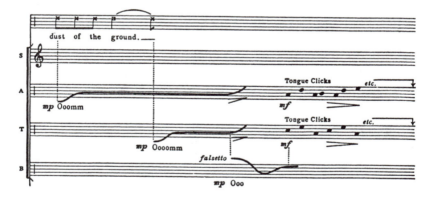

FIGURE 62 Excerpt from "The Creation" from *The Family of Man* by Michael Hennagin. (*a*) Approximate pitch level of vowel sound indicated by lines, and (*b*) special effects, such as tongue clicks. Copyright 1971, Walton Music Corp. Used by permission.

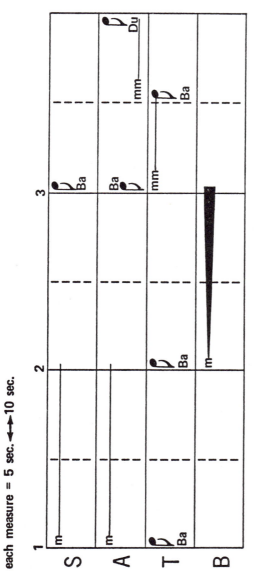

FIGURE 63 Excerpt from *Two Moves and the Slow Scat* by Dennis Kam. Dotted lines divide measures into two parts, with the solid line indicating the cue for the downbeat and the dotted line the cue for the upward beat. The size of each notehead indicates the relative dynamic level (*p, mf, f*) and its location within the box for each part indicates the pitch range (high, middle, low). The thickening of a line indicates a crescendo. Copyright 1973 by Belwin Mills Publishing Corp. Used by permission.

TOPICS FOR DISCUSSION

1. What are some problems one might encounter when trying to perform Baroque music as it was originally intended?
2. Discuss the benefits and the drawbacks of the old system of princely patronage of composers. What ideas have been advanced for the support of composers in our present-day society?
3. What specific techniques might a choral conductor use in teaching an appropriate style for any given period or composer? Discuss each historical period and cite particular composers and works.
4. How should the conductor's beat vary in conducting music of various periods?
5. In striving toward an authentic performance, to what extent should the conductor allow authenticity to give way to his personal idiosyncrasies?
6. Discuss the effect of geographical influences upon the style and mode of expression of particular composers.
7. The Romantic era has been referred to as a "period of opposites." What is meant by this expression, and what are the implications for understanding the music of particular composers?
8. What is meant by the term *an eclectic style?* Give some examples.

SELECTED READINGS

ALDRICH, PUTMAN C., "The 'Authentic' Performance of Baroque Music," in *Essays on Music in Honor of Archibald T. Davison*. Cambridge, Mass.: Harvard University Press, 1957.

APEL, WILLI, *The Notation of Polyphonic Music, 900–1600*. Cambridge, Mass.: Mediaeval Academy of America, 1942.

ARNOLD, DENIS, *The New Oxford Companion to Music* (2 vols.). Oxford, England: Oxford University Press, 1983.

ARTZ, FREDERICK, *From the Renaissance to Romanticism*. Chicago: University of Chicago Press, 1962.

BAKER, THEODORE, *Baker's Biographical Dictionary of Musicians* (7th ed., rev. Nicolas Slonimsky). New York: Schirmer Books, 1984.

BARRA, DONALD, *The Dynamic Performance: A Performer's Guide to Musical Expression and Interpretation*. Englewood Cliffs, N.J.: Prentice-Hall, 1983.

BLUME, FRIEDRICH, *Renaissance and Baroque Music*. New York: W. W. Norton & Co., Inc., 1967.

————, *Classic and Romantic Music*. New York: W. W. Norton & Co., Inc., 1970.

BORROFF, EDITH, *The Music of the Baroque*. Dubuque, Iowa: Wm. C. Brown, 1970.

BROWN, HOWARD, *Music in the Renaissance*. Englewood Cliffs, N.J.: Prentice-Hall, 1976.

BUKOFZER, MANFRED F., *Music in the Baroque Era: From Monteverdi to Bach*. New York: W. W. Norton & Co., Inc., 1947.

————, "On the Performance of Renaissance Music," *Music Teachers National Association, Volume of Proceedings*, 1941. Pittsburgh: The Association, 1942, pp. 225–35.

CALVOCORESSI, M. D., *A Survey of Russian Music*. Baltimore: Penguin, 1944.

DART, THURSTON, *The Interpretation of Music* (rev. ed.). London: Hutchinson Publishing Group Ltd., 1960.

DECKER, HAROLD A., AND JULIUS HERFORD, *Choral Conducting Symposium* (2nd ed.), chaps. 3, 4. Englewood Cliffs, N.J.: Prentice-Hall, 1988.

DOLMETSCH, ARNOLD, *The Interpretation of the Music of the XVIIth & XVIIIth Centuries*. London: Oxford University Press, 1946.

DONINGTON, ROBERT, *The Interpretation of Music*. London: Faber & Faber Ltd., 1963.

DORIAN, FREDERICK, *The History of Music in Performance*. New York: W. W. Norton & Co., Inc., 1942.

EINSTEIN, ALFRED, *The Italian Madrigal* (3 vols.). Princeton, N.J.: Princeton University Press, 1949.

———, *Music in the Romantic Era*. New York: W. W. Norton & Co., Inc., 1947.

ETHERINGTON, CHARLES L., *Protestant Worship Music: Its History and Practice*. New York: Holt, Rinehart & Winston, 1962.

FELLOWES, EDMUND H., *The English Madrigal Composers* (2nd ed.). London: Oxford University Press, 1948.

FLEMING, WILLIAM, AND ABRAHAM VEINUS, *Understanding Music: Style, Structure, and History*, pp. 309–10. New York: Holt, Rinehart & Winston, 1958.

GARRETSON, ROBERT L., "The Falsettists," *The Choral Journal*, XXIV, no. 1 (September 1983), 5–9.

GORE, RICHARD T., "The Performance of Baroque Church Music," *Music Teachers National Association, Volume of Proceedings*, 1950. Pittsburgh: The Association, 1953, pp. 155–63.

GROUT, DONALD JAY, *A History of Western Music* (3rd ed.). New York: W. W. Norton & Co., Inc., 1980.

Grove's Dictionary of Music and Musicians (5th ed., 9 vols.). New York: St. Martin's Press, Macmillan & Co. Ltd., 1954.

HANSEN, PETER S., *An Introduction to Twentieth Century Music* (2nd ed.). Boston: Allyn & Bacon, 1967.

HARMAN, R. ALEC, AND ANTHONY MILNER, *Late Renaissance and Baroque Music*. London: Barrie & Rockliff, 1959.

HEGER, THEODORE E., *Music of the Classic Period*. Dubuque, Iowa: Wm. C. Brown, 1969.

HOWERTON, GEORGE, *Technique and Style in Choral Singing*. New York: Carl Fischer, Inc., 1957.

JEPPESEN, KNUD, *The Style of Palestrina and the Dissonance*. Copenhagen: Ejnar Munksgaard, Publisher, 1946.

JORGENSEN, OWEN, *Tuning the Historical Temperaments by Ear*. Marquette: Northern Michigan University Press, 1977.

KENNEDY, MICHAEL, *The Oxford Dictionary of Music*. Oxford, England: Oxford University Press, 1985.

KJELSON, LEE, AND JAMES MCCRAY, *The Conductor's Manual of Choral Music Literature*. Miami: Belwin Mills Publishing Corp., 1973.

LANG, PAUL HENRY, *Music in Western Civilization*. New York: W. W. Norton & Co., Inc., 1941.

LEONARD, RICHARD, *A History of Russian Music*. New York: Macmillan, 1957.

LONGYEAR, REY M., *Nineteenth-Century Romanticism in Music* (3rd ed.). Englewood Cliffs, N.J.: Prentice-Hall, 1988.

MACCLINTOCK, CAROL, ed., *Readings in the History of Music in Performance*. Bloomington, Ind.: Indiana University Press, 1979.

MACHLIS, JOSEPH, *The Enjoyment of Music* (5th ed.). New York: W. W. Norton & Co., Inc., 1984.

———, *Introduction to Contemporary Music* (2nd ed.). New York: W. W. Norton & Co., Inc., 1979.

MANN, WILLIAM, *James Galway's Music in Time*. Englewood Cliffs, N.J.: Prentice-Hall, 1983.

MAY, JAMES D., *Avant-Garde Choral Music: An Annotated Selected Bibliography*. Metuchen, N.J.: Scarecrow, 1977.

MORLEY, THOMAS, *A Plain and Easy Introduction to Practical Music*. London, 1597. Modern edition by R. Alec Harman, London, 1952.

New Grove Dictionary of Music and Musicians, The, ed. Stanley Sadie (20 vols.). London: Macmillan Publishers, Ltd., 1980.

PALISCA, CLAUDE V., *Baroque Music* (2nd ed.). Englewood Cliffs, N.J.: Prentice-Hall, 1981.

PATTISON, BRUCE, *Music and Poetry of the English Renaissance*. London: Methuen & Company Ltd., 1948.

PAULY, REINHARD G., *Music in the Classic Period* (2nd ed.). Englewood Cliffs, N.J.: Prentice-Hall, 1973.

POOLER, FRANK, AND BRENT PIERCE, *New Choral Notation*. New York: Walton Music Corporation, 1971.

QUANTZ, JOHANN JOACHIM, *Versuch einer Anweisung die Flöte traversiere zu spielen*. Berlin, 1752. Translation and study by E. R. Reilly. Unpublished Ph.D. dissertation, University of Michigan, 1958.

RANDALL, DON MICHAEL, ed., *The New Harvard Dictionary of Music*. Cambridge, Mass.: Harvard University Press, 1986.

REESE, GUSTAVE, *Music in the Renaissance*. New York: W. W. Norton & Co., Inc., 1954.

ROBINSON, RAY, AND ALLEN WINOLD, *The Choral Experience: Literature, Materials, and Methods*, Part Four on Performance Practices. New York: Harper & Row, Pub., 1976.

ROSEN, CHARLES, *Classic Style*. New York: Viking, 1971.

ROTHSCHILD, FRITZ, *The Lost Tradition in Music: Rhythm and Tempo in J. S. Bach's Time*. New York: Oxford University Press, Inc., 1953.

————, *Musical Performance in the Times of Mozart and Beethoven: The Lost Tradition in Music*, Part II. New York: Oxford University Press, Inc., 1961.

SACHS, CURT, *Rhythm and Tempo: A Study in Music History*. New York: W. W. Norton & Co., Inc., 1953.

SALZMAN, ERIC, *Twentieth-Century Music: An Introduction* (2nd ed.). Englewood Cliffs, N.J.: Prentice-Hall, 1974.

SCOTT, CHARLES KENNEDY, *Madrigal Singing*. London: Oxford University Press, 1931.

SPARKS, EDGAR, *Cantus Firmus in Mass and Motet, 1420–1520*. Berkeley and Los Angeles: University of California Press, 1963.

STEVENSON, ROBERT, *Music before the Classic Era*. London: Macmillan & Co., Ltd., 1955.

STRUNK, OLIVER, ed., *Source Readings in Music History*. New York: W. W. Norton & Co., Inc., 1950.

SWAN, HOWARD, *Conscience of a Profession* (ed. Charles Fowler). Chapel Hill, N.C.: Hinshaw Music, Inc., 1987.

TARTINI, GIUSEPPE, "Treatise on Ornamentation" (trans. and ed. Sol Babitz), *Journal of Research in Music Education*, 4, no. 2 (Fall 1956), 75–102.

ULRICH, HOMER, *A Survey of Choral Music*. New York: Harcourt Brace Jovanovich, Inc., 1973.

————, AND PAUL A. PISK, *A History of Music and Musical Style*. New York: Harcourt Brace Jovanovich, Inc., 1963.

VINQUIST, MARY, AND NEAL ZASLAW, *Performance Practice: A Bibliography*. New York: W. W. Norton & Co., Inc., 1971.

YOUNG, PERCY M., *The Choral Tradition*. New York: W. W. Norton & Co., Inc., 1962.

4

Rehearsal Techniques

The success of the choral concert is determined in the rehearsal room. Effective musical results are dependent upon a conductor's well-defined concept of his musical objectives and upon his ability to transmit them to the members of the choral group. Although careful planning assists in the clarification of objectives, the conductor must possess various techniques for implementing his ideas. Through judicious employment of these devices, he will strive toward a consistently improved performance. Efforts in this direction will result in higher musical standards and increased satisfaction for both the performers and the audience.

PREREHEARSAL PLANNING

Choral directors are constantly asked to perform, and many, especially school music directors, feel that allocated rehearsal time is inadequate to develop their groups to the proper performance level. In view of this situation, rehearsals must necessarily be well planned if the director is to make the most effective use of his time. Careful prerehearsal planning is also likely to result in more meaningful learning experiences, which in turn provide the climate necessary for subsequent learning experiences. Following are some general suggestions concerning overall rehearsal planning.

A director should include in the choral rehearsal a variety of music from all historical periods. If choir members are to develop an understanding of, and appreciation for, various types of music, they should have some experience with choral music of the Renaissance, Baroque, Classic, Romantic, and Modern periods, as well as with folk music.[1] Furthermore, when variety is provided by alternating selections with contrasting styles, moods, and tempi, student interest is more readily maintained.

A conductor should never attempt to learn the music concurrently with his singers, but should study it carefully prior to each rehearsal. To familiarize himself with the music, he should read through the choral parts on the piano. He should note specific difficulties or pitfalls that the singers are likely to encounter, such as intricate rhythmic patterns, difficult intervals in the various parts, unusual harmonic progressions, and particular diction problems. It is helpful for the conductor to mark his score with a colored pencil, indicating the anticipated difficulties.

Consideration should be given, of course, to teaching procedures for clarifying and solving rhythmic and tonal problems, and specific conducting techniques should be analyzed and practiced. It is advisable to sing through any portions of the vocal parts that are likely to cause the singers difficulty, so that they may be demonstrated adequately to the choir. The conductor should also examine the text for words with an unusual pronunciation, and when in doubt, he should consult a dictionary. Any textual subtleties reflected in the score should also be noted as a basis for achieving the proper interpretation.

In addition, the conductor will want to draw upon all his resources and musical background in achieving an effective musical interpretation. The practical application of knowledge gained in music theory and history classes will at this point be of inestimable value. The conductor should apply his knowledge of musical styles in various historical periods and, more specifically, his understanding of the unique styles of individual composers.

In determining the procedures for accomplishing one's objectives, the director ought to prepare and write out a set of sample sentences on how to state what he desires to say or do. Such a procedure will enable the director to be more objective and precise about his procedures. Not too much should be said! Be succinct and consider the *impact* of what you plan to say or do! If you later find that your procedure is not really effective, then try another way. Your written plan will provide you with some basis for evaluating your actions.

There are three basic ways or procedures for achieving one's objectives: (1) through a verbal expression of what one desires; (2) through demonstration (singing to illustrate tone quality, pronunciation, enunci-

---

[1]For a chronological listing of choral composers, see Appendix.

ation, phrasing, and so on, and clapping or chanting to correct rhythmic difficulties); and (3) through some psychological device or motivation such as "let the tone float—just as light as a feather." The director must decide which of these three procedures will be most effective in solving the problem at hand.

It is important that the director utilize reinforcement through words of approval or positive actions. If students are to improve, they need to know what they have achieved and what problems still remain to be solved. In short, they need careful guidance. Some teachers feel they shouldn't comment upon progress until the rendition of a specific choral selection is almost perfect. This approach is not advisable—conductors should endeavor to give *some* approval whenever possible. Teachers, however, should make an honest assessment. Actually, progress occurs in degrees, and directors may likewise respond with varying degrees of approval ranging from minimal approval to great satisfaction. The following succinct statements are provided as examples.

Minimal approval—"That's better! You have the idea!"
Moderate approval—"That's good! Much improved!"
Maximum approval—"I like it! That's great!"

The young conductor may sometimes have a concept in mind as to how the music should sound and then conduct blithely away, seemingly oblivious to the reality of the situation. At times during a rehearsal he may wish to make corrections but is receiving so many stimuli that he is unable to find the words to express what he desires. By identifying potential problems—and this skill improves through experience—and writing out appropriate statements or ways of seeking solutions, the director is better able to respond to the situation. By writing out succinct statements the director will, it is hoped, avoid the opposite pitfall of saying too much—to the extent that the impact is lost and valuable rehearsal time is lost.

Prior to the rehearsal, the conductor should determine the order of the selections to be rehearsed and place them on the chalkboard. Singers, after they enter the rehearsal room, can then place their music in order, thus saving time and eliminating or at least minimizing any confusion prior to working on each selection.

Make certain that the accompanist is provided any new music in ample time prior to the rehearsal, with instructions as to tempo, dynamics, mood, and the like. The most carefully laid rehearsal plans can be of little avail if the accompanist is not adequately prepared.

After each rehearsal, it is desirable to take a few moments to evaluate the group's progress and to notate, either on the music or in a notebook, those points in the score that need further attention, and any approaches that might be effectively used in subsequent rehearsals.

THE SINGERS' RESPONSIBILITIES

To what extent do the singers in the choir share the director's objectives? Do they have a full understanding of what is expected of them? Do they realize that the conductor can achieve only so much without their complete understanding and support? While conductors can verbalize many of the choir's overall objectives with the singers, one must realize that the majority of persons are visually rather than aurally oriented. Therefore, it is suggested that directors prepare a list of objectives they consider most important. The list, prepared in the form of questions, should then be duplicated and distributed to the choir members, so that every singer can read and contemplate each question. Questions may deal, for example, with each singer's preparation for rehearsals, attention given to the director's instructions, attitudes about new music, encouragement of other singers in the choir, listening to one's own singing voice, understanding of the text of the music, efforts toward memorizing the music, visual attention to the director, efforts toward improving music reading skills, and expectations regarding the achievements of the choir.

All questions and statements serve to reinforce comments that the director has previously stated verbally. Singers are asked to evaluate themselves on each question and determine how they rate personally, and to periodically reassess their status. The list provides a basis for informal group discussions held preferably at the beginning of the year and periodically as occasions necessitate.

THE FIRST REHEARSAL

The success of a choral group depends to a great extent upon the success of the initial rehearsal. In recruiting members, one of the best advertisements is a group of inspired singers. The word soon gets around that choral singing is an exciting adventure, and the question "Why don't you join too?" may be frequently asked.

Young singers entering the rehearsal room for the first time may possess mixed feelings about choral singing—they may eagerly anticipate an activity that they feel will be exciting and enjoyable, and yet be somewhat dubious of the outcome or the wisdom of their choice. It is the responsibility of the director to plan the rehearsal so that it will move smoothly toward its objective.

After the group has been seated, the conductor should endeavor to set the group at ease with a few words of welcome. Next, it will be necessary to explain the general rehearsal procedures and tell the singers what they must do in order to retain their membership. Initial remarks, however, should be kept to a minimum, and the business of the actual rehearsal should be undertaken without unnecessary delay. Also it should be kept in mind that overemphasis upon technique in the beginning can have a deadly effect upon a young choral group. These details are generally best introduced as the requirements of music dictate—and only a few at a time.

In selecting the music for the first rehearsal, the conductor should consider the musical background of the group. Perhaps the singers have not been exposed to the standard choral literature and are generally unaware and unappreciative of its inherent beauties. In the beginning, it is helpful to concentrate upon a variety of folk-song arrangements of a rhythmical nature. In situations where the singers' backgrounds are extremely limited, it is desirable to intersperse a few easy rounds and canons with the rest of the repertoire. By providing the singers with music commensurate with their abilities and backgrounds, the conductor can minimize individual feelings of frustration, and a more successful and enjoyable rehearsal will result. In the beginning, the singers should be provided with music they like, as long as it is within the limits of good musical taste. There will be ample time for raising musical standards and improving individual tastes.

The importance of having the first concert as soon as possible cannot be underestimated. Individuals constantly need a goal before them to guide their work if they are to make strides toward a consistently improved performance. This is especially important in the early stages of the development of a newly organized group. Soon the singers will anticipate the rehearsals for the sheer beauty of the music itself and the enjoyment and satisfaction that they receive. At this point the conductor should implement his plans, on a gradual basis, for broadening the singers' musical interests and raising their tastes and musical standards.

INTRODUCING MUSIC

In teaching new music, the best procedures are those that facilitate learning and achieve artistic singing in the shortest period of time. Some choral directors employ what is called the "note approach"; that is, after an attempt is made to read the music, each part is worked out separately with the aid of the piano, and finally all the parts are sung together. Such a procedure is extremely tedious, discipline is often difficult to maintain, and artistic singing is not readily achieved. One of the greatest objections to this procedure is that few of the emotional qualities of the music survive this mechanical approach. The following suggestions are given in an attempt to remedy this dilemma.

If the singers have a fair amount of reading power, they should try to sing the entire number through from beginning to end (with or without the aid of the piano, depending upon the development of their musicianship). In this way, not only will the reading ability of the group improve, but also an overall concept of the music will be attained.

In presenting difficult compositions, the accompanist may play the music on the piano while each singer follows his part. If a good recording is available, it can be an invaluable aid in presenting new music. Although one would certainly not recommend that choral recordings be slavishly imitated by any group or conductor, they can serve as an extremely useful guide and rehearsal aid. After the choir members have been introduced to the music and have an overall conception of it, then various sections may be rehearsed in detail.

Many choral conductors have found through years of experience that once the rhythmic problems have been overcome, the notes and the parts come faster. In studying sections of the music, it is very helpful to have the singers recite together the text of the composition in correct musical rhythm. Such an approach helps to solve simultaneously problems of rhythm, diction, phrasing, and proper dynamics.

This procedure does not preclude the necessity for occasionally devoting special attention to a particular voice part. At a specific point in the rehearsal, this may be the only means of achieving the desired musical results. Difficulties do sometimes arise, however, when directors devote too much time to this procedure. Discipline problems may be lessened considerably if the director strives to maintain the group's interest at all times and if he stresses the importance of using all the rehearsal time to the group's best advantage. In achieving this objective, the director may use the following procedures alternately. First, while one part is being rehearsed, each of the other singers should be asked to study his part and listen to it in relation to the other parts. Second, all singers might be asked to sing a troublesome part in unison. This procedure also has value in developing an awareness of the relationships between parts. Third, request the choir members to *hum* their own parts softly while the troublesome part is being rehearsed.

Successful directors have found that effective rehearsals must be stimulating and must move quickly. When the director maintains a fast pace and the singers are kept busy, much more is accomplished and confusion is reduced to a minimum.

IMPROVING MUSIC READING

In most areas of learning, conceptual understandings are likely to be most meaningful when learning is through a discovery process and not through simply being told the answer. Similarly, in music, sight-reading skills will improve most when a singer has to struggle a bit to interpret the score. Once he hears the music through a recording or on the piano, he no longer needs to rely on his musical memory in an attempt to recall the correct rhythm and pitches, for he already *has* the answer. To improve music-reading skills, singers need to be provided with challenges involving a wide variety of rhythmic and tonal experience.

If individuals are to improve, they must recognize and feel a need for improvement. Some persons are strongly motivated toward achieving success in all areas and have a strong desire for self-improvement. Such minds are highly receptive to improving music-reading skills. However, everyone does not possess this degree of motivation, and the director can assist such persons best by helping them to feel the satisfaction of achievement. He should be positive in all his remarks and plan all music-reading experiences so that they are as challenging and interesting as possible. Any devices used should generally grow out of a problem in actually reading music. At least, they should relate to a specific problem of music reading. Abstract drills, unrelated in any way to actual music, can become most dull and serve little purpose.

If the sight-reading abilities of a choir are to be developed, attention must be given to their development during each rehearsal period. Sight reading can be improved only by practice, based upon musical understanding. Perhaps just past the midway point of each rehearsal, it is desirable to include at least one selection for sight-reading purposes. Procedures followed at music competition-festivals are suggested. The music should be carefully examined by the choir members while the director points out and discusses various pitfalls inherent in it. Upon first examination, singers should accustom themselves to looking first at the meter and key signatures and at the beginning chord, and then scanning their respective parts for intricate rhythmic patterns or figures, unfamiliar intervals (particularly wide ones), any chromatic alterations, and expression markings. Next, pitches should be given and the group should attempt to sing the music completely through from beginning to end without a break. General suggestions that the group should keep in mind are (1) keep the eyes moving ahead to grasp patterns or groups of notes; (2) respond to the pulse of the music in some way—perhaps by wiggling the toes inside the shoes;[2] (3) keep going and do not stop or fret about mistakes; (4) look for familiar patterns in the music both before and during the reading process. Following the initial reading, difficult aspects of the music should again be discussed, and, if time allows, the selection should be repeated in an effort to eliminate previous errors.[3]

[2]For other means of encouraging a response to the pulse of the music, see later in chapter under section titled "Attacks and Releases."

[3]To develop sight-reading skills, some directors like to use music selected from their choral libraries, while others prefer to use a methods book designed for this purpose. A recommended book is *The Jenson Sight Singing Course* by David Bauguess (New Berlin, Wis.: Jenson Publications, 1984).

In many instances, problems of rhythm and pitch arising from reading sessions will be dealt with simultaneously. In other cases, the learning process may be facilitated when each is dealt with separately. Suggestions for achieving rhythmic responsiveness and tonal awareness follow.

Rhythmic Responsiveness

A singer's perception of rhythmic patterns and the accuracy of his or her response constitute an important part of music-reading skills. The following approaches are suggested as a means of increasing a choir's responsiveness to rhythm.

1. Reciting the text of the music in correct musical rhythm, as discussed in the preceding section, is an excellent means of facilitating the learning of difficult rhythm patterns. To develop individual rhythmic responsiveness, however, the singers should be asked to peruse the rhythmic patterns silently by themselves before the group endeavors to chant them together.

2. Clapping the troublesome rhythm patterns is a good way to elicit a bodily response to rhythm. Opportunity should be provided for everyone to respond in various ways—individually, in quartets, or in sections, rather than just in the entire group.

3. The director may accumulate a number of rhythmic problems confronted by the singers. To encourage more careful listening coupled with bodily response, he should chant a one- or two-measure pattern, with the group responding immediately afterwards. The response is more effective if the group taps the heel or the toe prior to the chanting, and maintains this steady response to the pulse throughout the activity. Rhythmic patterns may vary from the simple to the complex and encompass all musical styles. (For an illustration of this idea, see the discussion on rhythmic precision as it relates to attacks and releases, and Figure 65, later in the chapter.)

4. Isolate particular rhythm problems in the music and write them on the chalkboard. Analyze them and then respond in some way by chanting or clapping, or by some counting system.

5. Some students have difficulty reading music in meters other than 3/4 and 4/4 because, as a result of their limited experience, they usually expect each beat to be a quarter note. To correct this misconception, and to broaden their experience, it is helpful to write on the chalkboard a familiar tune in a meter other than the original. A tune originally in 4/4 meter might be written, for example, in 4/8, 4/2, or 12/8 meter. The familiar tune serves as a common element and through singing and comparing different ways of notating a tune, students gain insight into the relatedness of rhythms.

6. Write a phrase of a familiar song on the chalkboard and, after the group has sung it through once, alter the rhythm in some way. Use simple rhythmic alterations, but soon include the more difficult until a considerable number of rhythm patterns have been experienced. The familiar song

provides a base from which to begin, so that attention may be focused on the rhythm and not on the tonal problems.

Tonal Awareness

The ability to perceive differences and relationships in pitch and to reproduce them accurately is essential to achieving any degree of skill in music reading. The following procedures are suggested as a means of developing greater tonal awareness.

1. A keen awareness of the tonal relationships between various intervals is essential to the achievement of good intonation, as well as to skill in sight reading. One suggested device is the singing in unison of various intervals without aid from the piano. The director may request the group to sing "up a major third" and back to the initial pitch, then "up a perfect fifth" and back, then "down a perfect fourth" and back, and so on, until various intervals have been sung. Extended over a period of time, this device may encompass a wide gamut of interval experience, which will contribute substantially to the singers' musicianship. The introduction of this procedure presupposes, of course, some preliminary instruction in the theoretical aspects of intervals, and some initial practice in singing them with the aid of the piano and observing them on the chalkboard as they are sung. The practicality of this device, in terms of improving sight-reading skills, lies in the singers' ability to establish the connection between this aural experience and the visual recognition of the intervals. Therefore, to establish the connection more firmly, the director should, during the rehearsal of certain selections, ask the singers to identify specific intervals, recall their relationships, and then sing them with a reasonable degree of accuracy.

    A related procedure is to train the group to sing the pitch A = 440 without aid from the piano. In the initial stages, periodical checking of the pitch with the piano will be necessary and will illustrate to the group their relative degree of success. After a while the singers will develop this skill and a degree of confidence will result from the accomplishment. Once the pitch has become firmly established in the singers' minds, a basic starting point is also provided for the singing of various intervals.

2. A procedure used to help cement tonal relationships is to relate the intervals to those found in the opening or beginning pitches of familiar songs. A list of suggested songs follows. If some of the singers don't know the songs, then teach them. Singers should learn the entire song so they can recall the intervals in their tonal context. Singers should also be encouraged to add to the list songs that they know and particularly enjoy. The director also should look for appropriate songs.

    The practical aspect of this procedure is to transfer this tonal "frame of reference" to the choral rehearsal where singers are reading new and unfamiliar music. When the group has difficulty with particular intervals, the director will ask the singers to (a) identify the musical interval, (b) recall one or more songs in which the interval occurs and sing the pitches, and (c) apply the sound to the intervals and the choral music they are reading.

INTERVALS

Half Steps (Semitones)

Ascending—   "Stardust" (Hoagy Carmichael)
Descending—   Theme from "MASH," "Habanera" (from *Carmen*, Bizet), "Ciribiribin" (Italian)

Major Seconds (Whole Tones)

Ascending—   "America," "Happy Birthday," "Polly Wolly Doodle"
Descending—   "Mary Had a Little Lamb," "I Dream of Jeannie" (Stephen Foster), "Turkey in the Straw"

Minor Thirds

Ascending—   Lullaby (Brahms), "Impossible Dream," "Angels We Have Heard on High" (3rd and 4th pitches)
Descending—   "This Old Man," "The Caisson Song," "Everytime I Feel the Spirit," "The Sidewalks of New York" (chorus)

Major Thirds

Ascending—   "On Top of Old Smoky," "For He's a Jolly Good Fellow," "Kum Bah Ya," "When the Saints Go Marchin' In," "I Heard the Bells on Christmas Day"
Descending—   "Swing Low, Sweet Chariot," "Blest Be the Tie That Binds"

Perfect Fourths

Ascending—   "The Farmer in the Dell," "Auld Lang Syne," "Here Comes the Bride," "Flow Gently Sweet Afton," "Taps"
Descending—   "I've Been Working on the Railroad," "Born Free," "March of the Three Kings" (Bizet)

Augmented Fourths

Ascending—   "Maria" (from *West Side Story*)

Perfect Fifths

Ascending—   "Twinkle, Twinkle, Little Star," "My Favorite Things" (from *The Sound of Music*)
Descending—   "My Home's in Montana," "Feelings"

Minor Sixths

Ascending—   "Go Down, Moses" (spiritual)
Descending—   "Love Story"

Major Sixths

Ascending—   "My Bonnie," "My Wild Irish Rose," "It Came Upon the Midnight Clear"
Descending—   "Nobody Knows the Trouble I've Seen"

Minor Sevenths

Ascending—   "Somewhere" (from *West Side Story*)

Major Sevenths

Ascending—   "Bali Hai" (from *South Pacific*) (1st and 3rd pitches)

Perfect Octaves

Ascending—   "Somewhere Over the Rainbow," "The Christmas Song"
(Mel Torme), "Annie Laurie" (3rd and 4th pitches)

The preceding procedure must be considered as a training technique and used for that purpose only, since it quite understandably can slow a rehearsal down. Through careful prerehearsal planning, however, the director can anticipate those portions of the music where intervallic difficulties are most likely to occur and can then utilize the procedure quickly and only where most appropriate. On other occasions, another approach is for the director to play on the piano the initial phrase of different songs and then ask the group to identify the opening or beginning intervals.

3. Ear-training devices are generally helpful in developing tonal awareness, but particularly those that increase a singer's sensitivity to half steps. The following exercise will contribute toward that objective.

a. Proceed upward by half steps, stopping periodically to tune chords.
b. Upon arrival at desired pitch level, proceed downward: alto down two half steps; soprano down one half step; tenor and bass down one half step and alto up one half step upon change to new chord. Repeat sequence, indicating each tonal change by cueing choir sections.
c. Use various vowel and consonant sounds: *oo, thum* or *doom* (for a detached sound), *mee, may, mah, moh, moo,* and so on.
d. Sing at various tempi from moderate to fast.
e. Begin the exercise from varying pitch levels.

4. Singing the resolutions of dominant seventh chords develops a feeling for tonality and for modulation to new keys and, as a result, has a direct relationship to music-reading skills. A seventh chord creates tension, and each pitch possesses a "pull" toward another. Initially, it is desirable for the choir to experience all the resolutions in the different inversions of the chord. Then, they may sing the key circle progression given in Figure 64. The use of notation, however, is not necessary. Each section is asked, upon signal, to move to the closest possible note that will create a feeling of rest. The soprano, alto, and tenor parts will move upward or downward either a half or a whole step, or they will remain on the same tone. The bass part moves downward a fifth and upward a fourth, except in third inversion chords (V$_2$) when the seventh is in the bass part. Begin on a major triad, then direct one of the upper voice parts doubling the root of the chord to move downward a whole step, thus creating the dominant seventh chord. Give the choir lots of time to feel the "pull" of their notes before resolving each seventh chord.

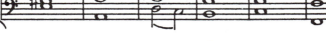

FIGURE 64   Resolving the dominant seventh.

5. An excellent device for developing tonal awareness is for the director to teach the choir members to recognize the chord progressions that they sing. A good starting place is to identify the cadences. Too many individuals sing the simple V-I cadence without knowing what it is. A few minutes of each rehearsal can be well spent in explaining to the group the function and purpose of the cadence, and the part each note plays in the chord. The director may want to take the chord progression out of context and drill each chord until it is perfectly in tune—each time making sure that the singers are able to identify the progression.

    As the group improves in their identification of chord sounds, the director will be able to extend the process to more complicated chord progressions and eventually even to modulation. Such a practice, if carried on over a long period of time, will most certainly show results not only in improved reading ability but also in better intonation and all-round musicianship.

6. When intonation difficulties occur within the group, the pitch variation is usually less than a half tone, since otherwise the group would be singing a wrong note, and many, but not all, individuals would recognize such a discrepancy. A helpful device is therefore to train the choir to sing *quarter tones*. First, select a note in the middle range and have the group sing downward a whole tone and back, then down two half steps and back, then down two *quarter tones* and back. Immediately check the pitch with the piano. In the beginning, the choir will find this procedure difficult, but after repeated daily attempts they will soon be able to sing quarter tones with comparative ease. One might ask, "Just what is the value of such an exercise?" After singers have developed an acute consciousness of pitch, the director often will be able to signal various sections of the choir to make the slight adjustments sometimes necessary for maintaining accurate pitch, especially when singing music *a cappella*.

7. Encourage the choir to maintain the pitches in their minds when they are stopped for corrections or suggestions. Do not always provide the pitch on the piano, but ask them to remember it and sing upon direction. At first they may flounder and begin to sing in a variety of keys. Soon, however, they will retain and recall the correct pitches. The general alertness necessary to remember the pitches will often have a beneficial effect on the rehearsal.

8. As a further means of developing tonal awareness, and as a check to determine how well the singers know their notes and if they are hearing them in tune, the device of "silent singing" is suggested.

First, give the pitch of a selection the group knows reasonably well. Then ask the choir to sing the music "silently" together at the tempo indicated by the conductor. At the appropriate time, the conductor should prepare the group to sing aloud with the verbal command, "Sing!" spoken on the previous beat. Initially, the group may sing silently for only four to eight measures, but as they become more proficient, the activity may be extended in length. The choir may also be directed to sing aloud at the beginning of a new phrase or, again as they develop proficiency, at any point within the phrase. The conductor will find silent singing to be an excellent means to stimulate concentration and alertness and to "rejuvenate" a sluggish choir.

ATTACKS AND RELEASES

Precision of attacks and releases is essential to artistic choral singing and is dependent upon several factors—namely, the general attentiveness of the group, the rhythmic response of the group, and the basic technique of the conductor.

A choral group with high morale, in which each individual possesses a feeling of "belonging" and exhibits a singleness of effort toward the group's objectives, is relatively easy to motivate toward a consistently improved performance. The attentiveness of the choral group depends to a very great extent upon this group morale and upon a high degree of motivation. Difficulties usually arise, not in the early stages of rehearsing a selection, but in the latter stages, just prior to the perfection of the number. The conductor should therefore be constantly in search of means to stimulate interest and capture the singers' imagination. Individuals who are highly motivated and desirous of improving their group's musical standards will not succumb to the pitfalls of slovenly body attitudes and the resultant lack of precision.

Rhythmic security in the music not only aids in the precision and the vitality of the performance, but also reduces to some extent excessive muscular tension and improves the tone quality of the group. Rhythmic security can be increased by encouraging a stronger rhythmic response to the music.

Here is an approach to rhythmic responsiveness that usually creates enthusiasm on the part of the singers. After setting the tempo,

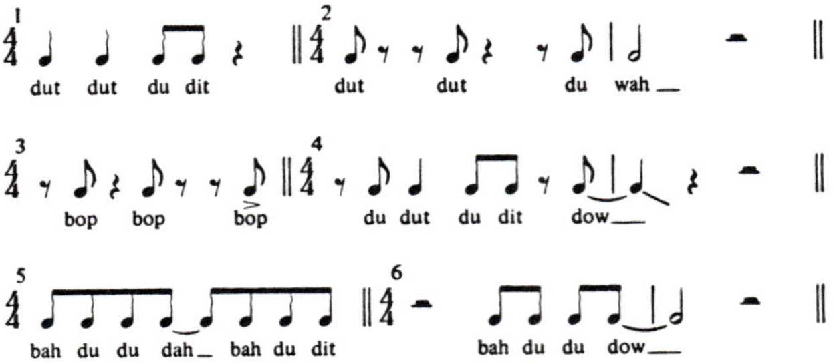

FIGURE 65   Patterns for developing singers' rhythmic responsiveness.

instruct the choir members to tap their feet (not too loudly) in response to this basic pulsation. Continue for several measures until the group is responding together precisely. While the group continues the tapping, the director sings a rhythmic or melodic pattern one or two measures long. In the following measure or measures, the group responds and imitates the pattern previously sung by the director (Figure 65). When figures extend to the last beat of a measure, it is best for the group to wait out a full measure and enter on the subsequent measure, often on the cue of the director. Patterns should be varied and may be sung on a single pitch or a melodic or "scat" pattern (see the section on scat singing in Chapter 5).

School-age youth especially enjoy responding to different rhythmic patterns. Try it—the possibilities are unlimited! In addition to evoking rhythmic response, this procedure is also beneficial as an ear-training device.[4]

Singers should develop a strong feeling for the pulsation of the music they are singing, especially if it is in a staccato or a marcato style. They are more likely to feel the pulsation if they make some large body movements while singing. Having the group either beat out the basic pulsation of the music on the knee or conduct the traditional conducting patterns can be exceedingly helpful.

The conductor should thoroughly prepare for all attacks and releases if they are to be clear to the performers. Many choral directors take too much for granted in this respect. Most singers soon learn to adjust to the indecisive movements of the conductor, yet as a group they are never quite sure of his intentions. The choral conductor's movements should be clear, precise, and rhythmical, and should reflect the

---

[4]This device is intended to be used in conjunction with music of a rhythmic, syncopated nature, such as the vigorous spiritual "Rock-a My Soul." It would provide an excellent means of evoking the necessary excitement and rhythmic awareness required for effective singing of this selection. Conversely, using the procedure immediately prior to a Bach chorale would by comparison make the chorale seem rather dull and would serve no purpose.

mood of the music. Daily practice in front of a mirror can be very helpful. *See if you can follow yourself!*

BALANCE AND BLEND

In achieving correct balance, one must consider the voice quality of the individual singers, the range in which the voices are singing, the number of persons singing the various parts, and the harmonic aspects of the chords and the relative importance of the various vocal lines.

Voices of unusual and distinct tone quality often protrude from their sections, thus destroying the choral balance and blend. These voices must be subdued and blended with the group if artistic choral singing is to be achieved. The director must be continually on the alert for such occurrences and should strive to develop the singers' awareness of the problem. Often the difficulty results from poor voice production and improper breath control. In such instances, especially in the case of a wide tremolo, individual assistance is often necessary to correct the problem.

The problem of the tremolo, or excessively wide vibrato, usually occurs when a person tries to sing with an overly large, dramatic quality and does so without the proper breath support. To eliminate this condition, the director should emphasize adequate breath support, a somewhat lighter tone quality, and practicing with a fairly straight tone. Through constant attention, the situation can be remedied.

When individuals are singing in the extreme high range of the voice, distortion is likely to occur. Voices with greater power and brilliance (resonance) in the upper registers must be subdued to the level of the entire group. If the proper balance and blend are to be maintained throughout the vocal range, choral groups should avoid using all their physical energy in an effort to sing "as loud as possible." Distortion cannot help but result. The best advice is always to save some energy in reserve by singing only up to approximately 75 percent of the maximum vocal effort, and by concentrating on resonance and improved tone quality. Maximum dynamic levels will, of course, vary from group to group, and the most effective dynamic ranges must necessarily be determined by the director for each specific group.

In music with divided parts, it may be necessary to redistribute some of the voices and assign them to the weaker parts in order to achieve the proper balance. It is suggested that a few selected voices in the chorus be designated as "roving" singers. This would mean, for example, that a few of the second sopranos need not be given a definite voice assignment, but may sing either the soprano or the alto part as the musical situation demands.

Moving parts, especially when they occur in the lower voices, should be emphasized and brought out. When some of the parts are sustained, these moving parts often indicate a change of harmony and are of special interest to the listener. A much more musical effect often can be created by emphasizing the rhythmical movement of the vocal line, rather than by just singing the part a little louder. The problem of bringing out the melody usually occurs when it is in the lower parts. In such instances it might be well to mark the melody on all the music. Close attention to dynamics is most essential in securing balance between the melodic line and the supporting harmonic parts.

Other factors influencing choral blend, aside from those previously mentioned, pertain specifically to uniform vowel production and tonal and harmonic awareness. In singing, the tone is sustained upon the various vowel sounds. Each vowel produced must be clear and distinct and uniform in production throughout the choir if any degree of blend is to be achieved. The choral director should stress the importance of *singing on the vowel*. As a basis for achieving good blend, it is suggested that the following two concepts be presented to the group and continually emphasized.

1. Following the initial consonant, move to the vowel sound as quickly as possible—and *sing on the vowel*.
2. Listen carefully and endeavor to blend your vowel sounds with the group.

Many directors have found it profitable to utilize all the primary vowel sounds in an exercise in which careful attention can be given to uniform production within the group. (See Exercise 17, for blending the vowels.)

EXERCISE 17

Mah may mee moh moo,   mah may mee moh moo,

1. Vocalize within the middle range of the voice only.
2. Move smoothly from one vowel to another.
3. Listen carefully—strive for uniform production within the group.

Some singers appear to be completely unaware of the other voices in the group. Good blend, balance, and intonation will not be achieved unless all the singers are trained to listen to the entire ensemble as well as to themselves.[5] Singers should be advised never to sing so loudly that

---

[5]For a further discussion of the importance of singing without accompaniment, see "Rehearsing A Cappella" later in the chapter.

they can't hear the individuals and the parts next to them. Humming the music sometimes will allow the singers to hear the other parts better. This device can be used to improve the blend of all the parts, especially in legato singing. On easy and familiar choral selections, it has been found profitable for the singers occasionally to switch parts. This helps to develop an awareness of the other parts and subsequently may improve the blend of the group.

A procedure that has been found to give the most immediate (and sometimes startling) results is to place the entire choral group in quartets (SATB), or in the arrangement known as the *scrambled setup.*[6] Achieving results from these arrangements presupposes that the students know their parts. These seating arrangements separate the students who lean upon each other and lessen the stridency in voices of students accustomed to sitting together. They generally result in a tone quality and a blend extremely satisfying to the group. In addition, they reveal the extent to which students have learned their parts.

A tape recorder can be put to very effective use in the choral rehearsal. Recordings of the group serve to reemphasize the suggestions made by the director. They are also valuable as a means of evaluating progress and determining future lines of endeavor.

PITCH AND INTONATION

Faulty pitch and intonation in choral groups are one of the most troublesome problems confronting choral directors today. Some have learned to live with the problem, so to speak, and have accepted it as being common to untrained voices. The majority, however, continue to strive for perfection, and many have achieved a reasonable consistency of performance in their groups.

Accurate pitch and intonation are basically dependent on (1) correctly produced tones, properly supported by the breath, and (2) the degree of tonal awareness that each individual singer possesses. In addition to these two basic factors, both previously discussed, there are other, varied causes of poor intonation, which the director should be cognizant of if he is to deal effectively with the problem.

The Slurring Attack

Attacking the notes from below and sliding or slurring to the proper pitch is a particularly obnoxious fault common to singers. The problem can be somewhat alleviated if the choir members are instructed to

---

[6]For diagrams of both these seating arrangements, see Plans 6 and 7 in Chapter 7.

think of approaching the notes from above, rather than from below, the pitch. Another helpful device is to think of singing the consonants on the same pitch as the vowels.

Repeated Tones and Scale Passages

Intonation difficulties frequently occur on repeated tones. Since there is sometimes a tendency to sing each repeated tone a bit lower, it is helpful if the singers are instructed to think of each repeated tone as being a bit higher.

Intonation difficulties also often occur on ascending and descending scale passages. Many individuals are likely to sing the ascending scale steps too small and the descending scale steps too large. Both practices, of course, result in flatting. It is therefore suggested that choir members be asked to think purposely of singing the ascending scale steps larger and of singing the descending scale steps smaller.

Diction

Lack of attention to careful enunciation of the words can create intonation difficulties. The best advice that can be given the singers in such instances is: "Vitalize your words," or "Be more precise in your tongue, lip, and jaw movements, and work for clarity of diction."

Breath Control

The problem of breath control usually occurs on long, extended phrases. Singers should be advised to refrain from using all their available breath supply, since this results in an irregular flow of the breath, which in turn results in gradations in volume and slight variations in the pitch. The group should be instructed in the "staggered" method of breathing. On long, extended phrases, each individual should drop out when in need of breath, take a full breath, and unobtrusively reenter. For best results, certain sections or groups probably should be told when to breathe in order that the best possible effect may be achieved.

Classification of Voices

Adolescent voices are unsettled and generally in a state of change. For this reason, and to protect the voices from unnecessary strain, it is advisable to retest each singer's voice frequently. Baritones singing tenor parts and altos singing soprano parts can lead to many difficulties.

Body Attitudes and Fatigue

Incorrect body attitudes, which generally reflect a lack of genuine interest, can have a decided effect upon performance. It behooves the director to be ever alert to this problem and to convince the choir members as best he can that they should maintain correct posture while singing. Correct posture and alert body attitudes are essential to properly supported tones, and when singers fully realize this fact they are usually more eager to cooperate. One idea found profitable in action is to insist that the group maintain correct posture only when singing; between numbers they should relax in a position most comfortable to themselves. Good posture can become a habit. Strive for it!

The best time of day for the choral rehearsal is believed to be the middle or late morning hours. Individuals generally do not sing as well immediately following lunch or late in the afternoon when body fatigue begins to occur. It is recognized that some school schedules prohibit the utilization of the most desirable hours for rehearsal and that many directors have little voice in determining the scheduling of classes. It is felt, however, that the director should at least discuss the problem with his school administrator. Administrators are eager to provide the best possible education for their students and if presented with a reasonable argument for making changes in the schedule, are usually most anxious to cooperate if they can.

When rehearsals become dull and uninteresting, body fatigue is bound to occur regardless of the time of day or the length of the rehearsal. Directors should, therefore, carefully plan and endeavor to make all rehearsals exciting events for the choir members.

Tempo

The tempo of the music can have a decided effect upon intonation. The tempo selected for a previous choral group—or the tempo originally chosen by the conductor—may not always be the best one. The conductor should become most sensitive to the problem and should determine through experimentation the tempo that is most suitable for his present group and, of course, for the most effective rendition of the music.

Seating Arrangements

In choral groups where a strict tryout is not mandatory for membership, there will usually exist a few voices that might be classified as "chronic flatters." If these individuals are allowed to sit together, their tone qualities are seemingly reinforced and can play havoc with the group's intonation. The problem, however, can be somewhat alleviated by judiciously placing each of those offenders between two or more stronger singers. In this way they are more likely to produce the tone qualities desired.

Acoustics

Many factors, including the size and the shape of the room and the finishing materials used, affect the acoustics of the rehearsal room or the auditorium stage. Again, the tempo at which the music is performed should be determined to some extent by the acoustical properties of the performance room. As a general rule, it will be found that in rooms with little reverberation, one should avoid singing the music too slowly if accurate pitch is to be maintained, whereas in rooms that are "exceedingly alive," one should avoid singing the music at too fast a tempo, lest the sounds emitted meet each other coming and going and produce a discordant and distasteful result.

Atmospheric Conditions

Atmospheric conditions also have their effect upon intonation. On dark, dismal days most individuals do not respond physically in the same way that they do on bright, clear days. At such times, spirits are sometimes low and the group does not always display an abundance of vitality. It has been said that a person's vitality is to some extent dependent upon the relative degree of humidity present in the atmosphere. During very humid days, body fatigue occurs sooner, the tone is generally not supported correctly, and intonation problems may result. What can be done to alleviate the situation? The director can only point out to the group the pitfalls that may occur and, through increased group effort, hope to avoid some of the difficulties. If this procedure does not produce the desired results, then all concerned would be wise to charge the difficulty to "just one of those days."

Ventilation

Poor ventilation in the rehearsal room creates a stuffy, stale atmosphere that can have a decidedly detrimental effect upon intonation. The director should recheck this condition periodically during the rehearsal. It is often advisable to assign the task to one or more interested and helpful persons.

Growing Stale

Most directors have experienced the problem of having choral selections grow stale. There is only one solution to this problem. Set the number aside and return to it at a later date. The problem can be avoided somewhat if the season's repertoire is planned early in the year. This provides ample time for singers to learn a new selection, which can then be set aside until rehearsals are renewed just prior to its presentation. This procedure can have a definite beneficial effect upon raising standards of musical performance.

OTHER REHEARSAL CONSIDERATIONS

The effectiveness of a given rehearsal begins from the moment the choir members enter the rehearsal room. The conductor should encourage the singers to secure their music folders and immediately take their seats so that the rehearsal may begin promptly with a minimum of confusion. This process is facilitated if each singer's music is kept in an assigned folder and stored in music cabinets near the entrance door. Following are suggestions that will contribute to more effective and satisfying rehearsals.

Rehearsal Pace

Rehearsals should move quite rapidly—when they lag, discipline problems may arise. Confusion between selections can be lessened if the rehearsal order is carefully planned and written on the chalkboard prior to the rehearsal. Choir members should not be given the opportunity to waste time. In most cases, they will appreciate the director's efforts to make efficient use of rehearsal time.

Warm-up Exercises and Ear-Training Devices

Many conductors prefer to begin their rehearsals with a warm-up exercise or an ear-training device. To avoid monotony, it is desirable to alternate these exercises and devices and, above all, to keep them *short*. Get to the music as soon as possible.

Establishing and Maintaining Rapport

It is advisable to begin rehearsals with *familiar* music of a reasonably vigorous nature that is straightforward, uncomplicated, and not too demanding vocally. Selections that are demanding vocally or that include various subtle nuances and shadings may be better dealt with later in the rehearsal when the singers are more adequately warmed up.

The conductor should study the technical aspects of the music before each rehearsal and know what he wants to accomplish. He should use the music as a reminder, glancing at it only when necessary. Thus he is free to concentrate upon maintaining eye contact with the group. Whenever possible, the conductor should inject a bit of humor into the rehearsals. A good laugh can lessen group tension and contribute substantially to the rehearsal's outcome. Through body attitudes, the conductor should project his enthusiasm for the music to the group and spur the singers toward greater musical accomplishments.

Maintaining Correct Posture

If tones are to be adequately supported, correct posture must be maintained while singing. Unless the singers are continually encouraged, they are likely to fall into poor posture habits. Since the length of many choral selections will average about three minutes, choir members should be expected to maintain 100 percent effort for this minimum length of time. Between selections they should be instructed to stretch and relax. This same philosophy applies to those individuals who feel they must communicate with each other during the singing of a specific selection. The following rule should apply: *No talking during actual rehearsal! Time between selections will be allotted for questions and communication regarding musical problems of concern to the group.*

Avoiding Fatigue and Vocal Strain

There is a limit to what can be accomplished with a given selection during a single rehearsal. When the singers show signs of fatigue and boredom, set the music aside and return to it at the following rehearsal.

It also is highly desirable for the director to provide a short break at the midway point in the rehearsal period. This time may be effectively utilized for special announcements, such as forthcoming concerts and musical events.

Rehearsing A Cappella

Too often singers become overly dependent upon the piano for tonal and rhythmic support. As a result, they listen primarily to this instrument and not to the other vocal parts. Therefore, it is absolutely essential to rehearse some of the choral selections without accompaniment. Only in this way will the maximum degree of vocal independence, rhythmic security, and effective blend and balance be achieved.

Making Corrections

Errors in rhythm, pitch, and phrasing should be corrected immediately, before they become habitual. The conductor, however, should not be overcritical or belittle the singers, for this may discourage the group. The director's remarks should be positive—commenting about progress already made, as well as about the portions of the music that still require improvement.

When the conductor resorts to excessive talking, however, the singers' enthusiasm is lessened and valuable rehearsal time is lost. Therefore, he should be succinct in his comments and proceed with the rehearsal as quickly as possible.

The conductor should concentrate on rehearsing the troublesome parts of a choral selection. Much time can be wasted by simply repeating the sections that the singers already know. It is also advisable to periodically hold sectional rehearsals for a choir. This practice is essential if minor discrepancies in rhythm and pitch are to be corrected and if sectional tone quality and blend are to be improved.

Prior to the repetition of selections, the conductor should avoid merely saying "Let's sing it again." If singers are to improve, they must know what they are striving for. Therefore, he should tell clearly what he wants in every repetition.

Consideration should be given to possible starting points after the choir is stopped for corrections. A general procedure is to identify the point by referring to first the *page*, then the *score*, the *measure*, and finally the *beat* within the measure. After the choir is reasonably familiar with the music, a particular word or phrase may be identified as the starting point. After the singers have gained even further knowledge of the musical score, starting points may be identified as, for example, (1) after the double bar, (2) at the key change, (3) at the tenor entrance (thus forcing the other singers to identify this portion of the music to orient themselves).

Although demonstrating desired musical improvements and occasionally singing certain entrances is justifiable, the director should avoid continually singing with the group. Instead, he should devote his attention to critical listening and assisting the group to a more effective interpretation of the music through his conducting technique.

Stimulating Concentration

It is important that singers give their undivided attention to the conductor and that they concentrate upon achieving artistic singing. Following are suggestions that will contribute toward this objective.

Rehearsing from a standing position Singers can become fatigued when rehearsing all the music from a sitting position. In addition, the maximum group effort cannot always be achieved unless the singers stand, assume the correct singing posture, and concentrate upon artistic singing. Therefore, alternate selections should be sung from a standing position.

As a further means of developing more careful attention, it is advisable for the conductor to time each selection with a stopwatch. While the resulting information is essential in planning the length of the final concert program, it has the added advantage of stimulating an extra group effort, particularly if the singers understand the purpose of the timing and the importance of being alert and responsive to the director's conducting movements.

"Erratic" conducting   When singers seemingly have their eyes glued to the music and are unresponsive to the subtleties of the conductor's movements, then it is helpful for him to purposely alter the tempo—faster and slower and employing the fermata at will. Singers enjoy this activity, and the challenge of "following" the conductor is an excellent means of developing attentiveness and responsiveness in a choir.

"Silent singing"   Mentally thinking together the pitch, rhythm, and tempo of a selection under a conductor's direction, before being asked to sing aloud at a designated point, is an excellent means of stimulating concentration and alertness. (For a more detailed discussion of this procedure, see end of section "Tonal Awareness" earlier in this chapter.)

Encouraging Individual Responsibility

The conductor should encourage the choir members to analyze their difficulties and to request assistance with particularly troublesome voice parts or sections of the music. Although the conductor must use discretion and be the final judge as to which problems should be undertaken first, he should encourage individual responsibility in regard to the various problems encountered in the music. Encouraging individual effort produces greater group solidarity, improved musicianship, and eventually a more effective interpretation of the music.

Ending the Rehearsal

The conductor should schedule a selection relatively familiar to the group during the final portion of the rehearsal—one that the singers particularly enjoy, so they will leave the rehearsal room with a feeling of genuine aesthetic accomplishment. The director should be prompt in ending the rehearsal, because most individuals have a demanding time schedule. Nevertheless, the dismissal time must be considered the director's prerogative—the singers should not be mere "clock watchers," but should wait to be dismissed.

INTERPRETATION

In achieving the artistic interpretation of choral music, a conductor must take into consideration a number of factors. The following suggestions will assist the conductor in achieving his goals.

Style of the Music

Prior to the initial rehearsal of a choral selection, the conductor should give ample thought to the style of the music. These considerations will provide a guide to the achievement of a more artistic interpretation. Essential points are the characteristics of music in various historical periods and the specific treatment of meter and stress, tempo, dynamics, texture, and expression. The unique characteristics of the music of each individual composer should also be understood.

Consideration should also be given to the stylistic features or characteristics of particular types of compositions, such as the chorale, the motet, the madrigal, the cantata, the oratorio, the mass, liturgical music, the folk song, the ballad or love song, and music in a popular idiom.

Another facet of style is the manner in which it is articulated—that is, legato, staccato, and marcato. The mood of the text as well as the musical markings will generally reveal these basic styles. Each musical selection requires a specific treatment in terms of diction, as well as in the projection of the mood or spirit of the song to the audience. The singers, therefore, must become aware of the differences in style if they are to interpret the music artistically.

Dynamic Range and Contrast

The dynamic range of a particular choral group depends upon the age level, physical maturity, and vocal development of the singers in the group. The relatively immature voices of a junior high school chorus, for example, are obviously unable to achieve the same full *fortissimo* effects as an adult choral group. Conductors should avoid being overambitious and striving for effects that may prove harmful to younger students' voices. Contrast of dynamics is, of course, one of the objectives of the conductor. One should remember, however, that dynamics are relative, and that to achieve this goal the dynamic extremes of one group need not necessarily equal those of another choral group. Through experimentation, a conductor should determine the maximum dynamic level that voices of his particular group may sing without distortion of sound and undue vocal strain—and then compensate at the other extreme of the dynamic range by reducing the level of the *pianissimo* effects. Although immature vocal groups will be unable to achieve the same *pianissimo* effects as an adult group, some adjustment toward the goal of achieving dynamic contrasts must necessarily occur at this end of the continuum. Only in this way will the voices be protected from undue vocal strain.

A director must devote considerable attention to the achievement of effective dynamic contrasts. Crescendo and decrescendo markings should be adhered to. In the absence of such markings a slight crescendo on ascending vocal lines and a slight decrescendo on descending vocal lines will generally enhance the effectiveness of the interpretation. When the director is in doubt about the general dynamic level, a thorough study of the text will reveal certain subtle implications—each suggesting, sometimes from phrase to phrase, a change in dynamic effects; to achieve effective interpretation the director must assist the singers in developing an awareness of the importance of dynamic contrasts. Through the use of teacher demonstrations, the tape recorder, choral recordings, and other means, the ineffective portions of a selection must be brought to the singers' attention, and the importance of dynamic contrasts should be continually stressed.

Tempo

Although choral conductors will often differ in their opinions concerning the "correct" tempo of a selection, the majority will agree that they must determine the most effective tempo for their own groups. Factors determining the proper tempo are the basic style of the music, the mood of the text, the given musical markings, the physical maturity of the group, and the acoustical properties of the rehearsal room and the auditorium. One may best advise the conductor to experiment in an effort to determine the most effective tempo for his particular group.

Nuances

Nuances may be defined as delicate changes in musical expression, either in tone, in color, in tempo, or in volume. The various nuances and shadings necessary for the most effective performance of the music quite naturally develop as the singers gain increased understanding of the text. The singers should recite and study the words of the music individually and as a group. Only through this approach will certain subtle, hidden meanings—essential to the best interpretation of the music—be revealed.

One type of nuance, perhaps obvious only to the director, is the slight degree of tension and relaxation within each phrase essential to the most effective interpretation of choral music. The tension or emotional surge is usually characterized by a slight quickening of one phrase, whereas the relaxation aspect of the cycle is reflected through a slight slowing down of the tempo. The tension is not only balanced but also complemented by the relaxation. Improvement of a problem moves through three stages: an awareness of the problem, an evaluation or appraisal of present progress, and a renewed effort toward improvement. Therefore, to implement these effects in the music, the conductor must demonstrate his desired objective by singing various vocal lines, and by playing back tape-recorded portions of the music so that the group may evaluate their performance.

Projecting the Mood

Projection of the mood or spirit of a song is essential to an effective choral performance. Capturing the proper mood of a selection may occur only through diligent study of the text. The director should discuss the implications of the text with the singers, the proper mood should be established for each selection, and an effort should be made to improve the projection with each subsequent rehearsal.

In achieving this goal, it is helpful to give special attention to the consonants. For example, in certain words, such as *thunder* and *glory,* the prevailing thought is quite dynamic. Therefore, the initial consonants should be stressed—almost "exploded." Often the advice "Sing these as *Capital Consonants*" assists in creating in the singers' minds the desired mental picture. Conversely, other initial consonants, in such words as *dreams, softly,* and *lullaby,* demand the opposite treatment and must be handled more subtly and sung in a smooth, legato style.

Finishing the Musical Phrase

Perhaps one of the most obvious differences between a professional and an amateur choral group is the seeming inability of the latter to complete their musical phrases. Often, because of lack of proper breath control, choral groups anticipate the release of the phrase ending. A choral director may eliminate this difficulty, to some extent, by employing what is called "staggered breathing," thus enabling the singers to sustain the phrase until it is released by the conductor. Singers often are inclined to anticipate the release of the phrase. It is often helpful if, during rehearsals, the director employs a slightly modified type of interpretation by holding certain phrases a bit longer than others. In this way, choir members are trained to watch the conductor more carefully, especially at the beginning and the end of phrases.

One of the most troublesome faults in choral singing is that groups do not finish their words. Such singing is slovenly and detrimental to an effective projection of the mood or spirit of the music. Singers should be trained to include the final consonants on all words, and should be especially careful to include the final consonant upon the release of the phrase by the conductor. For example, a problem often arises when one or more sections of the choir release the phrase at the end of the second beat, while another section begins a phrase on the third beat of the music. This is essentially a conducting problem, and the difficulty can be avoided if the singers are instructed that the attack for one section will serve as the release for the other section (Figure 66).

Eliminating Excessive Slurring

Exaggerated slurring or scooping is the scourge of effective choral singing. According to studies by the music psychologist Carl Seashore,

FIGURE 66   Excerpt from "April Is in My Mistress' Face" by Thomas Morley.

some degree of "gliding attack" is characteristic of the human voice and is even desirable.[7] However, definite steps should be taken to avoid excessive slurring. Most objectionable slurring occurs because the jaw is tight and rigid and the mouth is kept too tightly closed. Slurring can be eliminated, to a considerable extent, if the singers are requested to drop their jaws prior to the initial attack or prior to wide pitch changes. When choir members learn to anticipate wide pitch or interval changes, and properly adjust the vocal mechanism, choral singing can be much more effective.

Facial Expressions and Body Attitudes

Many choral concerts are rendered less effective as a result of the stoic, expressionless faces of the singers. Especially since the advent of television, choral directors are becoming more cognizant of the importance of facial expressions and body attitudes to the ultimate success of the concert program. A correct body attitude may be defined as "that entire body posture or stance which reflects the mood of the music." Appropriate facial expressions are equally important to the effective performance of a selection, and considerable attention must be devoted to each individual singer if the desired results are to be achieved.

[7]C. E. Seashore, *Psychology of Music* (New York: McGraw-Hill, 1938), p. 271.

Memorizing the Music

If the mood of the music is to be projected effectively to the audience, music performed for programs and concerts must be thoroughly memorized. When music is memorized, the singers are able to watch the director more closely and concentrate on the interpretative aspects. The director is able to establish better rapport with the group and to transmit the desired musical interpretation through conducting technique, body attitudes, and facial expressions.

Some choral groups are able to memorize music more quickly than others. Memorization can be facilitated through increased musical understanding and through the principle of association. Students with a greater understanding of the musical score—that is, knowledge of form, harmonic structure, styles of music, and the like—will memorize their parts more quickly. Memorization of the text may be facilitated by identifying particular key words in the text and associating them with various facets of personal experience. When one connection fails, often one can rely upon others to assist in the recall process.[8] Memorization is dependent upon a well-defined concept of the entire musical composition and upon the relationship of the various parts to the whole. In short, a systematic, well-planned program of instruction, designed toward the goal of improving the musicianship and the understanding of the singers, will reap many benefits—only one of which is improved memorization.

MENTAL ATTITUDES

Each individual hears "two voices" (Self 1 and Self 2) while he or she is engaged in any physical activity, including singing. One is the trained self, the other the natural self. The trained self is the one that will become hypercritical, and we are often inclined to pay so much attention to this inner voice that it sometimes overrides the natural self. The hypercritical attitude inhibits freedom in performance.[9]

Before a performance, individuals should let go of their critical attitudes and endeavor to enjoy themselves. Singers should be told to

[8]An approach to the identification of key words is as follows. Write the complete text of the choral selection on the chalkboard, and ask the group to follow it when singing, rather than the text in the octavo publication. Prior to the next repetition, erase certain nonessential words, such as *and, or,* and *to.* Then, gradually, on each subsequent repetition erase other words, until only a small group of key words remains. Then suggest to the group that they give vent to their imaginations and associate these key words with as many related ideas as possible. Finally, erase all the words from the chalkboard and test the singers' recall ability.

[9]W. Timothy Gallwey, *The Inner Game of Tennis* (New York: Random House, 1974), pp. 14–15.

stop being self-critical, to let loose and release tension and any negative attitudes that would inhibit a performance, since it is usually too late immediately prior to a performance to make major changes anyway. We are in an age when students expect or try to be perfect; the public media, including radio, television, and recordings, have created this unrealistic expectation. We need to encourage singers to accept their performance at all stages of its development and to see it as an improving activity— one in which being expressive is as good as being perfect. This approach is particularly applicable to the solo singer, but it has validity for choruses as well.[10]

During the final chorus rehearsal and also immediately prior to the first concert, the director should tell the choir, "We have worked diligently on technical matters in the music, and now they should take care of themselves. Let's don't continue to dwell on these matters, but enter into the concert in a joyful spirit, enjoy ourselves, and transmit our feelings to the audience. It will be helpful if you watch me closely, and I will maintain close eye contact with you to help facilitate the communication of musical ideas.[11] Think about the message of the text, use your imaginations, and communicate with the audience. Now let's all make beautiful music together!"

CONDUCTING CHORAL/ORCHESTRAL WORKS

A conductor who is planning to perform a work for chorus and orchestra must not only carefully rehearse the chorus, but also be prepared to conduct the orchestra. Among the many things he must be concerned with are a working knowledge of orchestral instruments, stringed instrument bowings, achieving proper balance and intonation, and efficient rehearsal procedures. He must also consider various arrangements in the concert hall for an effective performance.

The Orchestral Instruments

It is presumed that the conductor understands the nature of transposing instruments—that is, where particular pitches are written and where they actually sound—and that he is able to read the orchestral score to at least determine if the right notes are being played. Experi-

---

[10]For helpful ideas on assisting the solo performer, see Barry Green, *The Inner Game of Music* (Garden City, N.Y.: Anchor Press/Doubleday, 1986). See also the references at the end of this chapter.

[11]Maintaining eye contact with the singers is essential, not only for the interpretation of musical ideas, but also to help minimize tension in the singers. It helps them to "loosen up!"

ence with orchestral instruments will help conductors understand their timbre or tonal characteristics so they will know better the composer's expectations as regards the orchestral scoring. (If one didn't know the characteristics of voices, it would be difficult to conduct a choir.) If a conductor feels deficient in any of the aforementioned areas, he should make an effort to remedy the situation.

To become acquainted with the range and tonal characteristics, the technical abilities, and the limitations of particular instruments, conductors may review a book on orchestration.[12] However, nothing will substitute for actually hearing the instruments and discussing them with instrumentalists. So, talk with orchestral musicians about the nature of their specific instruments and the technical difficulties they might have. Be sure to ask about the physical capabilities and limitations of each instrument. Listen to recordings of numerous orchestral works, particularly choral/orchestral works. It is especially important, however, to listen to school orchestras in both rehearsals and concerts. Listen carefully and make some judgments, however tentative, about articulation, phrasing, balance, intonation, and so on. Would you do anything differently if you were the conductor?

In working with school, college, and community orchestras, having an adequate number of players for each part is generally not a problem. However, church and community choirs who do not have these resources at their disposal generally have to employ musicians if they want to perform a choral/orchestral work. In this case, where finances are of some concern, thought may be given to the minimum number of players that can effectively perform the work with the chorus. If the orchestra is very small, *never* use two players on the first and second violin parts. Use either one or three players on a part, because of the tight or close frequencies. The third player neutralizes pitch problems and facilitates the blend. The violas and the cellos can get by with only two players on a part if using only normal ranges. Under most circumstances, however, the suggested minimum-sized string section would be three first violins, three second violins, two violas, two violoncellos, and one string bass.

Bowings

String players need to utilize bowings that are the easiest to execute while achieving the desired musical effect. Different bowings achieve varying musical effects, and it is the responsibility of the conductor to

[12]See, for example, Kent Kennan and Donald Grantham, *The Technique of Orchestration*, 3rd ed. (Englewood Cliffs, N.J.: Prentice-Hall, 1983). This text also includes suggested music for listening to specific instruments. The Appendix includes a listing of different instruments, and where particular pitches are written and where they actually sound.

determine the desired result (the bowings should conform to the vocal phrasing and breathing). The bowings printed on the music may not always be acceptable, and in such instances, the conductor should provide a bowed score for the string parts prior to the first rehearsal, so that each part may be properly marked. In school situations, this will be the conductor's responsibility. In professional orchestras, the responsibility may be delegated to the concertmaster—subject, of course, to the approval of the conductor.[13]

The conductor should understand the importance of using the upper part of the bow for delicate, soft, and understated passages, and the lower part (where more weight is needed) for louder, heavier, and more dramatic passages. Also, know when to ask for the instrumentalists to play on or off the strings (spiccato or brush). Feel free to ask to hear it played both ways, and be guided by what you hear and what you want to hear. The conductor should make sure the string basses (bass viols) are placed prominently and play strongly, since these low vibrations do not project as well, yet supply the fundamentals for all the upper harmonic partials. At the same time they must be carefully monitored in order to avoid a "grunting" quality by stopping the heavy strings firmly and using longer, lighter bowing.

Balance and Intonation

In rehearsals, listen for a balance between instruments in one family and between sections of the orchestra. Again, note the markings in the score. What sounds right to you? Intonation, of course, is always a matter of concern. Following are some points to remember.

1. String players should use plenty of bow; if the sound is too loud, then reduce the pressure on the strings, not the amount of bow being used. As previously indicated, the bowing should conform to the vocal phrasing and breathing.
2. Brass players can often diminish their volume without losing intensity by directing the bells of their instruments into the music stands; conversely, they can add brilliance by raising the bells of their instruments.
3. Check balance especially carefully with instrumental parts that double vocal parts (for example, the trombones in Beethoven's Ninth Symphony, Choral Finale, 3/2 section).
4. In performing choral/orchestral works, it is particularly important that singers not have vocal scores blocking their faces; if they do, the sound will become lost and not be properly projected. Singers should know their parts well enough that they need the music for reference only and can keep their eyes and attention focused upon the conductor.
5. The conductor should be aware of the orchestra's tendency to go sharper

---

[13]For detailed information on bowings, see Elizabeth A. H. Green, *The Dramatic Orchestra* (Englewood Cliffs, N.J.: Prentice-Hall, 1987), chap. 6.

as instruments warm up, particularly with young orchestras. In some instances, the situation may necessitate retuning the orchestra between sections of a musical work. However, this problem may be minimized through adequate warm-up and tuning prior to the concert.

Rehearsals

If one has selected a musical work to perform and has either made arrangements with the school orchestra or employed some musicians for rehearsals and performance(s), then it is desirable to rehearse the orchestra well in advance of the combined choral/orchestra rehearsal(s). Prior to the first rehearsal, the conductor should familiarize himself with the seating arrangement of the orchestra or whatever instrumental ensemble will be performing.

Before working details in rehearsals try to read through the entire work or movement so the orchestra can get a good feel for the entire work—that is, how it all fits together. The subsequent detail work will be more effective and meaningful than if done out of context. During the read-through, some errors will be corrected by the players themselves and often acknowledged through eye contact with the conductor, thus eliminating any reason to stop the rehearsal at those points for corrections. Also, if you hear a wrong note, don't always assume that the player(s) made a mistake, but first check the score against their parts, particularly if the pitch is played by more than one player.

Choral directors are sometimes inclined to be too "fluid" in their gestures when directing a chorus. An orchestra often expects more precision and definition in the conductor's movements or gestures. To help clarify your gestures, conduct with a baton rather than with the hands only. Some orchestral instruments, such as the string basses and the lower brasses and woodwinds, "speak" more slowly, and to coordinate the ensemble's efforts, direct your gestures toward those instruments, particularly during entrances, as well as at other times when they are prominent. The players can also help by slight anticipation.

After each rehearsal, it is helpful to talk to the orchestra director about your conducting effectiveness with the orchestra. Are your conducting gestures understood by the orchestra? Ask for suggestions from the orchestra director! It is also helpful to record your orchestra rehearsals for later review. How do they square with your expectations of the chorus? Will they work together?

The conductor should memorize the choral score, so that he needs to make only minimal reference to it and so that he can focus upon the multiplicity of lines in the orchestral score. The chorus should become less and less dependent upon the conductor for the subtle gestures often given during choral concerts. It is suggested that the conductor begin to conduct the choral rehearsals from a full orchestral score well in advance of the combined choral/orchestral rehearsals. Thus, he can gradually give attention to the total ensemble, rather than using the full score only immediately prior to the orchestral rehearsals. In preparation for the choral/orchestral rehearsals, it is also desirable to have the singers mark the measure numbers at important selected points in their choral scores.

The appropriate and effective use of time is essential in the final choral/orchestral rehearsals. There can be nothing more frustrating to performers than to sit through any part of a lengthy rehearsal that does not directly involve them. Therefore, the conductor should continually evaluate a group's progress and plan to devote time to those players and singers who need special attention. For example, rehearse the soloists prior to the scheduled arrival of the chorus. Or, toward the end of a rehearsal, dismiss the singers and focus upon the improvement of specific instrumental parts. In certain instances, part of the orchestra may be dismissed if attention needs to be given to a particular orchestral section. Each choral/orchestral work is different and will need its own specific and particular plan. In the final dress rehearsal, however, the entire work must be rehearsed in sequence, so that all individual performers comprehend their relationship to the total work.

The Concert Hall and the Performance

Many modern auditoriums have an acoustical ceiling and side panels that surround the stage. If the facility is not thus equipped, then all sound-absorbing materials, such as curtains, should be pulled or drawn aside and an acoustical sound shell placed behind the singers. An effective performance necessitates a reflective surface from which sound can be reflected toward the audience and which will allow the singers and the orchestral musicians to more adequately hear themselves and each other.

As previously mentioned, the balance between the chorus and the orchestra is highly important. During the combined choral/orchestral rehearsals, an initial determination of this balance must be made. Singers, of course, have physical limits to the sound they can produce; therefore, achieving an appropriate balance usually necessitates softening the orchestra to whatever degree is necessary. The best determination can be made during final rehearsals in the concert hall, and it is often helpful to have a colleague stand at the rear of the hall to provide feedback on this matter.

If the singers are placed behind the orchestra they will, of course, usually be on standing risers. (On long, extended works, seated risers would be preferable; however, elevated platforms and chairs take much more space.) In orchestral concerts, the wind players are often elevated on platforms to facilitate balance, as well as to improve visual sight lines.

However, it is difficult for singers to project over the heads of orchestra members. Therefore, it is important that the wind players be seated on the floor rather than on risers. The only alternative to this arrangement is to place the singers on more highly elevated platforms. For example, standing choral risers may be placed on top of 4' × 8' portable staging, with two or more sections reversed to provide a straight, rather than a curved, stage arrangement. Portable 4' × 8' staging is available in elevations of 8, 16, 24, and 32 inches.[14]

When an auditorium has aprons in front of the proscenium arch, risers may be placed on each side of and in front of the orchestra to help achieve proper balance; however, the feasibility of this arrangement depends on the musical security of the group, as well as on the musical work being performed. A similar arrangement, except that all the singers are on the stage, is illustrated in Plan 3 on page 229. Another alternative is to place the chorus on the left side of the stage, as illustrated in Plan 2, page 228.

Singers should not have to stand any longer than is absolutely necessary; therefore, the orchestra should be seated, tuned, and ready to play before the chorus is asked to enter the stage. Following the concert, all performers should be recognized: first the soloists, then the chorus and the orchestra. After a limited amount of applause, the soloists and the conductor may leave the stage (or opt to remain on stage), only to return momentarily for continued recognition. At this point, after again recognizing the soloists and the chorus, the conductor should, with a hand motion, signal the orchestra to rise. Continue to accept the audience's applause for as long as possible. After all, the performers deserve it! Performers should *never* leave the stage as long as the audience is still showing its appreciation through applause.

MUSICAL TERMS FOR THE ORCHESTRAL PLAYER/CONDUCTOR

Arco: With the bow
Attacca: Proceed directly to next movement
A2 or zu 2: Double part (two players—on woodwind or brass parts)
Bouché: Stopped horn
Bratsche: Viola
Col legno: With the stick part of the bow
Concertmaster: The principal violinist of an orchestra; sets bowings, tunes the orchestra, and so on
Con sordino: With mute
Contra: Instrument sounding an octave below the written pitch

[14]With the use of portable staging, choral risers may be positioned to accommodate from nine to as many as twelve rows of singers. For further information on these plans, contact the Wenger Corporation, 555 Park Drive, Owatonna, MN 55060.

Corni: Horns
Crook: Tubing of a brass instrument
Détaché: A broad legato stroke (separate bows— ⊓ , ∨)
Divisi: Separated string parts; outside plays top, inside plays bottom or divided by stand
Doppio movimento: 2 × tempo, double the tempo
Down-bow (⊓):   A bowing stroke in which the bow is pulled down from the frog
Dur: Major
Fagott: Bassoon
Glissando: Sliding the fingers continuously in a smooth manner
Harmonic: A natural partial of a string
Leggiero: Light, delicate; generally implies a bouncing bow
Luftpause: "Air pause" (quick breath)
Marcato, Martelé: A sharp, accented stroke—literally, "well marked"
Moll: Minor
Non divisi: A double stop (stopping two or more strings at once)
Pizzicato: Plucked
Portamento: Gliding from one note to another
Saltato, Saltando: Ricochet bowing ("throwing" the bow so it will bounce a series of rapid notes)
Scordatura: The unusual tuning of any string instrument for special effects
Spiccato: Controlled bouncing bow
Staccato: Short, detached stroke
Sul ponticello: To play at or near the bridge of a stringed instrument, resulting in an eerie tone
Sul tasto, Sur la touche: Bowing near or above the fingerboard
Talon: The heel or nut or frog of the bow
Tremolo: A reiteration of the same note, produced by rapidly moving the bow back and forth on the same pitch
Tromba: Trumpet
Tromboni: Trombone
Unisoni: Marks the end of a divisi passage
Up-bow (∨):   A bowing stroke in which the bow is pushed up from the tip
Vibrato: A rapid, regular oscillation of pitch above and below the tone

TOPICS FOR DISCUSSION

1. What are some of the personal characteristics of successful choral directors you have known?
2. In your experience as a participant in various choral groups, have you ever sensed or felt that the director was unprepared for the rehearsal? What were your feelings? What was the reaction of the group?
3. Discuss the effects upon a chorus of a mechanistic approach to the teaching of new music.
4. Identify, if possible, the causes of poor pitch and intonation in some of the choral groups in which you have participated.
5. Recall the techniques utilized by the conductor for achieving effective interpretation in groups in which you have participated. Which techniques were most effective? Which were relatively ineffective?
6. Select a specific publication and try to analyze the difficulties that a particular group might encounter in rehearsals.
7. Why should accompanied selections be rehearsed, at least part of the time, without accompaniment?

8. Discuss the factors that prevent the attainment of effective balance and blend in a choral group. How would you remedy them?
9. Analyze the difficulties, if any, that hamper your memorization of music.
10. Should music be memorized for all performances? For what reasons would you have the chorus memorize the music? For what reasons would you have the chorus use the music at programs and concerts?

SELECTED READINGS

BAUGUESS, DAVID, *The Jenson Sight Singing Course* (2 vols.). New Berlin, Wis.: Jenson Publications, Inc., 1984. There is both a Student's Edition and a Teacher's Edition.

BOYD, JACK, *Rehearsal Guide for the Choral Director.* Champaign, Ill.: Mark Foster Music Company, 1977.

————, *Teaching Choral Sight Reading.* West Nyack, N.Y.: Parker Publishing Company, Inc., 1975.

CAIN, NOBLE, *Choral Music and Its Practice,* chaps. 9, 11, 12. New York: M. Witmark & Sons, 1942.

CHRISTY, VAN A., *Glee Club and Chorus,* chaps. 4, 5. New York: G. Schirmer, Inc., 1940.

DAVISON, ARCHIBALD T., *Choral Conducting,* chaps. 4, 5. Cambridge, Mass.: Harvard University Press, 1945.

EHRET, WALTER, *The Choral Conductor's Handbook,* chaps. 1–7. New York: Edward B. Marks Music Corp., 1959.

FINN, WILLIAM J., *The Art of the Choral Conductor,* chaps. 5–12. Boston: C. C. Birchard & Co., 1939.

HEFFERNAN, CHARLES W., *Choral Music: Technique and Artistry.* Englewood Cliffs, N.J.: Prentice-Hall, 1982.

HOGGARD, LARA G., *Improving Music Reading in the Choral Rehearsal.* Delaware Water Gap, Pa.: Shawnee Press, Inc., 1947.

JENNINGS, KENNETH, *Sing Legato.* San Diego, Calif.: Neil A. Kjos Music Co., 1982.

JONES, ARCHIE N., ed., *Music Education in Action: Basic Principles and Practical Methods,* pp. 172–84, 186–99. Boston: Allyn & Bacon, 1960.

KRONE, MAX T., *The Chorus and Its Conductor,* chaps. 3, 6, 7. San Diego: Neil A. Kjos Music Co., 1945.

MURRAY, LYN, *Choral Technique Handbook.* Great Neck, N.Y.: The Staff Music Publishing Co., 1956.

PFAUTSCH, LLOYD, "The Choral Conductor and the Rehearsal," in *Choral Conducting Symposium* (2nd ed.), ed. Harold Decker and Julius Herford. Englewood Cliffs, N.J.: Prentice-Hall, 1988.

SWAN, HOWARD, *Conscience of a Profession* (ed. Charles Fowler). Chapel Hill, N.C.: Hinshaw Music, Inc., 1987.

VAN BODEGRAVEN, PAUL, AND HARRY R. WILSON, *The School Music Conductor,* chaps. 2, 4, 5, 6. Chicago: Hall & McCreary Co., 1942.

WILSON, HARRY R., *Artistic Choral Singing,* chaps. 3, 4, 9, 11. New York: G. Schirmer, Inc., 1959.

References on Mental Attitudes

GALLWEY, W. TIMOTHY, *The Inner Game of Tennis.* New York: Random House, 1974.

GREEN, BARRY, AND W. TIMOTHY GALLWEY, *The Inner Game of Music.* Garden City, N.Y.: Anchor Press/Doubleday, 1986.

MALTZ, MAXWELL, *Psycho-Cybernetics.* New York: Pocket Books, 1969.

RISTAD, ELOISE, *A Soprano on Her Head.* Moab, Utah: Real People Press, 1982.

The Jazz/Show Choir

Following World War II, some choral directors began to add popular music to the repertoire of their small ensembles. Throughout the 1950s many professional groups appeared on television and gradually began to have an influence on the attitudes of school music directors. They came to recognize the range of possibilities as well as the educational benefits that might accrue to their singers. Since then, popular vocal music ensembles have steadily increased both in quantity and in quality and are presently widely considered to be an integral part of the choral music curriculum. Music publishers in turn have responded to the movement and currently offer high quality arrangements of music in various styles.

Some choral directors place their emphasis on vocal jazz, while others focus upon the show choir and the performance of popular music with choreography and staged productions. While some directors emphasize one or another type of music, there appears to be a growing tendency for directors to present a broader range of musical styles to their students so that their musical experiences may be as diverse as possible.

The vocal jazz ensemble movement, which is particularly strong in the Pacific Northwest, emphasizes the jazz idiom as exemplified by the stage band movement and stresses the importance of vocal improvisation—and thus creativity—necessitating an understanding of harmonic progressions and the development of an aural sensitivity to the essence of jazz. The show choir, on the other hand, may perform a variety of styles of music, including pop, rock, and Broadway show tunes as well as some vocal jazz, but with an emphasis on body movement that appropriately reflects and usually enhances the presentation of the music. Singing-dancing groups can be seen on television and provide ample illustration of effective choreography.

Both the vocal jazz ensemble and the show choir have valid educational concepts, and to allow students to experience all these varying styles and to gain proficiency and understanding is a tall order indeed. Whatever choices the director makes, however, the purposes of this chapter are to give some practical insights into the various problems that can arise with jazz and show choirs and to provide some procedures for working with these groups.[1]

Jazz and show choirs may range in size from twelve to twenty-four singers, depending on the available talent in the school and the director's philosophy about the ideal size to meet the group's objectives. Whereas vocal jazz ensembles generally perform on three-step risers, show choirs using active body movement need space in which to maneuver effectively. Therefore, twenty-four singers is generally considered the maximum number that can be accommodated.

AUDITIONS

Auditions should be held at a designated time of the year. Some conductors prefer to hold their auditions in the fall; many others prefer the late spring. The advantage of spring, particularly for secondary schools, is that the student body knows about the group and upper-class students are given first chance to audition. Spring auditions are also necessary for scheduling purposes. After the results are announced, discussions can be held to determine the outfits of the group, students can be sized, and the outfits can be ordered. During the summer the conductor and singers can peruse music; the conductor can make selections based on the ability of the group and can order the music. In addition, since participation in such a group is quite time consuming, those students who are not selected are free to make decisions about other activities, jobs, and the like. Furthermore, students who are selected may be motivated enough to begin private study of voice. If others are already studying, they may even want to increase their efforts.

---

[1]Readers may wish to write to music publishers listed in the Appendix and request catalogs of their current offerings in order to facilitate the choosing of music for jazz and show choirs.

In selecting members of the group, the director should keep several important criteria in mind: (1) the singer's vocal ability and musicianship; (2) each singer's experience, flexibility, and ability to learn and remember various body movements or dance routines[2] (students with "two left feet," so to speak, would be detrimental to the purposes and objectives of the group); and (3) proficiency with some musical instrument—for example, drums (trap set), guitar, electric or acoustical bass, flute, and so on. If students within the group have instrumental abilities, they can occasionally be drawn from the ensemble for certain selections to add variety and another dimension to the performance. (If the singers who audition do not have those abilities, then students who do should be sought out from the instrumental music department of the school.) Finally, although spring auditions are desirable, if the "right" singers do not audition, the conductor may opt not to choose the entire ensemble at that time, but to leave some openings for supplementary auditions in the fall or to modify somewhat the size of the group.

While conductors of jazz and show choirs in secondary schools generally prefer to hold their auditions in the spring, conductors of college groups often prefer to hold their auditions in the fall, immediately before the beginning of school, for the simple reason that in comparison to secondary schools, there is probably a larger percentage of students who don't return to school—for financial reasons, because of scholastic difficulties, or because they have transferred to another institution. Of those students remaining in school, some may develop class-schedule conflicts with established rehearsal times or decide to pursue other activities.

SELECTING MUSIC AND PROGRAMMING

Finding just the right music for a jazz/show choir can be a time-consuming task but one that is essential to the success of the group. Following are some suggestions for the director's consideration.

1. Contact music publishers (see Appendix for list) and ask to be placed on their mailing lists for announcements of all their new publications. Some publishers provide samplers of their latest publications (often photo-reduced), promotional records, or brochures on new releases, and some will provide sample examination copies. In writing publishers, it is desirable to do so on school letterhead stationery.[3]

---

[2]If the group is going to use choreography, then personal appearance is also an important factor to be considered. Appearance involves grooming, height-to-weight ratios, and how the singers use the qualities they have. Appearance in this sense does *not* mean looks or innate beauty.

[3]Some publishers offer a library plan whereby for a yearly fee one receives all their latest publications.

2. Many music stores maintain a single-copy file of music of various types and styles, generally in alphabetical order. Look through these files whenever possible and ask to be notified when new releases are obtained.

3. Keep in touch with the media (radio, newspapers, magazines, TV) on what is current—also check with the students, since they are well aware of the current favorites. Before purchasing the latest pop tune, ask yourself, "Will it last or will its popularity be only momentary?" While this is often difficult to predict, the director should, nevertheless, consider the matter. Take a chance on some of the latest pop music, but consider also the many tastefully done arrangements of the old standards; they are certainly much safer. However, the arrangements of some old standards done years ago are rather bland in comparison to the fresh and innovative ideas used today. Compare and decide!

4. Reading sessions and workshops are often sponsored by university and commercial establishments (sometimes in cooperation). Take advantage of these sessions whenever you hear about them.

5. Select quartets composed of students who can read fairly well, and review single copies of music that you have on approval. Solicit their opinions! Sometimes a second reading on another day will provide further insights. A director may, for example, feel that a particular tune or arrangement is "great," but if the students reject it, especially after it has been purchased, then both money and effort have been wasted.

6. In making your final decisions (always in consideration of the budget available), select a variety of types and styles of popular music including current pop tunes, old standards, and vocal jazz. Medleys are good and a number are available, some including the music of particular composers and others featuring the favorites of previous decades.[4] The rationale for selecting a variety of types and styles is the same for a jazz/show choir director as it is for the conductor of the concert chorale. Would you approve of performing a program of music from only one historical period? What would be the audience reaction? Variety helps the conductor to fulfill his educational mission better.

As to the length of programs, thirty to forty-five minutes is a range within which the director should operate. When working within a given time frame such as a school assembly, programs may be lengthened if necessary by including solos by members of the group. Don't use too many, however, and give consideration to their judicious placement between sets of selections by the group. Obviously, selections should not be included on a program if they are not adequately prepared.

As to the sequence of selections, begin with a rousing opener to establish rapport with the audience. Consider the intensity of the various selections and the impact each will have on the audience at a particular point in the program. It may be helpful to diagram the intensity of the music and rearrange the order whenever necessary or desirable.

Some directors prefer to write a narration for their programs; others do not. There are reasons to support either position. Persons

[4]See the Shawnee Press catalog.

opposed to narrated programs feel that this only interrupts the continuity or the flow from one number to the next. Those directors who advocate narration feel it may be used to link the separate musical numbers into a meaningful whole, sometimes with the use of a theme. If narration is used, comments should be relatively short and carefully conceived with a special effect in mind. Narration need not occur between every number, but between identifiable sets—with a definite purpose in mind. Thus, it should contribute to the continuity of the performance and never detract from it.

INTERPRETATION

In the interpretation of popular music, the conductor who has had no experience performing in an ensemble of this type, or in playing in a jazz ensemble, is somewhat at a disadvantage. His interpretation may be tabbed as somewhat "square"—in other words too stiff and unyielding or too loose and "sloppy." The effect in either case is unmusical. The same criticism has been leveled at instrumentalists during their initial experiences in playing in a jazz ensemble. The choral conductor who has had no experience with a jazz or show choir, however, can, with diligent study, develop proficiency in this area.

Rhythm

A basic aspect of interpretation pertains to the treatmentof eighth notes. In most pop/rock tunes they are usually performed with equal duration and are generally notated that way; for example:

The underlying even eighth-note pattern in the percussion part of the combo accompaniment is an integral part of the style and helps to perpetuate the rhythmic drive. (Certain performers even say that they feel the music in 8, or at least a strong *and*, or second half of the beat.) Some publications provide directions in various ways. For example, in "Crazy Rhythm" by Meyer and Kahn, arr. Ellis Bretton (Warner Bros.), the initial directions are "Funky Rock" (equal eighth notes)." In "Sausalito Strut" by Carl Strommen (Alfred Publishing Co.), the music is marked "Bright Rock (♩ = 120)" and the drum part is notated ⟨Light Rock beat⟩.

In "Just the Way You Are" by Billy Joel, arr. Ed Lojeski (Hal Leonard), under "Performance Notes" is the comment, "Rehearse slowly, counting

[5]From "Streets A-fire!" by Mark Brymer (Hal Leonard Publishing Co.).

each eighth note," and at measure 21 the percussion part includes the directions "Bossa Nova—rock feeling."[6] Eighth notes are also generally of equal length in music of a particularly slow tempo. Textual cues and notation within the total configuration of the music will usually enable the director to determine the proper desired effect. Directions and clues for performance in a pop/rock style may be found at various places in the music, and if none are there, then the director must make his own assessment of the musical style, listen to a current recording of the music, or both.

Singers should always strive to feel and respond to the pulse or forward drive of the music. Particularly after a rest, $\frac{4}{4}$ ♩ ♪ ♩. |, the entrance of the group must be together, which is not likely to occur unless the singers feel the pulse of the third beat and respond precisely on the rebound, or second half of the beat (pop/rock style).

In performing offbeat rhythms, $\frac{4}{4}$ ♪ ♩ ♪♪♪ ♪|♪♪ ♪♪♪ ♪|♪ , for example, such as occur in "Just the Way You Are" by Billy Joel, arr. Ed Lojeski (Hal Leonard) and "Baby Come Back to Me" by Nick Santamaria, arr. Jerry Nowak (Hal Leonard), singers should avoid simply trying to read individual notes and should try to develop a feel for the entire phrase. In pop/rock music the offbeat accents occur on the second half of the beat, while in vocal jazz they usually are held back and performed on the last third of the beat (see the following discussion on swing style). Directors should, therefore, determine the basic style and then assist their singers in its interpretation accordingly.

In music with a moderate tempo, there is a tendency for some singers to rush the figure ♪♩ ♪♩, particularly the eighth followed by the quarter note, thus creating a stiff or square effect.[7] Singers should be advised to stretch out or "lay back" on these two notes to create a more relaxed (and less corny) style.

In swing style, both equal eighth notes and dotted eighth and sixteenth notes are performed with a two-to-one, rather than a three-to-one, ratio. For example, the dotted-eighth-and-sixteenth-note pattern in the old standard "Louise," notated as $\frac{4}{4}$ ♫ ♫ ♩ ♫ | ♫ ♫ ♩ |, is not sung as indicated, but as $\frac{12}{8}$ ♩ ♪ ♩ ♪ ♩. ♩ ♪ | ♩ ♪ ♩ ♪ ♩ |. The three-to-one durational pattern would create a stiff or "square" effect, whereas the two-to-one relationship (as indicated in the example) makes the choir "swing." Another way of notating the two-to-one relationship is as fol-

---

[6]For an interpretation of this song by the singer/composer, see the album *The Stranger*, Columbia 34987.

[7]See, for example, "Georgia on My Mind" by Hoagy Carmichael, arr. Gene Puerling (Studio P/R).

lows: [musical notation] . However, in certain instances this notation can be somewhat difficult to read. An increasing number of arrangers are indicating on the score the style they desire. For example, in "I Hear Music" by Loesser and Lane. arr. Larry Lapin (Warner Bros.), the directions "Moderate Swing" ([musical notation]) are indicated. While all the eighth notes in this arrangement are written equally, the directions clearly indicate to the director that a two-to-one relationship is necessary in performance. If the music is not marked "swing style," then one may be inclined to assume that equal eighth notes should be performed as written. However, there can be exceptions to this, and the director must use his own musical judgment. In swing style, the dotted quarter note is similarly performed as: [musical notation] . Also in swing style, one may periodically encounter the rhythmic figure [musical notation] . As to the last two equal eighth notes, they have been performed in three ways: [musical notation] , and [musical notation] . In such situations, try the pattern several ways; that is, experiment, think about what you feel is the most effective or sensitive way, and then do it!

In the first measure of the introduction to the arrangement of "I Hear Music," each chord (syllable) is notated on the second half of the first, second, and fourth beats, respectively; however, they are performed on the last one-third of each of the beats indicated. (Note the directions by the arranger—"Moderate Swing [musical notation] .") For the singers to respond to the rhythm accurately, they must feel the beginning of each beat and "bounce off," so to speak, so the accents are as precise as possible.

The question is often asked why arrangers don't notate the music the way they would like it to sound. Figure 67 shows the notated rhythm of an excerpt from "I Hear Music" followed by notation indicating the correct performance style. The latter two ways are obviously more difficult to read than the first. For this reason the traditional means of musical notation is generally used, with an indication of "swing style" given. Once a person comprehends the basic swing style, he or she can usually read the notation quite easily.

In interpreting jazz rhythms, the director will encounter innumerable patterns. For further study, the reader is referred to Clark Terry and Phil Rizzo, *The Interpretation of the Jazz Language,* M.A.S. Publishing Co., Bedford, Ohio, 1977. In this publication, various rhythmic patterns are notated with a suggested appropriate jazz interpretation included on a line underneath.

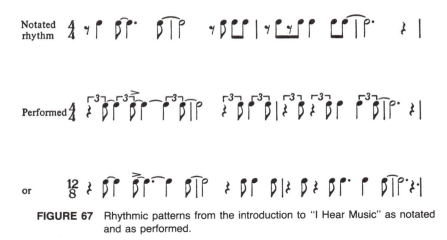

FIGURE 67 Rhythmic patterns from the introduction to "I Hear Music" as notated and as performed.

Tempo

In the rendition of any vocal jazz or pop tune, the finding of the "right groove" is essential for the most precise articulation and overall impact of music. Directors will find the metronome markings helpful, but they should experiment a bit because, for example, the personnel of a group and the acoustics of the performance hall may have a subtle effect on the tempo that will seem right for the group. Once this is determined and marked on the conductor's score, many conductors like to refer to a pocket metronome to make certain of the tempo before it is given to the group. Performance conditions can have subtle effects on the groups, and they should be advised to hold rigidly to the given tempo—that is, don't rush and don't drag; keep on the beat!

On up-tempo tunes, there is often a tendency for the group to drag, or sing behind the beat. Conversely, on medium to slow tempos there is sometimes a tendency for a group to rush the tempo. As previously mentioned, an inward response to the pulse of the music is essential to maintaining a steady beat. On up-tempo tunes the singers should keep on top of the beat, so to speak, and have a feeling of leaning forward; that is, they should anticipate and respond to the "front" side of the beat. (However, they should avoid rushing up-tempo tunes to the extent that articulation becomes blurred.) On slow tempos, singers should be advised to "lay back," relax, and respond to the back side of the beat.

Sometimes there is a tendency for singers to rush staccato notes that fall on the beat—for example, ⁴⁄₄ ♩ 𝄾 ♩ ♩ | ♩ ♩ ♫♫♫♩ ♩. They should be advised to "lay back" and allow for the separation that should occur between the quarter notes.

Tone Quality

In vocal jazz, as well as in most pop tunes, singers should be advised to sing with a straight tone during all unison passages and in those with close or tight harmony; otherwise, the intonation and the blend will be adversely affected. Note, for example, the voicing in measure 2 of the excerpt from "When I Fall in Love" (Hal Leonard), shown in Figure 68. With the bass, tenor, and alto parts an interval of a major second apart, the clarity of the chord structure would most certainly be "muddled" were any vibrato to be used. Some vibrato, however, may be used occasionally for coloring purposes, but primarily on solo passages.

The same basic principles of correct tone production as related in Chapter 2 generally apply to pop singing (see section titled "Developing Choral Tone" in particular). As to diction, initial consonants should be clearly and precisely articulated, though the intensity of *middle* and *final* consonants should be minimized. The consonant *t,* in particular, needs to be softened. For example, on the final consonant in *doot,* minimize the *t* and keep the tongue in contact with the palate. Also, the function of the *t* in *doot* is to stop the sound.

As to the treatment of diphthongs, the second vowel will usually be omitted or at least softened. One of the most troublesome problems of choral singers, regardless of the music style, seems to be their dogged determination to anticipate the second vowel in diphthongs and, of course, not all at the same time, thus resulting in problems with choral blend. Pop singers, however, have numerous models to whom they listen regularly, so the director can perhaps more readily make his point. In summary, tone and diction in pop style should not be forced, but should be somewhat relaxed and easygoing.

Vocal Jazz Articulations and Inflections

The following symbols are generally accepted as standard articulations and inflections for arrangements of vocal jazz ensemble music.

Accent markings—there are several types.

$\tilde{\r}$ = heavy accent held to fullest value. May occur on or off the beat.

$\hat{\r}$ = heavy accent, usually on the beat and held less than full value.

$\hat{\dot{\r}}$ = heavy accent, but short as possible.

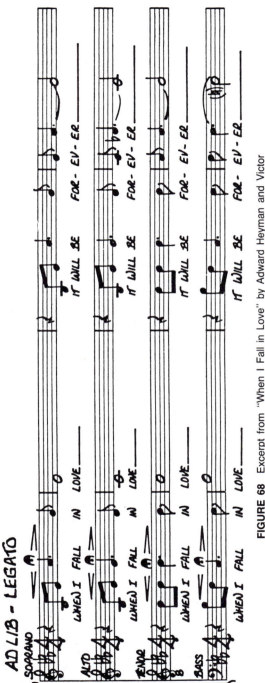

FIGURE 68 Excerpt from "When I Fall in Love" by Adward Heyman and Victor Young, arranged by Phil Azelton. © Copyright 1952, 1973 by Northern Music Corp., a division of MCA Entertainment, Inc., and Victor Young Publications. Used by permission.

Tenuto and staccato

$\bar{\rho}$ = note held to fullest value.

$\overset{\bullet}{\rho}$ = short and detached.

Shake

$\overset{\sim}{\rho}\cdot$ = a rather fast alternation between the written pitch and minimally a major second above. Some directors prefer a minor third or even a major third. Shakes need not be synchronized within the group.

Flip

    = sound first note written and just before its release raise the pitch and drop quickly to the next note.

Smear

    = a slide into a note from below, reaching the pitch just before the next note. The length of the smear, then, depends on the length of the note.

Falloff

    = a descending slide that may be either short or long, depending on the style and the tempo of the music. (The sigh is the essence of the falloff.)

Doit

    = an ascending slide of one to five steps.

Plop

    = a descending slide to the indicated note. Sing the main note at the last instant and "land" with force.

Indefinite sound (ghost notes)

    = an indefinite pitch for notes needing a soft but vital sound.

Glissando (Gliss)

= a slide from one pitch to another that may be up, down, short, or long. Some arrangers simply mark the music as .

Downward turn or dip

= an inflection, generally occurring on the first beat of a measure, in which the singers bend a note downward, usually a half step, and resume the original pitch.[8]

In rehearsing the jazz/show choir, there are many subtleties of interpretation of which the choral director should be aware. The following activities, therefore, are offered to enable the conductor to develop greater sensitivity by (1) listening to and analyzing recordings of outstanding popular groups; (2) discussing with his colleagues various matters of interpretation (most school systems have at least one person who has had experience with instrumental or vocal jazz ensembles); (3) attending concerts of other jazz/show choirs in the area; and (4) openly discussing interpretative matters with the students in the ensemble. Their "young ears" generally are tuned to the current popular music on radio and TV, and as a result, they often quite naturally interpret popular music in an acceptable manner, which, although perhaps not perfect, is stylistically preferable to the approach of the uninitiated conductor. Following are several performing groups whose recordings are suggested for listening and study: The Four Freshmen, Manhattan Transfer, Singers Unlimited, The Hi Lo's, Rare Silk, Phil Mattson & the P.M. Singers, Seawind, and Swingle II.

SCAT SINGING

Scat singing, or a free improvised solo, is an integral part of the vocal jazz movement and can be of benefit to those students who desire the opportunity for free creative vocal expression. It will be of special appeal to those students who have innovative ideas they would like to express but would find difficult to notate.

There is little question that the steps involved in learning to scat-sing can develop increased musical understanding and musicianship. Doug Anderson delineates six basic ingredients of scat singing.[9] They are

---

[8]For further performance suggestions, as well as musical examples for study purposes, see Kirby Shaw's *Vocal Jazz Style* (Milwaukee: Hal Leonard Publishing Corp., 1976).

[9]For further suggestions on these basic ideas, see Doug Anderson, *Jazz and Show Choir Handbook* (Chapel Hill, N.C.: Hinshaw Music, Inc., 1978), pp. 58–67.

1. Chord patterns—singers must know and hear the progressions underlying the music.
2. Chord structure—singers must understand and hear the notes or pitches involved in the basic chords in the progression.
3. Phrase form—singers should understand that phrases are like sentences, that they are statements of varying length (usually four measures), and that singers must fit their musical ideas into these phrases or time frames.
4. Melodic form—singers should construct their solos around the basic melody, and as skills develop (and not until) they may stray further from this basic melody.
5. Rhythm—singers should experiment with various rhythmic patterns ranging from sustained notes to intricate patterns. Listening to various recordings will increase students' understanding of the range of possibilities.
6. Inventive human sounds—the human voice is very flexible and the mind is very inventive. Experimentation with both the range and the variety of sounds can lead to the development of unique styles.

As a beginning point in teaching improvisation, try the twelve-bar blues (in 4/4 meter) with the following chord progression in successive measures:

B♭, B♭, B♭, B♭, E♭, E♭, B♭, B♭, F, E♭, B♭, B♭

1. As an instrumental group (or a recording) plays the basic chord progression shown, ask the group to listen for chord roots and then to sing them. Next, repeat the process on the third and then the fifth of the chord.
2. Devise some interesting rhythms for the group to sing using the root and the third of the chord.
3. Remember that music is a combination of sounds and silences, so see how effective the use of rests can be.
4. All chord roots have upper and lower neighbors. Experiment with them, but always return to the root of the chord.
5. Strive for variety in the use of different vowel and consonant sounds. Eventually use various words and phrases.

The preceding outline is only an introduction on getting started. For basic instructional books along with cassette tapes, see Scott Frederickson, *Scat Singing Method* (Alfred Publishing Co.), and Dominic Spera, *Blues and the Basics* (Hal Leonard). Another recommended book, available with a record, is Jamie Aebersold's *Nothin' But Blues* (JA-1211) (Studio P/R, Inc.).

CHOREOGRAPHY

The director of a show choir will want to involve the group in some type of movement that will enhance the effectiveness of the music. Choreography adds a new dimension to the total performance. If one has had relatively little experience with choreography, there are several avenues open to the director.[10] In some instances the director may find it helpful to enlist the help of a dance specialist in the physical education department. Or perhaps one is acquainted with a professional dance teacher in the community or with a dance major in a local or nearby college or university. Any of these persons may be willing to work with your group on ideas in basic movement, as well as choreographing special choral selections. Also, they may be willing to work with certain students in your group who are both interested in and capable of planning choreography.

After the program has been initiated, it may be found that some of the most unusual and effective ideas will come from the students in the ensemble, and if their pride is exceptional, they may even request that they, rather than a person from "outside" the group, be allowed the opportunity to choreograph the music. Students interested in developing the choreography for a particular song should be encouraged to do so and to bring their ideas to the director for evaluation before presenting them to the group. Through the development and utilization of individual talent within the group, the director is often able to identify and then appoint a "chief" choreographer who will coordinate other students' ideas in a way that contributes to the cohesiveness of the entire group. Some directors prefer to have both a male and a female choreographer to provide leadership and assistance whenever necessary to the members of their sections.

In evaluating choreography, several matters should be considered. Does the movement enhance or add to the effectiveness of a piece? If not, then how may it be modified? Certainly avoid the mistake of using too much body movement, which not only detracts from the music itself but also leaves the singers in a somewhat "breathless" state, unable to do justice vocally to the music. Remember that both singing and body movement take energy, and to do both well is difficult indeed! Some compromise, therefore, is needed. For up-tempo tunes, also make certain that the choral arrangement is not overly complex. Up-tempo tunes, including some unison and two-part harmony, may be all the group can handle musically, especially if involved with active choreography. Does the choreography relate to the tempo, the rhythm, the various textual cues, and the overall mood of the selection? Up-tempo tunes, especially showstoppers used for opening and closing programs, should have energetic movement. For moderate tempo tunes the movements should be more flowing, while slow ballads often are most effective with no movement at

---

[10]Choreography involves artistic body movement, but just as music is a combination of sounds and silences, choreography also has its moments of rest.

all. The contrast is appreciated by the audience, and the preceding and following numbers become even more effective by contrast.

Finally, when students are creating the choreography, the role of the director should be to guide them in every way possible. For example, a particular movement, although interesting and effective the first time you see it, can become terribly dull after excessive repetition. Therefore, the director should identify a basic step and ask the choreographer(s), "How many ways can this movement be modified or expressed?" In other words, take the same idea and modify or build upon it to add interest and variety to your routines.

When the choreographer presents the movements to a group, they need to be not only attentive but also open-minded. This is not the time for critical analysis; it may only result in chaos. Give the choreographer's ideas a chance, and then after the rehearsal they may be reevaluated. If necessary, the director or certain students may suggest modifications, but always in a positive manner.

During the introduction of the choreography, the singers should be advised not to ask questions but to *watch* and *listen!* This procedure helps to focus their powers of concentration. Students are often inclined to ask questions as a "stall"—that is, because they couldn't accomplish a particular move. Also, when student choreographers are used, have them write their schedules of free periods on the chalkboard so that the singers can get together with them for extra help if necessary.

Show choirs may differ considerably in the extent and the nature of their choreography. Some groups will use more active body movements than others; yet, basic to the consideration of any choreographer are the formations or positions out of which movement may most naturally evolve. Different formations are, of course, more appropriate for use with specific selections, where arrangements may range from somewhat stationary positions to those adaptable for active movement. As a point of departure consider the following:

1. The ensemble is arranged in pairs (boy–girl, boy–girl, and so on) in a semicircle formation (partners should be matched according to their relative heights). Tall pairs of partners are generally placed together and can be situated either on the outside or on the inside of the group; it is generally preferable, however, to place them on the inside so that the visual configuration of the ensemble from the view of the audience would appear to be reasonably uniform.

2. The boys stand behind the girls, but just a bit to one side, so that the boys' faces and a partial view of their bodies can be seen.

3. For slow ballads or music with complex harmony, the choir may be placed in a tableau or grouping to "make a picture." Another term to describe this is a *sculpture*—a shaping of artistic forms through a carefully considered placement of persons in the group. As a beginning point, try seating some of the singers on stools (thirty inches in height) with the remainder stand-

ing behind. Then experiment by moving people around until the right visual effect is achieved. For example, some of the singers on the stools may sit at a slight angle, and two singers may even share a stool back-to-back. Anything to avoid a stilted look!

4. The use of elevated platforms of differing levels, with portions of the group placed on each level, can create an interesting visual effect. At one point in the piece, the singers can either change levels (higher, lower) or move to the stage level. The gradual movement of the entire ensemble to the front of the stage can help create a dramatic effect.

5. The girls sit sideways on stools (thirty inches in height) with the heels placed on the bottom rung; the boys stand behind.

6. Props such as the stools just mentioned are most useful in enabling a group to create a variety of formations. Shorter stools (about twelve inches in height) are also desirable—for example, when a portion of the ensemble, either boys, girls or a combination of each, needs to be only slightly elevated for a special effect.

In determining body movements, remember to keep them simple, especially in the initial stages of a group's development, and vary them periodically throughout a selection. Among the simpler movements are the following:

Swaying (only slightly)

Holding and swinging hands (with minimal movement)

Boys' hands on girls' waists (particularly when assisting them on or off stools)

Boys and girls in a back-to-back position (sometimes with arms folded, perhaps to indicate disdain or poutiness) and then turning to face each other, indicating a complete change of mood

Girls walking slowly around the boys, with boys turning their heads to one side to watch their departure and then to the other side to anticipate their return

Boys hiding behind girls and "peeking" to one side or the other

Upraised arms to indicate joy and exultation

A "chorus line" kick of the right leg crossing in front of the left and then the left leg in front of the right.

Short side steps on each beat of 4/4: left, right, left, right toe touch (in front of left), then reverse direction—right, left, right, left toe touch (in front of right)

Slight shoulder movements: front to side on each beat (or every other beat), reversing sides on every other measure

Boys hold girls' hands straight above their heads while girls slowly turn about

Diagonal thrust of arms to left and right sides (alternate between measures)

Precise upward movement of arms one section at a time: left front, right back, right front, left back.

Singers should watch television variety shows, movie musicals, and musical theater productions whenever possible and make notes on movements that might be adapted to particular selections that the group is currently rehearsing. Ideas for choreographing choral selections seem to grow and to inspire still further ideas. The process becomes easier as the group gains experience.

Whether one brings in a dance specialist to do the choreography or whether students within the group are assigned this task, the director still has the ultimate responsibility for the final result. Therefore, he will want to become as knowledgeable as possible about dance and body movement. This may be accomplished by studying books and articles on the topic; by observing television variety shows involving choreography, movie musicals, and musical theater productions; by attending programs of show choirs from other high schools and colleges; by participating in special workshops offered by colleges and universities; or by enrolling in dance courses during the academic year or a summer session.

Directors should give consideration to the following teaching sequence.

1. The group must first learn and memorize the music. To introduce choreography before that is accomplished would be an exercise in futility! Besides, in teaching a new routine, the choreographer may periodically give word cues to clarify and facilitate the learning of the movement.
2. Teach the choreography in sections. Explain and demonstrate the movements; then have the group "walk through" the sequence. Make certain the group can execute the movements reasonably well before introducing a new section; in other words, don't try to teach too much at one time.
3. After the choreography has been introduced and reasonably well learned, return to a rehearsal of the music to focus entirely upon such matters as tone, blend, enunciation, pitch and intonation, balance, and so on. (Rehearsing by SATB quartets seated in a circle facilitates more careful listening.) If the music is not periodically focused upon, it can deteriorate in sound, thus negating the entire purpose of the choreography, which is to enhance the musical presentation.
4. Whenever necessary and appropriate, alternate rehearsals that emphasize the choreography with rehearsals that emphasize the music.
5. In the final rehearsal, especially on the day of a performance, don't sing at full voice, but save it! Work toward the achievement of both precision of movement and vocal articulation.

STAGE PRESENCE

Anything that affects the impact of the performance upon an audience, whether it be visual or aural, is important and must be considered, no matter how minute it may seem. Some of the nonmusical considerations are as follows:

1. *Facial expressions* The facial expressions of the singers must reflect the mood of the music. This is important for all choirs, but it is absolutely essential to the effectiveness of jazz and show choirs. Singers must "turn on" to up-tempo tunes and should avoid a solemn expression on ballads. The essence of the music's sensitively conceived text should be projected to the audience.

Most directors will face the problem of helping certain students with a stoical expression on their faces. Sometimes this occurs because they are trying too hard, which may be alleviated through the development of individual confidence. The director may periodically need to encourage them to relax, loosen up, and "smile a bit." He may also encourage them to select someone in a friendly audience (perhaps a parent or a student friend) and endeavor to transfer to that person the feeling or mood of the song—for example, happiness, sadness, or love.

2. *Eye contact* The singers should never forget their mission and role as performers: to project the essence of the poetic and musical ideas to the audience and to do so in an entertaining manner. Even when the body is turning sideways in choreographic movements, singers should keep their heads facing the audience as much as possible. The sound will project better too!

3. *Body language* All body attitudes—posture, positions, and movements—project a message to the audience—that is, how the singers feel about the music as well as about themselves. When they feel secure in their performance, they will project a more positive image. Normally, students who enjoy and "get into" the music as well as the choreography have less difficulty in this respect; however, most singers need a continual reminder about its importance. The director may advise the singers to "go home and sing to yourself in the mirror, and if you don't like what you see no one else will!"

Building confidence in the group's abilities is an important task of the director and will occur as a part of the growth process necessitating periodical reassessment and the establishment of immediate, as well as long-term, goals. It seems that progress occurs by degrees. The group may function on one plateau for a while, then move to a higher performance level. When this occurs it's time for a celebration!

While all the movements of a show tune may be precisely and effectively executed, what happens between selections? Consideration must be given to the movements to the new position so that they effect a smooth transition.

   4. *Acknowledgment of audience applause*   When and how often will the singers recognize the applause of the audience? At the end of each selection, the director may wish to recognize the applause if he feels it is necessary. Certainly one should not confuse the audience or do anything to keep them from applauding—they should be allowed to release the excitement they have built up. Some directors plan group bows at the end of sets of music; others prefer them at the end of the program. Two suggested ways are group bows from the waist (given on cue) and a ripple bow. Some groups like to use both types. On the waist bow, the movements must be together. It is helpful to designate a centrally located leader from whom the group will take its cue. Two waist bows may be executed with the group counting silently to themselves: down, two, three, four; up, two, three four; and down, two, three, four; up, two, three, four. After a brief pause the waist bow may be repeated or a ripple bow may be executed: Beginning at stage left, each singer bows in turn until the entire group has bowed; the "ripple" then reverses itself, and each individual successively assumes an erect position, beginning at stage right. To make the movements effective, each singer must be keenly aware of the movements of the singer next to him or her. An effective ripple bow should be as smooth as a gentle ocean wave.

   An alternative is for the director to give the bowing cues, provided he is in an appropriate position to do so. Following the singers' bows, the instrumentalists should be recognized by the director. (If carefully planned and coordinated they may also be recognized on cue by the singers as well.) In summary, all of the aspects of stage presence must be discussed with the singers and then thoughtfully considered and rehearsed. This will not happen through wishful thinking but only by diligent practice.

   To assist in the development of stage presence, videotaping the group is an excellent teaching aid. When students are able to see themselves as others see them, the conductor's comments become far more meaningful. Videotaping should be scheduled periodically; however, it is helpful if for at least one complete session, the camera focuses on the hands of the singers. (Singers often betray their nervousness through an awkward use of their hands. Once they surmount this obstacle, they will perform more confidently.) The director must be equally cognizant of the person who overacts. Videotaping often helps this type of person to identify his problem and to be better able to blend into the group.

   Social functions held periodically can also contribute to the development of group cohesiveness and help to dispel the self-consciousness that a particular member might feel.

IMPORTANCE OF SOLO PERFORMANCE

The jazz/show choir director should do all he can to encourage solo performances by each singer in the group. Such experience contributes to the individual, as well as to the ensemble, in the following ways.

1. It helps each singer to learn the strengths and the limitations of his or her voice.
2. It encourages listening to other singers and the development of one's unique style.
3. It develops vocal independence and provides valuable ear training that enables each singer to function more effectively in the larger group.
4. It develops self-confidence and the necessary ability to "sell" a song to an audience. The ability of a jazz/show choir to project enthusiasm as a group may be strengthened considerably through the singers' solo experiences.

In preparing their solos, singers may be helped by practicing their songs in front of a mirror. Videotaping the singers in the performance of their songs may help each person to gain a realistic perspective of his or her performance and can lead to a critical analysis that will foster improvement.

ACHIEVING SPECIAL EFFECTS

An important aspect of a choreographic venture is the costuming, which can be most creative if left to the imagination of the members of the group. Changes of costume between sets are often effective. When dresses are worn by the girls, they should be of a type that allows for freedom of movement. Many show tunes may be enhanced through the use of special props such as top hats and canes, small pastel-colored umbrellas for the girls and straw hats for the boys, and various other paraphernalia, depending on the character of the music. In addition, an imaginative stage crew, knowledgeable about special lighting effects, can contribute substantially to the overall effectiveness of a performance. Each selection has a specific mood, and color changes in the lighting can serve to highlight these moods.

Obviously, it is unnecessary for the director of such an ensemble to conduct a group during public performances, because that would only detract from the performance of the singers. The conductor is best advised to remain backstage and assist with the lighting effects and the overall timing or pacing of the show. Exceptions to the general rule will occur when the establishment of a precise tempo is essential to an effective performance. In such instances, the conductor may establish the tempo from the center or the side of the stage and then exit. The only other justification for the conductor's being onstage is to help singers effectively execute music with varying tempo changes when the singers are unable to do so without direction. The singers, however, should be given the opportunity to perform without the conductor in front of them. In this situation, they will necessarily have to listen to each other more carefully, and thus an opportunity is provided for the further development of their own musical sensitivities.

Most groups enhance their performances by utilizing a small instrumental combination, including piano, guitar, acoustical or electric bass, and drums to accompany the group.[11] Not only is the rhythm of the singers solidified as a result, but also the added "tonal color" of the instruments contributes substantially to the overall effectiveness of the presentation.

Groups such as jazz/show choirs are often used to provide variety on a school choral program and often appear on programs with the school chorus or choir. In other instances, however, when the repertoire of the group is sufficient, they are able to present complete programs by themselves. Again to provide variety, as well as a needed rest between sets, vocal and instrumental solos are often used. The performance demands on school choral programs are often excessive, and the organization and the utilization of a group such as a show choir not only relieves certain performance pressures for the other choral organizations, but more often than not is also the ideal group, in terms of both size and repertoire, to present performances before luncheon or dinner groups such as local service clubs.

One final word! Before any public performance is scheduled, the conductor must make certain that the choreography is just as well rehearsed as the music is. Although slight slips of memory in the music can sometimes be "covered up" (to the uninitiated ear, at least), miscues or mistakes in the choreography are obvious to everyone and embarrassing to the singers, as well as to the conductor. The dedication of both time and effort to perfecting all movements must match, if not exceed, that put forth during the music rehearsals if performances are to be even reasonably adequate and if the ensemble is to achieve its aesthetic goals. With a jazz/show choir, the mental preparation for a performance is highly important. The mental warm-up, or getting ready to perform, is even more important than the vocal warm-up.

TOPICS FOR DISCUSSION

1. List several of the specific criteria for the selection of new members in a jazz/show choir, and describe how auditions might be held.

[11]It is suggested that two piano accompanists be part of the total group, not just to cover illness, but also because on some selections it may be desirable to use a four-hand piano accompaniment.

2. When introducing choreography to singers, what means can be used to help ensure that they comprehend the movements and can learn to execute them with a minimum of confusion?

3. Describe various means by which singers can be assisted in overcoming certain inhibitions that are detrimental to the overall effectiveness of a group's performance.

4. Describe the tone quality appropriate for jazz/show choirs. Discuss means by which the "ideal" quality may be achieved.

5. Discuss various special effects that a jazz/show choir might achieve through unique costuming.

SELECTED READINGS

AEBERSOLD, JAMIE, *Nothin' But Blues* (JA-1211), book and record. Lebanon, Ind.: Studio P/R, Inc.

ALBRECHT, SALLY K., *Choral Music in Motion*. East Stroudsburg, Pa.: Music in Action, 1984.

ANDERSON, DOUG, "Improvisation for Vocal Jazz Ensembles," *Music Educators Journal*, 66, no. 5 (January 1980), 89–94.

————, *Jazz and Show Choir Handbook*. Chapel Hill, N.C.: Hinshaw Music, Inc., 1978.

BOWER, JORDAN HAMM, "Ideas from a Choreographer," *The Choral Journal*, December 1978, pp. 25–26.

DAVIDSON, JOHN, AND CORT CASADY, *The Singing Entertainer*. Sherman Oaks, Calif.: Alfred Publishing Co., 1980.

FREDERICKSON, SCOTT, *Scat Singing Method*. Sherman Oaks, Calif.: Alfred Publishing Co., 1985.

JACOBSON, JOHN, *Dance Warm-ups & Workouts for the Show Choir* (a Step-by-Step Instructional Book with Album). New Berlin, Wis.: Jenson Publications, Inc., 1984.

KYSAR, MICHAEL, DAVID CROSS, KEN KRAINTZ, AND FRANK DEMIERO, *Vocal Jazz Concepts*. Chapel Hill, N.C.: Hinshaw Music, Inc., 1976.

LEA, BARBARA, *How to Sing Jazz*. New York: Chappell Music Co., 1980.

LEATHERMAN, GARY, *Jazz Show Choirs*. Cherokee, Iowa: Rapid American Press, 1978.

LOCKHART, AILEENE, AND ESTHER E. PEASE, *Modern Dance: Building and Teaching Lessons*. Dubuque, Iowa: Wm. C. Brown, 1977.

MURRAY, ARTHUR, *How to Become a Good Dancer*. New York: Pocket Books, 1976.

OSTRANDER, ARTHUR, AND DANA WILSON, *Contemporary Choral Arranging*. Englewood Cliffs, N.J.: Prentice-Hall, 1986.

SHAW, KIRBY, *Vocal Jazz Style*. Milwaukee: Hal Leonard Publishing Corp., 1976. (Vocal Jazz Style Pak includes 1 teacher's manual, 20 student books, and 1 cassette tape.)

————, *Warm-ups for the Jazz and Show Choir*. Milwaukee: Hal Leonard Publishing Corp., 1978. (Pak includes 30 SATB student scores.)

SMALLWOOD, RICHARD, "Gospel and Blues Improvisation," *Music Educators Journal*, 66, no. 5 (January 1980), 100–4.

SPERA, DOMINIC, *Blues and the Basics*. Milwaukee: Hal Leonard Publishing Corp., 1975. (Pak includes book and cassette tape. Books available separately. C treble clef instrumental/vocal, C bass clef instrumental/vocal.)

————, *Making the Changes*. Milwaukee: Hal Leonard Publishing Corp., 1977. (Pak includes book and cassette tape. Books available separately. C treble clef instrumental/vocal, C bass clef instrumental/vocal.)

STROMMEN, CARL, *The Contemporary Choir: Jazz, Pop, and Rock*. Sherman Oaks, Calif.: Alfred Publishing Co., 1980.

TERRY, CLARK, AND PHIL RIZZO, *The Interpretation of the Jazz Language*. Bedford, Ohio: M.A.S. Publishing Co., 1977.

Programs and Concerts

Practically all choral conductors have at one time or another encountered difficulties in the preparation and presentation of choral programs. Problems of special concern include locating a variety of worthwhile choral materials, planning and staging programs of an artistic nature, and planning and implementing effective publicity. The individual conductor solves these problems as best he can and, in so doing, constantly obtains new ideas. Following are suggestions that may be helpful.

SELECTING THE MUSIC

The basic consideration in planning a choral program is selection of the music, since the success of the program depends to a great extent upon the quality and the appropriateness of the music performed. Following are criteria that will serve as a guide in selecting good, usable choral materials.

1. Is the text worthwhile? Does it contain a message of sufficient value?
2. Is the music artistically conceived, and does it reflect the mood of the text?
3. Does the selection fit the needs and the interests of the particular age

212

group for which it is being selected? Does the music have emotional appeal for the singers?

4. Does the music fit the physical limitations of the singers? Is the tessitura of the parts too high or too low? Are there extreme, awkward jumps in the voice parts that might prove difficult to execute?

5. Are the voice parts handled in such a manner as to make each part sufficiently interesting?

6. If the selection is an arrangement, is it done in an authentic musical style? Is the authenticity of the music sacrificed for clever musical effects? (This criterion applies to arrangements of the masters as well as to folk-song arrangements.)

7. Does the music justify the rehearsal time necessary to prepare it?

8. Are all the various types and styles of choral music being represented in your selections, so that the singers may have the broadest educational experience possible?

CONSIDERING THE AUDIENCE

The choral conductor should consider the audience in his selection of music for particular programs. Music has a variety of moods and must be appropriate to the occasion. Aside from individual musical tastes, the nature of the event quite often determines the receptivity of the group to various types of music. Performing at certain festive banquets, for example, quite often precludes the exclusive use of sacred music. If the occasion warrants the use of popular and novelty tunes, they should be used. This need not imply a lowering of musical standards, for to include in the program a variety of styles and types of music is often the most effective way of evoking enthusiastic audience reaction.

It is important to the success of the program that rapport be established as soon as possible between the audience and the performers. Prior to the beginning of the choral concert, the audience is usually unsettled, as evidenced by considerable shuffling around, coughing, and general confusion. To gain the complete attention of the audience, the conductor should begin the program with music that is reasonably straightforward and vigorous. Placing quiet and subdued selections at the beginning of the program should be avoided, for here their effect is lost. Such numbers are more effective if placed later in the program, when the audience is in a more receptive mood.

The conductor also should consider the audience in planning the length of the program. Fatigue decreases not only the efficiency of the singers but also the receptivity of the audience. Choral programs generally should not exceed an hour and a quarter, including intermission. It is desirable to end the program with the audience wanting to hear more, since that will promote more enthusiastic support of the choral organization.

ACHIEVING UNITY AND VARIETY

For an effective choral program, it is important that both unity and variety be maintained. Musical *variety* may be achieved by selecting numbers that contrast in style, mood, length, mode, and key. Variety in the program also may be obtained by

1. Featuring vocal or instrumental soloists, or both, either within or in addition to the choral selections.
2. Featuring either or both the male and the female voices in the choir in selected TTBB and SSA literature.
3. Presenting several of the school's music groups, both vocal and instrumental, in a combined program.

Unity, as well as variety, is often achieved in the choral program by selecting publications that fall into three or more groups and that have some definite literary or stylistic relationship to each other—for example, sacred music, folk songs, and contemporary music. A prevalent practice is to begin the program with a group of sacred selections, representing various historical periods, and to end the program with music of a lighter mood—either folk songs or contemporary music, depending upon the nature of the music. Many directors also like to include the composers' dates on the printed program to indicate to the listening audience, and to remind the singers of, the historical periods the music represents.[1] Program I illustrates these ideas.

The program sequence from serious to lighter moods and from early periods to contemporary compositions is, of course, heavily enmeshed in tradition and has many merits. However, some directors feel that the group of sacred songs is likely to be better received if it is placed later in the program. Furthermore, they believe that audience rapport may be more firmly established if the program is begun with music of a lighter mood. Program II is presented as an alternative approach. The use of a choral prelude and a choral postlude may contribute further to the overall effectiveness of the program.

Since any given audience will usually contain people with varied musical tastes, the conductor may wish to evoke maximum audience response and enthusiasm by including on the program a variety of musical styles and ensembles. In Program III, for example, Part I includes sacred choral literature from various periods. In Part II, while the singers are given a brief rest, the accompanist is featured in two piano selections. Including an extended choral work in Part III serves to highlight the first portion of the program, as well as providing a valuable musical experience for the participants. Following an intermission, it is

---

[1]See the Appendix for a chronological listing of composers from the Renaissance to the present.

Program I

I
SACRED MUSIC

Jubilate Deo . . . . Orlandus Lassus
(1532–1594)

Day by Day We Magnify Thee . . . . George F. Handel
(1685–1759)

Contentment . . . . W. A. Mozart
(1756–1791)

Nunc Dimittis . . . . Vassili S. Kalinnikov
(1866–1901)

The Last Words of David . . . . Randall Thompson
(1899–1984)

II
CONTEMPORARY MUSIC

It Is Good to Be Merry . . . . Jean Berger
(1909–   )

The Lobster Quadrille . . . . Irving Fine
(1914–1962)

Old Abram Brown . . . . Benjamin Britten
(1913–1976)

Sure on This Shining Night . . . . Samuel Barber
(1910–1981)

Whether Men Do Laugh or Weep . . . . Ralph Vaughan Williams
(1872–1958)

III
FOLK SONGS

My Pretty Little Pink . . . . American Folk Song
arr. Joyce Barthelson

Dance to Your Daddie . . . . Scottish Nursery Song
arr. Edmund Rubbra

I Know My Love . . . . Irish Folk Song
arr. Parker-Shaw

May Day Carol . . . . English Folk Song
arr. Deems Taylor

Didn't My Lord Deliver Daniel? . . . . Spiritual
arr. Ralph Hunter

Program II[2]

CHORAL PRELUDE

O Sing Your Songs .... Noble Cain

FOLK SONGS

Chiapanecas .... Mexican Dance Tune
arr. Harry R. Wilson

Shenandoah* .... Early American Barge Song
arr. Tom Scott

Soon-Ah Will Be Done† .... Spiritual
arr. William L. Dawson

Charlottown .... American Folk Song
arr. Charles F. Bryan

SACRED MUSIC

O Filii et Filiae .... Volckmar Leisring
Ave Verum Corpus .... W. A. Mozart
Salvation Is Created .... Paul Tschesnokov
Glory to God in the Highest .... Randall Thompson

CONTEMPORARY MUSIC

Younger Generation .... Aaron Copland
Old Abram Brown .... Benjamin Britten
Monotone .... Normand Lockwood
Stomp Your Foot (from *The Tender Land*) .... Aaron Copland

CHORAL POSTLUDE

Onward, Ye Peoples .... Jean Sibelius

[2]In this and subsequent programs, symbols indicate that selections are to be sung by (*) girls' glee club, (†) boys' glee club, and (‡) choir and audience. Undesignated selections are to be sung by the mixed chorus.

Program III

I

Cantantibus Organis . . . . Luca Marenzio

Cantate Domino Canticum Novum . . . . Heinrich Schütz

Plorate Filii Israel . . . . Giacomo Carissimi

Ave Maria . . . . Sergei Rachmaninoff

Alleluia . . . . Alan Hovhaness

II

Reflets dans l'eau . . . . Claude Debussy

Alborada del gracioso . . . . Maurice Ravel

Mary Jones, Pianist

III

Polovetzian Dance and Chorus
(from *Prince Igor*) . . . . Alexander Borodin

INTERMISSION

IV

Marching to Pretoria . . . . South African Veld Song
arr. Joseph Marais & Ruth Abbott

Ho-La-Hi . . . . German Folk Song
arr. Roger Fiske

Ching-A-Ring Chaw . . . . Minstrel Song
arr. Aaron Copland & Irving Fine

When Love Is Kind . . . . English Folk Song
arr. Salli Terri

Ezekiel Saw the Wheel . . . . Spiritual
arr. Harry Simeone

V

Josh'a Fit de Battle . . . . Spiritual
arr. Harvey Enders

Loch Lomond . . . . Scottish Folk Song
arr. Dede Duson

Men's Octet

VI

A Wonderful Day Like Today . . . . Leslie Bricusse
& Anthony Newley
arr. Norman Leyden

Am I Blue? . . . . Harry Akst
arr. Kirby Shaw

Just One of Those Things . . . . Cole Porter
arr. Roger Emerson

The Modernaires

VII

Neighbors' Chorus
(from La Jolie Parfumeuse) . . . . Jacques Offenbach

Broadway Spectacular . . . . arr. Roger Emerson

often desirable to include music of a less serious nature. A group of folk songs from various countries, therefore, is appropriate at this point (Part IV). Further variety may be achieved by featuring one or more smaller vocal ensembles. Part V includes music particularly suitable for a men's octet, while Part VI includes music most appropriate for a small mixed ensemble of twelve to sixteen voices. As the culmination of the program, the entire chorus is featured in music of a light character. Selections from light opera and Broadway musicals are particularly appealing to most audiences and generally are enthusiastically received.

Using a Theme

Another means of achieving unity is to build the choral program around some theme. In choosing a theme, the conductor should consider the various alternative subtopics around which the music may be grouped. Provided the text of the music under consideration is related to the central theme, a careful analysis of it will often reveal many possibilities for natural groupings. Christmas, Easter, and other important holidays or seasons provide a natural opportunity for this type of thematic treatment. For the imaginative choral director the possibilities are unlimited. Consider the following suggestions.

Christmas programs   A most effective Christmas choral program may be achieved by selecting numbers that fall into one of the following three categories: "The Advent," "The Nativity," and "The Rejoicing."

Program IV

CHORAL PRELUDE

Fanfare for Christmas Day .... Martin Shaw

THE ADVENT

While Shepherds Watch'd .... Old Yorkshire Carol
arr. Gustav Klemm

As Joseph Was A-Walking .... Don Malin

Lost in the Night .... Finnish Folk Melody
arr. F. M. Christiansen

The Three Kings .... Healey Willan

THE NATIVITY

Jesus, Jesus, Rest Your Head .... Appalachian Carol
arr. Niles-Warrell

Gentle Mary and Her Child .... Finnish Folk Melody
arr. Lundquist

Slumber Song of the Infant Jesus .... François Auguste Gevaert

Silent Night* .... Franz Gruber

THE REJOICING

Hodie Christus Natus Est .... Jan Pieters Sweelinck

Go Tell It on the Mountain .... Spiritual
arr. John W. Work

Glory to God in the Highest .... G. B. Pergolesi.

CHORAL POSTLUDE

Joy to the World‡ .... George F. Handel

By using this theme, directors will find their problems somewhat minimized, since most of the choral publications of Christmas music may be placed into one of these three important periods of the Christmas season. Program IV illustrates this idea.

Other categories that may be used in a similar manner for a Christmas program are "The Star of Bethlehem," "The Nativity of the Christ Child," and "Joy to the World."

"Christmas Around the World" is a flexible theme for a school assembly program. The program may be built around carols from all countries. The use of a narrator may further enhance the effectiveness of the program.

Whereas some directors prefer to use only sacred music at Christmas, others may wish to include some secular music, as well, on their programs. When this is done, the selections must be given careful consideration and judiciously placed on the program according to some particular plan. To help achieve this purpose, the theme "Music at Christmastide" is suggested. Appropriate categories for developing this theme are "Christmas Hymns and Carols," "Christmas Symbols and Greetings," and "Songs of Youth and Childhood." The program may be made even more effective through the use of an organ prelude, a brief choral prelude or "fanfare" prior to the processional, and the inclusion of selected masterworks for combined choirs immediately after the processional and just before the recessional. Further variety may be achieved by featuring different choral groups on all or part of each of the three major sections of the program. Program V illustrates this idea.

Program V

𝕸𝖚𝖘𝖎𝖈 𝖆𝖙 𝕮𝖍𝖗𝖎𝖘𝖙𝖒𝖆𝖘𝖙𝖎𝖉𝖊

ORGAN PRELUDE

Pastorale . . . . Arcangelo Corelli

Carol Rhapsody . . . . Richard Purvis

Organist: Mary Jones

CHORAL PRELUDE

Fanfare for Christmas Day . . . . Martin Shaw

PROCESSIONAL AND GLORIA

Adeste Fideles . . . . Old Latin Hymn

Gloria in Excelsis Deo . . . . Joseph Haydn

Combined Choirs

CHRISTMAS HYMNS AND CAROLS

Christmas Hymn . . . . 17th Century German

God Rest Ye Merry, Gentlemen . . . . Old English Carol

Still, Still, Still . . . . Austrian Carol
Carol of the Bells . . . . Ukrainian Carol
Concert Choir

CHRISTMAS SYMBOLS AND GREETINGS

Now Is the Caroling Season . . . . Dorothy Priesing
O Tannenbaum . . . . Traditional German
Silver Bells . . . . Jay Livingston
Mistletoe . . . . Fred Waring and Jerry Toti
Mixed Chorus

SONGS OF YOUTH AND CHILDHOOD

Sleigh Ride . . . . Leroy Anderson
Winter Wonderland . . . . Felix Bernard
Chestnuts Roasting on an Open Fire . . . . Torme and Wells
Toyland . . . . Victor Herbert
The Modernaires

CHORAL POSTLUDE AND RECESSIONAL

Hallelujah Chorus (from *Messiah*) . . . . George F. Handel
Combined Choirs
Joy to the World‡ . . . . George F. Handel
Audience and Combined Choirs

Other categories or titles for grouping choral selections are "Music of the Masters," "Now We Go A-Caroling!" "The Many Moods of Christmas," "Christmas Favorites," "Yuletide Carols," "Loud Their Praises Sing!" and "Carols from Faraway Lands."

Interfaith programs   In schools and colleges where the student body or the membership of a choral group is representative of several faiths, a particularly appropriate program may include music from various religions. Program VI illustrates this idea.

Easter program   An effective grouping of music for a sacred Easter program may be achieved by selecting music that falls into one of the following three categories: "The Holy Week," "The Crucifixion," and "The Resurrection."

Program VI

I

O Magnum Mysterium .... Tomas Luis da Vittoria

Verbum Caro .... Gaspar von Weerbeke

Angelus ad Pastores .... Hans Leo Hassler

Weihnachts Motette .... Luca Marenzio

II

Mi Yemalel (Who Can Retell?) .... Max Helfman

Saenu .... Yemenite Melody
arr. Charles Davidson

S'vivon (The Top) .... Folk Song
arr. Max Helfman

Light the Legend (A Song for Chanukah) .... Michael Isaacson

II

Break Forth, O Beauteous Heavenly Light .... J. S. Bach

Joseph Tender, Joseph Mine .... Seth Calvisius

Lo, How a Rose E'er Blooming .... Michael Praetorius

Hallelujah Chorus (from Messiah) .... George F. Handel

---

General sacred programs   Groupings that may be used for general sacred choral music programs are "The Spirit of Glorification," "The Spirit of Trust," and "The Spirit of Peace."

Secular programs   Appropriate groupings for a secular program are "Songs of Work," "Songs of Love," and "Songs of Play," or "Songs of Nature," "Songs of Love," and "Songs of Travel." "I Hear America Singing" may be used as an appropriate title for a spring concert in which both sacred and secular music is included (Program VII).

Memorial Day program   An effective Memorial Day program may be achieved by grouping the music into the categories "The Ideals," "The Men and the Women," and "The Land." Program VIII illustrates the use of this theme.

Program VII

I HEAR AMERICA SINGING

CHORAL PRELUDE

A patriotic selection

OF HER FAITH

Sacred music of various faiths

OF HER PEOPLE

Secular or sacred music about particular societal organizations
or famous individuals

PRAISE TO THE LAND OF THE FREE

Appropriate patriotic music

CHORAL POSTLUDE

America the Beautiful‡

PUBLICIZING THE CONCERT

Adequate publicity is essential to the overall success of concerts and
programs. Singers perform best before an interested and enthusiastic
audience; therefore, the director should continually search for means to
increase the size and the quality of the audience and to develop community support for the choral music program. Following are some suggested publicity techniques.

Newspaper Articles

Newspaper articles should be well written, giving all the vital information, such as date, time, place, soloists, and other special features of
the program. This information, along with a copy of the program,
should be forwarded to local newspapers well in advance of the program
date. Most newspaper editors welcome such information and are usually
willing to allot a limited amount of space in their publications as a public
or community service. The younger set may be best reached by placing

---

Program VIII

LEST WE FORGET

CHORAL PRELUDE

The Star-Spangled Banner‡ . . . . John S. Smith

THE IDEALS

Born to Be Free . . . . Ralph E. Williams
What Makes a Good American? . . . . Singer-Gearhart
Give Me Your Tired, Your Poor . . . . Irving Berlin

THE MEN AND THE WOMEN

Anchors Aweigh . . . . Miles & Zimmerman
The Caissons Go Rolling Along . . . . E. L. Gruber
The Marines' Hymn . . . . L. Z. Phillips
The U.S. Air Force Song . . . . Robert Crawford
Reading: *O Captain! My Captain!* . . . . Walt Whitman

THE LAND

This Is My Country . . . . Al Jacobs
Homeland . . . . Noble Cain
God Bless America . . . . Irving Berlin
America the Beautiful . . . . Samuel A. Ward

POSTLUDE

Taps‡ . . . . U.S. Army Bugle Call

---

articles and announcements in the school newspaper. To provide a desirable learning experience for secondary school students, the director should designate individuals in the choral organization to handle this latter aspect of public relations.

Radio Announcements

In communities displaying a high degree of interest in school, church, and community affairs, certain local radio stations have cooperated by broadcasting spot announcements of programs, sometimes during local news broadcasts, a few days before the event is to occur. Some radio stations provide this assistance as a public service, without charge. In certain instances, stations have been known to interview choir members on radio broadcasts concerning aspects of a coming musical event or program.

Complimentary Tickets

Perhaps one of the most effective means of publicity is the distribution of a specified number of complimentary tickets to concerts for which there normally would be no admission charge. Tickets may be mailed to selected persons, or a certain number may be provided each choir member for distribution. Individuals do not, as a rule, destroy so quickly items to which they attach some value; tickets may lie around a person's home in various conspicuous places or be shuffled daily from one coat pocket to another. In this way, the tickets are a constant reminder of the coming event.

Mailing of Programs

In many instances, a certain clientele may be lured by duplicated copies of the actual program. In contrast to the more formal appearance of a printed announcement, the actual program creates greater interest for the reader. Recognition of a familiar or a favorite choral selection sometimes provides the necessary extra motivation for one to leave the confines of a comfortable home on a cold winter night.

Posters

Attractive, eye-catching posters can also be an effective means of attracting attention and stimulating interest in choral programs. Posters may be printed by local printing shops for a nominal fee or in the school printing shop, where facilities exist. In most organizations there are a number of people with artistic ability who are willing to prepare some attractive posters. These same individuals will usually assume the task of distribution. Posters should be placed where traffic is heavy—in locations where they will be seen by the largest number of people—in schools, churches, stores, and various other locations in the community. Adequate study given to determining the best locations will reap later dividends.

Handbills and Public-Carrier Advertisements

Although handbills and public-carrier advertisements are used infrequently because of their prohibitive cost, the distribution of the former throughout a specified section of the community and the use of the latter posted inside or outside buses or other types of public transportation are additional means of publicity. Their use would probably be justified only for programs that are financially self-supporting and presented on several consecutive evenings.

A less expensive means that may be profitably utilized is the distribution of automobile bumper stickers that advertise a specific event.

"Word-of-Mouth"

For many performances, a large segment of the audience will always consist of parents, relatives, and friends. This group is motivated to attend programs and concerts largely because of their individual interests in particular members of the performing organization. The "personal touch" is exceedingly important in all areas of human relations. Effective results may be achieved, therefore, if each participant in the organization is requested to extend a cordial, verbal invitation to at least twenty-five people outside his immediate family. Each singer may be provided with a printed reminder, perhaps in the form of an invitation, to make certain that he remembers to pass the word.

THE FINAL REHEARSAL

When programs are to be presented in a school or church auditorium, it is of paramount importance that the final rehearsal be held there so that the choir members may become accustomed to the acoustics and to the routine of the performance. (Indeed, the final rehearsal for any concert should always be held at the place where the concert is to be given.) The group should even practice marching on and off the risers so that this may be accomplished with a minimum of confusion.

Not everyone in an audience is capable of judging the musical accomplishments of a choral group, but most will surely be impressed one way or another by the singers' general appearance. The importance of uniform dress is discussed in Chapter 7. In addition, the director should emphasize the importance of body attitudes and facial expressions that reflect the mood of the music. Concentration upon the emotional qualities of the music not only will result in an improved performance and greater audience appreciation, but also will serve to reduce excessive nervousness in the singers.

The choir should be advised always to keep their eyes on the conductor and not on the audience, never to turn their heads to look at the person next to them, never to call attention to any mistakes, and to maintain absolute silence between selections and when offstage. In short, the group should endeavor to be as "professional" as possible.

It is suggested that the director turn part of the rehearsal over to a student conductor or a qualified assistant and listen from the back of the auditorium for choral balance, blend, precision, intonation, and general effect. Most persons generally wish to do their best, and last-minute suggestions are sometimes taken more seriously than advice given during previous rehearsals.

When the music has been memorized, the singers are able to pay closer attention to the conductor and to his interpretative wishes. Most individuals will have memorized the music by the time it is perfected and ready for performance. There may be occasions, however, when it is necessary to use the music. In such instances the singers should be reminded to hold their music so that they can easily see the director—they should keep their noses out of the music and watch him as closely as possible, especially at the beginnings and ends of phrases.

Final instructions concerning the dress for the performance and the meeting time and place prior to the concert should be reiterated at the last rehearsal. To avoid any misunderstanding, it is advisable to place these final instructions on both the bulletin board and the chalkboard. When the performance involves a number of different school, church, or community groups, it has been found profitable to duplicate the instructions and distribute a copy to each individual involved.

The placement of the piano in relationship to the chorus must be considered if it is to enhance the effectiveness of the music and if the correct balance and maximum security of the singers are to be achieved. Generally, the best location for a grand piano is immediately in front of the chorus, rather than at either side. If it is in this position, generally all singers can hear equally well. If only an upright piano is available, then the risers may be divided in the middle and the piano placed between the two sections in such a position that the director can be easily seen. This arrangement has the obvious disadvantage of dividing the singers, but it is outweighed by the increased tonal and rhythmic security they receive.

When a band or an orchestral accompaniment is used, the chorus is usually placed on risers, or on the stage, immediately behind the band or orchestra (Plan 1). From the visual standpoint this arrangement is highly desirable. In addition, it usually enables all the performers to see the conductor more easily. The major problem that usually occurs with this arrangement lies in achieving a proper balance between the two groups. Unless an especially large choral group is performing, it is necessary to lessen considerably the volume of the instrumental group. This is sometimes best accomplished by assigning only one player to a part.

When a satisfactory balance still cannot be achieved, the problem can be lessened to some extent by placing the chorus on one side of the stage, as illustrated in Plan 2. This arrangement allows for a somewhat better projection of the voices.

PLAN 1

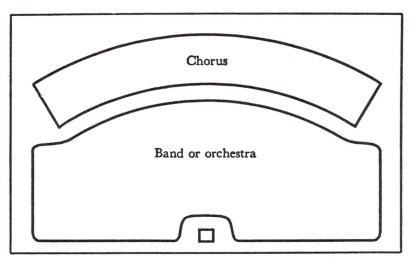

Still another possibility is to divide the chorus and place them on both sides of the instrumental group and to the front of the stage (Plan 3). This arrangement allows for the highest degree of voice projection but has the obvious disadvantage of lessening, to some 'extent, the tonal and rhythmic security of the singers.

Musical productions presented on a stage with adequate facilities can be made much more effective by using appropriate lighting. Through the use of various colors, such as amber, red, blue, green, and pink, during the various choral selections, the emotional effects of the music can be heightened considerably. Lighting color media (gels) for

PLAN 2

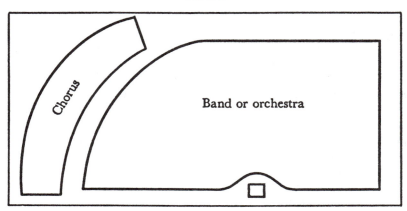

PLAN 3

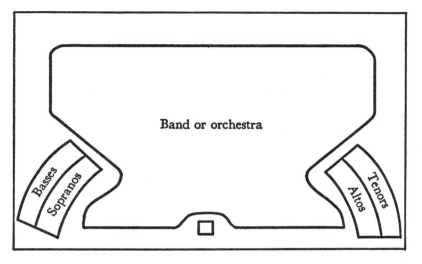

covering spot and stage lights may be obtained in a wide assortment of colors and hues (approximately ninety-five). The imaginative director will be able to identify the predominant color mood or moods of each selection by careful analysis of the music. A cue sheet or a marked copy of the program should be prepared for the electrician, and all lighting effects should be carefully set during the final rehearsal.

The director should stress the importance of an adequate warm-up before the performance. Choir members should be in the rehearsal room at least forty-five minutes prior to the concert. It is important that the temperature of the rehearsal room be approximately that of the auditorium stage. Extreme differences in temperature can have a detrimental effect upon the singers' voices.

A little time devoted to vocalization, reviewing general procedures, and renewing in the singers' minds the tempi and the general moods of the choral selections can prove a profitable aid in achieving an improved performance. It is especially important to review the order of the selections. It is helpful to start each number and sing at least the first phrase or so. This procedure helps the group accustom themselves to the routine of the program. Singers are often likely to be somewhat nervous and "on edge" immediately prior to the concert. The director, therefore, should endeavor to exert a calming influence on the group by talking and chatting informally with them in the warm-up room, prior to entering the auditorium stage.

Careful planning and attention to all the preceding details will contribute substantially to the overall effectivess of the choral concert.

TOPICS FOR DISCUSSION

1. Maintain a file of programs of various types. Discuss the aspects of particular programs you like or dislike, in terms of musical value, unity and variety, and general format.
2. Discuss the importance of achieving audience rapport. By what means may this be achieved?
3. As a class project, prepare individual programs using a unique thematic idea. Discuss the strengths and the weaknesses of these programs in terms of the purposes for which they were designed.
4. Discuss the lighting effects that you feel would enhance the effectiveness of a particular choral program.
5. Discuss the effects of a good program of public relations upon concert attendance and school–community relationships.
6. Recall from your past experience as a singer situations in which the director's careful attention to details during the final rehearsal contributed substantially to the effectiveness of the choral concert.

SELECTED READINGS

CAIN, NOBLE, *Choral Music and Its Practice,* chap. 13. New York: M. Witmark & Sons, 1942.

CHRISTY, VAN A., *Glee Club and Chorus,* chap. 8. New York: G. Schirmer, Inc., 1940.

DAVIS, ENNIS, *More Than a Pitchpipe,* chap. 8. Boston: C. C. Birchard & Co., 1941.

GARRETSON, ROBERT L., "Scheduling Choral Programs and Community Relations," *The Choral Journal,* XX, no. 2 (October 1979), 17–19.

GRAHAM, FLOYD F., *Public Relations in Music Education,* chap. 7. New York: Exposition Press, 1954.

KRONE, MAX T., *The Chorus and Its Conductor,* chaps. 9, 10. San Diego: Neil A. Kjos Music Co., 1945.

WILSON, HARRY R., *A Guide for Choral Conductors,* chap. 4. Morristown, N.J.: Silver Burdett, 1950.

7

Planning and Organization

A practical knowledge of planning and management procedures is as important to the choral director as the techniques of teaching: Many times, the ultimate success of the music program depends on it. The choral conductor is first an organizer, second a teacher, and finally a conductor. A conductor without an understanding of organizational procedures may be seriously impaired in his efforts to develop outstanding musical groups. Certain administrators often judge the effectiveness of the music director by his ability to plan and organize, rather than by his musicianship. They can generally assume that the music teacher has had an adequate training in music; they cannot, however, always assume that the person is an effective organizer.

RECRUITING MEMBERS

The organization and development of new choral groups in various educational institutions, or the improvement of established programs, may in some instances pose a considerable problem to the inexperienced director. A successful choral group demands at least a specific minimum membership, without which it is difficult to achieve any measurable degree of success; naturally the long-range development of a program depends to some extent upon this initial success. Following are suggestions that should prove profitable in the development of the choral music program.

Endeavor to show all individuals that singing can be an enjoyable and a rewarding experience—not an uninteresting mechanical ritual! In schools this may be approached, in the beginning, through well-planned but informal songfests, preferably in groups that are not too large so that effective rapport and communication can be achieved.[1] In churches, informal sings may be promoted as an integral part of the program provided or sponsored for various age groups—that is, boy and girl scouts, youth groups, young married couples' groups, singles' groups, men's organizations, and women's societies.

At the outset of this program, one should use many familiar songs, sung in unison. Singing in unison, with good tone quality and clear diction, can be a satisfying musical experience. This activity, plus the singing of many rounds and canons, provides the background for and serves as a means of stimulating interest in the later group harmonization of favorite songs. Although the emphasis should always be upon the recreational and not the technical aspects of the music, it is possible for the leader to stress the importance of good tone quality and clear diction as it relates to expressive singing. Remarks such as "When you open your mouths wide, you sound so much better," and "Enunciating your words makes this song more enjoyable to sing" contribute toward this end. Several highly successful choral programs were begun in this manner. From the musical seeds sown in these informal sings and assemblies grew a strong desire on the part of many to explore further the vast wealth of choral literature.

With particular reference to school situations the following suggestions are offered. Inviting outstanding choral groups from neighboring schools and from the community at large to present assembly programs may serve to stimulate interest in singing and provide further impetus to the choral music program. One of the local barbershop quartets might prove of special interest to the male students. If individuals are to improve, they must know what they are striving for. Hearing other choral groups provides a means through which students may evaluate their own attitudes and progress.

In certain schools, the biggest problem in recruiting students for choral groups is obtaining an adequate number of boys to sing four-part music for mixed voices (SATB). The reasons for this problem are many, including schedule conflicts with other school activities and athletics. The solution usually comes down to ferreting out the remaining number

[1]For a variety of songs for recreational singing, see the listing at the end of this chapter.

of boys, making the choral program so attractive that an adequate number of singers are drawn from conflicting activities, or both. The organization of a male quartet or octet that may be called upon to sing in the school assembly or elsewhere in the community can have a most desirable effect upon boys who consider choral singing to be a non-masculine activity. To combat this attitude, many successful directors have devoted special attention to establishing rapport with, and subsequently recruiting in the organizations, the leaders of the school athletic teams. Once this group has been won over, the problem of recruiting additional boys is, for obvious reasons, lessened considerably.

Enlisting the cooperation of other teachers in the school to be on the lookout for students who display an interest in music, and who from all indications will be able to meet the established membership qualifications, has in many cases proven most profitable. Some students, to a greater or lesser extent, desire to participate in choral groups, but either are unaware of their capabilities or lack courage enough to express their desires to the choral director.

It is advisable to heed the adage "Nothing succeeds like success." The director should believe in the success of his choral groups. In other words, he should always be optimistic; he should think in positive terms and avoid negative thoughts. A positive attitude is contagious and can have a decidedly beneficial effect on one's singers.

SELECTING ACCOMPANISTS

Capable accompanists are essential to effective rehearsals and to the success of the choir. The director should, of course, always be on the lookout for pianistic talents in the school. Some personal characteristics of a good accompanist are dependability, cooperativeness, and a desire to contribute to the school choral music program. Musical abilities include a piano technique sufficient to play the accompaniment to the choral music being performed, a reasonable ability to sight-read new and unfamiliar music, a sensitivity to the problems the choir is having, and, when the director stops the group for comments, knowing what pitches to provide the choir for a fresh start (this last ability may need to be developed through experience).

When auditioning prospective accompanists, ask each student to first play two selections (or portions thereof) of contrasting musical styles—to enable the director to determine the overall level of technique and musicianship. In other words, what is he or she pianistically capable of? To determine the student's sight-reading abilities, have him or her play the accompaniment to one or more of the choral pieces that the choir is presently performing or that the director is contemplating using. Other suggestions for sight reading are Bach chorales and accompaniments to art songs.

When an "ideal" accompanist is found, a director should feel fortunate; however, this will not always be the case. In high schools it is often desirable to have several accompanists, each of whom can be assigned to work on specific pieces and can substitute when one of the others is ill or absent. Also, more than one accompanist is necessary if sectional rehearsals are held periodically.

In schools with a relatively high socioeconomic level (where parents start their children studying piano at an early age), locating suitable accompanists may not be difficult. In less affluent schools, however, these conditions do not always exist, and the director may be forced to employ some capable adult within the community to accompany the choir(s). Also, directors should be in constant communication with teachers and students in "feeder" schools to encourage piano study and to inform younger students of the musical opportunities that exist for them when they reach high school.

In working with accompanists, the following procedures are very important.

1. Give the accompanists their new music well in advance of the time they will be expected to play it. At that time indicate or demonstrate appropriate tempi, dynamics, phrasing, and so on.
2. Meet with the accompanists prior to the first rehearsal of the new music, or the time they will be expected to play the accompaniments.
3. Identify any problems and apprise the students of their progress.
4. Be supportive and provide encouragement! Stimulate in each student the desire to improve his or her accompanying skills and to contribute to the choir.
5. Discuss with students the appropriate procedures for giving pitches (for example, individual pitches played slowly from the lowest to the highest, proper dynamic levels, and so on).

Accompanists' names should always be listed on printed programs, and proper acknowledgment should be given them during each choral concert.

STIMULATING INTEREST

Individuals are normally motivated in a variety of ways toward music participation. There are relatively few whose initial interest is entirely *intrinsic*—that is, whose desire to study music emerges primarily from a love of the music itself. Nevertheless, such interest not only is admirable, but also might well be considered one of the ultimate goals of music education. The skilled director who displays a great enthusiasm for music will normally make great strides in developing in individuals a love for music and the desire to explore and experience the vast wealth of music literature. It is not suggested, however, that the choir director depend entirely upon this intrinsic interest in the development of the choral music program. In a normal situation, one will find that everyone is interested in music to a greater or a lesser extent. The problem usually occurs with the half-interested person who either is "exploring" the activity or is merely anxious to remain in the company of his friends. The experienced director, however, takes a realistic attitude and utilizes many means to help accomplish his goal or purpose. Sometimes these techniques or methods are described as *extrinsic* means of motivation; that is, the director motivates such a person by taking advantage of interests that lie outside the music itself.

Following are suggestions that might be placed in either of the previously mentioned categories and, if utilized, will not only stimulate interest in music participation, but will also result in other values that contribute to the development of the choral music program.

Exchange Concerts

Exchange concerts with neighboring communities are valuable in that they provide the singers a "yardstick" for the evaluation of the progress of their own music groups, as well as serving as an introduction to varied types of music literature. In addition, valuable and lasting friendships are sometimes made with individuals from other schools or communities.

Guest Conductors

Using guest conductors for rehearsals and concerts can be a valuable musical experience for chorus members. As a result of this experience, singers necessarily become more alert to the conducting movements of the director and develop an awareness of varying types of musical interpretation. Such an arrangement can usually be made on an exchange basis with directors from neighboring institutions. Whenever financial arrangements can be made, however, it would seem highly desirable to invite a nationally known choral conductor to work with the choir or chorus for a day or two. These rehearsals may culminate in a public concert. A practice that is quite prevalent, and certainly more economical, is for a number of neighboring schools or churches to join together and direct their efforts toward one large musical festival. Between schools, lines of communication usually are set up by the principals; therefore, it is quite natural for those in the same activities conference to join together for this event.

Attending Concerts

Group solidarity and a feeling of belonging—so important to the ultimate success of an organization—are often facilitated when members of a choral organization attend as a group various musical events presented in the community or in nearby towns or cities. In addition, a broader understanding and a greater appreciation of music are often developed by the group.

Choral Recordings

Recordings of professional, collegiate, church, and community choral groups are often used to introduce new musical selections to the group, and as a means of studying various types of interpretation. A variety of listening experiences is helpful in broadening the singers' musical horizons and in improving their musical tastes.

Tape Recordings as a Rehearsal Aid

The use of a tape recorder during rehearsals can be a most effective means of facilitating the singers' musical development. As an aid in improving the interpretation of a musical selection it is in many ways unsurpassable. Often the well-chosen words of the director, expressing a specific desired effect, are comparatively ineffective, whereas the playback of a tape recording usually has a profound effect on the listeners.

Production and Sale of Recordings

Provided the musical development of the organization warrants it, it may be profitable to produce and sell recordings of the group. Such a project not only serves to stimulate the singers' interest, but also focuses the community's interest on the choral music program—certainly a most desirable objective.

Group Photographs

The experienced director is well aware of the enthusiasm created when organization pictures are taken. They have for a long time been utilized as a means of developing esprit de corps in groups. People of all ages enjoy pictures, but school-age youth are especially interested in photographs that include themselves and their peers.

The Rehearsal-Room Bulletin Board

The bulletin board may be used advantageously—for posting general announcements, magazine or newspaper articles of general interest, organization photographs, and various other types of pictures and cartoons dealing with music topics. All of these are effective means for stimulating interest in music.

Radio and Television Broadcasts

The choral group that is fortunate enough to participate in radio or television broadcasts will usually be highly motivated to prepare for the program.[2] As a result, most directors would agree that such opportunities are a profitable educational experience for the persons involved. Many local stations want to schedule programs of general public interest. Because the nature or the content of choral music programs is especially appropriate for programming during the Christmas and Lenten seasons, many community music groups may be heard at these times. Unfortunately, in some localities, opportunities such as these are not frequently available for all choral groups. In such instances, however, many directors endeavor to utilize these educational media in other ways—by announcing at rehearsals various noteworthy programs or posting notices of them on the bulletin board. In this way the choir members may benefit considerably from the programs themselves, as well as from discussions of them later.

Publication of Yearbooks or Newsletters

Many school music groups have found it extremely profitable, in terms of developing individual interest, to publish a yearly booklet in which photographs, comments on noteworthy performances, and various anecdotes about the organization's members are included. Other groups publish periodically a newsletter with equal success. In most groups there are people who have a keen interest in writing and who will benefit especially from this experience.

Awards

The presentation of letters, pins, or keys to outstanding students, or to students who have participated for a specified length of time, has long been an effective means of stimulating interest in school music groups. Some directors have found the establishment of a point system to be quite effective in implementing such a plan. That is, to receive an award a student must be credited with a specified number of points. For example, points may be given for attendance at regular and special rehearsals, participation in concerts and music festivals, or participation as a soloist or a member of an ensemble at competition-festivals or at various functions in the community. It is usually advisable for a commit-

---

[2]Choral conductors should acquaint themselves with the hand signals used in television studios. See the Appendix.

tee selected by the students to work with the director in setting up the system of awards.

Social Events

Dances, mixers, and parties provide a splendid opportunity for the development of esprit de corps and the feeling of belonging that can contribute so much to the eventual success of an organization. In addition to serving as a means of strengthening personal relationships within the group, they can be utilized as money-making activities.

Newspaper Publicity

Adequate newspaper coverage of concerts can be of considerable assistance in the development of the choral music program. Newspaper editors are eager to receive information concerning news events that they believe will be of special community interest. Many newspapers have a prescribed format to be followed in preparing news items. Learning and following these procedures will often facilitate communication and the release of the news item. Early submission of an item that has no particular release time enables a paper to use it whenever it will fit their makeup. The importance of maintaining friendly relationships with the local newspaper staff, and submitting articles that are carefully written, cannot be overemphasized.

Competition-Festivals

Music competition-festivals may contribute substantially to the development of the music program. Adjudicators' remarks may prove helpful to singers and director alike. Opportunity is also provided for hearing other school music groups and for making many lasting acquaintances with individuals from other communities. Perhaps the major criticism levied against contests—not the only one, however—is that too much emphasis is placed upon the competitive aspects, and that singers often become emotionally upset over the preparation, the performance, and the final ratings. In certain instances this criticism may be true; however, it should not be interpreted as a condemnation of contests. Prior to participation in such events, the director must prepare his groups emotionally for any eventual outcome. He will encourage concentrated effort during rehearsals and performances. Nevertheless, he will strive to develop in his singers a realistic life attitude. In our present-day society, too much emphasis is placed upon winning "first prize" in various fields of endeavor, or being named the star of the show or the hero of the game. Individuals failing to reach their goals often assume a defeatist attitude. The director can render a genuine service to his singers by helping them to develop a proper perspective.

THE EVALUATION OF CHORUS MEMBERS

The evaluation of choir members should be a continuous process from the first rehearsal to the end of each formal grading period. Without specific established criteria, directors may easily succumb to the pitfall of giving all the students the same grade. This is certainly an undesirable practice, for if a group is to progress at a desired level, then the students must be evaluated on the basis of their accomplishments.

For a group to be properly evaluated, students must know the course objectives and the teacher's expectations. In this respect, it is suggested that teachers prepare a course syllabus that includes the following: objectives of the course; content of the course—that is, music to be rehearsed and performed (this information is helpful to parents as well); expectations as regards attendance; performance dates, time, and place, and an indication of the total number that will occur during the school year; the importance of attitude toward the achievement of the group's performance objectives; the care of choir robes or other attire; and specific criteria that will be used in the grading procedure and the percentage allocated to each. For example:

Written examinations	40%
Performance (singing exams)	40%
Attendance, effort, and attitude	20%
Total	100%

Examinations are, of course, time consuming, both in their preparation and in the grading, but it is felt that there should be some balance between the written and the performance types, since both contribute to improved musicianship. Various types of written tests may be given. One might simply cover the text of the music. A particular phrase could be given with directions for the student to write, in the space provided, the words of the succeeding phrase. This type of quiz may be given periodically and is helpful in that it stimulates singers to make a special effort to memorize the words of a piece. Some students learn words quite readily; some, however, can sing a piece for an entire semester or even longer and not memorize the text by simple repetition. These students, in particular, need the stimulation of quizzes to force them to make a special effort. In the memorization of poetry, students are advised to identify and memorize the key words in each phrase to help trigger their recall.[3]

[3]For further suggestions or procedures on memorization, see the section titled "Memorizing the Music" near the end of Chapter 4.

Written exams or quizzes may also be given on such content as musical markings, texture, harmonic structure of a particular piece, rhythmic patterns, and melodic patterns (for example, "Circle the wrong pitch or note in the following phrase").

In evaluating performance capabilities, the director will want to consider each singer's tone quality, ability to carry his or her own part, and blend and balance with the other singers. To help set a procedure for determining this, the director may divide the entire choir into quartets (SATB) and during the evaluation period identify the quartet and the specific beginning point in a selected piece. The length of time each quartet sings will depend upon the director's having adequate time to focus upon each individual singer in the quartet and make a judgment on tone, blend, balance, phrasing, and the ability to carry his or her part. It is advisable to rotate the selections used for various quartets, and when exams are given periodically, the director will wish to note both the grade in his gradebook and a code number for the selection so that a different one may be used on the next exam. Some directors may prefer to set aside a particular time and have each quartet sing in his office; however, this is more difficult to arrange and certainly more time consuming. One advantage of the quartet assignment is that students may be encouraged to practice together during out-of-school hours in preparation for the next exam. When this occurs, many benefits may accrue to the singers as a result of this small ensemble experience where they all more readily hear their own parts, which will facilitate the development of improved tone quality, balance, blend, and general musicianship.[4]

TESTING AND CLASSIFYING VOICES

Among choral directors, it is accepted procedure to audition individuals before admitting them to membership in an organization. In some cases, the audition is used as a means of limiting membership and obtaining the best voices for the choir or chorus. Directors using the procedure primarily for this purpose justify it as a necessary means of providing the selected singers with the best possible musical experience. It is most desirable to develop and maintain highly selective choral groups, provided that the remaining individuals are not prevented from participating in some group as a result. Opportunity for participation in a wide variety of choral groups and ensembles should be provided, so that the musical and the social needs of *all* interested persons are met. Auditions also provide a means of determining the singer's vocal range and voice

[4]As an alternative to assigning students in quartets, the director may wish to play three parts on the piano, with the singer filling in the fourth part to make up the quartet.

quality so that he or she may be assigned the voice part to which he or she is best suited and by which that singer can make the best contribution to the group. Since most adolescent voices are quite unstable and are still in the process of change, it is advisable to retest voices periodically in order to avoid unnecessary strain from singing in an improper vocal range.

In classifying voices, the director must take two criteria into consideration—*range* and *quality*. The following procedure is suggested as a means of determining these factors.

1. Determine the approximate middle range of the student's voice and start there.
2. Using Exercise 18, vocalize upward, noting the point at which excessive strain occurs or at which the quality of the voice changes to any noticeable degree.

EXERCISE 18

3. Using Exercise 19, vocalize from the middle range downward, noting the point at which the quality of the voice changes. The low range is as important as the higher limits of the voice. Little benefit can come to a voice that is forced downward in an attempt to sing too low a part.

EXERCISE 19

The voice ranges in Figure 69 are only approximate classifications, and the ranges of many singers do not always fall easily into these categories. The vocal range of some individuals may be considerably smaller than, and some may conceivably cover the ranges of two or more of, the classifications presented. In any case, one must listen carefully to the quality of the voice and determine the range in which it sounds most natural—that is, where the person sings with the best voice quality and with the least amount of strain or effort. This is most readily accomplished by utilizing some easy song material. The well-known English folk song "Drink to Me Only with Thine Eyes" is excellent for this purpose, and may be found in many songbooks compiled for community singing.

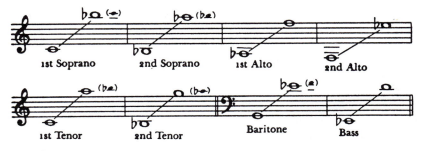

FIGURE 69   A general classification of voice ranges of untrained singers.

As a further guide in determining the proper voice classification of singers, the following voice qualities are considered characteristic.

First Soprano—light, flutelike, lyric quality.

Second Soprano—similar in range to the first soprano, but has a fuller, more dramatic voice quality.

First Alto—similar in quality to the second soprano, but has a more developed lower range.

Second Alto—a heavier, deeper voice quality, especially in the lower range, which is more developed than the first alto voice.

First Tenor—light, lyric quality, especially in the upper range limits.

Second Tenor—similar in range to the first tenor, but has a fuller, more dramatic voice quality.

Baritone—often similar in quality to the second tenor, yet has a more fully developed middle and lower range. (Initial voice characteristics may be deceiving; it is in this category that many true tenor voices may be identified and developed. Periodical retesting is recommended.)

Bass—a heavier, darker, deeper quality, especially in the middle and lower ranges of the voice.

In addition to determining voice quality and range, many directors like to test the singer's ability to read music and to carry a harmony part independently. The aforementioned song is also excellent for this purpose. A suggested procedure is as follows:[5]

1. For all female voices, request the person to sing the alto part. For male voices, request the individual to sing either the bass or the tenor part, depending upon the singer's vocal range and previous musical experience.

2. Provide the starting note or a short introduction. Accompany the singer, playing all the voice parts *except* the one he or she is requested to sing. (Omitting this part enables the director to determine more readily the extent to which a singer can carry a part without help from others in his

[5]It is assumed that the individual has been oriented to the song through singing the melody during the previous part of the audition.

section. This information is invaluable in assigning seating in an organization. "Followers" may be judiciously placed between "leaders," and from the reading standpoint the total effectiveness of the choral group will be enhanced.)

3. Because of some singers' lack of experience, it may occasionally be necessary to provide some assistance with their parts. This procedure is justifiable, since the director really wants to determine just how quickly the individuals "catch on." In some instances, repeating the song a time or two (with less assistance each time) will enable the director to determine the singer's musical memory and his ability to adjust to and profit from assistance provided during rehearsals.

Following is a suggested list of other songs that might be utilized for voice auditions. These selections may be located in most songbooks compiled for community singing.

All through the Night (old Welch air)
Tell Me Why (college song)
My Homeland (from *Finlandia*)
Believe Me if All Those Endearing Young Charms
Annie Laurie
Fairest Lord Jesus (German folk song)
Juanita (Spanish air)
Jacob's Ladder (spiritual)

Many choral conductors have found it advantageous to maintain a permanent record for each choir member. Readily available information, included on personnel cards, can be helpful in administering the total choral music program. Figure 70 shows a sample card, which may be altered or adapted to suit individual tastes.

SEATING ARRANGEMENTS

Choral conductors generally have found, through experimentation, that certain seating arrangements are preferable to others. The type of arrangement selected usually depends upon several factors, including the number of voices assigned to or available for each part, the comparative voice qualities of various members, and the relative musical experience of the singers. Plans 4–14 show several suggested seating arrangements for mixed voices, and the advantages of each are listed.

The advantages of the arrangement of Plan 4 are as follows:

1. One of the problems confronting choral directors seems to be the development of tenor voices. When placed in the front of the choir, the tenors are more easily heard and may therefore sing in a more natural voice, thus improving the blend of the group.

PERSONAL DATA

Name: _____

Address: _____

_____ Phone: _____

Previous musical experience: _____

Part(s) previously sung: S1, S2, A1, A2, T1, T2, B1, B2

Height:_____ Weight: _____ Chest Measurement: _____

. . . .

Range: _____

Voice timbre: S. A. T. B.

Comments: _____

Quality: 1 2 3 4 5   Part assigned: S1, S2, A1, A2

Intonation: 1 2 3 4 5   T1, T2, B1, B2

S. Reading: 1 2 3 4 5   Robe no. assigned: _____

FIGURE 70   A sample personal data card. The vocal range in which the individual sings with comparative ease may be indicated in red; the undeveloped part of the vocal range may be indicated in blue.

2. At times the tenor part may need to be reinforced. If some of the second altos need to be used for this purpose, they will be close enough to effect a reasonably good blend.

3. The soprano and the bass sections are relatively close together. The proximity of these two sections, which are the outside two parts of the harmonic structure, can effect a stability to the chord and thus help to improve intonation.

4. The placement of a limited number of girls behind the boys can assist in the development of a better blend among the various sections. Choral blend is dependent to a great extent upon the ability of the singers to hear the other parts adequately. This seating arrangement in which the female

PLAN 4

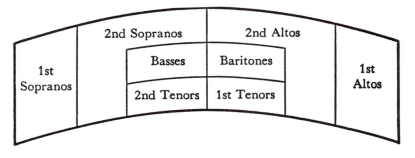

PLAN 5

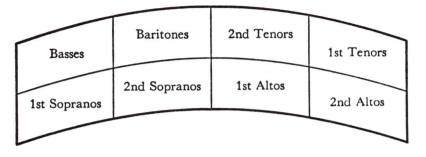

voices literally surround the male section increases the latter's awareness of the upper parts and provides increased tonal support, which is especially desirable for unstable adolescent male voices.

Plan 5 shows another suggested arrangement that may be used effectively when the membership of boys is adequate in both quantity and quality. The advantages of this arrangement are as follows:

1. With the taller students in each section standing toward the outside, a more uniform appearance is achieved—producing a total effect noticeably different from the first arrangement. The difference in height between the boys and girls is not accentuated, as it would be were they placed in the same row.
2. Both choirs are reasonably close together and may function as separate units if necessary. (In terms of providing variety to a choral program, the inclusion of numbers arranged exclusively for male or female voices is highly desirable.)
3. In the event that the first tenor part needs to be reinforced with altos, the proximity of the second alto section would provide the maximum support and enable the singers to achieve a reasonably good blend.
4. The proximity of the soprano and the bass sections effects a certain stability to the harmonic structure and assists in improving intonation.

The preceding arrangements have one advantage in common; that is, the grouping together of the voices on the same part provides a degree of security for the singers, particularly those in young choirs. However, with the security of singing next to others on the same part also goes the danger of some singers becoming overly dependent upon certain leaders within their section. If these leaders happen to be absent on a particular day, the effectiveness of the entire section is often hampered. It behooves the choral conductor, therefore, to seek ways to strengthen the aural sense of all the singers in his groups. The director's objective should be the development of individual security through vocal independence, not dependence. Seating arrangements may make their

PLAN 6

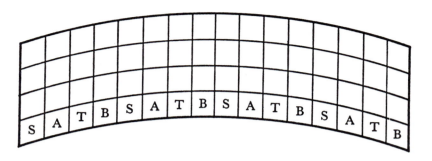

contribution to this end. After the choir members have had a certain minimal musical training, it is desirable for the director to experiment with different seating arrangements, in which each singer will be better able to hear himself or herself and to evaluate his or her efforts properly.

One arrangement, used for a number of years, is the placement of choir members by quartets; that is, SATB or any combination thereof, as shown in Plan 6.[6] The quartet seating arrangement usually results in the achievement of better balance and blend. Although the voice parts are arranged in rows from the front to rear of the choir, each singer is nevertheless able to hear himself or herself—and the other voice parts— better. Some conductors assign singers to quartets (or octets) on a continuing basis and utilize these groupings periodically for small ensemble practice. In school situations some conductors, at intervals of about six weeks, will request each quartet to sing a portion of selected music for evaluative purposes.

Another arrangement involves placing each singer as far as possible from another singing the same part, thus enabling each to hear his or her own voice better and to evaluate his or her efforts toward improved tone quality, diction, balance and blend, and intonation. This arrangement, used by Robert Shaw, has been designated the *scrambled setup* by Louis Diercks. Plan 7 is for a choir of nine first sopranos, seven second sopranos, eight first altos, seven second altos, five first tenors, seven second tenors, eight baritones, and seven basses.[7]

One of the most striking results of the use of this arrangement is improved balance and blend. The weaker singers are not in a position to affect the others in the section adversely, all singers can hear themselves

---

[6]Some directors use the arrangement TSAB, whereas others prefer BSAT.

[7]Louis H. Diercks, "The Individual in the Choral Situation," *The NATS Bulletin,* 17, no. 4 (May 15, 1961), 7. Used by permission.

PLAN 7

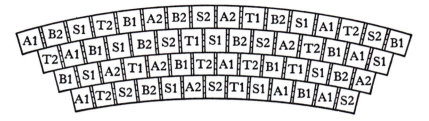

better, and, with the sound of any particular part coming from all areas of the choir, there seems to be a better fusion of sound.[8]

Because the voices in the front row are nearest to and the first to reach the audience, Diercks suggests placing the more select singers in this position to serve as a "mask" to the choir.[9] Also, when a sufficient number of choir risers are available, it is desirable to space the singers slightly farther apart than usual. This also contributes to the objectives of this arrangement.

Some conductors prefer to use either the quartet arrangement or the scrambled setup exclusively, even when introducing new music. Others prefer to use a more conventional setup until they feel that the singers possess at least a minimal understanding of, and ability to sing, their parts. For the latter group, Plan 8 is suggested. While the singers are learning the music in their respective sections, the voice parts are at least divided or arranged so as to achieve a somewhat better blend, or fusion of sound, than in some of the traditional arrangements.

Directors of junior high school choirs often use SAB music arrangements because of a lack of well-developed tenor voices. Plan 9 is suggested for this voice combination. Because of the insecurity of the male voices of this age group, it is desirable to place them toward the front of the choir where they will be nearly surrounded by the female voices. This will ensure their being heard more easily and will result in a better balance and blend. As the group progresses, and as the individual voices mature, it will become feasible to introduce some easy four-part (SATB) music. At this particular stage of development, the tenor voices are likely to be especially insecure, and perhaps fewer in number. Therefore, seating this group of voices in front of the baritones will also contribute to the balance and blend of the group.

[8]Both the quartet arrangement and the scrambled setup are desirable for use primarily with music of a homophonic texture. When performing polyphonic music, the choir should use a traditional formation, because the beauty of polyphony results from the interplay of the voice parts stemming from various sections of the choir.

[9]Diercks, "The Individual in the Choral Situation," p. 7.

PLAN 8

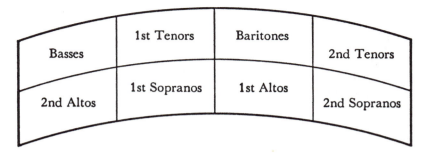

PLAN 9

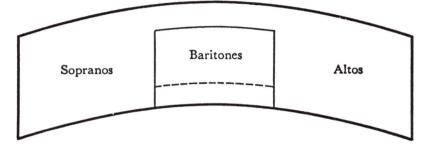

For directors of treble voice choirs, the seating arrangements shown in Plans 10, 11, and 12 are suggested. Plan 10 is for grade school choirs comprising selected fifth- and sixth-grade students. This plan allows for flexibility in rehearsing and programming a variety of music suitable for this age group. The repertoire will usually include a combination of two- and three-part music, some of which is learned in the general music class. When singing two-part music, the group placed in the center will sing their respective soprano or alto parts. When singing

PLAN 10

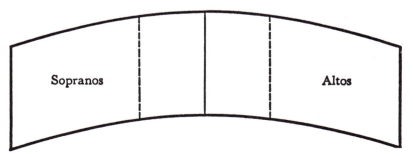

PLAN 11

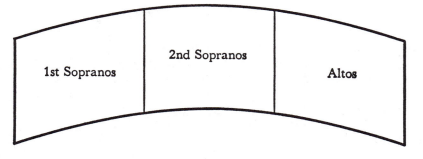

three-part music, they will sing the second soprano part. The group of students for this shifting, flexible role should be carefully selected through auditions held prior to the first rehearsal.

Plan 11 is suggested for girls' glee clubs in junior and senior high school, and for women's choruses on the college or adult level. Although a sufficient amount of three-part music is available for girls' glee clubs, the more proficient organizations may ultimately desire to include some SSAA music in their repertoire because of the more complete harmonic effects. In such instances, the alto parts will necessarily have to divide, as indicated in Plan 12.

Since both SSA and SSAA arrangements may be utilized in a given program, both Plan 11 and Plan 12 will be found practical because of the adjacency of the second soprano and the alto parts. To achieve an adequate balance, it may be necessary, for example, to assign a few second sopranos, designated as "roving singers," to the first alto part. Or, in other instances, a few altos may be used to bolster the second soprano part. These two seating arrangements allow for a flexible assignment of adjacent parts to meet the requirements of the music being performed.

Plans 13 and 14 are suitable for use with male glee clubs. The arrangement shown in Plan 13 generally will be the more suitable, es-

PLAN 12

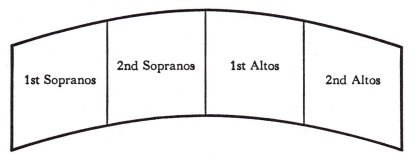

PLAN 13

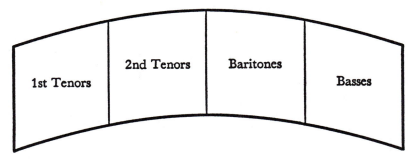

pecially when an adequate number of boys is available to balance the parts. However, when there is a definite lack of tenor voices, Plan 14 may provide an alternative solution. When the tenor voices are placed toward the front, they are more likely to be heard, and a more effective balance may be achieved.

In seating the students, it is advisable to place the stronger voices and some of the better readers toward the back of the group. In such a position they will be better able to assist the rest of the singers. It is also advisable to scatter some of the better readers throughout the choir, in order to stabilize the group.

In an effort to achieve the best choral blend, it is advisable to place singers with strident voices between singers with a more natural vocal production. Individuals are inclined to simulate or assume the voice qualities of the persons nearest them. When several singers of a similar voice quality are seated together, this particular quality is sometimes strengthened and the resultant tone becomes stronger and out of proportion to the number of singers with that particular quality. The same principle may also adversely affect intonation. When several chronic flatters (caused by faulty voice production) are seated together, intonation problems are sometimes magnified. When these singers are dis-

PLAN 14

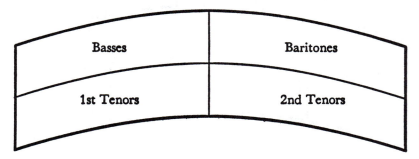

tributed within the group, intonation problems are usually lessened considerably.

Another factor to take into consideration is the height of the choir members. It is recommended that the taller individuals be placed toward the outside and the back of the group. Especially when the singers are on choral risers, this arrangement will enable them to see better the conducting movements of the director and will result in greater security of the entire group.

Directors will find it highly profitable to experiment with a variety of seating arrangements. Given plans may be more effective with certain groups than with others, and periodic changes in arrangements will sometimes contribute to the betterment of the choral organization.

THE CHORAL CURRICULUM

The development of music education in America has been marked by different emphases during various periods or decades. During the 1930s, for example, there was much emphasis on the *a cappella* choir, and the choral literature of the time reflected this emphasis on unaccompanied singing. During the 1940s and the 1950s, the emphasis was on diction and methods and means of improving choral tone. Concurrently during the 1950s, certain educators expounded upon the beauty and the spiritual values of choral music as a means of fulfilling a basic human need. During the 1960s, and perhaps related to the effect of "Sputnik" upon the American educational system, music began to be considered as an "academic discipline." In a way, many subjects in the school curriculum needed to prove their worth and be justified, particularly in view of the continually increasing costs of education. During this period, and also during the 1970s, choral music fulfilled the dual purpose of not only providing worthwhile aesthetic experiences, but also (perhaps to keep pace with the other subject-matter areas) developing a definite subject-matter content of its own. An important aspect of these dual objectives focused upon the adherence to authentic performance practices. This emphasis has been extended and perhaps intensified in the 1980s.

Fortunately, musicologists have provided the choral profession with considerable insight into the performance practices of music from various historical periods, while music theorists have developed college courses in musical styles (or analytical techniques) that develop the prospective teacher's capacities to analyze, create, and more thoroughly understand the music of particular composers, as well as the more generalized characteristics of the music of different historical periods. Thus a sizable body of course content has developed for choral conductors, one that not only enhances the aesthetic experience, but also provides students with insights and understanding of the stylistic aspects of music of various historical periods. Students also gain a comprehension of the ongoing social, economic, and political forces during the life of a particular composer and how these served as a "framework" for his creative output.

To develop student understanding of musical style and specific performance practices, the conductor need not resort to extensive lectures, which might prove "deadly" and defeat his purposes. Rather, he should endeavor to relate, in a succinct manner, pertinent information as it applies to the performance of a particular musical selection. As a result, musical enjoyment can be increased, students will gain a greater understanding of their musical heritage, and the artistic level of musical performances may be increased substantially. The conductor with adequate college preparation can achieve these goals without undue effort, providing he plans carefully for all his rehearsals.

Whereas dietitians and physicians speak of a balanced nutritional diet, musicians refer to a balanced musical diet—that is, the development of a choral curriculum that will provide students with some experience and comprehension of music of all types and styles, including music from the Renaissance, Baroque, Classical, Romantic, and Modern periods, folk music, and music of a popular, stylized nature. Often one particular choral group is unable to cover literature this broad in scope. Therefore, various groups are sometimes included in the choral curriculum, each with a slightly different focus, but all designed to meet the varied musical needs and interests of students.

In developing a balanced choral music program, the director may frequently ask himself, "How many and what types of choral groups should I have?" Certainly the answer to this question depends upon the situation as it exists in a specific school. The size of the school and the existing need are both determining factors. The most successful school choral programs usually include a selected mixed choir or chorus with other junior groups used as "feeders" to the advanced group. This does not mean to suggest the exclusion of particular students from the advanced groups. Rather, it implies the necessity for choral experience commensurate with the level of each singer's musical development. The choral program should be based upon meeting the needs of all students, and everyone with the desire should have the opportunity to participate in some choral group.

Students enter the junior high school with a variety of previous experience and backgrounds. Although most of them have benefited from the general music program in the elementary school, certain pupils may have been fortunate enough to participate in grade school choruses comprising selected fifth- and sixth-grade students. Figure 71 illustrates

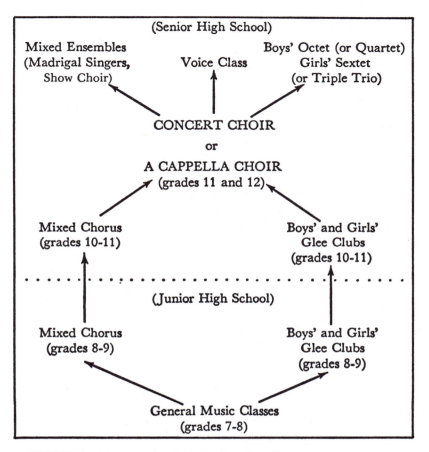

FIGURE 71 A junior-senior high school vocal music program.

the type and the variety of choral groups that the secondary school may endeavor to maintain. It also illustrates two alternative approaches in the basic pattern of organization. Both programs are predicated upon the philosophy of meeting the needs of all students—that is, providing an opportunity for all students who so desire to participate in choral singing.

The general music class is usually required by most junior high schools. In some instances this class is required only of seventh-grade pupils, while being optional or elective for eighth-grade students. In general music classes, students are provided the opportunity to explore special music areas of particular interest. Although some schools enroll seventh-grade students in selective choral groups, it is desirable to delay this particular experience until the eighth grade. At this point the music program usually becomes more selective, and students are encouraged to participate in some activity of special interest, whether it be choral or instrumental music, fine or industrial arts, home economics, or some other area. In the late spring, before the close of school, seventh-grade students may be offered the opportunity of auditioning for the more selective eighth- and ninth-grade choral groups.

Junior High School Choral Groups

As indicated in Figure 71, the organization of special groups may follow one of several patterns. Some schools organize a boys' and girls' glee club for eighth- and ninth-grade students. Where school enrollments are particularly large, separate boys' and girls' glee clubs are often maintained for *both* eighth- and ninth-grade students. This plan of organization is predicated on the belief that during early adolescence boys and girls enjoy participating in activities with their own sex. Another reason advanced is that the music composed or arranged for boys' and girls' glee clubs is more closely in line with their particular interests and musical tastes. Advocates of this position advance the argument that these types of musical experience differ considerably from the standard choral literature for mixed voices, and should be an integral part of the junior high school students' background.

Administrators and music educators in other schools feel that boys and girls should have experiences that bring them together under socially desirable conditions; thus they advocate the *mixed chorus* as the most ideal plan of organization. Still other schools, recognizing the values of both glee clubs and mixed groups, compromise between these two alternatives and thus capitalize upon the strong points of both plans of organization. In such instances, the girls' glee club rehearses during school hours on Monday and Wednesday, and the boys' glee club on Tuesday and Thursday. Then on Friday the two groups rehearse together.[10] Thus, during their separate rehearsals the students have the opportunity to become better acquainted with the literature for either male or female voices and also to rehearse separately their parts for the SATB (or SAB) music, which they will rehearse jointly on Fridays. For junior high schools this plan is advocated as the one that best meets the needs of the majority of students.

Senior High School Choral Groups

In the senior high school, the "combined" plan may also be followed for the "junior" groups, but owing to scheduling difficulties stu-

---

[10]Under this plan of organization, each student has the opportunity to participate in choral music activities for three periods a week—that is, either M-W-F or T-Th-F. On alternate days he or she may be scheduled to participate in physical education, art, home economics, industrial arts, or some other class, depending upon the particular school situation.

dents generally participate in either a mixed chorus or a boys' or a girls' glee club. (In certain schools, where the enrollment is exceptionally large, both types of organizations may be maintained.) It is desirable to schedule these groups for a minimum of three periods a week. In four-year high schools (grades 9–12), the membership in the mixed chorus (sometimes referred to as the junior choir) and the glee clubs generally comprises ninth- and tenth-grade students. In three-year high schools (grades 10–12), the membership in these organizations will consist primarily of tenth-grade students, plus a limited number of eleventh-grade students who were not accepted for membership in the advanced choir. Because of the greater variety and amount of literature available for mixed voices, and since in many cases it may be more practical to schedule one organization than two, the mixed chorus is felt to be the most flexible arrangement. In addition, since all "senior" or advanced choral groups depend upon a "feeder" organization for their ultimate success, student experiences in singing music for mixed voices, prior to membership in the advanced choir, may contribute substantially to the degree of proficiency that the latter organization is able to achieve.

The "Concert Choir" and the "A Cappella Choir" are two names commonly given the selective choral group in the high school.[11] By maintaining a selective choral group, higher musical standards may be achieved and the participating singers will benefit from a higher quality of musical experiences. Because the school's musical groups provide a "bridge of understanding" between the school and the community, it is highly desirable to develop and maintain a choral group that achieves and maintains high musical standards. The membership will usually consist of eleventh- and twelfth-grade students (juniors and seniors). A selective choral group, to achieve the maximum degree of musical proficiency, should rehearse at least five days a week, Monday through Friday. The most effective rehearsal time is during the morning, since students often become overly fatigued during the afternoon hours.

Small Vocal Ensembles

For particularly talented and interested students, experience in various small ensembles should also be provided. Participation in either an octet or a quartet will provide an outlet for boys who desire male companionship and the opportunity to explore the literature composed

[11]Although the term *a cappella* choir is still used as a name for mixed choral groups in particular schools, it should be noted that the term is somewhat archaic and a "holdover" from several decades ago, when the trend was to perform music *a cappella* (without accompaniment) almost exclusively. Today, the practice is to choose the repertoire for its musical worth, and as a result, conductors generally achieve a reasonable balance between unaccompanied music and music with instrumental accompaniment—that is, with either piano, organ, string, wind, or percussion instruments, or an ensemble of instruments in various combinations.

and arranged especially for male voices. Participation in a sextet or a triple trio will provide a similar opportunity for the especially talented girls in the school.

The mixed ensemble, however, may provide a unique musical experience. Many schools organize a group of "madrigal singers," with a membership usually of twelve to sixteen voices. These groups generally devote themselves to a thorough study of madrigal singing and related types of choral literature. Other schools may organize a show choir, ranging from sixteen to twenty-four voices, devoted to the study and performance of popular, stylized arrangements. Although the latter group is given various names, the title "The Modernaires" is descriptive of the choral music performed (see Chapter 5 on the jazz/show choir). Often the school enrollment and the degree of student interest necessitate the maintenance of both types of small mixed choral ensembles— that is, both a madrigal group and a "jazz" or "show" choir. If only enough students are available for one mixed ensemble, however, the group should study, rehearse, and perform a wider variety of choral literature, rather than devote itself to only one type or style of choral music.

Small vocal ensembles should rehearse at least twice weekly. In some cases the singers will find a "free" period during the day in which rehearsals can be scheduled. When this is not possible, rehearsals will have to be scheduled before or after school hours or during the noon period. The smaller ensembles, such as trios, quartets, sextets, and octets, may be encouraged to schedule, during the evening hours, an additional weekly rehearsal at one of the members' homes. Although the most desirable arrangement would have the director meet with the singers during every rehearsal, his busy schedule may not permit him to do so. Thus these evening rehearsals, if deemed necessary or desirable according to the local situation, may be conducted by one of the more talented student leaders. Such opportunity provides valuable experience for students who may eventually enter teacher training programs.

The Voice Class

The high school voice class is an adjunct of the choral program. It is usually taught by the choral director and may serve as a valuable training ground for student soloists in the advanced choir. Membership in the voice class should be selective and limited to those students who possess at least a reasonable degree of innate vocal and musical ability, and who display a keen interest in developing vocal proficiency. The particular value of the class approach to vocal training lies in the opportunity for singers to observe each other and discuss, as a group, common vocal difficulties. Although private vocal study is highly desirable, it may be financially prohibitive to many students; in addition, the opportunity for valuable group experience does not present itself. Therefore, by meeting the needs of a particularly interested and musically talented group, the high school voice class makes its unique contribution to the balanced vocal music curriculum.

THE MUSIC BUDGET

The cost of educating our children and running our schools has risen almost continually since World War II, and with continuing inflation, the problem is sure to become more and more acute. School administrators, therefore, must become more watchful of the amount of the budget allotted to each department. Departments not demonstrating a definite need for the funds allotted them are likely to suffer a decrease. Many music educators are especially concerned with the problem because, as their program develops and more students participate in it, additional funds are needed to purchase music and equipment necessary to provide the best musical education for the students. One bright spot: The more students enrolled, the lower the per capita cost.

Among administrators there seems to be a growing interest in a performance type of budget, in which the emphasis is upon values received rather than upon facts and figures. It might, therefore, prove most profitable for the music educator to discuss with his administrator the benefits of music study in terms of its aesthetic, expressive, cultural, personal, social, avocational, and vocational values. Although most administrators are familiar with these benefits, it is nevertheless desirable for them to understand the music educator's particular point of view.

It is suggested that music educators demonstrate an interest in matters of budget. They should familiarize themselves with the proper procedures for requisitioning materials and keeping accounts and records. They should set up a system of filing and maintaining music materials, and should demonstrate knowledge of how to repair music. If administrators feel that the music educator is spending money wisely, and if they feel that materials are well cared for, they are more inclined to grant a request for an increase in the music department budget.

After careful planning and estimating of future choral department needs, the director should discuss the budget problem with his administrator, emphasizing the fact that the quality of instruction depends to a great extent upon adequate teaching materials and equipment. A long-term approach to departmental needs is highly recommended. The budget for the approaching school year might be divided into three categories: "Desirable and Helpful," "Highly Desirable," and "Essential" for the operation of the program during the ensuing school year. Admin-

Budget 1 CHORAL MUSIC DEPARTMENT

Proposed Budget for the Academic Year _____.

A. *Essential and Necessary Items*[*]   *Amount*
1. Octavo music (SATB, SSA, TTBB) .... $ ____
2. Music folders ....
3. Music storage boxes ....
4. Choir-robe maintenance and repairs ....
5. Equipment maintenance ....
6. Choral recordings and magnetic tapes ....

    Total .... $ ____

B. *Highly Desirable Items*[†]
1. Additional storage cabinets .... $ ____
2. Photographs (for publicity purposes) ....
3. Additional rehearsal-room risers ....
4. Additional chairs (for rehearsal room) ....
5. Additional standing risers (for concerts) ......
6. New bulletin board ....

    Total .... $ ____

C. *Desirable and Helpful Items*[‡]
1. Film rentals .... $ ____
2. New tape-recording equipment ....
3. Stereophonic record player ....
4. Transportation expenses (festivals and
   contests) ....
5. Additional piano (for student practice) ....
6. Visiting conductors' fees ....

    Total .... $ ____

    Grand Total .... $ ____

[*]Essential for operation of the department or activity during the ensuing school year.
[†]Highly desirable for the future growth of the program.
[‡]Desirable and helpful in terms of providing the best educational experiences for the students.

istrators are generally most appreciative of such a businesslike approach to the budget problem. (See Budget 1.)

Another approach to the budget problem is simply to list the items under two, rather than three, categories. Under "Operating Expenses," list the items necessary for the efficient functioning of the department for the ensuing year. Under "Nonrecurring Expenses" (or "Capital Equipment Needs"), list the items that are important to the further development of the program. Since the funds for special purchases are not likely to be available in any one year for the acquisition of all special

Budget 2 CHORAL MUSIC DEPARTMENT

Proposed Budget for the Academic Year _____.

A. *Operating Expenses*   *Amount*
 1. Octavo music .... $ _____
 2. Music folders ....   _____
 3. Music storage boxes ....   _____
 4. Choir robe maintenance ....   _____
 5. Equipment maintenance ....   _____
 6. Choral recordings and magnetic tapes .... _____
 7. Photographs ....   _____
 8. Film rentals ....   _____
 9. Transportation expenses ....   _____

     Total .... $ _____

B. *Nonrecurring Expenses*
 1. Additional chairs (for rehearsal room) .... $ _____
 2. Additional risers ....   _____
 3. Additional piano ....   _____
 4. Additional storage cabinets ....   _____
 5. Choir robe replacements ....   _____
 6. New tape-recording equipment ....   _____
 7. Stereophonic record player ....   _____

     Total .... $ _____

     Grand Total .... $ _____

needs, the items in this category should be listed in the order of importance. This will be of considerable assistance to the administrator in making his final budget allotments. Any items that the school is unable to acquire in a particular year may be included on the following year's budget request and perhaps ranked proportionately higher in their order of importance. Sample Budget 2 illustrates this idea.

Regardless of the form used, it is helpful to attach to the proposed budget a concise description of each item and the reasons for its need. This information will minimize questions of a general nature and thereby will facilitate the budget conference held between the choral director and the school administrator. Whenever conferences are held with administrators, a businesslike approach to the budget problem will be appreciated by the administrators and will be to the director's advantage. Choral directors should study carefully their groups' needs and be prepared to explain the importance of each item. They should be thoroughly familiar with the exact specifications of each requested item and be able to explain its desirability over other products of a similar nature but lower in cost.

CARE OF CHORAL MUSIC

Indexing and Storing

A practical method of indexing and storing choral music has many advantages. It protects the music from unnecessary wear and tear, selections are more easily located, and a much neater appearance is usually created in the rehearsal or storage room. In general, choral directors find one of the following two methods more suitable for their particular situations. Some directors prefer to place each choral selection into a separate 9 × 12-inch manila filing envelope, and to file the music alphabetically by title in a metal filing cabinet. So that selections may be easily located, the title is placed in the upper left-hand corner of the envelope, along with other pertinent information such as the composer, the arranger, the voice arrangement, and the number of available copies. For easy reference, these data may also be kept on 3 × 5-inch cards and maintained in a metal file box.

Other music directors prefer to file their music in 7½ × 11-inch reinforced cardboard boxes and to place them on conveniently situated shelves. (Boxes are available in 1-, 2-, and 3-inch widths.) Each box is labeled and numbered so that selections may be easily located. Again, all pertinent information, as previously described, should be placed on 3 × 5-inch cards, along with the number of the box in which the music is stored. All cards are filed alphabetically by title in a file box so that pertinent data or particular selections may be easily located. A separate index by composers is often helpful in quickly locating certain selections. Although file boxes are slightly more expensive than manila envelopes, the latter system will be less expensive to maintain. As the music library grows, it will be slightly less expensive to build additional shelves for storing music than to purchase additional filing cabinets.

Distribution

Choral directors distribute the music in various ways. Most find it a practical timesaver to insert the music in a folder of some type. Some use a plain 9 × 12-inch manila filing folder; others use a folder with cloth reinforced edges (8½ × 11-inch) with flaps that hold the music in place and prevent it from falling out. This type of folder, although a bit more expensive than manila folders, is well worth the investment; it is described in several music distributors' catalogs. Some directors utilize the services of student librarians to distribute the choral folders. Others file the music in a music cabinet near the door, so that each student may pick up a folder as he enters the room (cabinets may be constructed or purchased ready-made for this purpose). Choir members are instructed to leave the music in the same place when they leave the room. This procedure saves the director a great deal of time and energy and is a practice far superior to collecting music left haphazardly about the rehearsal room.

Repair

After choral selections have been removed from the folders and before they are filed, they should be examined carefully and repaired with mending tape whenever necessary. When selections have been numbered, they should be replaced in order and filed in their appropriate locations. Disorderly piles of music not only are unsightly, but also can make a poor impression upon school administrators.

Many of the duties just described can be assigned to responsible students. In this way, desirable training can be provided younger persons and the director can be freed from many time-consuming chores, thus having more time to coordinate and develop the total choral music program.

SELECTING CHOIR APPAREL

Uniformity of dress has always been an important consideration for choirs and choruses because it contributes to developing the group into a unified and cohesive whole. It minimizes attention on individuals, which could be distracting during a performance, and focuses upon the total ensemble.

By attending an American Choral Directors Association convention or a state music competition-festival, one will observe the wide variety of apparel in use today. With each passing year, it seems even more options become available. Outfits chosen, however, will range from the very simple to the highly elaborate, depending upon the age level of the singers, the sophistication of the group, and the financial resources of individuals or the group.

In schools where finances are of immediate concern, the director will want to consider inexpensive options, including some items of clothing that singers may already have in their wardrobes. For example, some children's choirs have looked very appropriate in blue jeans and T-shirts, particularly for their age group. For high school groups, most boys usually have a sport coat, slacks, and matching shirts and ties. Girls usually have a white blouse (with long sleeves), and they can make a floor-length skirt or have one made. First, determine the color and the material most appropriate, and how much will be needed. Before purchasing, inquire about a discount on a quantity order of material. Then provide each girl with the necessary amount of material and a skirt pattern (several may be shared). Make certain, however, that a qualified person is doing the cutting and distribution of the material. Some girls have the ability to make the skirts themselves, while others may require help from parents or from a local seamstress. When members leave the chorus upon graduation or for other reasons, they may sell their skirts to incoming members, and a choir apparel committee or the director may serve as a liaison for these arrangements. (This type of apparel is often worn by college and adult women as well, but the men appear in formal wear.) For a splash of color with white blouses and dark skirts, consider adding a maroon cummerbund, or a scarf in dark red or some other tasteful color. A dark red scarf also seems to work nicely with an all-black dress.

In considering unique apparel for a choir, first look at the broad field. A wide variety of attire is available, including multicolored women's dresses and men's tuxedos in various shades such as black, white, silver grey, charcoal grey, light blue, navy blue, burgundy, brown, and cream, as well as tux shirts, bow ties, and cummerbunds in different colors. The uniqueness of available apparel will be appealing to all choirs. Initially, explore the wide range of possibilities and their costs. Send for catalogs and secure bid prices, and specific terms of payment, from manufacturers or distributors (see the Appendix for a listing of manufacturers/distributors of choir apparel and their addresses). Consult with local merchants to determine what they might be able to supply. Consider the quality of the material and the tailoring, as well as the cost per outfit. Better materials usually wear longer and often look much better.

It is desirable to utilize a special student committee (of not more than three persons) to study the varied possibilities and narrow the options down to a few reasonable choices to present to the choir for discussion. Then, secure sample outfits from firms. Request specific sizes for a male and a female singer and have the outfits modeled before the choir. Let the group consider (1) flexibility of uses, (2) taste and style, (3) cost (to each individual, the school, or a combination), and (4) availability of the apparel in the future. In other words, will replacements for new members be available?

Allow ample time for discussion, and encourage everyone to be candid but courteous. The members must all realize that this is a costume and not an outfit designed specifically for themselves. Suggest that they all keep an open mind before making a choice. Then take a straw vote and think about the decision for a while. If individual members are to assume the cost, then be certain that they discuss the matter with their parents. In course descriptions, state that part of the course requirement is that members furnish a portion or all of their performing attire. That way, students know beforehand all the course expectations. The final selection may be voted upon by the choir, or the decision may be made by the choir apparel selection committee in consultation with the choir director (in most cases a preferable option). Of course, involved in this decision-making process is the question of who is to pay for each outfit— the individual students, the school, or a combination of the two (that is, through school funds and monies acquired through fund-raising activities). If the school decides to purchase the outfits, then it is always helpful to purchase a few extra sizes to accommodate future members who wear unusual sizes and to allow for any increase in choir membership.

Fund-raising activities are frequently necessary to pay for uniforms. Various concerts may be designated and advertised for this purpose, with each choir member being responsible for selling a specified number of tickets. Another option, particularly appropriate in colleges and universities, is for the school to purchase the attire with monies from a school revolving account or to borrow the funds from a school foundation, or an alumni association, with the understanding that the monies will be repaid within a specified number of years. If each student pays a minimum yearly rental fee of 20 to 25 percent of the total cost, then the outfits could be paid for in four or five years. Continued rental charges, at a reduced rate, will also help to build a fund for the future replacement of outfits, as well as providing funds for a limited number of extra outfits of unusual sizes each year. Such a plan should initially be applied to the purchase of men's tuxedos and accessories, since these are much more expensive than women's outfits and since no option usually exists for less expensive attire, as it does for the women's outfits.

Once attire has been purchased, rules should be established as to the maintenance of outfits, dry cleaning, and so on. All statements of policy should be put in writing and distributed to the choir members to minimize any possible misunderstandings. For example, what should be done about a lost outfit that belongs to the school? How and when is it to be paid for? The policy should state the dates that school-owned outfits are to be returned and what will be done about an unreturned outfit. It is also suggested that all students sign a checkout card that specifies their responsibility and their agreement to specific conditions.

Choir Robes

While choir robes will necessarily be the choice of apparel for most church choirs, they are also a practical option for school choirs. Choir robes provide a comparatively cool garment, which may be donned with little effort and in a minimum amount of time. This advantage is especially important when program schedules allow only a limited amount of time for warming up and dressing. Following is information to help in choosing this type of attire.

Color   To obtain individuality, many directors select robes and accessories in school colors. Two-tone color effects and pleasing color harmony may be achieved through the use of various accessories that can be worn with the choir robe. There are also robes now available that are constructed entirely of one material, but in a combination of two colors.

Many church choir directors purchase robes that blend with the interior decorations of the church. Some time ago, the Protestant church would not select choir robes in any color except black. However, today the trend is to use color in their choir apparel—color that is pleasing and that will complement and blend with the interior of the church.

According to manufacturers, the most popular colors are shades of (1) blue, (2) gold, (3) green, (4) maroon and cardinal, and (5) black. White is sometimes used on special festive occasions such as Christmas and Easter, and also during the summer months. In addition to these colors, a wide range of delicate pastels is now available and is becoming increasingly popular. You may choose from such colors as pale yellow, powder blue, ivory, mint green, and aqua, to name a few.

Style   Styles are available to fit many individual tastes. There are robes designed specifically for children's, intermediate, and adult choirs. After the director determines his needs, he should consult various manufacturers' catalogs before making the final decision. Upon request, manufacturers will provide detailed pictures, swatches of material, sample robes, and other pertinent information. Also available are special robes for the director, the pianist, and the organist. They are altered by changing the sleeve construction to allow greater hand visibility and freedom.

Fabric   In areas of the country where there is heavy industry, unless the material is specially treated, various chemical gases in the air will affect the robes, causing the color to fade. In such an area, the director should take great care to determine if the fabric has been treated to prevent fading. Question the manufacturer before making a purchase. The quality of the fabric will determine the price of any given style. The better fabrics wear longer, retain their shape, are more comfortable, have better draping qualities, do not fade, and are less subject to wrinkling. A "wash and wear" fabric for robes is not necessarily practical. Some of the new polyester materials are well suited for robes; others are not. Check the quality carefully by examining samples.

Yoke   The foundation of any robe is the yoke, and the importance of its construction should not be overlooked. The yoke should be constructed of a substantial material so that it will hold its shape and prevent the body of the robe from drooping. It should be made of a strong yet lightweight material—lightweight for comfort, but possessing strength so that the body will retain its shape. The yoke shouldn't shrink, and should lie flat when dry-cleaned.

Fluting The fluting gathers the fullness of the robe over the shoulders and across the back, allowing the robe to hang in attractive folds. It is most desirable to purchase robes that have ample fullness so that large or small persons can wear them.

Closures Various companies recommend different kinds of closures. Here are some of the advantages and disadvantages of each: (1) zipper—faster and looks neater; care must be taken that clothes are not snagged; (2) hook and eye—hooks may pull out, causing some gapping; (3) snap placket—snaps may pull out if they are merely tacked on; however, if care is taken they are quite satisfactory; and (4) Velcro— sometimes difficult to align properly and not as serviceable as a zipper, but far less destructive should a robe get caught in a door while being worn.

Robe sizes and assignments Choir robes should be purchased in a range of sizes that will fit the average group. If funds are available, a few extra robes should be bought, because it may not be possible to purchase the same material in future years to replace damaged robes or to increase the quantity. The mill that manufactures the fabric may discontinue it, and in dyeing new fabrics, it may not be possible to match the shade exactly.

Computer programs are now available to fit robes to members so that the length above the floor is uniform. Programs also allow for a printout that may be posted on the door of the robe closet.[12]

Care and repair When robes are purchased, it is wise to sew in a numeral near the label; robes can then be assigned by number, and choir members can more easily locate their own robes. The director can maintain a list of all the choir members and the robe number that is assigned to each member.

All robes should be treated as one would treat fine clothes. To be protected against moths, they should be stored when not in actual use; they should be kept in a closet, away from light, since light will fade some robes as it will other fabrics. All robes should be dry-cleaned at least once

---

[12]A particularly good program is called "Robematch," and is available from Buchanan Software, 2190 West Drake, No. 320, Fort Collins, CO 80526.

a year, preferably by the same firm. If proper care is taken, choir robes should last ten years or more. The proper maintenance and upkeep of robes is a wise way in which to protect one's investment.

TOPICS FOR DISCUSSION

1. Try to recall your personal reactions to hearing an outstanding choral group from a neighboring community. In what way did this experience serve as a means of motivating your own music study?

2. What musical experiences or events in high school made the greatest impression upon you? In your opinion, why did these experiences make such a lasting impression?

3. Why are certain seating arrangements more effective with some choral groups than with others?

4. From a psychological basis, why is it more desirable to schedule music classes every day, rather than, for example, only twice a week?

5. Outline an instructional program in choral music designed to meet the musical and social needs of a specific school or church. What choral groups and ensembles would you organize, and what membership requirements would you specify?

6. In what way is the budget problem related to the scheduling problem?

7. Discuss the types of attire available for various choral groups. Discuss the appropriateness of attire in relation to various types of musical programs and in relation to particular occasions.

8. Utilizing the criteria of purpose, price or cost, and durability, discuss the strengths and the weaknesses of essential musical equipment, such as pianos, risers, tape recorders, record players, directors' stands, music folders, music storage cabinets, choir robes (and storage cabinets), and other suitable attire.

9. What supplies and equipment do you consider basic to the effective operation of a balanced choral program?

SELECTED READINGS

CAIN, NOBLE, *Choral Music and Its Practice*, chaps. 6, 7, 8. New York: M. Witmark & Sons, 1942.

CHRISTY, VAN A., *Glee Club and Chorus*, chaps. 2, 3. New York: G. Schirmer, Inc., 1940.

DIERCKS, LOUIS H., "The Individual in the Choral Situation," *The NATS Bulletin*, 17, no. 4 (May 15, 1961), 6–10.

DYKEMA, PETER W., AND KARL W. GEHRKENS, *The Teaching and Administration of High School Music*, chaps. 29, 30. Evanston, Ill.: Summy-Birchard Company, 1941.

GARRETSON, ROBERT L., "Music Curricula," in *International Encyclopedia of Education*, vol. 6, pp. 3457–63. Oxford, England: Pergamon Press, Ltd., 1985.

——, "Scheduling Choral Programs and Community Relations," *The Choral Journal*, XX, no. 2 (October 1979), 17–19.

GRAHAM, FLOYD F., *Public Relations in Music Education*, chap. 3. New York: Exposition Press, 1954.

KLOTMAN, ROBERT H., *Scheduling Music Classes*. Vienna, Va.: Music Educators National Conference, 1968.

KRONE, MAX T., *The Chorus and Its Conductor,* chaps. 1, 2. San Diego: Niel A. Kjos Music Co., 1945.

MENC Committee on Music Rooms and Equipment, Elwyn Carter, Chairman, *Music Buildings, Rooms, and Equipment,* (rev. and enlarged ed.). Vienna, Va.: Music Educators National Conference, 1955.

SNYDER, KEITH D., *School Music Administration and Supervision* (2nd ed.), chaps. 7, 8, 9. Boston: Allyn & Bacon, 1965.

SUNDERMAN, LLOYD F., *Choral Organization and Administration.* Rockville Centre, N.Y.: Belwin Mills, Inc.,1954.

———, *Organization of the Church Choir,* chaps. 2, 6. Rockville Centre, N.Y.: Belwin Mills, Inc., 1957.

VAN BODEGRAVEN, PAUL, AND HARRY R. WILSON, *The School Music Conductor,* chaps. 10, 12. Minneapolis: Schmitt, Hall & McCreary Co., 1942.

WILSON, HARRY R., *Artistic Choral Singing,* chap. 10. New York: G. Schirmer, Inc., 1959.

———, AND JACK L. LYALL, *Building a Church Choir,* chap. 5. Minneapolis: Schmitt, Hall & McCreary Co., 1957.

SONGS FOR RECREATIONAL SINGING[13]

Introductory Songs

Hello! (*Sing Together,* p. 160)

How D'ye Do (*357 Songs We Love to Sing,* p. 217)

Laugh Provoker, A (*357 Songs We Love to Sing,* p. 226)

More We Get Together, The (*The Biggest Little Song Book,* p. 75)

Sweetly Sings the Donkey (*The Biggest Little Song Book,* p. 75)

Viva l'Amour (*Singing Time,* No. 79)

Action Songs

Alouette (*The Golden Book of Favorite Songs,* p. 127)

Daisy Bell (*Singing Time,* p. 150)

Little Tom Tinker (*The Biggest Little Song Book,* p. 75)

MacDonald's Farm (*357 Songs We Love to Sing,* p. 217)

Oh! Susanna (*357 Songs We Love to Sing,* p. 224)

She'll Be Comin' Round the Mountain (*The Biggest Little Song Book,* p. 64)

Sweetly Sings the Donkey (*The Biggest Little Song Book,* p. 75)

Rounds and Canons

Alleluia (*Rounds and Canons,* No. 24)

Alphabet, The (*Rounds and Canons,* No. 41)

Are You Sleeping? (*357 Songs We Love to Sing,* p. 215)

Bell Doth Toll, The (*357 Songs We Love to Sing,* p. 23)

De Bezem (The Broom) (*357 Songs We Love to Sing,* p. 105).

Dona Nobis Pacem (*Singing Time,* No. 103)

[13]In organizing a "community sing," it is suggested that at least one song be selected from each of the categories listed.

Down in the Valley (*The Biggest Little Song Book*, p. 56)
Early to Bed (*Silver Book*, p. 135)
Fare Thee Well (*Sing Together*, p. 172)
French Cathedrals (*Sing Together*, p. 101)
Frog Round (*Sing Together*, p. 167)
Ifca's Castle (Carl Fischer Octavo, No. CM 4708)
Little Tom Tinker (*The Biggest Little Song Book*, p. 75)
Lovely Evening (*The Golden Book of Favorite Songs*, p. 70)
Merrily, Merrily (*357 Songs We Love to Sing*, p. 11)
Merry Lark, The (*Sing Together*, p. 169)
Morning Is Come (*Sing Together*, p. 169)
Old Hungarian Round (*Sing Together*, p. 171)
Reuben and Rachel (*357 Songs We Love to Sing*, p. 200)
Rise Up, O Flame (Praetorius) (*Sing Together*, p. 11)
Row, Row, Row Your Boat (*The Biggest Little Song Book*, p. 74)
Scotland's Burning (*357 Songs We Love to Sing*, p. 30)
Sing Together (*Sing Together*, p. 41)
White Coral Bells (*Sing Together*, p. 180)
Wise Old Owl (*Singing Time*, No. 142)

Combined Songs

Are You Sleeping–Three Blind Mice (*357 Songs We Love to Sing*, pp. 215, 152)
Old Folks at Home/Humoresque (*Singing Time*, pp. 64, 75)
Solomon Levi–The Spanish Cavalier (*357 Songs We Love to Sing*, pp. 210, 211)
Tipperary–Pack up Your Troubles (Chappell & Co., Inc.)
Yankee Doodle–Dixie (*357 Songs We Love to Sing*, pp. 229, 238)

Songs for Harmonizing

All Through the Night (*357 Songs We Love to Sing*, p. 35)
Annie Laurie (*Singing Time*, No. 68)
Battle Hymn of the Republic (*357 Songs We Love to Sing*, p. 240)
Carry Me Back to Old Virginny (*Singing Time*, No. 27)
Clementine (*Singing Time*, No. 132)
Down by the Old Mill Stream (Forester Music Publishers)
Down in the Valley (*Singing Time*, No. 50)
Good-bye, My Lover, Good-bye (*357 Songs We Love to Sing*, p. 191)
Home on the Range (*Singing Time*, No. 60)
In the Evening by the Moonlight (*Singing Time*, No. 62)
I've Been Workin' on the Railroad (*Singing Time*, No. 130)
Jacob's Ladder (*Singing Time*, No. 124)
Little Annie Rooney (*Singing Time*, No. 83)
My Bonnie (*357 Songs We Love to Sing*, p. 215)

Old Folks at Home (*The Golden Book of Favorite Songs*, p. 27)
On Top of Old Smoky (*Singing Time*, No. 6)
Standin' in the Need of Prayer (*Singing Time*, No. 120)
Tell Me Why (*Singing Time*, No. 74)

Closing Songs

All Through the Night (*357 Songs We Love to Sing*, p. 35)
America (*The Golden Book of Favorite Songs*, p. 3)
Auld Lang Syne (*357 Songs We Love to Sing*, p. 29)
Fare Thee Well (*Sing Together*, p. 172)
God Be with You (*357 Songs We Love to Sing*, p. 52)
God Bless America (Irving Berlin, Inc.)
Good Night Canon (*Sing Together*, p. 49)
Good Night, Ladies (*357 Songs We Love to Sing*, p. 200)
Good Night to You All (*Rounds and Canons*, No. 60)
Jacob's Ladder (*Singing Time*, No. 124)
Now the Day Is Over (*The Biggest Little Song Book*, p. 32)
So Long, It's Been Good To Know Ya! (Folkway Music Publishers)
Softly Now the Light of Day (*Silver Book of Songs*, No. 170)
Taps (*The Gray Book of Favorite Songs*, p. 3)

Community Songbooks

Aloha Oe. Miami Beach: Hansen House, 1983.
Amazing Grace. Miami Beach: Hansen House, 1983.
Biggest Little Song Book, The (comp. John Christopher). Miami: McAfee Music Pub., n.d.
Christmas Caroler's Book in Song and Story (arr. Torstein O. Kramme). Miami: Schmitt, Hall & McCreary, 1935.
Christmas in Song (arr. Theo Preuss). Miami: Rubank, Inc., 1947).
Fred Waring Song Book (comp. and ed. Hawley Ades). Delaware Water Gap, Pa.: Shawnee Press, Inc., 1962.
Golden Book of Favorite Songs, The. Miami: Schmitt, Hall & McCreary, 1923.
Good Fellowship Songs. Delaware, Ohio: Cooperative Recreation Service.
Gray Book of Favorite Songs, The. Miami: Schmitt, Hall & McCreary, 1941.
Joy to the World. Miami Beach: Hansen House, 1982.
Rounds and Canons (ed. Harry R. Wilson). Miami: Schmitt, Hall & McCreary, 1943.
Silver Book of Songs. Miami: Schmitt, Hall & McCreary, 1935.
Sing Around the Clock (arr. Howard Ross). Miami Beach: Hansen House, 1955.
Singing Time (arr. Ruth Heller and Walter Goodell). Miami: Schmitt, Hall & McCreary, 1952.
Sing Together (3rd ed.). New York: Girl Scouts of the U.S.A., 1973.
Spirituals (arr. William Stickles). Miami Beach: Hansen House, 1946.
357 Songs We Love to Sing. Miami: Schmitt, Hall & McCreary, 1938.

Appendix:
Source
Information

CHORAL COMPOSERS

This chronological list does not presume to be complete, but it does include most of the major contributors to choral literature from approximately 1400 to the present. Although some composers may be known as well or perhaps even better for compositions other than choral music, all have made contributions significant enough to justify inclusion herein. This list was developed primarily from the choral compositions listed in the Appendix. For representative compositions of these composers, see lists under sections titled Choral Octavo Publications, Choral Collections, and Extended Choral Works.

PRE-RENAISSANCE (ca. 1200–1400)

Perotin (Perotinus Magnus)	b. France	ca. 1183–ca. 1238
Adam de la Halle	b. Arras, France	ca. 1240–1287
Guillaume de Machaut	b. France	ca. 1304–1377

RENAISSANCE PERIOD (ca. 1400–1600)

John Dunstable	b. Dunstable, England	ca. 1370–1453
Gilles Binchois	b. Mons, Belgium	ca. 1400–1460
Guillaume Dufay	b. Hainaut, Belgium	ca. 1400–1474
Johannes Okeghem	b. East Flanders, Belgium	ca. 1430–1495
Pierre de La Rue	b. Tournai, Belgium	ca. 1430–1518
Heinrich Isaac	b. Brabant, Belgium	ca. 1450–1517
Josquin Després	b. Hainaut, Belgium	ca. 1450–1521
Jacob Obrecht	b. Berg-op-Zoom, Netherlands	ca. 1452–1505
Loyset Compère	b. ?	ca. 1455–1518
Jean Mouton	b. Haut-Wignes, France	ca. 1470–1522
Antoine Brumel	b. Flanders	ca. 1475–1520
Martin Luther	b. Eislenben, Germany	1483–1546
Clément Janequin	b. Châtellerault, France	ca. 1485–1560
Ludwig Senfl	b. Zurich, Switzerland	ca. 1490–ca. 1543
Costanzo Festa	b. Rome, Italy	ca. 1490–1545
Nicolas Gombert	b. Flanders	ca. 1490–1556
Thomas Créquillon	b. Ghent, Belgium	?–1557
Claudin de Sermisy	b. France	ca. 1490–1562
Passereau	Early 16th-century French composer	?–?
Adrian Willaert	b. Bruges, Belgium	ca. 1490–1562
Robert Carver	b. Scotland	ca. 1491–ca. 1546
Johann Walther	b. Kahler, Thuringia	1496–1570
Cristóbal Morales	b. Seville, Spain	ca. 1500–1553
Christopher Tye	b. England	ca. 1500–ca. 1572
Jacob Arcadelt	b. Liège, Belgium	ca. 1505–1560
Claude Goudimel	b. Besançon, France	ca. 1505–1572
Mattheus Le Maistre	b. near Liège, Belgium	ca. 1505–1577
Thomas Tallis	b. Leicestershire (?), England	ca. 1505–1585
Jacobus Clemens	b. Ypres, Belgium	ca. 1510–1556

Antonio Scandello	b. Brescia, Italy	1517–1580
Noé Faignient	b. Flanders, Belgium	?–1595
Hubert Waelvant	b. Tongerloo, Belgium	ca. 1517–1595
Andrea Gabrieli	b. Venice, Italy	ca. 1520–1586
Philippe de Monte	b. Mons, Belgium	1521–1603
Fernando Franco	b. La Serena, Mexico	ca. 1525–1585
Giovanni Pierluigi da Palestrina	b. Palestrina, Italy	ca. 1525–1594
Claude Le Jeune	b. Valenciennes, France	1528–1600
Richard Farrant	b. England	ca. 1530–1581
Guillaume Costeley	b. Pont-Audemer, France	1531–1606
Orlando di Lasso	b. Mons, Belgium	1532–1594
Cornelius Freundt	b. Plauen, Germany	1535–1591
Giaches de Wert	b. Weert, Netherlands	ca. 1535–1596
Andries Pevernage	b. Courtrai, Belgium	1543–1591
William Byrd	b. Lincolnshire (?), England	ca. 1543–1623
Marco Antonio Ingegneri	b. Verona, Italy	1545–1592
Giovanni Maria Nanino	b. Tivoli, Italy	1545–1607
François-Eustache Du Caurroy	b. Beauvais, France	1549–1609
Tomás Luis de Victoria	b. Avila, Spain	ca. 1549–1611
Francesco Suriano	b. Soriano, Italy	1549–ca. 1621
Jacobus Gallus (Jacob Handl)	b. Reifnitz, Austria (now Yugoslavia)	1550–1591
Orazio Vecchi	b. Modena, Italy	ca. 1550–1605
Giovanni Macque	b. Valenciennes, France	ca. 1550–1614
Luca Marenzio	b. Coccaglio, Italy	1553–1599
Johannes Eccard	b. Mühlhausen, Germany	1553–1611
Bartholomeus Gesius	b. Müncheberg, Germany	ca. 1555–1613
Sethus Calvisius	b. Gorsleben, Germany	1556–1615
Giovanni Gastoldi	b. Caravaggio, Italy	ca. 1556–1622
Thomas Morley	b. England	1557–1602
Jacques Mauduit	b. Paris, France	1557–1627
Giovanni Croce	b. Chioggia, Italy	ca. 1560–1609
Don Carlo Gesualdo	b. Naples, Italy	ca. 1560–1613
Felice Anerio	b. Rome, Italy	ca. 1560–1614
Melchior Vulpius	b. Wasungen, Germany	ca. 1560–1615
Hieronymus Praetorius	b. Hamburg, Germany	1560–1629
Peter Philips	b. England	ca. 1561–1628
Jacobo Peri	b. Florence, Italy	ca. 1561–1633
Jan Pieterszoon Sweelinck	b. Deventer (or Amsterdam), Netherlands	1562–1621
John Dowland	b. Ireland, possibly in County Dublin	ca. 1562–1626
John Bull	b. Somersetshire, England	ca. 1562–1628
Francis Pilkington	b. England	ca. 1562–1638
Gregor Aichinger	b. Regensburg, Germany	1564–1628
Ludovico da Viadana	b. Viadana, Italy	1564–1645
Michael Cavendish	b. England	ca. 1565–1628
Peter Philips	b. England	ca. 1565–1638
Adriano Banchieri	b. Bologna, Italy	1568–1634
Paul Peurl	b. Austria	ca. 1570–1624
Salamone Rossi	b. Mantua, Italy	1570–ca. 1630
Thomas Tomkins	b. St. David's, England	ca. 1572–1656

John Wilbye	b. Diss, England	1574–1638
Thomas Weelkes	b. England	ca. 1575–1623
Steffano Bernardi	b. Verona, Italy	1576–1636
Melchior Franck	b. Zittau, Germany	ca. 1579–1639
Michael East	b. London, England	ca. 1580–ca. 1648
Thomas Ford	b. England	ca. 1580–1648
Orlando Gibbons	b. Oxford, England	1583–1625
Adrian Batten	b. London, England	ca. 1585–1637

BAROQUE PERIOD (ca. 1600–1750)

Giulio Caccini	b. Rome, Italy	ca. 1546–1618
Giovanni Gabrieli	b. Venice, Italy	ca. 1557–1612
Hans Leo Hassler	b. Nuremberg, Germany	1564–1612
Claudio Monteverdi	b. Cremona, Italy	1567–1643
Michael Praetorius	b. Kreuzberg, Germany	ca. 1571–1621
Richard Deering	b. Kent, England	ca. 1580–ca. 1630
Gregorio Allegri	b. Rome, Italy	1582–1652
Melchior Teschner	b. Fraustadt, Austria	1584–1635
Adrian Batten	b. England	1585–1637
Heinrich Schütz	b. Kostritz, Germany	1585–1672
Johann Hermann Schein	b. Grünhain, Germany	1586–1630
Salamone Rossi	b. Mantua, Italy	ca. 1587–ca. 1630
Samuel Scheidt	b. Halle, Germany	1587–1654
Thomas Ravenscroft	b. England	ca. 1590–ca. 1633
Johann Cruger	b. Grossbreece, Germany	1598–1662
John Hilton	b. Oxford, England	1599–1657
Pier Francesco Cavalli	b. Crema, Italy	1602–1676
Orazio Benevoli	b. Rome, Italy	ca. 1605–1672
Giacomo Carissimi	b. Marino, Italy	ca. 1605–1674
Andreas Hammerschmidt	b. Brüx, Bohemia	1612–1675
Guillaume Bouzignac	Early 17th-century French composer	?–?
Franz Tunder	b. Burg auf Fehmarn, Germany	ca. 1614–1667
Matthew Locke	b. Exeter, England	ca. 1630–1677
George Jeffries	b. England	?–1685
Jean-Baptiste Lully	b. Florence, Italy	ca. 1632–1687
Marc-Antoine Charpentier	b. Paris, France	ca. 1634–1704
Dietrich Buxtehude	b. Helsingør, Denmark	ca. 1637–1707
Johann Christoph Bach	b. Erfurt, Germany	ca. 1642–1703
Johann Wolfgang Franck	b. Unterschwaningen, Germany	1644–ca. 1710
Pelham Humfrey	b. England	1647–1674
Michael Wise	b. Salisbury, England	ca. 1648–1687
Johann Michael Bach	b. Arnstadt, Germany	ca. 1648–1694
John Blow	b. Newark-on-Trent, England	1649–1708
Johann Pachelbel	b. Nuremberg, Germany	1653–1707
Philipp Heinrich Erlebach	b. Esens, Germany	1657–1714
Giuseppe Pitoni[1]	b. Rieti, Italy	1657–1743
Henry Purcell	b. London, England	1659–1695

[1]Although Pitoni lived during the Baroque period, he was of the Roman school, which rejected the styles and forms of Baroque music and directed their efforts toward composing liturgical music in the style of Palestrina.

Johann Kuhnau	b. Geising, Germany	1660–1722
Alessandro Scarlatti	b. Palermo, Italy	1660–1725
André Campra	b. Aix, France	1660–1744
Giacomo Antonio Perti	b. Crevalcore, Italy	1661–1756
Antonio Lotti	b. Venice, Italy	1667–1740
François Couperin	b. Paris, France	ca. 1668–1733
Antonio Vivaldi	b. Venice, Italy	ca. 1669–1741
Antonio Caldara	b. Venice, Italy	1670–1736
D. Pompeo Canniciari	b. Rome, Italy	ca. 1670–1744
William Croft	b. Nether Ettington, England	ca. 1678–1727
Georg Philipp Telemann	b. Magdeburg, Germany	1681–1767
Jean-Philippe Rameau	b. Dijon, France	1683–1764
Bohuslav Cernohorsky	b. Nimburg, Czechoslovakia	1684–1742
Francesco Durante	b. Frattamaggiore, Italy	ca. 1684–1755
Johann Sebastian Bach	b. Eisenach, Germany	1685–1750
George Frideric Handel	b. Halle, Germany	1685–1759
Benedetto Marcello	b. Venice, Italy	ca. 1686–1739
Niccola Antonio Porpora	b. Naples, Italy	1686–1768
Johan Helmich Roman	b. Stockholm, Sweden	ca. 1694–1758
Maurice Green	b. London, England	1696–1755
Georg Gottfried Wagner	b. Mühlberg, Germany	ca. 1698–1756
Johann Ernst Eberlin	b. Jettingen, Germany	1702–1762
Karl Heinrich Graun	b. Wahrenbrück, Germany	ca. 1704–1759
Giovanni Battista Pergolesi	b. Jesi, Italy	1710–1736
Thomas Arne	b. London, England	1710–1778

CLASSIC PERIOD (1750–1820)

Wilhelm Friedemann Bach	b. Weimar, Germany	1710–1784
Gottfried August Homilius	b. Rosenthal, Germany	1714–1785
Christoph Willibald Gluck	b. Erasbach, Germany	1714–1787
Karl Philipp Emanuel Bach	b. Weimar, Germany	ca. 1714–1788
Johann Heinrich Rolle	b. Quedlinburg, Germany	1716–1785
Johann Christoph Altnikol	b. Bevna, Silesia	1719–1759
Johann Ernst Bach	b. Eisenach, Germany	1722–1777
Christian Friedrich Gregor	b. Dirsdorf, Germany	1723–1801
Johann Adam Hiller	b. Wendisch-Ossog, Germany	1728–1804
Johann C. Geisler	b. Germany	1729–1815
Johann C. F. Bach	b. Leipzig, Germany	1732–1795
Franz Joseph Haydn	b. Rohrau-on-the-Leitha, Austria	1732–1809
Michael Haydn	b. Rohrau, Austria	1737–1806
Carl Michael Bellman	b. Stockholm, Sweden	1740–1795
Quirino Gasparini	b. Bergamasco, Italy	?–1778
William Billings	b. Boston, Massachusetts	1746–1800
Johann Friedrich Peter	b. Heerendijk, Holland	1746–1813
Andrew Law	b. Milford, Connecticut	1749–1821
Dimitri S. Bortniansky	b. Glukhov, Russia	1751–1825
Jacob French	Early American composer	1754–18??
Wolfgang Amadeus Mozart	b. Salzburg, Austria	1756–1791
Luigi Cherubini	b. Florence, Italy	1760–1842
Joseph Eybler	b. Schwechat (near Vienna), Austria	1764–1846

Thomas Attwood	b. London, England	1765–1838
John Wall Callcott	b. London, England	1766–1821
Samuel Wesley	b. Bristol, England	1766–1837
Ludwig van Beethoven	b. Bonn, Germany	1770–1827

ROMANTIC PERIOD (1800–1900)

Ignaz von Seyfried	b. Vienna, Austria	1776–1841
Johann Kaspar Aiblinger	b. Wasserburg, Germany	1779–1867
Konradin Kreutzer	b. Messkirch, Germany	1780–1849
Konrad Kocher	b. Ditzinger, Germany	1786–1872
Gioacchino Rossini	b. Pesaro, Italy	1792–1868
Franz Schubert	b. Lichtenthal, Austria	1797–1828
Alexis F. Lvov	b. Reval, Russia	1798–1870
Hector Berlioz	b. Côte-Saint-André, France	1803–1869
Mikhail Glinka	b. Novosspaskoye, Russia	1804–1857
Felix Mendelssohn	b. Hamburg, Germany	1809–1847
Robert Schumann	b. Zwickau, Germany	1810–1856
Samuel Sebastian Wesley	b. London, England	1810–1876
Franz Liszt	b. Raiding, Hungary	1811–1886
Richard Wagner	b. Leipzig, Germany	1813–1883
Giuseppe Verdi	b. Le Roncole, Italy	1813–1901
Robert Franz	b. Halle, Germany	1815–1892
Charles François Gounod	b. Paris, France	1818–1893
Jacques Offenbach	b. Cologne, France	1819–1880
Franz Abt	b. Eilenburg, Germany	1819–1885
Louis Lewandowski	b. Wreschen (near Posen), Poland	1821–1904
César Franck	b. Liège, Belgium	1822–1890
Peter Cornelius	b. Mainz, Germany	1824–1874
Anton Bruckner	b. Ansfelden, Austria	1824–1896
Johann Strauss (Jr.)	b. Vienna, Austria	1825–1899
Stephen Collins Foster	b. Pittsburgh, Pennsylvania	1826–1864
François Auguste Gevaert	b. Huysse, Belgium	1828–1908
Jean-Baptiste Fauré	b. Mouline, France	1830–1914
Johann von Herbeck	b. Vienna, Austria	1831–1877
August Soderman	b. Stockholm, Sweden	1832–1876
Alexander Borodin	b. St. Petersburg, Russia	1833–1887
Johannes Brahms	b. Hamburg, Germany	1833–1897
César Antonovitch Cui	b. Vilna, Russia	1835–1918
Camille Saint-Saëns	b. Paris, France	1835–1921
John Farmer	b. Nottingham, England	1836–1901
Mily A. Balakirev	b. Nizhny-Novgorod, Russia	1837–1910
Alfred Robert Gaul	b. Norwich, England	1837–1913
Theodore Dubois	b. Rosnay, France	1837–1924
Georges Bizet	b. Paris, France	1838–1875
Modest p. Moussorgsky	b. Karevo, Russia	1839–1881
Peter Ilich Tchaikovsky	b. Kamsko-Votkinsk, Russia	1840–1893
John Stainer	b. London, England	1840–1901
Antonin Dvořák	b. Mühlhausen, Czechoslovakia	1841–1904
Arthur Sullivan	b. London, England	1842–1900
Edvard Grieg	b. Bergen, Norway	1843–1907

Herman Schroeder	b. Quedlinburg, Germany	1843–1909
Nikolai A. Rimsky-Korsakov	b. Tikhvin, Russia	1844–1908
Gabriel Urbain Fauré	b. Pamiers, France	1845–1924
Alexander Arkhangelsky	b. Penza, Russia	1846–1924
Gustav Schreck	b. Zeulenroda, Germany	1849–1918
Vincent D'Indy	b. Paris, France	1851–1931
Hugo Jungst	b. Dresden, Germany	1853–1923
Alexander A. Kopylov	b. St. Petersburg, Russia	1854–1911
Engelbert Humperdinck	b. Siegburg, Germany	1854–1921
Leos Janáček	b. Hukvaldy, Czechoslovakia	1854–1928
Stevan S. Mokranjac	b. Negotin, Yugoslavia	1855–1914
Sergei I. Taneyev	b. Vladimir, Russia	1856–1915
Alexander Kastalsky	b. Moscow, Russia	1856–1926
Edward Elgar	b. Broadheath, England	1857–1934
Reginald De Koven	b. Middletown, Connecticut	1859–1920
Mikhail M. Ippolitov-Ivanov	b. Gatchina, Russia	1859–1935
Edward MacDowell	b. New York, New York	1861–1908
Horatio Parker	b. Auburndale, Massachusetts	1863–1919
Pietro Mascagni	b. Leghorn, Italy	1863–1945
Richard Strauss	b. Munich, Germany	1864–1949
Alexander T. Gretchaninov	b. Moscow, Russia	1864–1956
Jean Sibelius	b. Tavastehus, Finland	1865–1957
Vassili S. Kalinnikov	b. Voin, Russia	1866–1901
Enrique Granados	b. Lérida, Spain	1867–1916
Granville Bantock	b. London, England	1868–1946
Louis Vierne	b. Pointiers, France	1870–1937
Franz Lehar	b. Komorn, Hungary	1870–1948
Henry Hadley	b. Somerville, Massachusetts	1871–1937
F. Melius Christiansen	b. Eidsvold, Norway	1871–1955
Max Reger	b. Brand, Germany	1873–1916
Sergei V. Rachmaninoff	b. Oneg, Russia	1873–1943
Hugh S. Roberton	b. Glasgow, Scotland	1874–1952
Samuel Coleridge-Taylor	b. London, England	1875–1912
Nikolai D. Leontovich	b. Monastirsh, Russia	1877–1921
Paul G. Tschesnokov	b. Vladimir, Russia	1877–1921

MODERN PERIOD (1890 TO PRESENT)
___

Claude Debussy	b. St. Germain-en-Lave, France	1862–1918
Frederick Delius	b. Bradford, England	1862–1934
Erik Satie	b. Honfleur, France	1866–1925
Henry Thacker Burleigh	b. Erie, Pennsylvania	1866–1949
Ralph Vaughan Williams	b. Down Ampney, England	1872–1958
Gustav Holst	b. Cheltenham, England	1874–1934
Arnold Schoenberg	b. Vienna, Austria	1874–1951
Paul Pierné	b. Metz, France	1874–1952
Charles Edward Ives	b. Danbury, Connecticut	1874–1954
Maurice Ravel	b. Ciboure, France	1875–1937
Martin Shaw	b. London, England	1875–1958
Ernest Bloch	b. Geneva, Switzerland	1880–1959
Healey Willan	b. Balham, England	1880–1968
Béla Bartók	b. Nagy Szent Miklós, Rumania	1881–1945
Robert Nathaniel Dett	b. Drummondville, Quebec, Canada	1882–1943

Zoltán Kodály	b. Kecskemet, Hungary	1882–1967
Igor Stravinsky	b. Oranienbaum, Russia	1882–1971
Anton Webern	b. Vienna, Austria	1883–1945
Marcel Dupré	b. Rouen, France	1886–1971
Konstantin N. Shvedov	b. Moscow, Russia	1886–?
Norris Lindsay Norden	b. Philadelphia, Pennsylvania	1887–1956
Heitor Villa-Lobos	b. Rio de Janeiro, Brazil	1887–1959
Ernst Toch	b. Vienna, Austria	1887–1964
Hall Johnson	b. Athens, Georgia	1887–1970
Božidar Sirola	b. Zakanj, Yugoslavia	1889–1956
Joseph W. Clokey	b. New Albany, Indiana	1890–1960
Heinrich Lemacher	b. Solingen, Germany	1891–1966
Arthur Honegger	b. Le Havre, France	1892–1955
Darius Milhaud	b. Aix-en-Provence, France	1892–1974
Felix Labunski	b. Ksawerynów, Poland	1892–1979
John Jacob Niles	b. Louisville, Kentucky	1892–1980
Bernard Rogers	b. New York, New York	1893–1968
Peter Warlock (Philip Heseltine)	b. London, England	1894–1930
Walter Piston	b. Rockland, Maine	1894–1976
Paul Hindemith	b. Hanau, Germany	1895–1963
Albert Hay Malotte	b. Philadelphia, Pennsylvania	1895–1964
Leo Sowerby	b. Grand Rapids, Michigan	1895–1968
William Grant Still	b. Woodville, Mississippi	1895–1978
Carl Orff	b. Munich, Germany	1895–1982
Gordon Jacob	b. London, England	1895–1984
Richard Kountz	b. Pittsburgh, Pennsylvania	1896–1950
Howard Hanson	b. Wahoo, Nebraska	1896–1981
Virgil Thomson	b. Kansas City, Missouri	1896–
Henry Cowell	b. Menlo Park, California	1897–1965
Alexander Tansman	b. Lodz, Poland	1897–
Roy Harris	b. Lincoln County, Oklahoma	1898–1979
William L. Dawson	b. Anniston, Alabama	1898–
Hugh Ross	b. Langport, England	1898–
Francis Poulenc	b. Paris, France	1899–1963
Carlos Chávez	b. Mexico City, Mexico	1899–1978
Alexander Tcherepnin	b. St. Petersburg, Russia	1899–1977
Randall Thompson	b. New York, New York	1899–1984
George Antheil	b. Trenton, New Jersey	1900–1959
Aaron Copland	b. Brooklyn, New York	1900–
Otto Luening	b. Milwaukee, Wisconsin	1900–
Gerald Finzi	b. London, England	1901–1956
Harry Robert Wilson	b. Salina, Kansas	1901–1968
Olaf C. Christiansen	b. Minneapolis, Minnesota	1901–1984
Jester Hairston	b. North Carolina	1901–
Edmund Rubbra	b. Northampton, England	1901–
William Walton	b. Oldham, England	1902–1983
Maurice Duruflé	b. Louviers, France	1902–
Jenö Takács	b. Siegendorf, Austria	1902–
Undine Smith Moore	b. Jarrett, Virginia	1905–
Paul Creston	b. New York, New York	1906–1985
Dmitri Shostakovitch	b. St. Petersburg, Russia	1906–1975
Normand Lockwood	b. New York, New York	1906–
Miklos Rozsa	b. Budapest, Hungary	1907–
Hugo Distler	b. Nuremberg, Germany	1908–1942

Elliot Carter	b. New York, New York	1908–
Halsey Stevens	b. Scott, New York	1908–
Jean Berger	b. Hamm, Germany	1909–
Samuel Barber	b. West Chester, Pennsylvania	1910–1981
Julius Chajes	b. Lwow, Poland	1910–
William Howard Schuman	b. New York, New York	1910–
Franz Reizenstein	b. Nuremberg, Germany	1911–1968
Alan Hovhaness	b. Somerville, Massachusetts	1911–
Gian Carlo Menotti	b. Cadegliano, Italy	1911–
Benjamin Britten	b. Lowestoft, England	1913–1976
Norman Dello Joio	b. New York, New York	1913–
Jan Meyerowitz	b. Breslau, Germany	1913–
Gardner Read	b. Evanston, Illinois	1913–
Irving Fine	b. Boston, Massachusetts	1914–1962
Gail Kubik	b. South Coffeyville, Oklahoma	1914–1984
Cecil Effinger	b. Colorado Springs, Colorado	1914–
Knut Nystedt	b. Oslo, Norway	1915–
Vincent Persichetti	b. Philadelphia, Pennsylvania	1915–1987
Houston Bright	b. Midland, Texas	1916–1970
Alberto Ginastera	b. Buenos Aires, Argentina	1916–1983
Gordon Binkerd	b. Lynch, Nebraska	1916–
Scott Huston	b. Tacoma, Washington	1916–
Ulysses S. Kay	b. Tucson, Arizona	1917–
Leonard Bernstein	b. Lawrence, Massachusetts	1918–
Vaclav Nelhybel	b. Czechoslovakia	1919–
Paul Fetler	b. Philadelphia, Pennsylvania	1920–
William Bergsma	b. Oakland, California	1921–
Lloyd Pfautsch	b. Washington, Missouri	1921–
Lukas Foss	b. Berlin, Germany	1922–
George Walker	b. Washington, D.C.	1922–
Anton Heiller	b. Vienna, Austria	1923–1979
Daniel Pinkham	b. Lynn, Massachusetts	1923–
Ned Rorem	b. Richmond, Indiana	1923–
Kirke Mecham	b. Wichita, Kansas	1925–
Gunther Schuller	b. New York, New York	1925–
Carlisle Floyd	b. Latta, South Carolina	1926–
Arnold Freed	b. New York, New York	1926–
Dominick Argento	b. York, Pennsylvania	1927–
Emma Lou Diemer	b. Kansas City, Missouri	1927–
Donald Erb	b. Youngstown, Ohio	1927–
Samuel H. Adler	b. Mannheim, Germany	1928–
Ron Nelson	b. Joliet, Illinois	1929–
Richard Felciano	b. Santa Rosa, California	1930–
Gilbert Trythall	b. Knoxville, Tennessee	1930–
Wendell P. Whalum	b. Memphis, Tennessee	1931–
Krzysztof Penderecki	b. Debiça, Poland	1933–
Nicolas Roussakis	b. Athens, Greece	1934–
Eugene Butler	b. Durant, Oklahoma	1935–
David Eddleman	b. Winston-Salem, North Carolina	1936–
Michael Hennigan	b. The Dalles, Oregon	1936–
James E. McCray	b. Kankakee, Illinois	1938–
John Rutter	b. London, England	1945–

CHORAL OCTAVO PUBLICATIONS

The octavo publications in this appendix have been included because they are particularly suitable for nonprofessional choral groups. SAB publications are included for junior high school choruses; also listed are SSA and TTBB publications that are particularly appropriate for high school as well as college glee clubs. SATB publications have been included for use with high school, college or university, church, and community choirs and choruses. In addition, there are listed selections that are appropriate for chorus and band and/or orchestra.

Because of the comparatively large number of publications included for use with mixed voices (SATB), all the music is listed under various categories so that directors may easily locate the selections they seek. These categories are "Christmas," "Easter and Lent," "Folk Songs and Spirituals," "Special Occasions," "General: Sacred and Secular," "Music with Electronic Tape/Nonconventional Notation," and "Music for Jazz/Show Choirs." For the other voice classifications (SAB, SSA, TTBB), publications are included under three categories: "Sacred," "Secular," and "Folk Songs and Spirituals."

Following the title, composer, and/or arranger, the publishers and the catalog number are given. This information is provided to facilitate the ordering of music. Since the director will wish to know if the selection is to be performed *a cappella* or with accompaniment, this information is also provided. All publications have been graded according to difficulty, using the following terms: Easy, Moderately easy, Medium, Moderately difficult, and Difficult. Also indicated are those publications having incidental solos. Prices have not been included since they are subject to change. It is suggested that current prices be requested from local dealers immediately prior to placing an order; in this way, both billing and budgeting problems may be minimized. In selecting music, it is suggested that directors obtain for examination purposes single copies of particular octavo selections from the publisher or their local dealer, whichever is more convenient. The lists below provide a helpful starting point, but only through careful analysis of each selection in relation to the needs of a specific choral group will the most effective programming be achieved.

As the demand for particular choral publications increases, they can sometimes become temporarily out-of-stock. Therefore, music dealers should be asked to ascertain an approximate date of availability. In some other cases, music may become permanently out-of-print. If a director has a single reference copy, he may write to the Director of Choral publications of the music publisher who holds the copyright and request permission to duplicate a specific number of copies. For this privilege, publishers usually charge a nominal fee per copy, and after the required amount has been submitted to a publisher, the director may duplicate the specified number of copies, but *not* until written permission has been received.[2]

PUBLICATIONS FOR MIXED VOICES (SATB)

Christmas (Sacred and Secular)

A La Nanita Nana (Spanish carol tune)—arr. Ehret.   Shawnee Press No. A-674.   Piano accompaniment.   Moderately easy.

And the Trees Do Moan (Carol of the Mountain Whites)—arr. Gaul.   Oliver Ditson No. 332.   Optional accompaniment.   Moderately easy.

Angelus ad pastores ait—Gabrieli.   C. F. Peters No. 5930.   Two choirs—12 parts.   Optional accompaniment.   Difficult.

As Dew in Aprille (from *A Ceremony of Carols*)—Britten, arr. Harrison.   Boosey & Hawkes No. 1829.   Accompanied.   Medium.

Behold a Star from Jacob Shining—Mendelssohn, arr. Davison.   E. C. Schirmer No. 1683.   Organ accompaniment.   Medium.

Birds and the Christ Child, The (Czechoslovakian carol)—arr. Krone.   Carl Fischer No. CM 4612.   *A cappella*.   Easy.

Boy Was Born, A—Britten.   Oxford No. X92.   *A cappella*.   Medium.

Break Forth, O Beauteous Heavenly Light—J. S. Bach.   Oliver Ditson No. 13744.   Accompanied.   Easy.

Carol of the Bells (Ukrainian carol; secular)—Leontovich, arr. Wilhousky.   Carl Fischer No. CM 4604.   *A cappella*.   Easy.

Carol of the Birds (traditional French Christmas carol)—arr. Cain.   Schmitt, Hall & McCreary No. 1507.   Optional accompaniment.   Moderately easy.

Carol of the Italian Pipers (traditional carol)—arr. Zgodava.   Shawnee Press No. A-967.   Optional accompaniment.   Moderately easy.

Carol of the Pifferari (old Neapolitan Christmas air)—arr. Christy.   Belwin Mills No. 2190.   *A cappella*.   Easy.

Carol of the Russian Children (White Russian carol)—arr. Gaul.   G. Schirmer No. 6770.   Optional accompaniment.   Moderately easy.

Child Said, A—McCray.   National Music Publishers No NMP-151.   Piano and oboe.   Optional solo.   Moderately easy.

Chocolate Burro, The (Mexican carol)—arr. Ringwald.   Shawnee Press No. A-1318.   Piano accompaniment.   Moderately easy.

Christmas Carol, A (Hungarian traditional tune)—arr. Kodály.   Oxford No. 84.091.   *A cappella*.   Moderately easy.

Christmas Gift—Hairston.   Bourne No. S1033.   Piano accompaniment.   Moderately easy.

Christmas Song, The—Torme and Wells, arr. Ehret.   Edwin H. Morris No. E9822a.   Piano accompaniment.   Moderately easy.

Christmas Spirituals (Mary Had a Baby and Rise Up, Shepherd)—arr. Scandrett.   Carus-Verlag.   *A cappella*.   Moderately easy.

Das neugeborne Kindelein (The Newborn Child)—J. S. Bach.   National Music Publishers No. NMP-175.   Piano or organ accompaniment.   Medium.

Enter the Stable Gently (Spanish carol)—arr. Hopson.   Music 70 No. M70-249.   *A cappella*.   Moderately easy.

Fanfare for Christmas Day—Shaw.   G. Schirmer No. 8745.   Optional organ accompaniment.   Moderately easy.

[2]*An Appeal from music publishers*—"The unofficial copying of music has the effect of reducing the number of works available in print, and very often those works that are available become more expensive because of reduced print runs and subsequent higher costs. In order to protect our choral repertoire (our choral heritage), adherence to copyright law is essential."

Fum, Fum, Fum (Catalonian carol)—arr. Parker and Shaw. G. Schirmer No. 10182. *A cappella*. Medium.

Gentle Mary and Her Child (Finnish folk melody)—arr. Lundquist. Elkan-Vogel No. 1152. *A cappella*. Easy.

Glory to God in the Highest—Pergolesi. Wood No. 289. Organ accompaniment. Moderately difficult.

Gloucestershire Wassail (traditional old English yule song)—arr. Scott. Shawnee Press No. A45. Accompanied. Bass or alto solo. Medium.

God Rest You Merry, Gentlemen (old English Christmas carol)—arr. Stevens. Pro Art No. 1420. Accompanied. Easy.

Good Christian Men, Rejoice (traditional German)—arr. Parker and Shaw. G. Schirmer No. 10183. *A cappella*. Moderately easy.

Go Tell it on the Mountain (Christmas spiritual)—arr. Work. Galaxy No. 1532. *A cappella*. Soprano and tenor solos. Medium.

Hawaiian Lullaby—Sargent. Oxford No. X85. *A cappella*. Medium.

He Is Born (Il est né)—arr. Roger Wagner. Lawson-Gould No. 663. *A cappella*. Easy.

Here 'mid the Cattle (Alsatian carol)—arr. Butler. Carl Fischer No. CM 8065. Piano or organ accompaniment. Baritone solo. Moderately easy.

Here We Come A-Wassailing (traditional)—arr. Goodrich. National Music Publishers No. WHC-129. *A cappella*. Moderately easy.

Hodie Christus natus est—Sweelinck. Edw. B. Marks No. MC 4301. *A cappella*. Moderately difficult.

Holly and the Ivy, The (traditional English)—arr. Parker and Shaw. G. Schirmer No. 10187. *A cappella*. Moderately easy.

Holy Child, The (Puerto Rican carol)—arr. Hruby. Pro Art No. 2687. Accompanied. Easy.

How unto Bethlehem (traditional Italian)—arr. Parker and Shaw. G. Schirmer No. 10194. *A cappella*. Moderately easy.

Hunter, The—Brahms. E. C. Schirmer No. 1680. *A cappella*. Moderately easy.

I Heard an Angel—Krenek. Rongwen No. 3540. *A cappella*. Medium.

Infant Sweet and Gentle, An (Polish carol)—arr. Ehret. Presser No. 312-40765. Accompanied. Moderately easy.

In Fields Not Far from Bethlehem (Austrian carol)—arr. Ehret. Elkan-Vogel No. 362-03117. Accompanied. Moderately easy.

I Saw Three Ships (traditional English)—arr. Parker and Shaw. G. Schirmer No. 10188. *A cappella*. Moderately easy.

It's the Most Wonderful Time of the Year—Pola and Wyle, arr. Ades. Shawnee Press No. A-1101. Piano accompaniment. Moderately easy.

I Wonder As I Wander (Appalachian carol)—arr. Niles and Horton. G. Schirmer No. 8708. Optional accompaniment. Soprano or tenor solo. Medium.

Jesus, Jesus, Rest Your Head (Appalachian carol)—arr. Niles and Warrell. G. Schirmer No. 8302. *A cappella*. Moderately easy.

Jesus' Christmas Lullaby (Bohemian folk song)—arr. Ehret. Elkan-Vogel No. 1140. Accompanied. Moderately easy.

Joseph Dear, Oh Joseph Mild—Calvisius. Associated No. A-396. *A cappella*. Medium.

La Virgen Lava Panales—arr. De Cormier and Sauter. Lawson-Gould No. 52227. Piano accompaniment. Medium.

Let Heaven Rejoice and Sing (German carol)—arr. Ehret. Sam Fox No. CC7. Accompanied. Easy.

Lo, How a Rose E'er Blooming—Praetorius. G. Schirmer No. 2484. *A cappella*. Easy.

Los Reyes Magos (The Three Kings)—Ramirez. Lawson-Gould No. 51748. Harpsichord, percussion, and guitar accompaniment. Moderately easy.

Lost in the Night (Finnish folk melody)—arr. F. M. Christiansen. Augsburg No. 119. *A cappella*. Soprano solo. Moderately difficult.

Love Came Down at Christmas—Pfautsch. Lawson-Gould No. 52278. *A cappella*. Medium.

Maiden Most Gentle, A (French tune)—arr. Carter. Oxford No. X266. Organ accompaniment. Easy.

Mary Had a Baby—William L. Dawson. Kjos No. T118. *A cappella.* Soprano solo. Medium.

Masters in This Hall (traditional French)—arr. Parker and Shaw. G. Schirmer No. 10192. *A cappella.* Medium.

O filii et filiae—Leisring, arr. Row. R. D. Row No. 283. *A cappella.* Medium.

Old Polish Christmas Carol—arr. Liszniewski. Huntzinger No. 4049. *A cappella.* Easy.

O magnum mysterium (O Wondrous Nativity)—Vittoria. G. Schirmer No. 7626. *A cappella.* Medium.

O Sanctissima (Sicilian folk melody)—arr. Parker and Shaw. G. Schirmer No. 10194. *A cappella.* Medium.

Our Day of Joy Is Here Again (Swedish folk melody)—arr. Lundquist. Elkan-Vogel No. 1151. *A cappella.* Easy.

Quem vidistis pastores? (Shepherds, Tell Us Your Story)—arr. Felis. Edw. B. Marks No. 4491. Optional accompaniment. Medium.

Saviour Is Born, The (Austrian carol)—arr. Warner. Summy-Birchard No. 1578. Accompanied. Easy.

Shepherds All, and Shepherdesses (Allon, gay, gay)—Costeley. Oxford No. OCS 1667. *A cappella.* Medium.

Shepherds' Chorus (from *Amahl and the Night Visitors*)—Menotti. G. Schirmer No. 10801. Accompanied. Soprano and bass solos. Medium.

Silent Night—arr. Sargent. Oxford No. OCS 876. *A cappella.* Moderately easy.

Sleep in Peace, O Heavenly Child—Michael Haydn. G. Schirmer No. 11043. Accompanied. Moderately easy.

Slumber Song of the Infant Jesus, The—Gevaert. E. C. Schirmer No. 1163. *A cappella.* Easy.

So Blest a Sight (English traditional)—arr. Parker and Shaw. G. Schirmer No. 10196. *A cappella.* Moderately easy.

Songs of Praise the Angels Sang (Swedish folk melody)—arr. Lundquist. Elkan-Vogel No. 1145. *A cappella.* Easy.

Still, Still, Still—Luboff. Walton No. 3003. Accompanied. Easy.

Sweet Mary Tends Her New-Born Son (German carol)—arr. Ehret. Elkan-Vogel No. 362-03116. Accompanied. Medium.

Sweet Was the Song (old English tune)—arr. Clausen. Mark Foster No. MF 550. *A cappella.* Moderately easy.

There Shall a Star from Jacob—Mendelssohn. Carl Fischer No. CM 6228. Accompanied. Medium.

This Little Babe (from *A Ceremony of Carols*)—Britten, arr. Harrison. Boosey & Hawkes No. 1830. Harp or piano accompaniment. Moderately easy.

Three Far-Eastern Carols—Sargent. Oxford No. X73. *A cappella.* Moderately easy.

Three Kings, The—Willan. Carl Fischer No. OCS 718. *A cappella.* Medium.

Three Old English Carols—arr. Holst. Schmidt No. APS 15171. Accompanied. Moderately easy.

'Tis the Time of Yuletide Glee—Morley. Music 70 No. M70-235. *A cappella.* Moderately easy.

Two Folk Carols (Star in the South and Zither Carol)—arr. Sargent. Oxford No. X50. *A cappella.* Moderately easy.

We Wish You a Merry Christmas (English folk song; secular)—arr. the Krones. Kjos No. 4006. Accompanied. Easy.

What Child Is This? (old English)—arr. Parker and Shaw. G. Schirmer No. 10199. *A cappella.* Moderately difficult.

While by My Sheep (17th-century Christian hymn)—arr. Jungst. G. Schirmer No. 2532. *A cappella.* Easy.

Ye Watchers and Ye Holy Ones (17th-century German melody)—arr. Davison. E. C. Schirmer No. 1780. Accompanied. Moderately easy.

Easter and Lent

Alleluia—Thompson. E. C. Schirmer No. 1786. *A cappella.* Moderately difficult.

Alleluia, Alleluia—Buxtehude. Presser No. 312-40668. Accompanied. Medium.

All Glory, Laud and Honor (Palm Sunday)—Teschner, arr. Cain. Flammer No. 81127. Accompanied. Easy.

Ave verum corpus—Byrd. Associated No. NYPMA 7. *A cappella.* Medium.

Cheer Up, Friends and Neighbors (old French Easter carol)—arr. Paget. Lawson-Gould No. 52334. *A cappella.* Easy.

Christ Is Arisen—Hassler. Edw. B. Marks No. 26. *A cappella.* Moderately easy.

Christ Is Arisen—Schubert. E. C. Schirmer No. 2686. *A cappella.* Moderately easy.

Christ ist erstanden (Christ Is Arisen)—Schubert. National Music Publishers No. CH-4. *A cappella.* Medium.

Crucifixus (from Mass in B minor)—J. S. Bach. E. C. Schirmer No. 1174. Accompanied. Medium.

Ecce, quomodo moritur—Jacobus Gallus (Jacob Handl). G. Schirmer No. 8424. *A cappella.* Moderately easy.

Four Chorales from the *Saint Matthew Passion*—J. S. Bach, ed. Ehret. Lawson-Gould No. 686. *A cappella.* Moderately easy.

God So Loved the World—Stainer. G. Schirmer No. 3798. *A cappella.* Easy.

Go to Dark Gethsemane—Noble. Gray No. CMR 501. *A cappella.* Medium.

He Never Said a Mumbalin' Word (spiritual)—arr. Wilson. Paull Pioneer. *A cappella.* Moderately easy.

Hosanna (Palm Sunday)—F. M. Christiansen. Augsburg No. 57. *A cappella.* Difficult.

Lamb of God (Chorale 1540)—arr. F. M. Christiansen. Augsburg No. 133. *A cappella.* Easy.

Lamb of God—Hassler. Lawson-Gould No. 800. *A cappella.* Moderately easy.

Light Divine (scene and prayer from *Cavalleria Rusticana*)—Mascagni. G. Schirmer No. 5959. Accompanied. Moderately difficult.

Magdalena—Brahms. G. Schirmer No. 9953. *A cappella.* Medium.

My Savior Dear, What Woe of Soul—J. S. Bach, arr. Lundquist. Willis No. 5503. *A cappella.* Medium.

O Jesus, Crucified for Man—Schubert. National Music Publishers No. CH-10. Accompanied. Medium.

O Lamb of God—Kalinnikov, arr. Ehret. Pro Art No. 1513. *A cappella.* Moderately easy.

Osterlied (Easter Song)—Schubert. National Music Publishers No. CH-9. Accompanied. Easy.

Palms, The (Palm Sunday)—Fauré, arr. Howorth. Belwin Mills No. 790. Accompanied. Medium.

Ride On! Ride On! (Palm Sunday)—Thompson. Gray No. CMR 1154. *A cappella.* Medium.

Sunrise Alleluia—Bright. Shawnee Press No. A-852. Accompanied. Moderately easy.

Surely, He Bore Our Sorrows (Lent)—Victoria. E. C. Schirmer No. 2217. *A cappella.* Medium.

Surely He Hath Borne Our Griefs (from *Messiah*)—Handel. G. Schirmer No. 6598. Accompanied. Medium.

Surrexit Pastor Bonus (The Shepherd Has Arisen)—Lasso. G. Schirmer No. 7685. *A cappella.* Medium.

This Is the Day Which the Lord Hath Made—Bortniansky. Bourne No. BL3041. *A cappella.* Medium.

Three Lenten Poems of Richard Crashaw—Pinkham. E. C. Schirmer No. 2693. Accompanied. Medium.

Tree of Sorrow—Chávez. Mercury No. MP-113. *A cappella.* Difficult.

Were You There? (spiritual)—arr. Burleigh. Ricordi No. NY423. Optional accompaniment. Medium.

Folk Songs and Spirituals

Ain'-a That Good News? (spiritual)—arr. Dawson. Kjos No. T103. *A cappella.* Moderately easy.

All Beauty within You (Italian love song)—arr. Riley. Music 70 No. M70-261. Accompanied. Moderately easy.

All My Trials, Lord (spiritual)—arr. Swenson. Galaxy No. 1.2824.1. Accompanied. Moderately easy.

Ash Grove, The (Welsh air)—arr. Jacob. Oxford No. F9. *A cappella.* Easy.

Black Is the Color of My True Love's Hair (Appalachian folk song)—arr. Churchill. Shawnee Press. Accompanied. Moderately easy.

Carmela (traditional Mexican song)—arr. Schillio. Presser No. 312-40740. Accompanied. Easy.

Charlottown (Southern folk song)—arr. Bryan. J. Fischer No. 8136. *A cappella.* Medium.

Chilly Waters (spiritual)—arr. Roberton. Curwen No. 61420. *A cappella.* Easy.

Ching-A-Ring Chaw (minstrel song)—arr. Copland and Fine. Boosey & Hawkes No. 5024. Accompanied. Medium.

Cicirinella (Italian folk song)—arr. Krone. Witmark No. 5-W2592. Accompanied. Easy.

Cindy (American folk song)—arr. Ehret. Presser No. 312-41186. Accompanied. Easy.

Climbin' up the Mountain (spiritual)—arr. Smith. Kjos No. 1001. *A cappella.* Easy.

Czechoslovakian Dance Song—arr. Krone. Witmark No. 5-W2608. Optional accompaniment. Moderately easy.

Dance to Your Daddie (Scottish nursery song)—arr. Rubbra. Belwin Mills No. 322. *A cappella.* Moderately easy.

Dark-Eyed Sailor, The (English folk song)—arr. Vaughan Williams. Galaxy No. 128. *A cappella.* Medium.

Deer Chase, The (American folk song)—arr. Luboff. Walton No. W3053. Accompanied. Moderately easy.

Didn't My Lord Deliver Daniel? (spiritual)—arr. Hunter. Lawson-Gould No. 957. Accompanied. Moderately easy.

Drei Volkslieder (Three folk songs)—arr. Mendelssohn. European American No. EA 413. *A cappella.* Medium.

Drunken Sailor, The (sea chantey)—arr. Schumann and Erickson. Bourne No. C3004. *A cappella.* Medium.

Each Little Flower (Swedish folk melody)—arr. Lundquist. Elkan-Vogel No. 1150. *A cappella.* Easy.

Early One Morning (English folk song)—arr. Christy. Schmitt, Hall & McCreary No. 1115. *A cappella.* Moderately easy.

Elijah Rock (spiritual)—arr. Hairston. Bourne No. S 1017. Optional accompaniment. Medium.

Every Time I Feel de Spirit (spiritual)—arr. Murray. Boosey & Hawkes No. 1737. Accompanied. Moderately easy.

Ezekiel Saw the Wheel (spiritual)—arr. Simeone. Shawnee Press No. 0130. Accompanied. Moderately difficult.

Farewell (Swedish folk song)—arr. Luboff. Walton No. W3095. *A cappella.* Moderately easy.

Farmer's Daughters, The (traditional English)—arr. Williams. G. Schirmer No. 8116. *A cappella.* Easy.

Fireflies (Russian)—arr. Clough and Leighter. E. C. Schirmer No. 1178. *A cappella.* Easy.

Frankie and Johnny (traditional)—arr. De Cormier. Lawson-Gould No. 52040. *A cappella.* Soprano, alto, tenor, and baritone solos. Medium.

Gay Fiesta (Mexican folk song)—arr. Riegger. Flammer No. 81149. Accompanied. Moderately easy.

Gentle Annie—Foster, arr. Eliot. Beckenhorst Press No. BP 113. Accompanied. Easy.

Gently, Johnny, My Jingalo (English folk song)—arr. Parker and Shaw. Lawson-Gould No. 643. *A cappella.* Moderately easy.

Girl with the Buckles on Her Shoes, The (Irish traditional)—arr. Nelson. G. Schirmer No. 10968. Accompanied. Moderately easy.

Good Night (German folk song)—arr. Manney. Wood No. 292. Accompanied. Moderately easy.

Goodnight Ladies (college song)—arr. Luboff. Walton No. W3097. *A cappella.* Moderately easy.

Great Angelic Host, The (Norwegian folk song)—arr. Grieg. Carl Fischer No. CM 530. *A cappella.* Medium.

Hawaiian Lullaby—arr. Sargent. Oxford No. X85. *A cappella.* Medium.

Ho-La-Hi (German folk song)—arr. Fiske. Oxford No. F53. *A cappella.* Easy.

How Good It Is (Hebrew folk song)—arr. Goldman. Lawson-Gould No. 51821. Accompanied. Moderately easy.

Ifca's Castle (Czechoslovakian folk song)—arr. Harley-Aschenbrenner. Carl Fischer No. CM 4708. *A cappella.* Easy.

I Know My Love (Irish folk song)—arr. Parker and Shaw. Lawson-Gould No. 657. Accompanied. Moderately easy.

I'm Goin' to Sing (spiritual)—arr. Parker and Shaw. Lawson-Gould No. 51101. *A cappella.* Moderately easy.

In Dat Great Gittin' Up Mornin' (Negro folk song)—arr. Hairston. Bourne No. B206516-357. *A cappella.* Tenor solo. Moderately easy.

I Ride an Old Paint—arr. Bright. Shawnee Press No. A-661. *A cappella.* Moderately easy.

Island Sheiling Song, An (folk song from the Hebrides)—arr. Arch. Boosey & Hawkes No. 5669. *A cappella.* Moderately easy.

I Sowed the Seeds of Love (Hampshire folk song)—arr. Holst. G. Schirmer No. 11149. *A cappella.* Medium.

I Won't Kiss Katy (Yugoslavian folk song)—arr. Smith and Aschenbrenner. Carl Fischer No. CM4596. *A cappella.* Moderately difficult.

Jacob's Ladder (spiritual)—arr. Wilson. Ricordi No. NY1476. Optional accompaniment. Moderately easy.

Jesus on the Water Side (spiritual)—arr. Aschenbrenner. Fitzsimons No. 1032. *A cappella.* Moderately difficult.

Jesus Walked This Lonesome Valley (spiritual)—arr. Harris. Music 70 No. M70-361. *A cappella.* Easy.

Just As the Tide Was Flowing (English folk song)—arr. Vaughan Williams. Galaxy No. 1.5020.1 *A cappella.* Medium.

Keys of My Heart, The (North country traditional song)—arr. Warrell. G. Schirmer No. 8474. *A cappella.* Moderately easy.

Lark on the Morn, The (folk song from *Sommersetshire*)—arr. Thompson. E. C. Schirmer No. 1782. *A cappella.* Easy.

Linden Lea (old English folk song)—Vaughan Williams, arr. Salter. Boosey & Hawkes No. 1401. Accompanied. Moderately easy.

Little Duck in the Meadow (Russian folk song)—arr. Nikolsky. G. Schirmer No. 6669. *A cappella.* Moderately easy.

Marching to Pretoria (South African veld song)—arr. Marais and Abbott. G. Schirmer No. 10423. Four-hand piano accompaniment. Easy.

Mary Had a Baby (spiritual)—arr. Dawson. Kjos No. T118. *A cappella.* Moderately easy.

Mayday Carol (English folk song)—arr. Taylor. J. Fischer No. 4838. Accompanied. Moderately easy.

Miner's Lament (Tune: Lilly Dale)—arr. De Cormier. Lawson-Gould No. 51975. *A cappella.* Moderately easy.

Moan to the Moon (Estonian folk song)—arr. Hunter. Lawson-Gould No. 954. Accompanied. Moderately easy.

Morning Now Beckons (Czechoslovakian folk song)—arr. Manney. Wood No. 355. Accompanied. Easy.

My Lord, What a Mornin' (spiritual)—arr. Burleigh. Ricordi No. 412. *A cappella.* Medium.

My Pretty Little Pink (American folk song)—arr. Barthelson. Lawson-Gould No. 792. Accompanied. Moderately easy.

Nine Hundred Miles from Home (Appalachian Mountain folksong)—arr. Schillio. Associated No. A-712. Accompanied. Moderately easy.

Oh, Dear! What Can the Matter Be? (English folk song)—arr. Bantock. Joseph Williams, Ltd. No. 19. *A cappella.* Moderately easy.

Oh! Susanna—Foster, arr. Hayes. Shawnee Press No. A-1745. Accompanied. Moderately easy.

Oh, What a Beautiful City (spiritual)—arr. Dawson. Kjos No. T100. *A cappella.* Medium.

Old Woman and the Peddler, The (old English)—arr. Kinscella. G. Schirmer No. 7819. *A cappella.* Moderately easy.

Peasant and His Oxen (Yugoslavian folk song)—arr. Smith and Aschenbrenner. Carl Fischer No. 4595. *A cappella.* Medium.

Prince Charlie's Farewell (traditional English air)—arr. Robertson. G. Schirmer No. 8512. *A cappella.* Moderately easy.

Red, Red Rose, A (Scottish folk tune)—arr. Parker and Shaw. Lawson-Gould No. 645. *A cappella.* Tenor solo. Medium.

Ride the Chariot (spiritual)—arr. Smith. Kjos No. 1015. Optional accompaniment. Medium.

Rock-a My Soul (spiritual)—arr. De Vaux. Bourne No. B-211128. Accompanied. Moderately easy.

Russian Picnic (based on Russian folk tunes)—arr. Enders. G. Schirmer No. 9544. Accompanied. Moderately easy.

Saenu (Yemenite melody)—arr. Davidson. Transcontinental No. 990744. Optional accompaniment. Moderately easy.

Sakura Sakura (Japanese folk song)—arr. Hairston. Bourne No. J1. Optional accompaniment. Moderately easy.

See the Gipsies (Hungarian folk song)—arr. Kodály. Oxford No. X61. *A cappella.* Medium.

Shenandoah (sea chantey)—arr. Moore. Mark Foster No. MF 3011. Optional accompaniment. Moderately easy.

She's like the Swallow (Newfoundland folk song)—arr. Chapman. Oxford No. X64. *A cappella.* Moderately easy.

Silver Moon Is Shining, The (Italian folk song)—arr. Davis. E. C. Schirmer No. 1754. *A cappella.* Moderately easy.

Soon-Ah Will Be Done (spiritual)—Dawson. Kjos No. T102. Optional accompaniment. Medium.

Spring of the Year, The (English folk song)—arr. Vaughan Williams. Galaxy No. 129. *A cappella.* Moderately easy.

S'vivon (The Top)—arr. Helfman. Transcontinental No. 991501. *A cappella.* Moderately easy.

Tchum Bi-Ri Tchum (Israeli folk tune)—arr. Goldman. Lawson-Gould No. 51888. Accompanied. Moderately easy.

Tender Love (Cajun folk song)—arr. Luboff. Walton No. 3070. Accompanied. Moderately easy.

There Is a Balm in Gilead (spiritual)—arr. Dawson. Kjos No. T105. *A cappella.* Soprano solo. Medium.

There's a Lit'l' Wheel a-Turnin' in My Heart (spiritual)—arr. Dawson. Kjos No. T121. *A cappella.* Medium.

Tomorrow Shall Be My Dancing Day (traditional English carol)—arr. Willcocks. Oxford No. 84.141. *A cappella.* Medium.

Turtle Dove, The (English folk song)—arr. Vaughan Williams. G. Schirmer No. 8105. *A cappella.* Baritone solo. Moderately easy.

Twenty Eighteen (English folk song)—arr. Taylor. J. Fischer No. 4846. Accompanied. Easy.

Two Macedonian Folk Songs—arr. Srebotnjak. G. Schirmer No. 11315. *A cappella.* Moderately easy.

Two Negro Spirituals (Deep River and Dig My Grave)—arr. Burleigh. G. Schirmer No. 5815. *A cappella.* Medium.

Wade in the Water (spiritual)—arr. Kirk. Carl Fischer No. CM 8022. *A cappella.* Solo. Easy.

Waltzing Matilda (Australian song)—arr. Wood. Oxford No. OCS 790. *A cappella.* Medium.

Waters Ripple and Flow (Czechoslovakian folk song)—arr. Taylor. J. Fischer No. 5675. Accompanied. Soprano and baritone solos. Moderately difficult.

Weep, O Willow (mountain tune)—arr. Lekberg. Summy-Birchard No. 5009. *A cappella.* Soprano solo. Medium.

Well-Beloved, The (Armenian folk song)—arr. Taylor. J. Fischer No. 4844. Accompanied. Soprano solo. Moderately easy.

When Love Is Kind (English folk song)—arr. Terri. Lawson-Gould No. 843. *A cappella.* Moderately easy.

When the Saints Go Marching In (spiritual)—arr. Luboff. Walton No. 3068. Accompanied. Moderately easy.

Ya Ba Bom (Jewish folk tune)—arr. Goldman. Lawson-Gould No. 51814. Piano accompaniment, with optional string bass and drums. Medium.

Yarmouth Fair (English folk song)—arr. Warlock. Oxford No. X37. *A cappella.* Moderately easy.

Zum Gali (Israeli folk tune)—arr. Goldman. Lawson-Gould No. 52026. Accompanied. Medium.

Special Occasions (Commencement, Thanksgiving, Patriotic Holidays)

Battle Hymn of the Republic (patriotic)—Steffe, arr. Ringwald. Shawnee Press No. A 0028. Accompanied. Moderately easy.

Battle Hymn of the Republic (patriotic)—Steffe, arr. Wilhousky. Carl Fischer No. CM 4743. Accompanied. Medium.

Come, Let Us Sing to the Lord (Thanksgiving)—Schvedov, arr. Cain. Boosey & Hawkes No. 1800. *A cappella.* Difficult.

Give Me Your Tired, Your Poor (patriotic or commencement)—Berlin, arr. Ringwald. Shawnee Press No. A 0119. Accompanied. Medium.

Give Thanks (Thanksgiving)—Williams. Flammer No. 84191. Accompanied. Soprano solo. Easy.

In Solemn Silence (memorial anthem)—Ippolitov-Ivanov, arr. Wilhousky. Carl Fischer No. 635. *A cappella.* Medium.

Land of Hope and Glory (commencement)—Elgar. Boosey & Hawkes No. 1161. Accompanied. Moderately easy.

Let All Creatures of God His Praises Sing (Thanksgiving)—Kalinnikov, arr. Cain. Boosey & Hawkes No. 1801. *A cappella.* Medium.

Now Thank We All Our God (Thanksgiving)—Cruger, arr. Holst. Kjos No. 5138. Accompanied. Moderately easy.

Now Thank We All Our God (Thanksgiving)—R. Thompson. E. C. Schirmer No. 4008. Accompanied (keyboard or orchestra). Moderately easy.

Onward, Ye Peoples! (commencement)—Sibelius, arr. Lefebvre. Galaxy No. 938–10. Accompanied. Medium.

Prayer of Thanksgiving (Netherlands folk song; Thanksgiving)—arr. Kremser. G. Schirmer No. 4345. Accompanied. Easy.

Recessional (Memorial Day)—DeKoven. Presser No. 322-35015. Accompanied. Moderately easy.

To Music (commencement)—Schubert, arr. Wilson. Schmitt, Hall & McCreary No. 1070. Accompanied. Moderately easy.

General: Sacred

Absalom—Tomkins. Chappell No. 6140. *A cappella.* Medium.

Adoramus Te—Corsi, arr. Greyson. Bourne No. ES15. *A cappella.* Moderately easy.

Adoramus Te—Gasparini. Belwin Mills No. 2148. *A cappella.* Medium.

Adoramus Te—Lassus. Music Press No. MP-76. *A cappella.* Medium.

Adoramus Te—Mozart. G. Schirmer No. 9932. Optional accompaniment. Moderately easy.

Adoramus Te, Christe—Palestrina. Carl Fischer No. CM 6578. *A cappella.* Easy.
Agnus Dei (Lamb of God)—Di Lasso. Raymond A. Hoffman No. R-2002. *A cappella.* Moderately easy.
Agnus Dei—Hassler. Shawnee Press No. A-1482. *A cappella.* Easy.
Agnus Dei—Lotti. Edw. B. Marks. No. 4365. *A cappella.* Moderately easy.
Agnus Dei—Morley, arr. Greyson. Bourne No. ES36. *A cappella.* Medium.
Agnus Dei—Pergolesi. Mercury No. MC 147. Accompanied. Medium.
Agnus Dei (from *Deutsche Messe*)—Schubert. Piedmont No. 4449. Accompanied. Medium.
Agnus Dei—Victoria. Lawson-Gould No. 925. *A cappella.* Medium.
All Breathing Life (from the motet *Sing Ye to the Lord*)—J. S. Bach. G. Schirmer No. 7470. Optional accompaniment. Difficult.
Alleluia (from the motet *Exsultate, Jubilate*)—Mozart, arr. Rosenberg. Carl Fischer No. 541. Accompanied. Medium. (Soprano solo, difficult.)
Alleluia—Thompson. E. C. Schirmer No. 1786. *A cappella.* Moderately difficult.
Alleluja—J. S. Bach. C. F. Peters No. 6106a. Accompanied. Medium.
Alleluia, Alleluia—Buxtehude. Presser No. 312-40668. Accompanied. Medium.
All Glory Be to God on High (melody of Gregorian origin)—arr. Malin. Summy-Birchard No. 345. Accompanied. Moderately easy.
All Hail the Power—Vaughan Williams. Oxford. Accompanied. Moderately difficult.
All the Earth Doth Worship Thee—Handel. Ricordi No. NY2030. Accompanied. Moderately easy.
All This Night—Finzi. Boosey & Hawkes No. 5127. *A cappella.* Medium.
Almighty and Everlasting God—Gibbons. Bourne No. ES35. *A cappella.* Moderately easy.
Almighty Father (Chorale from *Mass*)—Bernstein. G. Schirmer No. 11948. *A cappella.* Moderately easy.
Almighty God, Who Hast Me Brought—Ford. C. F. Peters No. 1558. *A cappella.* Moderately easy.
Amen—Scarlatti, arr. Ehret. European American No. EA 231. Organ or piano accompaniment. Moderately easy.
And Draw a Blessing Down (from *Theodora*)—Handel, arr. Malin. Edw. B. Marks No. 4535. Accompanied. Medium.
Angelic Greeting, The—Brahms, ed. Mattfeld. E. C. Schirmer No. 2477. *A cappella.* Medium.
Ave Christe, Immolate—Desprez. Éditions Salabert No. MC 531. *A cappella.* Medium.
Ave Maria—Bach-Gounod, arr. Tolmadge. Staff No. 243. Accompanied. Easy.
Ave Maria—Brahms. C. F. Peters No. 66136. Accompanied. Medium.
Ave Maria—Bruckner. Edw. B. Marks No. 47. *A cappella.* Moderately easy.
Ave Maria—Franck, arr. Borucchia. McLaughlin & Reilly No. 1072. Organ accompaniment. Moderately easy.
Ave Maria—Mouton. Music Press No. DCS 40. *A cappella.* Moderately easy.
Ave Maria—Rachmaninoff. Oliver Ditson No. 332-14564; Lawson-Gould No. 52344. *A cappella.* Medium.
Ave Maria—Tchaikovsky. Boston Music Co. No. 1064. *A cappella.* Moderately easy.
Ave Maria—Verdi. C. F. Peters No. 4256a. *A cappella.* Moderately difficult.
Ave Maria—Victoria. Music Press No. MP-79. *A cappella.* Moderately easy.
Ave Maria, gratia plena—Desprez. Associated No. 28. *A cappella.* Medium.
Ave Maria No. 20—Villa-Lobos, new text by H. R. Wilson. Consolidated. *A cappella.* Medium.
Ave Maris Stella—Desprez. Associated No. 35. *A cappella.* Medium.
Ave Maris Stella—Hassler. Kjos No. 5012. *A cappella.* Moderately easy.
Ave Regina Coelorum—Lassus. Associated No. A-406. *A cappella.* Medium.
Ave Regina Coelorum—Willaert. Ricordi No. NY1887. *A cappella.* Medium.
Ave verum corpus—Byrd. Bourne No. ES44. *A cappella.* Moderately easy.
Ave verum corpus—Mozart. G. Schirmer No. 5471. Organ accompaniment. Moderately easy.

Awake the Harp (from *The Creation*)—Haydn, ed. Neuen. Lawson-Gould No. 51982. Accompanied. Medium.

Beautiful Savior (Silesian folk tune)—arr. F. M. Christiansen. Augsburg No. 51. *A cappella.* Medium.

Behold a Hallowed Day—Handl. Concordia No. 98-1690. *A cappella.* Medium.

Be Joyful, Be Joyful—Homilius. Sam Fox No. MM5. Accompanied. Moderately easy.

Benedixisti (Thou Hast Been Gracious, Lord)—G. Gabrieli. G. Schirmer No. 7625. *A cappella.* Medium.

Best of Rooms, The—Thompson. E. C. Schirmer No. 2672. *A cappella.* Medium.

Blessed Are the Faithful—Schütz, ed. Shaw and Speer. G. Schirmer No. 10114. *A cappella.* Moderately difficult.

Blessed Savior, Our Lord Jesus—Hassler. G. Schirmer No. 7563. *A cappella.* Medium.

Bless the Lord for Ever and Ever—Mozart, arr. Hilton. Mercury No. 352-00459. Accompanied. Moderately easy.

Blest Be the Lord—Haydn. McLaughlin & Reilly Co. No. 2217. Accompanied. Medium.

Brother James' Air (Marosa)—Jacob. Carl Fischer No. OCS763. *A cappella.* Easy.

Call to Mary—Brahms, ed. Mattfeld. E. C. Schirmer No. 2480. *A cappella.* Medium.

Call to Remembrance—Farrant, arr. Greyson. Bourne No. ES 17. *A cappella.* Moderately easy.

Cantate Domino—Pitoni. Bourne No. ES 5. *A cappella.* Moderately easy.

Cantate Domino—Schütz. Arista No. AE 356; Bourne No. B201889. *A cappella.* Moderately difficult.

Cantique de Jean Racine—Fauré. Broude Bros. No. 801. Accompanied. Moderately easy.

Cherubic Hymn (Greek liturgy)—arr. Aliferis. Witmark No. 5-W3063. *A cappella.* Moderately difficult.

Cherubim Song—Glinka. Music 70 No. M70-423. *A cappella.* Moderately easy.

Cherubim Song—Gretchaninov, arr. Cain. Hoffmann No. 46012A. *A cappella.* Medium.

Cherubim Song No. 3—Tchaikovsky. G. Schirmer No. 2561. Piano or organ accompaniment. Moderately difficult.

Cherubim Song No. 7—Bortniansky, arr. Tchaikovsky. G. Schirmer No. 2560. *A cappella.* Easy.

Christus factus est pro nobis—Bruckner. C. F. Peters No. 6316. *A cappella.* Moderately difficult.

Clap Your Hands—Eddleman. Carl Fischer No. CM 8039. Optional percussion. Moderately easy.

Come, Blessed Rest—J. S. Bach. Kjos No. 2004. *A cappella.* Medium.

Come, Then, O Holy Breath of God—Palestrina. Piedmont No. 4414. *A cappella.* Medium.

Come Let Us Start a Joyful Song—Hassler. Bourne No. ES 74. *A cappella.* Moderately easy.

Come Thou, O Savior—J. S. Bach. Summy-Birchard No. 5203. *A cappella.* Moderately easy.

Comfort All Ye My People—Fauré, arr. Hopson. Carl Fischer No. CM 8017. Piano or organ accompaniment. Moderately easy.

Contentment—Mozart. Lawson-Gould No. 937. Accompanied. Soprano solo. Moderately easy.

Corporis mysterium (Sacrament of Priceless Worth)—Palestrina. Ricordi No. NY1852. *A cappella.* Moderately easy.

Create in Me, O God, a Pure Heart—Brahms, arr. Williamson. G. Schirmer No. 7504. *A cappella.* Moderately easy.

Crucifixus (from B. Minor Mass)—J. S. Bach. Hope Publishing Co. No. CY 3356; E. C. Schirmer No. 1174. Accompanied. Medium.

Crucifixus—Mozart. National Music Publishers No. WHC-141. Accompanied. Medium.

Dance Alleluia—Freed. Hansen Publications No. C566. Accompanied (piano, string bass, bongos, and wood block). Moderately easy.

David's Lamentation—Billings. C. F. Peters No. 66336. Optional accompaniment. Moderately easy.

Day by Day We Magnify Thee—Handel. Lawson-Gould No. 797; Edw. B. Marks No. 4516. Accompanied. Medium.

De profundis (Out of the Deep)—Thompson. Weintraub. *A cappella.* Moderately difficult.

Der Gott, unsers Herrn, Jesu Christi (To God, Our Lord and Saviour)—Telemann. Lawson-Gould No. 52207. Accompanied. Medium.

Dies irae (from Requiem)—Mozart. G. Schirmer No. 10016. Accompanied. Medium.

Dies sanctificatus—Palestrina. National Music Publishers No. RCS-102. *A cappella.* Medium.

Dona nobis pacem—Beethoven. National Music Publishers No. WHS-143. *A cappella.* Medium.

Ehre sei Dir, Christe (Christ, Be Thine the Glory!)—Schütz. G. Schirmer No. 10123. Optional accompaniment. Medium.

Et misericordia—Vivaldi, arr. Kjelson. Belwin Mills No. 2236. Accompanied. Moderately easy.

Every Thing You Do—Buxtehude. Sam Fox No. CM 19. Accompanied. Medium.

Exaltabo Te, Domine—Palestrina. G. Schirmer No. 7620. *A cappella.* Medium.

Exultate Deo (Sing and Praise Jehovah)—Palestrina. G. Schirmer No. 7672. *A cappella.* Medium.

Exultate Deo—Scarlatti. G. Schirmer No. 11001. *A cappella.* Medium.

Exultate justi—Viadana, ed. Klein. G.I.A. No. G-2140. *A cappella.* Medium.

Glaube, Hoffnung und Liebe (Faith, Hope and Love)—Schubert. National Music Publishers No. NMP-185. Accompanied. Medium.

Gloria (from Mass No. 3 in G minor)—J. S. Bach. Gentry No. JG2021. Accompanied. Medium.

Gloria—Vivaldi. National Music Publishers No. NMP-132. Accompanied. Medium.

Gloria in excelsis (from *Harmoniemesse*)—Haydn. Hal Leonard No. 08679600. Accompanied. Medium.

Gloria in excelsis—Mozart. G. Schirmer No. 3515. Accompanied. Medium.

Gloria—Only Begotten Son—Gretchaninov, arr. Tellep. Boosey & Hawkes No. 5097. *A cappella.* Medium.

Gloria Patri (Glory to God)—Palestrina, arr. Greyson. Bourne No. ES46. *A cappella.* Easy.

Glory—Lotti. Edw. B. Marks No. 4366. *A cappella.* Moderately easy.

Glory and Honor Are Before Him—J. S. Bach. Kjos No. 5150. A cappella. Medium.

Glory and Worship—Purcell. E. C. Schirmer No. 1108. Organ accompaniment. Moderately easy.

Glory Be to God—Rachmaninoff, arr. Tkach. Kjos No. 6528. *A cappella.* Medium.

Glory to God—Bach, ed. Wilson. Ricordi No. NY1397. Optional accompaniment. Moderately difficult.

Glory to God—Bortniansky. Witmark No. 5-W2743. *A cappella.* Moderately easy.

Glory to God—Handel. Lawson-Gould No. 796. Accompanied. Medium.

Glory to God in the Highest—Thompson. E. C. Schirmer No. 2470. *A cappella.* Medium.

Graduale—Sancta Maria—Mozart. Broude Bros. No. 77. Accompanied. Medium.

Grant unto Me the Joy of Thy Salvation—Brahms. G. Schirmer No. 7506. *A cappella.* Moderately difficult.

Great and Glorious—Haydn. Wood No. 316. Accompanied. Medium.

Haec dies—Byrd. Oxford No. TCM 50. Optional accompaniment. Moderately difficult.

Hail, Thou Gladdening Light—Gretchaninov. Wood No. 594. *A cappella.* Moderately difficult.

Hail, Thou Holy One—Tchaikovsky, arr. Cain. Boosey & Hawkes No. 1979. *A cappella.* Medium.

Hallelujah (from *Mount of Olives*)—Beethoven. G. Schirmer No. 2215. Accompanied. Difficult.

Hallelujah—Handel. Music 70 No. M70-330. Accompanied. Medium.

Hallelujah, Amen (from *Judas Maccabaeus*)—Handel. G. Schirmer No. 9835. Optional accompaniment. Medium.

Hear, O Lord, Hear My Prayer—Lasso, arr. Lundquist. Elkan-Vogel No. 1110. *A cappella.* Moderately easy.

Hear My Prayer—Kopylov. Boston Music Co. No. 1294. *A cappella.* Medium.

Hear Our Supplication—Mozart, arr. Hilton. Mercury No. 352-00378. Accompanied. Medium.

Heavenly Light—Kopylov, arr. Wilhousky. Carl Fischer No. CM 497. *A cappella.* Moderately easy.

Heavens Are Declaring, The—Beethoven. G. Schirmer No. 3032. Accompanied. Easy.

Heavens Are Telling, The (from *The Creation*)—Haydn, arr. Phillips. Carl Fischer No. CM 127. Organ accompaniment. Moderately difficult.

Here Is Thy Footstool—Creston. G. Schirmer No. 11146. *A cappella.* Medium.

He Shall Rule from Sea to Sea—Rorem. Boosey & Hawkes No. 5651. Accompanied. Medium.

He Watching over Israel (from *Elijah*)—Mendelssohn. G. Schirmer No. 2498. Accompanied. Moderately difficult.

He Who with Weeping Soweth—Schütz. G. Schirmer No. 10115. Optional accompaniment. Moderately difficult.

Hide Not Thy Face, O My Savior (Finnish folk melody)—arr. Lundquist. Willis No. 8469. *A cappella.* Moderately easy.

Hodie nobis coelorum Rex—Bright. Shawnee Press No. A-812. Accompanied. Medium.

Holy, Holy, Holy (Sanctus and Hosanna)—Haydn. Mercury No. 352-00469. Accompanied. Moderately easy.

Holy, Holy, Holy (Sanctus)—Lotti. E. C. Schirmer No. 2216. *A cappella.* Medium.

Holy, Holy, Holy—Scarlatti. Chappell No. 6141. *A cappella.* Medium.

Holy Is the Lord—Schubert. Presser No. 312-21416. Accompanied. Easy.

Honor and Glory—J. S. Bach. Plymouth No. SC10. Accompanied. Moderately easy.

Hosanna in excelsis Deo—Gounod. Gentry No. G-136. Accompanied. Medium.

Hospodi Pomilui—von Lvov, ed. Wilhousky. Carl Fischer No. CM 6580. *A cappella.* Medium.

How Lovely Is Thy Dwelling Place—Brahms. G. Schirmer No. 5124. Accompanied. Moderately difficult.

Humility before Thee—C.P.E. Bach, arr. Ehret. Elkan-Vogel No. 1268. Piano or organ accompaniment. Medium.

Hundredth Psalm, The—Mendelssohn, ed. Hines. Concordia No. 98-2215. *A cappella.* Moderately difficult.

Hymn to Saint Peter—Britten. Boosey & Hawkes. Organ accompaniment. Soprano solo. Moderately difficult.

Hymn to the Trinity—Kopylov. Kjos No. 5337. *A cappella.* Easy.

If I Flew to the Point of Sunrise—Berger. Kjos No. ED 5992. *A cappella.* Medium.

If Ye Love Me, Keep My Commandments—Tallis. E. C. Schirmer No. 2269. *A cappella.* Medium.

Incline Thine Ear, Oh Lord—Arkhangelsky. Witmark No. 5-W2689. *A cappella.* Medium.

In excelsis Deo (from *Mass in C*)—Mozart. Presser No. 312-41198. Accompanied. Medium.

In memoria aeterna (from *Beatus Vir*)—Vivaldi, ed. McEwen. Hinshaw No. HMC-179. Accompanied. Medium.

In omnem terram—Campra, arr. Castle. Wood No. 44-964. Organ or piano accompaniment. Moderately difficult.

In Thee Is Joy—J. S. Bach. Somerset Press No. MW 1229. Accompanied. Moderately easy.

Iustorum animae—Byrd. E. C. Schirmer No. 327. *A cappella.* Medium.

I Will Clothe Thy Priests with Salvation—Peter, arr. Kroeger. Boosey & Hawkes No. 6004. Accompanied. Medium.

Jesu, Joy of Man's Desiring—J. S. Bach. E. C. Schirmer No. 317. Organ accompaniment. Moderately easy.

Jesu dulcis memoria—Victoria. G. Schirmer No. 5573. *A cappella*. Easy.

Jesus, Now to Thee I Turn Me—Cherubini, arr. Lundquist. Elkan-Vogel No. 1159. *A cappella*. Easy.

Jubilate Deo—Lassus. Mercury No. MP-80. *A cappella*. Moderately easy.

Jubilate Deo—Mozart. Pro Art No. 1007. *A cappella*. Moderately easy.

Justum deduxit Dominus (Lord, God Has Led the Righteous Man)—Mozart. Lawson-Gould No. 52137. Accompanied. Moderately difficult.

King of Glory—Mozart, ed. Ehret. Gentry No. G-345. Accompanied. Medium.

Kyrie—Mozart, ed. Landon. G. Schirmer No. 12067. Accompanied. Medium.

Kyrie (from Mass in G)—Schubert. Kjos No. ED 5989. Accompanied. Soprano solo. Medium.

Kyrie eleison—Durante. Pro Art No. 2279. *A cappella*. Moderately easy.

Kyrie eleison—Haydn, arr. Ehret. Heritage No. H 94. Accompanied. Moderately easy.

Lacrymosa—Cherubini, ed. De Pietto. Lawson-Gould No. 51853. Accompanied. Medium.

Lacrymosa (from Requiem)—Mozart. G. Schirmer No. 10017. Accompanied. Medium.

Lasciatemi morire—Monteverdi. Ricordi No. NY841. *A cappella*. Moderately easy.

Last Words of David, The—Thompson. E. C. Schirmer No. ?294. Accompanied. Medium.

Laudate Dominum—Sweelinck. Concordia No. 97-5450. Optional accompaniment. Medium.

Laudate pueri—Mozart. Lawson-Gould No. 51166; Associated No. A-683. Accompanied. Medium.

Lend Thine Ear to My Prayer—Arkhangelsky, arr. Wilhousky. Carl Fischer No. CM 613. *A cappella*. Moderately difficult.

Let All Mortal Flesh Keep Silence—Holst. Galaxy No. 3.2309.1. Accompanied. Medium. 3.2309.1. Accompanied. Medium.

Let Every Nation His Praises Sing—Franck. Sam Fox No. CM 20. *A cappella*. Medium.

Let My Prayer Come Up (Offertorium)—Purcell. Gray No. 1527; Mercury No. 352-00440. Accompanied. Moderately easy.

Let Nothing Ever Grieve Thee—Brahms. C. F. Peters No. 6093. Accompanied. Moderately easy.

Let Their Celestial Concerts All Unite (from *Samson*)—Handel. E. C. Schirmer No. 312. Accompanied. Moderately difficult.

Let Thy Holy Presence—Tchesnokov, arr. Cain. Summy-Birchard No. 12. *A cappella*. Medium.

Libera me—Fauré. Belwin Mills No. 2032. Accompanied. Medium.

Light the Legend (A Song for Chanukah)—Isaacson. Transcontinental No. 991024. Accompanied. Moderately easy.

Like As the Hart—Palestrina. G. Schirmer No. 3509. *A cappella*. Moderately easy.

Lo, I Am the Voice of One Crying in the Wilderness—Schütz. G. Schirmer No. 10116. Optional accompaniment. Moderately difficult.

Locus iste a Deo factus est—Bruckner. C. F. Peters No. 6314. *A cappella*. Easy.

Lord, Have Mercy upon Us—Beethoven. Chappell No. 6145. Accompanied. Moderately easy.

Lord, Hear Our Prayer (from *Otello*)—Verdi, arr. Huguelet. Carl Fischer No. CM 616. Optional accompaniment. Medium.

Lord, How Lovely Is Your Dwelling Place—Gretchaninov, arr. Hopson. Carl Fischer No. CM8214. *A cappella*. Medium.

Lord, Remember Not—Mendelssohn. Walton No. 6010. Optional accompaniment. Medium.

Lord, We Love the Place—Graun. Sam Fox No. MM 6. Accompanied. Medium.

Lord Bless You and Keep You, The—Lutkin. Summy-Birchard No. 1089. *A cappella*. Easy.

Lord Christ, Son of God (Christe Dei Soboles)—Lasso. G. Schirmer No. 9414 *A cappella.* Medium.

Lord God, in Power and Glory—Haydn. Curwen No. 80782. Optional accompaniment. Moderately easy.

Lord Is My Shepherd, The—Thompson. E. C. Schirmer No. 2688. Accompanied. Moderately easy.

Lord of Love, to Thee I Flee—Cornelius. Sam Fox No. MM 26. Accompanied. Medium.

Lord Shall Be unto Thee, The (from Requiem)—Thompson. E. C. Schirmer No. 2641. *A cappella.* Medium.

Lovely Appear (from *The Redemption*)—Gounod. G. Schirmer No. 2013. Accompanied. Medium.

Magnificat—Gabrieli. Curwen No. 10565. *A cappella.* Three choirs. Difficult.

Magnificat—My Soul Doth Magnify the Lord—Buxtehude. C. F. Peters No. 66288. Accompanied. Moderately difficult.

Magnificat and Nunc dimittis—Purcell. C. F. Peters No. 66266. Optional accompaniment. Medium.

May We Ever Praise the Father—Handel. Lawson-Gould No. 52235. Optional accompaniment. Moderately easy.

Mighty Fortress Is Our God, A—Luther. Witmark No. 5W2835. Optional accompaniment. Moderately easy.

Miserere mei—Lotti. Boosey & Hawkes No. 1938. *A cappella.* Easy.

Miserere mei—Pergolesi. Walton No. 6011. Accompanied. Medium.

Mi Yemalel (Who Can Retell?)—Helfman. Transcontinental No. 991500. *A cappella.* Moderately easy.

My Heart Overflows—Harrer, ed. Frank. Sam Fox No. MM 1. Piano or organ accompaniment. Medium.

Ne irascaris—Byrd. Alexander Broude No. 216-9. *A cappella.* Moderately difficult.

Now God Be Praised in Heav'n Above—Vulpius. E. C. Schirmer No. 1693. Optional accompaniment. Moderately easy.

O, Lord in Thee Have I Trusted—Handel. Kjos No. 5481 C. Accompanied. Medium.

O, Love Divine (from *Theodora*)—Handel, arr. Malin. Edw. B. Marks No. 4543. Accompanied. Moderately difficult.

O Be Joyful! (Freut Euch, Freut Euch)—Mozart. Sam Fox No. MM 9. Accompanied. Medium.

O Be Joyful in the Lord—Rutter. Oxford No. A 346. Accompanied. Medium.

O Blessed Lord—Tchaikovsky. Wallace Gillman No. 4001. Optional accompaniment. Moderately easy.

O bone Jesu—Palestrina. Oliver Ditson No. 332-03070. *A cappella.* Easy.

O Cast Me Not Away from Thy Countenance—Brahms. G. Schirmer No. 7505. *A cappella.* Moderately difficult.

O Clap Your Hands—Vaughan Williams. Galaxy No. 222. Organ accompaniment. Moderately difficult.

O Divine Redeemer—Gounod, arr. Cain. Schmitt, Hall & McCreary No. 1602. Accompanied. Moderately easy.

O Glorious One—Gretchaninov, arr. Cain. Hoffman No. 46,339. *A cappella.* Moderately easy.

O God, I Thank Thee—Schumann, arr. Lundquist. Willis No. 8466. *A cappella.* Easy.

O God Who Reigns in Heav'n Above—Byrd, arr. Ehret. Gentry No. JG-439. Optional accompaniment. Moderately easy.

Oh, Blest Are They—Tchaikovsky, arr. Cain. Remick No. 3024. *A cappella.* Moderately difficult.

O Hear Me When I Call on Thee—Schubert. E. C. Schirmer No. 2684. Accompanied. Medium.

O Jesu, Salvator—Alberti, ed. Boyd. Lawson-Gould No. 51843. Accompanied. Medium.

O Lord, Have Mercy on Us (Kyrie eleison)—Buxtehude. Sam Fox No. CM 6. Optional accompaniment. Medium.

O Lord, Hear Thou My Prayer—Schumann, arr. Goldman. Lawson-Gould No. 51968. Piano or organ accompaniment. Soprano solo. Medium.

O Lord Most Holy (Panis angelicus)—Franck. Summy-Birchard No. 396. Accompanied. Medium.

O magnum mysterium—Rorem. Boosey & Hawkes No. 6006. *A cappella.* Medium.

O Mighty Hand (Dor Nifia)—Goldman. Transcontinental No. 991033. Organ or piano accompaniment. Moderately easy.

Omnipotence, The—Schubert. G. Schirmer No. 10146. Accompanied. Medium.

Once I Had Hoped from Thee—De Monte. Piedmont No. 4427. *A cappella.* Medium.

Onward, Ye Peoples!—Sibelius, arr. Lefebvre. Galaxy No. 938-10. Accompanied. Moderately easy.

O Rejoice, Ye Christians, Loudly—J. S. Bach. Carl Fischer No. CM 6600. *A cappella.* Moderately easy.

O Savior, Throw the Heavens Wide (Motet, Op. 74, No. 2)—Brahms. G. Schirmer No. 8545. *A cappella.* Moderately difficult.

O Sing unto the Lord—Hassler. G. Schirmer No. 10872. *A cappella.* Moderately easy.

O Sing unto the Lord—Purcell. E. C. Schirmer No. 1103. Organ accompaniment. Moderately easy.

O Sing unto the Lord a New Song—Piston. Associated No. A-640. Accompanied. Moderately difficult.

Os justi—Bruckner. G. Schirmer No. 8121. *A cappella.* Medium.

Our Father—Gretchaninov, English text by Kimball. Presser No. 332-13000. *A cappella.* Moderately difficult.

Our Soul Doth Wait upon the Lord—Antes, arr. Kroeger. Boosey & Hawkes No. 5941. Organ accompaniment. Medium.

O vos omnes—Correa. Lawson-Gould No. 52225. *A cappella.* Easy.

O vos omnes—Victoria. Ricordi No. NY1875. *A cappella.* Medium.

Pater Noster—Stravinsky. Boosey & Hawkes No. 1833. *A cappella.* Medium.

Pater Noster (Our Father)—Tchaikovsky. G. Schirmer No. 5475. *A cappella.* Moderately easy.

Plorate filii Israel (from *Jeptah*)—Carissimi. Bourne No. ES 34; Kjos No. ED 29; E. C. Schirmer No. 1172. Accompanied. Medium.

Praise Be to Thee—Palestrina, arr. Lundquist. Willis No. 5678. *A cappella.* Easy.

Praise Him—J. S. Bach, arr. Steele. Raymond A. Hoffman No. H-2005. Accompanied. Moderately easy.

Praise Him, Praise Ye the Lord—Caldara, ed. Ehret. Elkan-Vogel No. 362-03145. Piano or organ accompaniment. Soprano, alto, tenor, and bass solos. Moderately easy.

Praise the Lord in Song—Constantini. Music 70 No. M70-341. *A cappella.* Moderately easy.

Praise Ye the Lord—McCray. Music 70 No. M70-374. *A cappella.* Medium.

Prayer and Chorale—Mendelssohn. Lawson-Gould No. 849. *A cappella.* Moderately easy.

Psallite—Praetorius, arr. Greyson. Bourne No. ES 21. *A cappella.* Easy.

Psalm 43—Mendelssohn. Hope Publishing Co. No. APM 006. *A cappella.* Medium.

Psalm 92—Schubert. Alexander Broude No. AB 823. *A cappella.* Baritone solo. Moderately difficult.

Psalm CL (Praise Ye the Lord)—Franck. Oliver Ditson No. 332-14082. Organ accompaniment. Medium.

Psalm 150 (Hallelujah, Praise Ye the Lord)—Lewandowski. Schmitt, Hall & McCreary No. 1640; Transcontinental No. 990792. Optional *a cappella.* Medium.

Psalm 61—Hovhaness. C. F. Peters No. 6255. Organ accompaniment. Medium.

Quando corpus (from *Stabat Mater*)—Rossini, ed. Van Camp. Music 70 No. 205. *A cappella.* Medium.

Rejoice in the Lord—Amram. C. F. Peters No. 66517. *A cappella.* Medium.

Rejoice in the Lord Always—Purcell. Novello No. 1581. Accompanied. Moderately easy.

Religious Meditation—Berlioz, ed. Prussing. Tetra No. AB 833. Organ accompaniment. Medium.

Requiescat—Schuman. G. Schirmer No. 8926. Accompanied. Medium.

Salvation Is Created—Tschesnokov, arr. Norden. J. Fischer No. 4129. *A cappella.* Medium.

Salve Regina—Lasso. Music Press No. MP-73. *A cappella.* Medium.

Sanctum Domini Dei nomen est—Caldara. E. C. Schirmer No. E.C.S. 3076. Optional accompaniment. Medium.

Sanctus (from B Minor Mass)—J. S. Bach. G. Schirmer No. 5654. Accompanied. Difficult.

Sanctus (from C Major Mass)—Beethoven. Walton No. 6014. Accompanied. Medium.

Sanctus (from Requiem)—Fauré. Fitzsimons No. 2119. Accompanied. Easy.

Sanctus (from 16th Mass)—Haydn, arr. Hilton. Mercury No. MC 399. Accompanied. Medium.

Sanctus (from Mass VII)—Lotti. G. Schirmer No. 9407. *A cappella.* Moderately easy.

Sanctus—Rossini, ed. Ferguson. Lawson-Gould No. 51890. Accompanied. Moderately difficult.

Sanctus—Victoria. Music 70 No. M70-212. *A cappella.* Medium.

Sanctus and Hosanna—Pergolesi. Music 70 No. M70-405. Accompanied. Medium.

Send Out Thy Light (Emitte Spiritum Tuum)—Schuetky. Carl Fischer No. CM 548. *A cappella.* Moderately easy.

Serve the Lord with Gladness—Handel. Lawson-Gould No. 794. Accompanied. Medium.

Sicut Moses serpentem—Schütz. Associated No. A-412. Accompanied. Difficult.

Sing a New Song—Michael Haydn. Flammer No. A-5970. Accompanied. Moderately easy.

Sing to the Lord (Gloria in excelsis Deo)—Haydn. G. Schirmer No. 5414. Accompanied. Moderately easy.

Sing unto the Lord Most High—Pergolesi. Boosey & Hawkes. *A cappella.* Easy.

Sing We All Now with One Accord—Praetorius. G. Schirmer No. 7543. Accompanied. Moderately easy.

Sing with Gladness—Sweelinck, ed. Sateren. AMSI No. 337. *A cappella.* Moderately difficult.

Sing Ye to the Lord (Jauchzet dem Herrn)—Pachelbel. Music 70 No. M70-192. Accompanied. Moderately easy.

Sixty-seventh Psalm—Ives. Associated No. A-274. *A cappella.* Moderately difficult.

Song of Galilee (El Yivneh Hagalil)—transcribed by Chajes. Transcontinental No. TCL 214. Accompanied. Medium.

Song of Repentance—J. S. Bach. Broude Bros. No. 65. *A cappella.* Medium.

Sound the Cymbal—Schubert. Schmitt, Hall & McCreary No. 1745. Accompanied. Medium.

Stabat Mater—Schubert. Belwin Mills No. 2164. Accompanied. Moderately easy.

Surgens Jesus—di Lasso. Arista No. AE 309. *A cappella.* Medium.

Tarry Here and Watch—Pitoni, arr. Kingsbury. Tetra No. A.B. 757. *A cappella.* Medium.

Te Deum—Schuman. G. Schirmer No. 9453. *A cappella.* Medium.

This Is the Record of John—Gibbons, ed. Parker and Shaw. Lawson-Gould No. 550. Organ accompaniment. Tenor solo. Medium.

Thou Art the King of Glory—Handel. Kjos No. 5481A. Accompanied. Moderately easy.

Thou Art Worthy of Praise—Haydn. Sam Fox No. MM 13. *A cappella.* Moderately easy.

Thou Must Leave Thy Lowly Dwelling (from *Childhood of Christ*)—Berlioz. Gray No. 1898. Accompanied. Medium.

To Him Who Never Faileth—Altnikol, ed. Frank. Sam Fox No. MM 3. Accompanied. Moderately easy.

Tribulationes civitatum—Thomson. Weintraub. *A cappella.* Moderately difficult.

Tribus miraculis—Marenzio. Available—World Library. *A cappella.* Medium.

Turn Back, O Man—Holst. Galaxy No. 6. Accompanied. Medium.

Tu solus qui facis mirabilia—Després. Mercury No. 352-00045. *A cappella.* Medium.

Twenty-Third Psalm, The—Wilson. Bourne No. 703. *A cappella.* Medium.

Unto Thee I Lift My Spirit—Hiller. Sam Fox MM No. 7. Accompanied. Moderately easy.

Veni Jesu—Cherubini, arr. Riegger. Flammer No. 84189. Accompanied. Medium.

Venite, exsultemus Domino (O Come Let Us Sing)—Sweelinck. Summy-Birchard No. 5517. Optional accompaniment. Medium.

Veni Virgo Sacrata—Reutter, ed. Young. Broude Bros. No. MGC 21. Organ accompaniment. Medium.

Von Himmel hoch (From Highest Heav'n)—J. S. Bach. Lawson-Gould No. 903. *A cappella.* Medium.

Vouchsafe, O Lord—Gretchaninov. Galaxy No. 1356. Optional accompaniment. Medium.

We Adore Thee (Adoramus Te)—Lotti. Chappell No. 6149. *A cappella.* Moderately easy.

We Have No Other Help—Arkhangelsky, arr. Gnotov. Witmark No. 5-W3005. *A cappella.* Moderately easy.

We Pledge You Forever (from Cantata No. 208)—J. S. Bach, ed. Malin. Belwin Mills No. 2406. Accompanied. Moderately difficult.

We Praise and Bless Thee (from *Messe Solennelle*)—Gounod, arr. Witford. Oliver Ditson No. 332-40049. Accompanied. Moderately easy.

We Praise Thee—Gretchaninov, arr. Cain. Hoffman No. 46,335. *A cappella.* Easy.

We Will Rejoice in Thy Salvation—Handel, ed. Malin. Belwin Mills No. 2407. Accompanied. Moderately difficult.

While As a Stone, Yet Living—Marenzio. Piedmont No. 4485. Optional accompaniment. Moderately easy.

Who Shall Separate Us—Schuetz. Chantry Music Press. Organ or piano accompaniment. Medium.

Who With Grieving Soweth—Schein. Mercury No. 19. *A cappella.* Moderately difficult.

With a Voice of Singing—Shaw. G. Schirmer No. 8103. Accompanied. Moderately easy.

With Sorrow Shaken—K.P.E. Bach. Elkan-Vogel No. 362-01303. Piano or organ accompaniment. Alto solo. Moderately easy.

Ye Are Not of the Flesh (from the motet *Jesus meine Freude*)—Bach. Lawson-Gould No. 785. Accompanied. Difficult.

Your Voices Tune (from *Alexander's Feast*)—Handel, ed. Malin. Belwin Mills No. 2408. Accompanied. Medium.

General: Secular

Adieu, Sweet Amarillis—Wilbye, ed. Kaplan. Lawson-Gould No. 51865. *A cappella.* Medium.

Ah, Love, to You I'm Crying—Hassler, ed. Ehret. Tetra No. A.B. 759. *A cappella.* Medium.

Anima mia perdona—Monteverdi, ed. Malin. Belwin Mills No. 2380. *A cappella.* Medium.

Anthony O Daly—Barber. G. Schirmer No. 8909. *A cappella.* Medium.

April Is in Her Lovely Face—Morley. Ricordi No. 1398; E. C. Schirmer No. 1612. *A cappella.* Moderately easy.

As Long As Beauty Shall Remain—Brahms, arr. Christy. Schmitt, Hall & McCreary No. 1172. *A cappella.* Easy.

As Torrents in Summer—Elgar, arr. Cain. Flammer No. 81068. *A cappella.* Moderately easy.

Aug dem See (On the Lake)—Mendelssohn. National Music Publishers No. NMP-184. *A cappella.* Medium.

Autumn Rain—Adler. Associated No. A-263. *A cappella.* Medium.

Ballad of Green Broom—Britten. Boosey & Hawkes No. 1875. *A cappella.* Moderately difficult.

Beggar's Canon (from *The Brigands*)—Offenbach. Broude Bros. No. 117. Accompanied. Medium.

Blow, Blow, Thou Winter Wind—Rutter. Oxford No. 52.024. Accompanied. Moderately easy.

Chanson on *Dessus le Marche d'Arras*—di Lasso. Associated No. NYPM 32. *A cappella.* Medium.

Choose Something like a Star—Thompson. E. C. Schirmer No. 2487. Accompanied. Moderately easy.

Chorus of the Hebrew Captives (from *Nabucco*)—Verdi. Music 70 No. 224. Accompanied. Medium.

Chorus of the Office Clerks (from *Fortunio's Song*)—Offenbach. Broude Bros. No. 4066. Accompanied. Medium.

Come, Let Your Hearts Be Singing—Gastoldi, arr. Greyson. Bourne No. ES 26. *A cappella.* Moderately easy.

Come and Sing (from *Die Fledermaus*)—Strauss. Carl Fischer No. CM 4628. Accompanied. Moderately difficult.

Coolin, The—Barber. G. Schirmer No. 8910. *A cappella.* Moderately difficult.

Dedication—Franz, arr. Riegger. Flammer No. 81043. *A cappella.* Medium.

Der Gang zum Liebchen (Journey to My Love)—Brahms. National Music Publishers No. WHC-132. Accompanied. Medium.

Dixie—Emmett, arr. Luboff. Walton No. 3004. *A cappella.* Medium.

Early Spring—Mendelssohn. Music 70 No. M70-259. *A cappella.* Medium.

Eloquence (Die Beredsamkeit)—Haydn. Elkan-Vogel No. 1133. Accompanied. Medium.

Evening—Kodály. Boosey & Hawkes No. 1710. *A cappella.* Difficult.

Fable, A—Dello Joio. Carl Fischer No. CM 6299. Accompanied. Moderately easy.

Face to Face (from *Ten Songs*)—Shostakovitch. G. Schirmer No. 12121. *A cappella.* Moderately difficult.

Fair Is the Crystal—di Lasso. Piedmont No. 4384. *A cappella.* Medium.

Fall, Leaves, Fall—Bright. Shawnee Press No. A-945. *A cappella.* Medium.

Farewell, The (Horch, der Wind klagt in den Zweigen)—Brahms. Sam Fox No. RC 2. Accompanied. Moderately easy.

Farmer's Wife Lost Her Cat—Mozart. Edw. B. Marks No. 1. *A cappella.* Moderately difficult.

Fa una canzone—Vecchi. Lawson-Gould No. 556. *A cappella.* Easy.

From Grief to Glory (Verse II—Love in Grief)—F. M. Christiansen. Augsburg No. 175. *A cappella.* Difficult.

Frühzeitiger Frühling (Early Spring)—Mendelssohn. National Music Publishers No. NMP-167. *A cappella.* Medium.

Geographical Fugue (speaking chorus)—Toch. Belwin Mills No. 347. Difficult.

Glory (March from *Aida*)—Verdi. Willis No. 2892. Accompanied. Moderately difficult.

Gondoliers, The (Finale)—Gilbert and Sullivan. E. C. Schirmer No. 356. Four-hand piano accompaniment. Medium.

Happiness (O Seligkeit)—Schubert, ed. Freed. Sam Fox No. RC 4. Accompanied. Moderately easy.

Have Courage, Friends (from *Ten Songs*)—Shostakovitch. G. Schirmer No. 12118. *A cappella.* Medium.

Herbstlied (Autumn Song)—Mendelssohn. Lawson-Gould No. 52180. *A cappella.* Medium.

Hunting Song—Mendelssohn. Sam Fox No. RC 9. *A cappella.* Medium.

If All My Heartfelt Thinking—Brahms. Associated No. A-407. *A cappella.* Medium.

If I Should Part from You—Monteverdi. Presser No. 312-40939. *A cappella.* Moderately easy.

I Myself When Young Did Eagerly Frequent—Diemer. Boosey & Hawkes No. 5778. *A cappella.* Medium.

In Silent Night—Brahms. G. Schirmer No. 5848. *A cappella.* Easy.

In Swift Light Vessels Gliding (Opus 2)—Webern. Universal No. E6643A. *A cappella.* Moderately difficult.

In the Quiet Night—Mennin. Carl Fischer No. CM 6417. *A cappella.* Medium.

In These Delightful, Pleasant Groves—Purcell. Novello No. M. T. 1. *A cappella.* Medium.

In Winter—Hindemith. Associated No. AS 19432V. *A cappella.* Medium.

It Is Good to Be Merry—Berger. Kjos No. 5293. *A cappella.* Medium.

Je pleure (I Weep)—Le Jeune. Éditions Salabert No. 23-6. *A cappella.* Moderately easy.

Je serais enchanté (I Should Be Overjoyed)—Gounod. Alexander Broude No. 252-3. Accompanied. Moderately easy.

Jig for Voices—Rowley. Boosey & Hawkes No. 1699. Optional accompaniment. Medium.

Joyful Day—Handel. National Music Publishers No. NMP-143. Accompanied. Medium.

Lady, So Fair Thou Seemest—de Wert. Belwin Mills No. 60778. *A cappella.* Moderately easy.

Lark, The (Lerchengesang)—Mendelssohn. Music 70 Publishers No. M70-252. *A cappella.* Moderately easy.

Las Agachadas—Copland. Boosey & Hawkes. *A cappella.* For solo group and eight-part chorus. Moderately difficult.

Lebenslust (Joy of Living)—Schubert. Alexander Broude No. 258. Accompanied. Medium.

Life Is Happiness Indeed (from *Candide*)—Bernstein, arr. Page. G. Schirmer No. 12024. Accompanied. Medium.

Lonely Boat Drifts Slowly, A—Schumann. Broude Bros. No. 135. Soprano solo, flute, and horn. Medium.

Lost Youth (Verlorene Jugend)—Brahms. Presser No. 312-40946. *A cappella.* Medium.

Love Is a Blue Star—McCray. National Music Publishers No. WHC-137. *A cappella.* Medium.

Love Song—Brahms, arr. Wilson. Ricordi No. NY1475. Optional accompaniment. Moderately easy.

Lullaby (Wiegenlied)—Mozart. Associated No. A-84. Accompanied. Soprano solo. Moderately easy.

Madrigal—Gesualdo. Edw. B. Marks No. 52. *A cappella.* Medium.

Matona, Lovely Maiden—Lasso. Carl Fischer No. CM 4637. *A cappella.* Moderately easy.

Modern Music—Billings. C. F. Peters No. 66340. *A cappella.* Medium.

Monotone—Lockwood. Kjos No. 8. *A cappella.* Medium.

Music the Comforter (Trösterin Musik)—Bruckner. Sam Fox No. MM 12. Accompanied. Moderately easy.

My Love Dwelt in a Northern Land—Elgar. G. Schirmer No. 2366. *A cappella.* Moderately easy.

Neighbors' Chorus—Offenbach. Broude Bros. No. 130. Accompanied. Medium.

Nightingale, The—Mendelssohn, ed. Mason. Walton No. 7010. Optional accompaniment. Moderately easy.

Nuptial Chorus (from *The Guardsman*)—Tchaikovsky, ed. Malin. Belwin Mills No. 2405. Accompanied. Medium.

O, Dearest Love of Mine (Herzlieb zu Dir allein)—Hassler. Boston Music Co. No. 13703. *A cappella.* Medium.

O Be Joyful Ye Lands—Purcell. Gentry No. JG-459. Accompanied. Easy.

O Care, Thou Wilt Despatch Me—Weelkes. Boston Music Co. No. 13705. *A cappella.* Moderately easy.

O Death, Pray Come—Monteverdi. Boston Music Co. No. 2890. *A cappella.* Medium.

Oh, When My Husband Comes Back Home—di Lasso. Pro Art No. 2365. *A cappella.* Moderately easy.

Oh Love Divine (from *Theodora*)—Handel. Carl Fischer No. ZCM108. Accompanied. Medium.

Old Abram Brown—Britten. Boosey & Hawkes No. 1786. Accompanied. Easy.
Old Joe Has Gone Fishing (from *Peter Grimes*)—Britten. Boosey & Hawkes No. 1784. Accompanied. Moderately difficult.
Old Man, The (Der Greis)—Haydn. Associated No. A-618. *A cappella.* Medium.
O Lovely Mai (O Sussex Mai)—Brahms. Belwin Mills No. 2174. *A cappella.* Moderately easy.
On the Way to My Sweetheart—Brahms, arr. Matesky. Gentry No. G-4007. Accompanied. Moderately easy.
O Swiftly Glides the Bonny Boat—Beethoven. National Music Publishers No. CMS-126. Violin, cello, and piano accompaniment. Moderately easy.
O voi che sospirate a migliore note—Marenzio. Dartmouth Publications No. A-977. *A cappella.* Medium.
O Wondrous Harmony—Haydn. Lawson-Gould No. 52065. Accompanied. Medium.
O World, I Now Must Leave Thee (Innsbruck, ich muss dich lassen)—Isaac. Alexander Broude No. 251-3. *A cappella.* Medium.
Party of Lovers at Tea, A—Argento. Boosey & Hawkes No. 5712. *A cappella.* Medium.
Pavane pour une infante défunte—Ravel. Broude Bros. No. 100. Accompanied. Moderately difficult.
Placido e il mar (from *Idomeneo*)—Mozart. Belwin Mills No. 2403. Accompanied. Medium.
Pleasure Awaits Us (from *La Finta Gardiniera*—Mozart. Belwin Mills No. 2403. Accompanied. Medium.
Prelude—Schuman. G. Schirmer No. 8929. *A cappella.* Soprano solo. Moderately difficult.
Primrose, The (*Die Primel*)—Mendelssohn. Associated No. A-382. *A cappella.* Medium.
Promise of Living, The (from *The Tender Land*)—Copland. Boosey & Hawkes No. 5020. Piano duet accompaniment. Moderately difficult.
Rest, Sweet Nymphs—Pilkington. National Music Publishers No. CMS-121. String quartet or recorder consort accompaniment. Moderately easy.
Rise Up, Oh Flame—Praetorius, arr. Harley and Aschenbrenner. Carl Fischer No. CM 4712. *A cappella.* Moderately easy.
Road Not Taken, The—Thompson. E. C. Schirmer No. 2485. Accompanied. Moderately easy.
Roses of the South—Strauss, arr. Gibb. Homeyer No. 437. Accompanied. Moderately easy.
See How Aurora Comes with Brow All Glowing—Marenzio. Piedmont No. 4438. *A cappella.* Medium.
Sigh Goes Stirring through the Wood, A—Brahms. Associated No. A-379. *A cappella.* Medium.
Since All Is Passing—Hindemith. Schott No. AP 37. *A cappella.* Moderately easy.
Sing a Song of Sixpence—Bright. Shawnee Press No. A-851. *A cappella.* Medium.
Sing of Spring—Gershwin. Lawson-Gould No. 51964. Accompanied. Medium.
Six Balletti—Gastoldi. C. F. Peters, Set I, No. 6877a. *A cappella.* Moderately easy. Set II, No. 6877b. *A cappella.* Medium.
Six Love Songs—Brahms. Summy-Birchard. Four-hand accompaniment. Moderately difficult.
Skylark's Song, The—Mendelssohn. Belwin Mills No. 2181. Optional accompaniment. Moderately easy.
Song of the Lark (Lerchengesang)—Mendelssohn. Sam Fox No. RC 11. *A cappella.* Moderately easy.
Songs Filled My Heart—Dvořák. Presser No. 312-40813. Accompanied. Moderately easy.
So wahr die Sonne scheinet (As Surely As the Sun Shines)—Schumann. National Music Publishers No. WHC-117. Accompanied. Medium.
Springtime—Hindemith. Schott No. 19432, IV. *A cappella.* Moderately difficult.
Stomp Your Foot (from *The Tender Land*)—Copland. Boosey & Hawkes No. 5019. Piano duet accompaniment. Moderately difficult.
Strings in the Earth—Adler. Associated No. A-264. *A cappella.* Medium.

Sunrise—Taneyev. G. Schirmer No. 2623. *A cappella.* Difficult.
Sure on This Shining Night—Barber. G. Schirmer No. 10864. Accompanied. Moderately easy.
Swan, A—Hindemith. Schott No. 19432, II. *A cappella.* Medium.
Sweet Day—McCray. J. Fischer No. 10132. *A cappella.* Moderately easy.
These Are My Heartfelt Tears (madrigal)—Palestrina. Lawson-Gould No. 51029. *A cappella.* Moderately easy.
This World (from *Candide*)—Bernstein, arr. Page. G. Schirmer No. 12027. Accompanied. Medium.
Thought like Music, A—Brahms, arr. Suchoff. Plymouth No. A. S. 103. Accompanied. Moderately easy.
Three Nocturnes—Chávez. G. Schirmer No. 9522. *A cappella.* Moderately difficult.
To All, To Each—Schuman. Presser No. 342-40013. *A cappella.* Medium.
To All Our Hearts Are Now Returning (from *Julius Caesar*)—Handel. Belwin Mills No. 2404. Accompanied. Medium.
To Music—Carter. Peer International. *A cappella.* Moderately difficult.
Tones Enchanted (Durch der Töne)—Schubert. Kenbridge Music No. K-103. Accompanied. Medium.
Trysting Place, The (Der Gang zum Liebchen)—Brahms. E. C. Schirmer No. 391. Accompanied. Medium.
Under the Willow Tree (from *Vanessa*)—Barber. G. Schirmer No. 10861. Accompanied. Soprano solo. Moderately difficult.
Up Sprang a Birch Tree Overnight—Dvořák. Mercury No. 312-40816. *A cappella.* Medium.
Valse (Speaking Chorus)—Toch. Belwin Mills No. 60564. Optional percussion. Medium.
Voix Célestes (humming chorus)—Alcock. Chappell No. 2055. *A cappella.* Medium.
Walking on the Green Grass—Hennagin. Boosey & Hawkes No. 5443. *A cappella.* Medium.
Warm Was the Sun (Scaldava il sol)—Marenzio. Piedmont No. 4545. *A cappella.* Medium.
Warning—Diamond. Elkan-Vogel No. 362-03143. Accompaniment. Moderately difficult.
We Are Brave Matadors (from *La Traviata*)—Verdi. G. Schirmer No. 5435. Accompanied. Medium.
Welcome Sweet May (Wohl kommt der Mai)—de Lasso. Carl Fischer No. CM 7566. *A cappella.* Moderately easy.
When Evening Comes Chimes Fill the Forest—Dvořák. Mercury No. 312-40814. Accompanied. Medium.
When the Bright Sun—Byrd. Belwin Mills No. A-202. *A cappella.* Moderately easy.
Whether Men Do Laugh or Weep—Vaughan Williams. Oxford No. X66. Accompanied. Medium.
Woman Is a Worthy Thing, A—Chávez. G. Schirmer No. 9611. *A cappella.* Medium.
Wonderful Life, A (Lebenslust)—Schubert. Sam Fox No. MM 8. Accompanied. Medium.
Younger Generation—Copland, arr. Swift. Boosey & Hawkes No. 1723. Accompanied. Moderately easy.
Zamba for You—Ramirez. Lawson-Gould No. 52242. *A cappella.* Medium.
Zigeunerleben (Gypsy Life)—Schumann. Walton No. 2706. Accompanied. Moderately easy.

PUBLICATIONS FOR MIXED VOICES (SAB)

Sacred

Adoramus Te, Christe (We Adore Thee)—Corsi, arr. Ehret. Carl Fischer No. CM 8208. *A cappella.* Moderately easy.
Alleluja (from the motet *Exsultate, Jubilate*)—Mozart, arr. Riegger. Flammer No. 88522. Accompanied. Moderately difficult.

As Torrents in Summer—Elgar, arr. Cain. Flammer No. 88046. Optional *A cappella.* Easy.

Ave Maria—Gounod, arr. Downing. G. Schirmer No. 9450. Accompanied. Moderately easy.

Blessing, Glory and Wisdom—J. S. Bach, arr. Ehret. Elkan-Vogel No. 362-03118. Optional accompaniment. Medium.

Bless the Lord, O My Soul—Ippolitov-Ivanov, arr. Richardson. Boston Music Co. No. 2801. *A cappella.* Moderately easy.

Canon of Praise—Pachelbel, arr. Hopson. Somerset Press No. MW 1226. Accompanied. Moderately easy.

Cherubic Hymn, The (Opus 29)—Gretchaninov, arr. Howorth. Pro Art No. 1031. *A cappella.* Moderately easy.

Cherubim Song No. 7—Bortniansky, arr. Tchaikovsky. G. Schirmer No. 9753. Accompanied. Moderately easy.

Christus resurgens (Christ Being Raised)—Viadana. Leeds No. L-441. Organ accompaniment. Moderately easy.

Come Souls, Behold Today—Bach, arr. Nelson. Augsburg No. 1171. *A cappella.* Moderately easy.

Dona nobis pacem (old German canon)—arr. Wilson. Schmitt, Hall & McCreary No. 5510. *A cappella.* Moderately easy.

For the Beauty of the Earth—Kocher, arr. Davis. Remick No. 4-R3231. Accompanied. Easy.

God So Loved the World—Stainer, arr. Martin. Schmitt, Hall & McCreary No. 5509. *A cappella.* Easy.

Heavens Are Declaring, The—Beethoven, arr. Kountz. Witmark No. 2565. Accompanied. Easy.

Heavens Are Declaring, The—Beethoven, arr. Mueller. G. Schirmer No. 10670. Accompanied. Easy.

Heavens Are Telling, The—Haydn, arr. Wilson. Lorenz No. 7020. Accompanied. Moderately easy.

In God Rejoice—Tchaikovsky. Carl Fischer No. CM 8220. Accompanied. Moderately easy.

Jesu, Joy of Man's Desiring (from Cantata No. 147)—J. S. Bach. G. Schirmer No. 10023; Remick No. R3279. Accompanied. Easy.

Jesu, Son of God (Ave verum corpus)—Mozart. Schmitt, Hall & McCreary 5502. Accompanied. Moderately easy.

Lead Me, O Lord—Wesley, arr. Pitcher. Willis No. 8493. Accompanied. Easy.

Legend, A (from the cycle *Songs for Young People*)—Tchaikovsky, arr. Deis. G. Schirmer No. 10035. Accompanied. Medium.

Let Our Gladness Know No End (old Bohemian Christmas carol)—arr. Ryg. Belwin Mills No. 1761. *A cappella.* Moderately easy.

Lift Thine Eyes (from *Elijah*)—Mendelssohn, arr. Pitcher. Willis No. 8486. Optional accompaniment. Moderately easy.

Moon Shines Bright, The (old English carol)—arr. Wilson. Bourne No. T8. Accompanied. Moderately easy.

O Give Thanks unto the Lord—Haydn, arr. Hines. Raymond A. Hoffman No. H-2030. Accompanied. Moderately easy.

O Little Jesus (16th-century German carol)—arr. Gordon. Belwin Mills. No. 1873. Accompanied. Easy.

O Lord, Our God—Schvedov, arr. Wilson. Bourne No. T5. Optional accompaniment. Medium.

O Lord Most Holy—Franck, arr. Pitcher. Willis No. 8489. Accompanied. Easy.

Praise the Almighty, My Soul, Adore Him—Zipp. Concordia No. CH 1086. *A cappella.* Moderately easy.

Praise Ye the Father—Gounod, arr. Pitcher. Willis No. 8482. Accompanied. Moderately easy.

Prayer for Peace, A (Panis angelicus)—Franck, arr. Hoffman. Hoffman No. 46,107. Accompanied. Moderately easy.

Send Out Thy Light—Gounod, arr. Mueller. G. Schirmer No. 8695. Accompanied. Medium.

Shepherd of Eager Youth—Roff. Elkan-Vogel No. 507. Accompanied. Moderately easy.

Sing to the Lord, Our God (Cantate Domino)—Asola. Music 70 No. M70-350. *A cappella.* Medium.

Sing Ye Praises unto the Father—Mozart. Gentry No. G-151. Accompanied. Medium.

To Realms of Glory—Schein, arr. Nelson. Augsburg No. 1169. *A cappella.* Easy.

Turn Thy Face from My Sins—Attwood, arr. Pitcher. Willis No. 8487. Accompanied. Easy.

Secular

Bells of St. Mary's—Adams, arr. Stickles. Chappell No. 7006. Accompanied. Easy.

Bells of the Sea—Solman, arr. Wilson. Sam Fox No. 542. Accompanied. Moderately easy.

Carol of the Bells (Ukrainian carol)—Leontovich, arr. Wilhousky. Carl Fischer No. 4747. Optional *a cappella.* Easy.

Come Sirrah Jack Ho—Weelkes. National Music Publishers No. CMS-122. Clarinet trio accompaniment. Medium.

Danse Macabre—Saint-Saëns, arr. Lorenz. Lorenz No. 7098. Accompanied. Moderately difficult.

Dedication—Franz, arr. Wilson. Paull Pioneer. Accompanied. Moderately easy.

Down South—Myddleton, arr. High. Edw. B. Marks No. 403. Accompanied. Easy.

Follow Me, Sweet Love—East. National Music Publishers No. CMS-120. Recorder consort accompaniment. Moderately easy.

Follow the Drinking Gourd (source unknown)—arr. Horman. Somerset Press No. SP782. Accompanied. Moderately easy.

Green Cathedral—Hahn, arr. Montrose. Presser No. 322-35447. Accompanied. Easy.

Homing—Del Riego, arr. Stickles. Chappell No. 7007. Accompanied. Easy.

Kentucky Babe—Giebel, arr. Stickles. Edwin H. Morris No. 8003. Accompanied. Easy.

Ol' Man River—Kern, arr. Stickles. Chappell No. CR77. Accompanied. Moderately easy.

Pines of Home—Luvaas. Carl Fischer No. 6452. Optional *a cappella.* Moderately easy.

Prayer from *Hansel and Gretel*—Humperdinck, arr. Riegger. Flammer No. 88019. Accompanied. Easy.

Shortnin' Bread—Wolfe, arr. Riegger. Flammer No. 88088. Accompanied. Moderately easy.

Sing, Sing a Song for Me—Vecchi, arr. Greyson. Bourne No. ES 53C. Optional accompaniment. Moderately easy.

Sing Songs of Jubilation—Pachelbel, arr. Petker. Gentry No. JG-474. Accompanied. Medium.

Three Madrigals from the XVIIth Century:
1. Your Shining Eyes—Bateson.
2. As Late in My Accounting—Weelkes.
3. Follow Me, Sweet Love—East.
J. Fischer No. 9455. *A cappella.* Medium.

Tickling Trio (Vadasi via di qua)—Martini. Witmark No. 4-W2750. *A cappella.* Moderately easy.

To Music—Schubert, arr. Wilson. Schmitt, Hall & McCreary No. 5011. Accompanied. Moderately easy.

Turn Ye to Me—Wilson, arr. Churchill. Belwin Mills No. 1619. Accompanied. Moderately easy.

Folk Songs and Spirituals

Certainly, Lord (spiritual)—arr. Kirk. Pro Art No. 1834. Accompanied. Moderately easy.

Cindy (American folk song)—arr. Barthelson. Belwin Mills No. 1984. Accompanied. Moderately easy.
Cindy (American folk song)—arr. Ehret. Presser No. 312-41185. Accompanied. Moderately easy.
Cowboy's Meditation, The (American folk song)—arr. Wilson. Paull Pioneer. Accompanied. Moderately easy.
Ezekiel Saw de Wheel (spiritual)—arr. Cain. Belwin Mills No. 1131. Accompanied. Medium.
From Lucerne to Weggis Fair (Swiss folk song)—arr. Harris. Pro Art No. 2369. Accompanied. Medium.
Gonna Ride Up in the Chariot (spiritual)—arr. Richardson. Presser No. 312-41187. Accompanied. Easy.
He Never Said a Mumbalin' Word (spiritual)—arr. Wilson. Paull Pioneer. Optional accompaniment. Moderately easy.
I Ain't Gonna Grieve My Lord No More (spiritual)—arr. Ehret. Belwin Mills No. 1661. Accompanied. Medium.
I Got Shoes (spiritual)—arr. Cain. Flammer No. 88047. Accompanied. Easy.
Jennie Jenkins (American dialogue song)—arr. Churchill. Belwin Mills No. 1893. Accompanied. Easy.
John Anderson, My Jo (Scottish folk song)—arr. Gordon. Belwin Mills No. 1494. Accompanied. Moderately easy.
Little David, Play on Your Harp (spiritual)—arr. Cain. Flammer No. 88054. Accompanied. Moderately easy.
Night Herding Song (country folk ballad)—arr. Barker. Belwin Mills No. 1828. Optional accompaniment. Moderately easy.
Rock-a My Soul (spiritual)—arr. Wilson. Bourne No. T 11. Accompanied. Moderately easy.
Rocking Carol (Czech carol)—arr. Graham. Presser No. 312-40698. Optional accompaniment. Moderately easy.
Russian Picnic (based on Russian folk tunes)—arr. Enders. G. Schirmer No. 9632. Accompanied. Medium.
Simple Gifts (American Shaker tune)—arr. Kirk. Pro Art No. 2662. Accompanied. Moderately easy.
Turtle Dove, The (English folk song)—arr. Ahrold. Presser No. 312-40700. Accompanied. Moderately easy.
Vreneli (Swiss folk song)—arr. Ehret. Presser No. 312-41189. Accompanied. Easy.
Water Boy (Negro work song)—arr. Pitcher. Boston Music Co. No. 2359. Accompanied. Baritone solo—melody in baritone. Easy.
Were You There (spiritual)—arr. Wilson. Bourne No. T 2. Accompanied. Medium.

PUBLICATIONS FOR TREBLE VOICES (SSA)

Sacred

Adoramus Te (We Adore Thee)—Palestrina, arr. Swift. Belwin Mills No. 1655. Accompanied. Moderately easy.
Alleluia—Mozart, arr. Riegger. Flammer No. 89024. Accompanied. Medium.
Angel Ever Bright—Handel, arr. Overby. Augsburg No. 1013. Optional accompaniment. Moderately easy.
Angels and the Shepherds—Kodály. Universal No. 312-40593. A cappella. Medium.
Angelus ad pastores ait and Hodie Christus natus est (from *Sacrae Cantiunculae*)—Monteverdi. Mercury No. 352-000-24. A cappella. Medium.
Ave Maria—Arcadelt. Bourne No. ES 3. A cappella. Moderately easy.
Ave Maria—Kodály. Universal No. 312-40592. A cappella. Moderately easy.
Ave verum—Després, arr. Greyson. Bourne No. ES 88A. A cappella. Moderately easy.
Away in a Manger (traditional carol)—arr. Terri. Lawson-Gould No. 666. A cappella. Moderately easy.
Bless Ye the Lord—Ippolitov-Ivanov, arr. Wilhousky. Carl Fischer No. 639. A cappella. Moderately easy.

Blest Is the Man—Lasso. Augsburg No. PS603. *A cappella.* Moderately easy.

Bring a Torch, Jeannette, Isabella (old French carol)—arr. Nunn. E. C. Schirmer No. 496. *A cappella.* Moderately easy.

Call of the Shepherds, The (French Noël)—arr. Malin. B. F. Wood No. 826. *A cappella.* Moderately easy.

Cantate Domino—Pitoni. Flammer No. 89181. *A cappella.* Moderately easy.

Carol of the Italian Pipers (traditional carol)—arr. Zgodava. Shawnee Press No. B-321. Accompanied. Moderately easy.

Cherubic Hymn—Musitcheskoo. Boosey & Hawkes No. 5026. Accompanied. Medium.

Christ Is Born (Ukrainian carol)—arr. Boberg. Carl Fischer No. 7455. *A cappella.* Moderately easy

Christmas Hymn (17th century)—arr. Jüngst. G. Schirmer No. 9890. *A cappella.* Moderately easy.

Come, O Jesus, Come to Me—Cherubini, arr. Ehret. Plymouth No. S.C. 201. Accompanied. Moderately easy.

Come, Ye Gay Shepherds—Costeley, arr. Cramer. Edw. B. Marks No. 4482. Optional accompaniment. Moderately easy.

Come, Ye Lofty, Come, Ye Lowly (Breton carol)—arr. Malin. Summy-Birchard No. 1419. Accompanied. Moderately easy.

Come to Me—Beethoven, arr. Aslanoff. G. Schirmer No. 8711. Accompanied. Easy.

Coventry Carol (English carol)—arr. Stone. Belwin Mills No. 2070. Accompanied. Moderately easy.

Crucifixus—A. Gabrieli, ed. Ehret. Edw. B. Marks No. 4332. *A cappella.* Medium.

Glory to God in the Highest!—Pergolesi, arr. Riegger. Flammer No. 89041. Accompanied. Medium.

God of Abraham Praise, The (traditional Hebrew melody)—arr. Malmin. Augsburg No. 1238. Accompanied. Easy.

God Rest You Merry, Gentlemen (English carol)—arr. Scholin. Belwin Mills No. 1625. Accompanied. Moderately easy.

Hear Our Supplication—Mozart, arr. Hilton. Mercury No. 352-00460. Accompanied. Moderately easy.

Holy Infant's Lullaby, The—Dello Joio. Edw. B. Marks No. 4392. Accompanied. Moderately easy.

How Far Is It to Bethlehem?—Chesterton. World Library No. AC-595-3. *A cappella.* Easy.

Hush My Babe—Rousseau-Stone. Belwin Mills No. 2067. Accompanied. Easy.

Incline Thine Ear, O Lord—Arkhangelsky, arr. Krone. Witmark No. 3220. *A cappella.* Medium.

Jesu, Joy of Man's Desiring—Bach, arr. Treharne. G. Schirmer No. 8388. Accompanied. Easy.

Lacrymosa—Mozart. Carl Fischer No. CM 6945. Accompanied. Medium.

Legend, A—Tchaikovsky. Carl Fischer No. CM 6325. Accompanied. Moderately easy.

Lift Thine Eyes (from *Elijah*)—Mendelssohn. Willis No. 698. *A cappella.* Moderately easy.

Lo, A Voice to Heaven Sounding—Bortniansky, arr. Davis. E. C. Schirmer No. 1079. *A cappella.* Moderately easy.

Lord Is My Shepherd, The—Schubert, arr. Watson. Remick No. 2-G1646. Accompanied. Moderately difficult.

O Little Jesus (16th-century German carol)—arr. Gordon. Belwin Mills No. 1874. Accompanied. Moderately easy.

Once in Royal David's City (Finnish folk melody)—arr. Lundquist. Elkan-Vogel No. 3079. *A cappella.* Easy.

Praise to the Lord (17th-century German tune)—arr. Whitehead. Gray No. 2095. Organ accompaniment. Moderately easy.

Praise Ye the Lord—J. S. Bach, arr. Trusler. Plymouth No. TR-103. Piano or organ accompaniment. Moderately easy.

Praise Ye the Lord of Hosts—Saint-Saëns. Belwin Mills No. 698. Accompanied. Easy.

Prayer of Thanksgiving (old Dutch melody)—arr. Kremser. G. Schirmer No. 6812. Accompanied. Easy.
Puer natus est—Morales. Bourne No. ES 73. Optional accompaniment. Medium.
Rejoice, Holy Mary (French carol)—arr. Malin. Belwin Mills No. 693. Accompanied. Moderately easy.
Send Out Thy Light—Balakirev. Boosey & Hawkes No. 1924. *A cappella*. Medium.
Shepherd's Carol—Billings. Gray No. 3024. Accompanied. Moderately easy.
Slumber of the Infant Jesus—Gevaert, arr. Davis. E. C. Schirmer No. 1088. *A cappella*. Medium.
This Little Babe (from *A Ceremony of Carols*)—Britten. Boosey & Hawkes No. 5138. Accompanied. Moderately easy.
To Our Little Town (French carol)—arr. Malin. Belwin Mills No. 692. *A cappella*. Moderately easy.
To Us There Comes a Little Child (German melody)—arr. Malin. Belwin Mills No. 704. Accompanied. Moderately easy.
Two Czech Carols—arr. Peloguin. McLaughlin & Reilly No. 2047. *A cappella*. Moderately easy.
Vere languores nostros—Lotti. Bourne No. ES 22. *A cappella*. Moderately easy.
While Shepherds Watched (17th-century melody)—arr. Tkach. Kjos No. 6044. Accompanied. Easy.
Whither Going, Shepherd? (Hungarian folk song)—arr. Taylor. J. Fischer No. 5054. Accompanied. Moderately easy.
Wolcum Yole! (from *A Ceremony of Carols*)—Britten. Boosey & Hawkes No. 1755B. Accompanied. Medium.
Ya Ba Bom (Jewish folk tune)—arr. Goldman. Lawson-Gould No. 51958. Piano and percussion accompaniment. Medium.

Secular

Adelaide—Beethoven. Boston Music Co. No. 3045. Accompanied. Moderately easy.
Adieu, Mignonne, When You Are Gone—Dello Joio. Carl Fischer No. 6784. Accompanied. Moderately difficult.
Amarilli, Mia Bella—Caccini, arr. Taylor. J. Fischer No. 4375. Accompanied. Medium.
An Offering—Baldwin, arr. Watson. Witmark No. 5W3362. *A cappella*. Moderately easy.
As Fair as Morn—Wilbye. Edw. B. Marks No. 4331. *A cappella*. Moderately easy.
As from the Earth a Flower Grows—Monteverdi, arr. Zipper. Edw. B. Marks No. 45. *A cappella*. Moderately easy.
Bird Flew, A—Clokey. J. Fischer No. 5506. Accompanied. Medium.
Bois épais—Lully, arr. Taylor. J. Fischer No. 4562. Accompanied. Moderately easy.
Calm As the Night—Boehm, arr. Cain. Schmitt, Hall & McCreary No. 2016. Accompanied. Moderately easy.
Carol of the Bells (Christmas)—Leontovich, arr. Wilhousky. Carl Fischer No. 5276. Optional accompaniment. Medium.
Come, Let Us Start a Joyful Song—Hassler. Bourne No. ES 31. Optional accompaniment. Moderately easy.
Come, Sirrah Jack Ho—Weelkes. E. C. Schirmer No. 840. *A cappella*. Medium.
Come, You Maidens—Tchaikovsky. Boosey & Hawkes No. 5031. Accompanied. Moderately easy.
Danza, Danza—Durante, arr. Taylor. J. Fischer No. 4378. Accompanied. Medium.
Dreams—Wagner, arr. Shelley. Presser No. 10687. Accompanied. Medium.
Enchanting Song—Bartók. Boosey & Hawkes No. 1954. *A cappella*. Medium.
Go 'Way from My Window—Niles, arr. Ross. G. Schirmer No. 9805. Accompanied. Soprano solo. Medium.
Hark! Hark! the Lark—Schubert, arr. Bliss. Willis No. 2338. Accompanied. Easy.
He Came to Me—Franz. Schmitt, Hall & McCreary No. 2127. Accompanied. Easy.
In Summer Fields—Brahms. Boston Music Co. No. 3044. Accompanied. Moderately easy.

In the Mill—Rebikoff, arr. Sammond. J. Fischer No. 5689. *A cappella.* Medium.
In These Delightful Pleasant Groves—Purcell. Bourne No. ES 28; Gray No. 519. *A cappella.* Moderately easy.
Invocation of Orpheus—Peri. Witmark No. W 2728. Accompanied. Medium.
Lass with the Delicate Air, The—Arne, arr. Chambers. Gray No. 515. Optional accompaniment. Moderately easy.
Let Us Sing—Rameau. Witmark No. 2-W 2988. Accompanied. Medium.
Linden Lea—Vaughan Williams, arr. Harrison. Boosey & Hawkes No. MFS 219. Accompanied. Moderately easy.
Little White Hen, A (Ein Hennelin weiss)—Scandello, arr. Greyson. Bourne No. ES 29A. Optional accompaniment. Medium.
Loafer—Bartók. Boosey & Hawkes No. 1671. Accompanied. Moderately easy.
Love Song—Brahms, arr. Gibb. Boston Music Co. No. 3046. Accompanied. Moderately easy.
Marienwürmehen (My Lady Bird)—Schumann, arr. Robinson. G. Schirmer No. 10743. Accompanied. Medium.
Mocking of Youth—Bartók. Boosey & Hawkes No. 1955. *A cappella.* Medium.
Mother, I Will Have a Husband—Vautor. Bourne No. ES 11. Optional accompaniment. Moderately easy.
Musetta's Waltz Song (from *La Bohème*)—Puccini. Boosey & Hawkes No. 5120. Accompanied. Moderately easy.
My Mistress Frowns—Hilton, arr. Stoufer. National Music Publishers No. CMS-123. *A cappella.* Recorder consort accompaniment.
Nightingale, The—Weelkes, arr. Leslie. E. C. Schirmer No. 1008; Gray No. 671. *A cappella.* Medium.
O Lovely Spring—Brahms, arr. Grant. Belwin Mills No. 1839. Accompanied. Medium.
Over the Gods Love Holds His Sway—Arcadelt, ed. Malin. Belwin Mills No. 2413. *A cappella.* Moderately easy.
Pat-a-Pan (Burgundian carol; Christmas)—arr. Davis. E. C. Schirmer No. 1052. *A cappella.* Medium.
Prayer from *Hansel and Gretel*—Humperdinck, arr. Riegger. Flammer No. 83087. Accompanied. Easy.
Pretense—Clokey. J. Fischer No. 7361. Accompanied. Moderately easy.
Robin Loves Me—De La Halle. Edition Musicus No. 014. Optional accompaniment. Easy.
Silent Strings—Bantock, arr. O'Shea. Boosey & Hawkes No. 1467. Accompanied. Moderately easy.
Silver Swan, The—Gibbons, arr. Greyson. Bourne No. ES 12A. *A cappella.* Moderately easy.
Sing Songs of Jubilation—Pachelbel, arr. Petker. Gentry No. JG-460. *A cappella.* Medium.
Slumber, Beloved One—Ravel, arr. Douty. Presser No. 21434. Accompanied. Moderately difficult.
Slumber Song—Gretchaninov. G. Schirmer No. 7510. Accompanied. Moderately easy.
Smith, The—Brahms. Presser No. 312-40035. Accompanied. Easy.
Song from Ossian's Fingal—Brahms. E. C. Schirmer No. 495. Horn and harp accompaniment. Medium.
Song of Sorrow—Schumann. Leeds Music No. L-423. Optional accompaniment. Moderately easy.
Songs My Mother Taught Me—Dvořák, arr. Cain. Flammer No. 83097. Accompanied. Moderately easy.
Spanish Serenata—Granados, arr. Harris. G. Schirmer No. 7814. Accompanied. Moderately difficult.
Sweet Day—Vaughan Williams, arr. Pasfield. Galaxy No. 695. Optional accompaniment. Moderately easy.
Tambourine, The—Schumann. Leeds Music No. L-428. Optional accompaniment. Medium.

To Schumann with Love (Three Songs from the *Dichterliebe*)—Schumann, arr. Harris. National Music Publishers No. WHC-119. Accompanied. Medium.

Weep, O Mine Eyes—Wilbye. E. C. Schirmer No. 841. *A cappella*. Moderately easy.

While the Birds Are Singing—Boccherini, arr. Ambrose. Schmidt No. 747. Accompanied. Moderately difficult.

Who Is Sylvia?—Schubert. G. Schirmer No. 733. Accompanied. Moderately easy.

Within My Heart Breathes Music—Brahms, arr. Gibb. J. Fischer No. 9158. Accompanied. Moderately easy.

You Lovers That Have Loves Astray—Hilton, arr. Stoufer. National Music Publishers No. CMS-119. Recorder consort accompaniment. Medium.

Younger Generation—Copland, arr. Swift. Boosey & Hawkes No. 1722. Accompanied. Medium.

Folk Songs and Spirituals

Ay, Ay, Ay!—Freire, arr. Malin. Piedmont No. 4372. Accompanied. Moderately easy.

Charlottown—Bryan. J. Fischer No. 7993. *A cappella*. Medium.

Chiapanecas (Mexican dance song)—arr. Marlowe. Huntzinger No. 2039. Accompanied. Moderately easy.

Czechoslovakian Dance Song—arr. Row. R. D. Row No. 234. *A cappella*. Easy.

Dancing-Song (traditional Hungarian)—Kodály. Oxford No. 54.942. *A cappella*. Medium.

Dove on the Lily Tree, The (Swedish folk song)—arr. Vené. Carl Fischer No. CM 6280. Accompanied. Easy.

Down by the Sally Gardens (old Irish air)—arr. Donovan. Galaxy No. 555. Accompanied. Moderately easy.

Early One Morning (old English folk song)—arr. Scott. Shawnee Press. Accompanied. Medium.

Eriskay Love Lilt, An (folk song from the Hebrides)—arr. Arch. Boosey & Hawkes No. 5665. Accompanied. Moderately easy.

Farewell (Austrian folk song)—arr. Kanitz. Carl Fischer No. CM 6397. Accompanied. Easy.

Goin' to Boston (Kentucky folk song)—arr. Davis. Summy-Birchard No. 1573. Accompanied. Medium.

Good Night (German folk song)—arr. Malin. Wood No. 830. Accompanied. Moderately easy.

Gute Nacht (German folk song)—arr. G.W.W. E. C. Schirmer No. 819. Accompanied. Medium.

Hi, Ho, Sing Gaily (Swiss folk tune)—arr. Luvaas. Summy-Birchard No. 1505. Accompanied. Moderately easy.

Ifca's Castle (Czechoslovakian folk song)—arr. Harley and Aschenbrenner. Carl Fischer No. 5223. *A cappella*. Moderately easy.

I Got Shoes (spiritual)—arr. Cain. Flammer No. 83206. Accompanied. Moderately easy.

I Live Not Where I Love (traditional English tune)—arr. Parry. Oxford No. W45. Accompanied. Easy.

Keel Row, The (Tyneside air)—arr. Fletcher. Curwen No. 71227. Optional accompaniment. Medium.

Lass from the Low Country, The (British folk song)—arr. LaMance. Lawson-Gould No. 52187. French horn accompaniment. Medium.

Linden Lea—Vaughan Williams. Boosey & Hawkes No. MFS 219. Accompanied. Moderately easy.

Little Bird (Mexican folk song)—arr. Grant. Belwin Mills No. 1723. Accompanied. Moderately easy.

Little David, Play on Your Harp (spiritual)—arr. Cain. Flammer No. 83178. Accompanied. Easy.

Little Sandman, The (German folk song)—arr. Harley & Aschenbrenner. Carl Fischer No. CM 5280. *A cappella*. Easy.

Little White Hen, A—Scandello, arr. Greyson. Bourne No. ES 29A. Optional accompaniment. Moderately easy.

Lollytoodum (American folk song)—arr. Bell. Shawnee Press No. B 0096. Accompanied. Medium.

May Day Carol (English folk song)—arr. Taylor. J. Fischer No. 4872. Accompanied. Moderately easy.

Meadows, Grow Ye Greene (Austrian folk song)—arr. Kanitz. Carl Fischer No. CM 6395. Accompanied. Easy.

Memories (Irish folk tune)—arr. Luvaas. Summy-Birchard No. 374. *A cappella.* Easy.

Meneate, buena moza (Spanish folk song)—arr. Malin. Piedmont No. 4374. Accompanied. Moderately easy.

My Desert Flower (North African folk song)—arr. Marshall. Belwin Mills No. 1821. Accompanied. Moderately easy.

O Can Ye Sew Cushions? (old Scottish cradle song)—arr. Mansfield. Belwin Mills No. 711. Accompanied. Moderately easy.

Old Woman and the Pedlar, The (English air)—arr. Davis. E. C. Schirmer No. 1060. *A cappella.* Medium.

O Little Star in the Sky (Swedish folk tune)—arr. Davis. E. C. Schirmer No. 1065. Accompanied. Medium.

O Mary, Don't You Weep (spiritual)—arr. Siegmaster and Ehret. Bourne No. 25. Accompanied. Medium.

Rock-a My Soul (spiritual)—arr. De Vaux. Bourne No. 195. Accompanied. Medium.

Shy Love (Ukrainian folk song)—arr. Boberg. Kjos No. 6088. Accompanied. Easy.

Song of a Happy Heart (Ukrainian folk song)—arr. Boberg. Kjos No. 6091. Accompanied. Easy.

Swallow's Wooing, The (Hungarian children's song)—arr. Kodály. Oxford No. 542. *A cappella.* Medium.

Swing Low, Sweet Chariot (spiritual)—arr. Burleigh. Ricordi No. 116469. Accompanied. Moderately easy.

Three Hungarian Folk Songs—Bartók, arr. Suchoft. Boosey & Hawkes No. 5488. Accompanied. Medium.

Three Songs from Sweden—arr. Hallstrom. Shawnee Press No. B-215. Accompanied. Moderately easy.

Vreneli (Swiss folk song)—arr. Lester. Belwin Mills No. 1830. Accompanied. Moderately easy.

Waters Ripple and Flow (Czechoslovak folk song)—arr. Taylor. J. Fischer No. 5065. Accompanied. Moderately difficult.

We Wish You a Merry Christmas (English folk song)—arr. Krone. Kjos No. 1211. Optional accompaniment. Medium.

When Love Is Kind (traditional English or Austrian)—arr. Trinkaus. Carl Fischer No. 6139. Accompanied. Moderately easy.

PUBLICATIONS FOR MALE VOICES (TTBB)

Sacred

Adoramus Te—Palestrina, arr. Greyson. Bourne No. ES 16. *A cappella.* Easy.

Adoramus Te, Christe—Corsi, arr. Cain. Choral Art No. R180. *A cappella.* Moderately easy.

Alleluia—Handel, arr. Dawe. G. Schirmer No. 9412. Accompanied. Tenor solo. Moderately difficult.

All Glory Be to God on High (chorale melody of Gregorian origin)—arr. Malin. Summy-Birchard No. 1538. Accompanied. Moderately easy.

Ave Maria (Give Ear unto my Prayer)—Arcadelt, arr. Greyson. Bourne No. ES 4. Optional accompaniment. Moderately difficult.

Ave, maris stella (Hail, O Star; Christmas)—Grieg, arr. Pitcher. Summy-Birchard No. 881. *A cappella.* Moderately difficult.

Babe, So Tender, A (old Flemish carol)—arr. Manton. E. C. Schirmer No. 543. *A cappella.* Medium.

Beautiful Savior (Silesian folk tune)—arr. F. M. Christiansen and Wycisk. Augsburg No. 263. *A cappella.* Moderately easy.

Behold That Star (spiritual; Christmas)—arr. Cunkle. Shawnee Press No. 10. *A cappella.* Bass solo. Medium.

Cantate Domino—Hassler, arr. Beveridge. E. C. Schirmer No. 2194. *A cappella.* Medium.

Carol of the Russian Children (White Russian carol)—arr. Gaul. G. Schirmer No. 7363. Optional accompaniment. Medium.

Christ Is Born of Maiden Fair (ancient carol)—ed. H. Clough-Leighter. E. C. Schirmer No. 515. *A cappella.* Medium.

Christmas Hymn (17th century)—arr. Jüngst. G. Schirmer No. 1414. *A cappella.* Moderately easy.

Come, Sweet Death—Bach, arr. Reed. G. Schirmer No. 8956. *A cappella.* Moderately easy.

God Rest You Merry, Gentlemen (English carol)—arr. the Krones. Kjos No. 1117. Optional accompaniment. Moderately easy.

Hallelujah (from *Mount of Olives*)—Beethoven. G. Schirmer No. 10774. Accompanied. Moderately difficult.

Hallelujah, Amen—Handel, arr. Davison. E. C. Schirmer No. 38. Accompanied. Medium.

Heart Worships, The—Holst, arr. Duey. Boston Music Co. No. 2952. Accompanied. Medium.

Heavenly Light—Kopylov, arr. Wilhousky. Carl Fischer No. CM 611. *A cappella.* Moderately difficult.

I Wonder As I Wander (Appalachian carol)—arr. Niles and Horton. G. Schirmer No. 9292. *A cappella.* Medium.

Jacob's Ladder (spiritual)—arr. Wilson. Ricordi No. NY1680. Optional accompaniment. Medium.

Joseph, Dear One, Joseph Mine (German carol)—arr. Barrow. E. C. Schirmer No. 2158. *A cappella.* Moderately easy.

Joyous Christmas Song, A (Norwegian carol)—arr. Hokanson. Summy-Birchard No. 3142. *A cappella.* Moderately easy.

Let All Give Thanks to Thee—J. S. Bach, arr. Treharne. G. Schirmer No. 8342. *A cappella.* Moderately easy.

Let Nothing Ever Grieve Thee—Brahms. C. F. Peters No. 6009. Accompanied. Medium.

Let Thy Holy Presence—Tschesnokov, arr. Ehret. Boosey & Hawkes No. 5022. *A cappella.* Moderately easy.

Matthew, Mark, Luke, and John (West Country folk song)—arr. Holst. Curwen No. 50616. *A cappella.* Tenor solo. Moderately easy.

May Now Thy Spirit—Schuetky, arr. Treharne. Willis No. 5641. *A cappella.* Medium.

May Thy Blessed Spirit—Tschesnokov, arr. Cookson. Fitzsimons No. 4062. *A cappella.* Medium.

Nature's Praise of God—Beethoven. G. Schirmer No. 6566. Optional accompaniment. Moderately easy.

Noel, Noel—Gevaert, arr. Grayson. Kjos No. 5513. Accompanied. Easy.

Now Thank We All Our God—Cruger, harmonized by Mendelssohn. Boston Music Co. No. 471. Organ accompaniment. Easy.

O bone Jesu—Palestrina. Bourne No. ES 45. *A cappella.* Easy.

O Light Divine—Arkhangelsky, arr. Bement. Oliver Ditson No. 15182. *A cappella.* Medium.

O Lovely, Holy Night (Christmas)—Kremser, arr. Biedermann. J. Fischer No. 3344. *A cappella.* Medium.

Praise the Name of the Lord—Ivanoff, arr. McKinney. J. Fischer No. 9166. *A cappella.* Medium.

Release Them, Lord (Absolve Domine)—Cornelius. Music 70 No. M70-303. *A cappella.* Medium.

Requiem aeternam—Cherubini. Edition Musicus No. 1013. *A cappella.* Moderately easy.

Since Christ Our Lord Was Crucified—Schütz, arr. A.T.D.   E. C. Schirmer No. 88.   *A cappella.* Moderately difficult.
Sleep of the Child Jesus—Gevaert, arr. Lefebvre.   Franco Colombo No. NY773.   *A cappella.* Easy.
Stars, The—Schubert, arr. Larson.   Summy-Birchard No. 5021.   *A cappella.* Tenor solo. Medium.
Tell Me, Shepherds, Dear (Polish carol)—arr. H.G.M.   E. C. Schirmer No. 2105.   *A cappella.* Medium.
Thanks Be to Thee—Handel, arr. Lefebvre.   Galaxy No. 1222.   Accompanied.   Tenor solo. Easy.
Then Round About the Starry Throne (from *Samson*)—Handel.   E. C. Schirmer No. 907.   Accompanied. Medium.
They Sang That Night in Bethlehem—Schubert, arr. Deis.   G. Schirmer No. 8292.   *A cappella.* Medium.
Thou Must Leave Thy Lowly Dwelling—Berlioz.   Galaxy No. 2065.   Accompanied. Medium.
Who Ne'er His Bread with Tears Did Eat—Schubert.   Lawson-Gould No. 876.   Accompanied. Medium.
With a Voice of Singing—Shaw.   G. Schirmer No. 10454.   Piano or organ accompaniment.   Medium.
Ye Watchers and Ye Holy Ones (17th-century German melody)—arr. Davison.   E. C. Schirmer No. 65.   Piano or organ accompaniment.   Medium.
Your Voices Raise—Handel, arr. A.T.D.   E. C. Schirmer No. 86.   Accompanied. Difficult.

Secular

Aura Lee—Poulton, arr. Hunter, Parker, and Shaw.   Lawson-Gould No. 527.   *A cappella.* Moderately easy.
Battle Hymn of the Republic—Steffe, arr. Ringwald.   Shawnee Press No. A 0028.   Four-hand piano accompaniment.   Baritone solo.   Medium.
Brothers, Sing On!—Grieg, arr. McKinney.   J. Fischer No. 6927.   *A cappella.* Medium.
By the Sea—Schubert, arr. Bantock.   Belwin Mills No. 1145.   *A cappella.* Moderately easy.
Crown of Roses, The—Tchaikovsky, arr. Bell.   Belwin Mills Music No. 1085.   *A cappella.* Medium.
Death Came Knocking—Floyd.   Boosey & Hawkes No. 5368.   Accompanied. Moderately difficult.
Dreams—Wagner, arr. Scherer.   Gray No. 436.   Accompanied.   Medium.
Gambler's Lament, The—Niles.   G. Schirmer No. 10305.   Accompanied.   Medium.
Good Fellows Be Merry—Bach, arr. Duey.   Boston Music Co. No. 2944.   Accompanied. Difficult.
Holiday Song—Schuman.   G. Schirmer No. 9866.   Accompanied.   Moderately easy.
Hunting Song (Jaglied)—Mendelssohn, arr. Mueller.   G. Schirmer No. 12074.   *A cappella.* Medium.
In the Doorways I Will Linger—Schubert, arr. Rider.   Lawson-Gould No. 875.   Accompanied. Medium.
Laura Lee—Foster, arr. Parker and Shaw.   Lawson-Gould No. 874.   *A cappella.* Moderately easy.
Liebe—Schubert.   Mark Foster No. MF 1059.   *A cappella.* Medium.
Night, The (Die Nacht)—Schubert.   Lawson-Gould No. 786.   *A cappella.* Medium.
Nocturne—Mendelssohn, arr. Treharne.   Boston Music Co. No. 2987.   Accompanied. Moderately difficult.
Passing By—Purcell, arr. Parker-Shaw.   Lawson-Gould No. 967.   *A cappella.* Moderately easy.
Pilgrims' Chorus (from *Tannhäuser*)—Wagner, arr. Dawson.   Kjos No. 5490.   *A cappella.* Medium.
Pilgrim's Song—Tchaikovsky, arr. Treharne.   G. Schirmer No. 8802.   Accompanied. Moderately difficult.

Rain Has Kissed the Rose, The—Schumann. G. Schirmer No. 412. *A cappella.* Moderately easy.

Red, Red Rose, A—Schumann, arr. Pfautsch. Lawson-Gould No. 781. *A cappella.* Medium.

Rest (Du bist die Ruh)—Schubert, arr. Bantock. Belwin Mills No. 1146. *A cappella.* Medium.

Rhapsodie—Brahms. Boston Music Co. No. 229. Accompanied. Alto solo. Moderately difficult.

Serenade—Haydn, arr. Schultz. G. Schirmer No. 1087. *A cappella.* Easy.

Sophomoric Philosophy—Dvořák. Remick No. 9G 1108. *A cappella.* Moderately easy.

Stopwatch and an Ordinance Map, A—Barber. G. Schirmer No. 8799. Kettledrum accompaniment. Moderately difficult.

Stouthearted Men—Romberg, arr. Scotson. Harms, Inc. No. 9-H1184. Accompanied. Moderately easy.

Swan, The—Saint-Saëns, arr. Boyce. G. Schirmer No. 10527. Humming chorus with violin solo and piano accompaniment. Medium.

Sweet Love Doth Now Invite—Dowland. Bourne No. ES7. Optional accompaniment. Moderately easy.

To All You Ladies Now on Land—Callcott. E. C. Schirmer No. 533. *A cappella.* Moderately easy.

Winter Song—Bullard. Oliver Ditson No. 10160. Accompanied. Moderately easy.

Woods So Dense—Lully, arr. Sodero. G. Schirmer No. 8568. *A cappella.* Moderately easy.

Folk Songs and Spirituals

Ain'-a That Good News (spiritual)—arr. Dawson. Kjos No. T104. *A cappella.* Medium.

All through the Night (old Welsh song)—arr. Ringwald. Shawnee Press No. C-21. Optional accompaniment. Medium.

A-Roving (sea chantey)—arr. Wagner. Lawson-Gould No. 791. *A cappella.* Baritone solo. Medium.

Aura Lee—Poulton, arr. Parker-Shaw. Lawson-Gould No. 527. *A cappella.* Moderately easy.

Believe Me, If All Those Endearing Young Charms (old Irish air)—arr. Hunter, Parker, and Shaw. Lawson-Gould No. 528. *A cappella.* Medium.

Blow the Man Down (English sea chantey)—arr. Parker and Shaw. Lawson-Gould No. 51055. *A cappella.* Bass solo. Moderately difficult.

Boar's Head Carol, The (English secular carol)—arr. Parker and Shaw. G. Schirmer No. 10179. *A cappella.* Easy.

Carol of the Bells (Ukrainian carol; Christmas)—Leontovich, arr. Wilhousky. Carl Fischer No. CM 2270. *A cappella.* Moderately easy.

Climbin' up the Mountain (spiritual)—arr. Smith. Kjos No. 1101. *A cappella.* Medium.

De Animals a-Comin' (Negro spiritual)—arr. Bartholomew. G. Schirmer No. 8046. *A cappella.* Medium.

Down among the Dead Men (old English air)—arr. Vaughan Williams. Belwin Mills No. 1142. *A cappella.* Medium.

Down in the Valley (Kentucky folk tune)—arr. Mead. Galaxy No. 1716. Accompanied. Moderately easy.

Drink to Me Only with Thine Eyes (old English air)—arr. Hunter, Parker, and Shaw. Lawson-Gould No. 530. *A cappella.* Moderately difficult.

Go Tell It on the Mountain (spiritual)—arr. Huntley. Fitzsimons No. 4067. *A cappella.* Medium.

Green Grow the Rushes O! (Scottish folk song)—arr. Roberton. R. D. Row No. 519. *A cappella.* Medium.

Hickory Stick, The (American folk song)—arr. Sheppard. Boston Music Co. No. 13042. Optional accompaniment. Medium.

I Got Shoes (spiritual)—arr. Bartholomew. G. Schirmer No. 7144. *A cappella.* Moderately easy.

I Wished to Be Single Again (English folk song)—arr. Ricketts. Somerset Press No. SP748. *A cappella.* Baritone solo. Medium.

John Peel (old English hunting song)—arr. Andrews. Gray No. 31. *A cappella.* Moderately easy.

Lincolnshire Poacher, The (English folk song)—arr. Bantock. Belwin Mills. *A cappella.* Medium.

Little Innocent Lamb (spiritual)—arr. Bartholomew. G. Schirmer No. 9907. *A cappella.* Moderately easy.

Loch Lomond (Scottish folk song)—arr. Duson. Kjos No. ED.5564. *A cappella.* Medium.

Lord Randall (British folk song)—arr. Duey. Boston Music Co. No. 2954. *A cappella.* Baritone or tenor solo. Medium.

Marianina (Italian folk song)—arr. Parker and Shaw. Lawson-Gould No. 974. *A cappella.* Tenor solo. Medium.

My Johnny Was a Shoemaker (English folk song)—arr. Taylor. J. Fischer No. 4834. Accompanied. Medium.

My Lord, What a Mornin' (spiritual)—arr. Burleigh. Franco Colombo No. NY1713. *A cappella.* Moderately easy.

Night Herding Song (cowboy song)—arr. Luboff. Walton No. 1006. Accompanied. Easy.

Old Chisholm Trail, The (Western folk song)—arr. Cain. Pro Art No. 1483. Accompanied. Easy.

On Top of Old Smoky (American folk song)—arr. Stone. Pro Art No. 1347. Accompanied. Easy.

O Tannenbaum (traditional German)—arr. Parker and Shaw. G. Schirmer No. 10195. *A cappella.* Moderately easy.

Over Here (Irish folk song)—arr. Roberton. Boosey & Hawkes No. 1987. *A cappella.* Moderately easy.

Poor Lonesome Cowboy (cowboy song)—arr. Luboff. Walton No. 1007. *A cappella.* Moderately easy.

Poor Man Lazrus (spiritual)—arr. Hairston. Bourne No. S1022. *A cappella.* Medium.

Rantin' Rovin' Robin (Scottish folk song)—arr. Davison. E. C. Schirmer No. 84. Accompanied. Baritone solo. Moderately easy.

Rebel Soldier, The (American folk song)—arr. Sheppard. Boston Music Co. No. 3081. *A cappella.* Moderately easy.

Ride the Chariot (spiritual)—arr. Smith. Kjos No. 1102. *A cappella.* Tenor solo. Moderately easy.

Rio Grande (sea chantey)—arr. Dougherty. G. Schirmer No. 10414. Accompanied. Moderately easy.

Scissors-Grinder, The (Flemish folk song)—arr. Jungst. G. Schirmer No. 10414. Accompanied. Moderately easy.

Shenandoah (sea chantey)—arr. Wagner. Lawson-Gould No. 848. *A cappella.* Baritone solo. Moderately easy.

Sister Mary Wore Three Lengths of Chain (spiritual)—arr. Bartholomew. G. Schirmer No. 10243. *A cappella.* Medium.

Soon-Ah Will Be Done—Dawson. Kjos No. T101A. *A cappella.* Moderately difficult.

Sourwood Mountain (Kentucky mountain song)—arr. Hall. G. Schirmer No. 8140. *A cappella.* Medium.

Steal Away (spiritual)—arr. Richardson. Mark Foster No. MF 1011. *A cappella.* Moderately easy.

Swansea Town (Hampshire folk song)—arr. Holst. Curwen No. 50615. *A cappella.* Medium.

Turtle Dove, The (folk song)—arr. Vaughan Williams. Curwen No. 50570. Accompanied. Baritone or tenor solo. Medium.

We Wish You a Merry Christmas (English folk song; secular)—arr. the Krones. Kjos No. 1114. Optional accompaniment. Moderately easy.

What Shall We Do with a Drunken Sailor? (traditional sea chantey)—arr. Bartholomew. G. Schirmer No. 7422. Accompanied. Easy.

PUBLICATIONS FOR TWO PARTS (SA OR TB)

Achieved Is the Glorious Work—Haydn, arr. Davies. Oxford No. E111. Accompanied. Medium.

Ah, Lovely Meadows (Czech folk song)—arr. Kjelson. Belwin Mills No. 1901. Accompanied. Easy.

Ash Grove, The (Welsh folk song)—arr. Stone. Belwin Mills No. 2199. Accompanied. Moderately easy.

As Lately We Watched (Austrian carol)—arr. Stocker. Kjos No. ED.6144. Piano and optional instrumental accompaniment. Moderately easy.

At the Gates of Heaven (Basque folk song)—arr. Kjelson. Belwin Mills No. 1903. Accompanied. Moderately easy.

Bright Star (Polish carol)—arr. Ehret. Edw. B. Marks No. 4407. Accompanied. Moderately easy.

Christ Is Born to You Today (German folk song)—arr. Ehret. Edw. B. Marks No. 4408. Accompanied. Moderately easy.

Cielito Lindo (Mexican folk song)—arr. Tate. Oxford No. T72. Accompanied. Medium.

Cindy (American folk song)—arr. Barthelson. Belwin Mills No. 1746. Moderately easy.

Come, All Ye Lads and Lassies (old English melody)—arr. Howorth. Belwin Mills No. 1874. Medium.

Coventry Carol (English carol)—arr. Stone. Belwin Mills No. 2142. Accompanied. Moderately easy.

Cuckoo, the Nightingale, and the Donkey, The—Mahler. Oxford No. T75. Accompanied. Medium.

Cuckoo Cries, The—Möller, arr. Swift. Belwin Mills No. 1436. With solo voices. Medium.

De Gospel Train (spiritual), and There's Music in the Air (G. F. Root)—arr. Rhea. Bourne No. MD2. Easy.

Drill, Ye Tarriers, Drill (American ballad)—arr. Kjelson. Belwin Mills No. 1904. Moderately easy.

Dyby Byla Kosa Nabróšená (If There Were a Sharpened Scythe)—Dvořák. National Music Publishers No. WHC-91. Accompanied. Easy.

Elephant and the Flea, The (nonsense song)—arr. Barthelson. Belwin Mills No. 1747. Moderately easy.

Go Tell It on the Mountain (Christmas spiritual)—arr. Barthelson. Belwin Mills No. 1833. Moderately easy.

He's Goin' Away (American folk song)—arr. Howorth. Belwin Mills No. 1848. Moderately easy.

He's Got the Whole World in His Hands (spiritual)—arr. Howorth. Belwin Mills No. 1777. Optional solo. Moderately easy.

Holding Wonder—Goldsmith. Flammer No. E-5242. Accompanied. Easy.

I Love Little Willie (Southern mountain song)—arr. Barthelson. Belwin Mills No. 1748. Easy.

I'm Goin' Leave Old Texas Now (cowboy song)—arr. Pitcher. Belwin Mills No. 1835. Easy.

Jesus Christ Our Saviour Is Born (Lithuanian carol)—arr. Gordon. Belwin Mills No. 1844. Moderately easy.

Kentucky Babe—Giebel, arr. Churchill. Belwin Mills No. 1836. Easy.

Little Cradle Rocks Tonight in Glory, The (spiritual)—arr. Walker. Concordia No. 98-2139. Xylophone and percussion accompaniment. Moderately easy.

My Heart Ever Faithful—J. S. Bach, arr. Bampton. Presser No. 312-40474. Accompanied. Moderately easy.

O Come, All Ye Children (German Christmas carol)—arr. Gordon. Belwin Mills No. 1720. Easy.

O Thou Good and Faithful Servent (Serve bone)—Charpentier, arr. McCray. Mark Foster No. MF 805. Accompanied. Moderately easy.

Patapan (Burgundian carol)—arr. Jacques. Oxford No. T86. Accompanied. Easy.

Serve bone—di Lasso. Mark Foster No. MF 801. *A cappella.* Moderately easy.

Shenandoah (sea chantey)—arr. Stone. Belwin Mills No. 2141. Accompanied. Moderately easy.

Sing Hallelujah, Praise the Lord (Moravian melody)—arr. Mueller. G. Schirmer No. 10754. Moderately easy.

Sing Ye Praises unto the Father—Mozart, arr. Ehret. Gentry No. JG-524. Accompanied. Medium.

So Far Away (Wie kann ich froh und lustig sein?)—Mendelssohn. Gentry No. JG-527. Accompanied. Medium.

Standin' in the Need of Prayer (spiritual)—arr. Kjelson. Belwin Mills No. 1902. With solo voice. Moderately easy.

Still, Still (German carol)—arr. Sumner. Scholin No. 2021. Easy.

Sweet Betsy from Pike (American folk song)—arr. Swift. Belwin Mills No. 1622. Moderately easy.

There's a Little Wheel a-Turnin' (spiritual)—arr. Vance. Belwin Mills No. 1898. Optional third voice and solo. Medium.

Today with Loud Rejoicing—Mozart, arr. Heinrich. Boston Music Co. No. 3117. Easy.

Velvet Shoes—Thompson. E. C. Schirmer No. 2526. Accompanied. Easy.

Viennese Lullaby (Viennese popular song)—arr. Wilson. Bourne No. B214056. Easy.

PUBLICATIONS FOR COMBINED CHORUS AND BAND AND/OR ORCHESTRA

All Glory, Laud and Honor—Teschner, arr. Cain. Flammer. SATB—for chorus and band; chorus and orchestra.

Ave Maria—Bach and Gounod, arr. Tolmadge. Staff. SATB—for chorus and band.

Battle Hymn of the Republic—Steffe, arr. Ringwald. Shawnee Press. SATB; TTBB—for chorus and band; chorus and orchestra.

Battle Hymn of the Republic—Steffe, arr. Wilhousky. Carl Fischer. SSATTBB—for chorus and band; chorus and orchestra.

Beautiful Dreamer—Foster, arr. Frangkiser. Boosey & Hawkes. SATB; TTBB—for chorus and band.

Break Forth, O Beauteous Heavenly Light—Bach. G. Schirmer. SATB—for chorus and orchestra (orchestra parts available from publisher on rental only).

Chorale: St. Antoni—Haydn and Brahms, arr. Tolmadge. Staff. SATB—for chorus and band.

Chorale: King of Glory—J. S. Bach. Staff. SATB—for chorus and band; chorus and orchestra; chorus, band, and orchestra.

Chorale: St. Martin—arr. Gardner. Staff. SATB—for chorus and band.

Chorale from *Organ Symphony No. 3*—Saint-Saëns. Staff. SATB—for chorus and band.

Choral Procession (Finale to Cantata *The Song of Man*)—Kountz, arr. Campbell and Watson. Witmark. SATB—for chorus and band.

Christmas Day—Holst. Gray. SATB—for chorus and orchestra (orchestral parts available from publisher on rental only).

Fantasie on Christmas Carols—Vaughan Williams. Galaxy. SATB, with bar. solo—for chorus and orchestra (orchestra parts available from publishers on rental only).

Festival Finale—Maddy. Kjos. SATB—for chorus and band; chorus and orchestra; chorus, band, and orchestra.

Festival Song of Praise—Mendelssohn, arr. Wilson and Harris. Bourne. SATB—for chorus and orchestra.

Gloria in excelsis (from Twelfth Mass)—Mozart. Presser. SATB—for chorus and orchestra.

Glory—Rimsky-Korsakov. Witmark. SSAATTBB—for chorus and orchestra.

Glory and Triumph—Berlioz. Mercury. SATB—for chorus and band; chorus and orchestra.

Glory to God in the Highest—Pergolesi, arr. Houseknecht. Kjos. SATB—for chorus and band.

God of Our Fathers—arr. Gearhart. Shawnee Press. SATB—for chorus, with three trumpets, percussion, four-hand piano and organ accompaniment.

Hail, Glorious Day—Elgar, arr. Schaefer.   Boosey & Hawkes.   SATB—for chorus and band.

Hallelujah Chorus (from *Messiah*)—Handel.   Carl Fischer.   SATB—for chorus and orchestra; chorus and band.

Heavens Are Telling, The—Haydn.   Carl Fischer.   SATB—for chorus and orchestra.

Holy, Holy, Holy—arr. Ledizén.   Bourne.   SATB—for chorus and band.

How Lovely Is Thy Dwelling (from Requiem)—Brahms.   G. Schirmer.   SATB—for chorus and orchestra (orchestral parts available from publisher on rental only).

Hymn of Freedom—Brahms, arr. Tolmadge.   Staff.   SATB—for chorus and band.

Hymn of Praise—Mozart, arr. Tolmadge.   Staff.   SATB—for Chorus and Band.

Hymn to America—McKay.   Schmitt, Hall & McCreary.   SATB—for chorus and band.

Land of Hope and Glory—Elgar.   Boosey & Hawkes.   SATB; SSA—for chorus and band; chorus and orchestra.

Largo from *New World Symphony* (choral parts: "Behold Our God")—Dvořák. Belwin Mills.   SATB—for chorus and band.

Let All Mortal Flesh Keep Silence—Holst.   Galaxy.   SATB—for chorus and orchestra.

Magnificat—Vaughan Williams.   Oxford.   SSA, with contralto solo—for chorus and orchestra (orchestral parts available from publisher on rental only).

Mannin Veen (Dear Isle of Man)—Wood.   Boosey & Hawkes.   SATB; SAB; SSA—for chorus and orchestra; chorus and band.

Mighty Fortress Is Our God, A—Luther.   Staff.   SATB—for chorus and band; chorus and orchestra; chorus, band, and orchestra.

Nation's Creed, The—Williams.   Schmitt, Hall & McCreary.   SATB—for chorus and band.

Now Thank We All Our God—R. Thompson.   E. C. Schirmer.   SATB—for chorus and orchestra.

O Clap Your Hands—Vaughan Williams.   Galaxy.   SATB—for chorus, brass choir and percussion.

Omnipotence, The—Schubert.   G. Schirmer.   SSAATTBB; TTBB; SSA—for chorus and orchestra (orchestral parts available from publisher on rental only).

One World—O'Hara, arr. Wilson and Leidzen.   Bourne.   SATB; TTBB; SSA—for chorus and band; chorus and orchestra.

Onward, Christian Soldiers—arr. Simeone.   Shawnee Press.   SATB; TTBB—for chorus and band; chorus and orchestra.

Onward, Ye Peoples—Sibelius, arr. Lefebvre.   Galaxy.   SATB; SSA; TTBB—for chorus and band; chorus and orchestra.

Pomp and Circumstance—Elgar.   Staff.   SATB—for chorus and band; chorus and orchestra; chorus, band, and orchestra.

Rhapsody in Blue (choral finale)—Gershwin, arr. Warnick.   Harms, Inc.   SSATTBB—for chorus and band; chorus and orchestra.

Song of Destiny—Brahms.   Staff.   SATB—for chorus and band.

To Music—Schubert, arr. Wilson.   Schmitt, Hall & McCreary.   SATB; SAB; SSA—for chorus and orchestra.

Trumpet Voluntary—Purcell.   Staff.   SATB; SAB, SSA; SA—for chorus and band; chorus and orchestra; chorus, band, and orchestra.

Turn Back, O Man—Holst.   Galaxy.   SATB—for chorus and orchestra (orchestral parts available from publisher on rental only).

Voice of Freedom—Rubinstein, arr. Caillet.   Boosey & Hawkes.   SATB; TTBB—for chorus and band; chorus and orchestra.

With a Voice of Singing—Shaw.   G. Schirmer.   SATB—for chorus and orchestra (orchestral accompaniment available from publisher on rental only).

CHORAL MUSIC WITH ELECTRONIC TAPE/NONCONVENTIONAL NOTATION

Aleatory Psalm—Gordon H. Lamb.   World Library Publications No. CA-4003-8. SATB.

Alleluia, Acclamation and Carol—Daniel Pinkham.   E. C. Schirmer Nos. 2954 and 2955.   SATB, timpani, percussion, and electronic tape.

All the Ways of a Man—Knut Nystedt. Augsburg No. 11-9004. SATB.
Amens—Daniel Pinkham. E. C. Schirmer No. 3016. SATB and electronic tape.
Call of Isaiah, The—Daniel Pinkham. E. C. Schirmer No. 2911. SATB with organ and electronic tape.
Collect—Leslie Bassett. World Library Publications No. CA2000-8. SATB, electronic tape.
Creation, The (from *The Family of Man*)—Michael Hennagin. Walton No. W2186. SATB.
Dialogue—Robert Karlén. A.M.S.I. No. AMS 175. SATB, tape recorder.
Emperor of Ice Cream, The—Roger Reynolds. C. F. Peters. Eight singers, piano, percussion, bass; multimedia.
Etude and Pattern—Brock McElheran. Oxford. SSAATBB unaccompanied.
Etude and Scherzo—Brock McElheran. Oxford. SSAATBB unaccompanied.
Evergreen—Daniel Pinkham. E. C. Schirmer No. 2962. Unison chorus, electronic tape, and optional instruments (Autoharp, bells, harp, guitar, piano, and organ).
God Love You Now—Donald Erb. Merion No. 342-40099. SATB, speaker, assorted instruments, reverberation device.
Hymn of the Universe—Richard Felciano. E. C. Schirmer No. 2944. SAB and electronic sounds.
In the Beginning of Creation—Daniel Pinkham. E. C. Schirmer No. 2902. Mixed chorus, electronic tape.
In the Presence—Gilbert Trythall. Edw. B. Marks No. 4495. SATB, electronic tape.
I Saw an Angel—Daniel Pinkham. E. C. Schirmer No. 2973. SATB and electronic tape.
Kyrie—Donald Erb. Merion No. 342-40026. SATB, piano, percussion, electronic tape.
Out of Sight—Richard Felciano. E. C. Schirmer No. 2909. SATB, organ, and electronic tape.
Pentecost Sunday—Richard Felciano. World Library Publications No. EMP-1532-1. Unison male chorus, organ, electronic tape.
Praise to God—Knut Nystedt. Associated No. A-597. Mixed voices, *a cappella.*
Praise Ye the Lord—Gardner Read. Lawson-Gould No. 51871.
Psalm 27 (Part III)—Robert Karlen. A.M.S.I. No. 160. SATB.
Pshelley's Psalm—Richard Felciano. E. C. Schirmer No. 2930. SATB.
Sic transit—Richard Felciano. E. C. Schirmer No. 2903. SAB chorus, organ, electronic tape, light sources.
Signs—Richard Felciano. E. C. Schirmer No. 2927. SATB, electronic tape and one, two, or three film strip projectors.
Susani—Richard Felciano. E. C. Schirmer No. 3002. Mixed voices, organ, percussion, and electronic tape.
Three-in-One-in-Three—Richard Felciano. E. C. Schirmer No. 2910. Chorus, organ, tape.
Time to Every Purpose, A—Gilbert Trythall. Edw. B. Marks No. 4586. SATB, electronic tape.
Two Moves and the Slow Scat—Dennis Kam. Belwin Mills No. 2282. SATB.
Two Public Pieces—Richard Felciano. E. C. Schirmer No. 2937. Unison voices and electronic sounds.
Words of St. Peter—Richard Felciano. World Library Publications No. CA-2093-8. Mixed voices, organ, and electronic tape.

MUSIC FOR JAZZ/SHOW CHOIRS
(Broadway Musicals/Popular/Vocal Jazz)

Alexander's Ragtime Band—Berlin, arr. Simeone. Shawnee Press No. 0638. Piano accompaniment. Moderately easy.
Am I Blue—Akst, arr. K. Shaw. Warner Bros. No. 441-01044. *A cappella.* Moderately easy.
Another Op'nin', Another Show (from *Kiss Me Kate*)—Porter, arr. Cable. Hal Leonard No. 00346038. Piano accompaniment. Moderately easy.
A Wonderful Day Like Today—Bricusse and Newley, arr. Leyden. Musical Comedy Productions No. S7029. Piano accompaniment. Moderately easy.

Baby Come Back to Me—Santamaria, arr. Nowak. Hal Leonard No. 07357521. Piano with optional rhythm section. Medium.

Beautiful City (from *Godspell*)—Schwartz, arr. Lojeski. Hal Leonard No. 08200630. Piano with optional percussion, guitar, and string bass. Moderately easy.

Bill Bailey, Won't You Please Come Home—Cannon, arr. K. Shaw. Jenson No. 441-02014. Piano and optional rhythm section. Moderately easy.

Black and Blue (from *Ain't Misbehavin'*)—Waller, arr. Elliott. Chappell No. 3893. Piano accompaniment. Medium.

Blues Down to My Shoes—K. Shaw. Hal Leonard No. 07852435. Piano, bass, and drums. Moderately easy.

Blue Skies—Berlin, arr. Emerson. Jenson No. 403-02094. Piano and optional rhythm section. Medium.

Broadway Spectacular (What I Did For Love, Tomorrow, Put On a Happy Face, Hello Dolly, Mame)—arr. Emerson. Jenson No. 403-02044. Piano and optional rhythm section. Moderately easy.

Bye Bye Blues—Hamm, Bennett, Lown, and Gray, arr. Simeone. Shawnee Press No. A-0523. Piano accompaniment. Medium.

Celebration—Bell, arr. Chinn. Jenson No. 457-03014. Piano and optional rhythm section. Moderately easy.

C'est si bon (It's So Good)—Betti, arr. Weir. Hal Leonard No. 08623371. Piano, bass, and percussion, with optional jazz ensemble. Difficult.

Corner of the Sky (from *Pippin*)—Schwartz, arr. Cacavas. Belwin Mills No. OCT 02288. Piano accompaniment. Moderately easy.

Crazy Rhythm—Meyer and Kahn, arr. Bretton. Warner Bros. No. H2210. Piano, guitar, and bass. Moderately easy.

Cute—Hefti, arr. Averre. Warner Bros. No. 487-41008. Piano, bass, and drums. Moderately easy.

Day by Day (from *Godspell*)—Schwartz, arr. Leyden. Columbia Pictures No. 0014DC1X. Piano, drums, and guitars. Moderately easy.

Don't Take Away the Music—Tawney, arr. Lojeski. Hal Leonard No. 08212800. Piano, guitar, percussion, and electric bass. Medium.

Ease on Down the Road (from *The Wiz*)—Smalls, arr. Beard. Shawnee Press No. A-1374. Piano accompaniment. Moderately easy.

Everybody Loves My Baby—Palmer and Williams, arr. K. Shaw. Hal Leonard No. 0865781. Piano and optional instrumental accompaniment. Medium.

Everybody Rejoice (from *The Wiz*)—Vandross, arr. H. Ades. Shawnee Press No. A-1402. Piano accompaniment. Moderately easy.

Gene Puerling Sound, The (Am I Blue, April in Paris, Autumn in New York, Dancing in the Dark, Indian Summer)—arr. G. Puerling. Shawnee Press No. A-1291. Optional piano accompaniment. Medium.

Georgia on My Mind—Carmichael, arr. Puerling. Studio P/R No. VGP 8001. Piano, bass, and drums. Moderately difficult.

Georgia on My Mind—Carmichael, arr. Strommen. Studio P/R No. SV 8337. Piano and guitar accompaniment. Medium.

Getting to Know You (from *The King and I*)—Rogers, arr. Puerling. Hal Leonard No. 07359124. Piano with optional rhythm section. Medium.

Go for the Good Times—Brymer. Jenson No. 445-07054. Piano and optional rhythm section. Medium.

Got to Get You into My Life—Lennon and McCartney, arr. Strommen. Alfred No. 6823. Piano with optional guitar, bass, and drums. Stage band accompaniment also available. Medium.

Home (from *The Wiz*)—Smalls, arr. Hayward. Shawnee Press No. A-1394. Piano accompaniment. Moderately easy.

How Lucky Can You Get—Kander and Ebb, arr. Jennings. Warner Bros. No. 408-08014. Piano accompaniment. Moderately easy.

I Hear Music—Lane, arr. Lapin. Warner Bros. No. CH 0926. Piano with optional guitar, bass, and drums. Moderately difficult.

Impossible Dream, The (from *Man of La Mancha*)—Leigh, arr. Ringwald. Shawnee Press No. A-0885. Piano accompaniment. Medium.

In the Mood—Garland, arr. Sterling. Shawnee Press No. A-1533. Piano with optional guitar, string bass, and drums. Moderately easy.

I've Got the Music in Me—Boshell, arr. Billingsley. Jensen No. 432-09024. Piano and optional rhythm section. Medium.

I've Got You under My Skin—Porter, arr. Mattson. Hal Leonard No. 08603340. Piano, bass, and drums. Medium.

Jailhouse Rock—Leiber and Stoller, arr. K. Shaw. Hal Leonard No. 08657893. Piano with optional instrumental accompaniment. Moderately easy.

Jubilation—Anka and Harris, arr. K. Shaw. Hal Leonard. No. 07981226. Piano, electric bass, drums, trumpet, alto saxophone, and trombone. Medium.

Just One of Those Things—Porter, arr. Emerson. Warner Bros. No. 403-10104. Piano accompaniment. Easy.

Just the Way You Are—Joel, arr. Lojeski. Hal Leonard No. 08234875. Piano, guitar, percussion, and electric bass. Medium.

King and I Medley, The—Rogers, arr. Kerr. Hal Leonard No. 08565671. Piano and optional instrumental accompaniment. Moderately easy.

Let the Sunshine In—K. Shaw. Jenson No. 441-12014. Piano and optional rhythm section. Medium.

Love Is the Answer—Hannisian. Shawnee Press No. A-1382. Piano accompaniment. Moderately easy.

Magic to Do (from *Pippin*)—Schwartz, arr. Fisher. Belwin Mills No. OCT 02302. Piano with optional bass, guitar, and drums. Moderately easy.

Mama Told Me (Not to Come)—Newmann, arr. K. Shaw. Hal Leonard No. 08658250. Piano, trumpet, alto saxophone, electric guitar, electric bass, and drums. Medium.

Maybe God Is Trying to Tell You Somethin'—Crouch, Jones, Maxwell, and Del Sesto, arr. K. Shaw. Warner Bros. No. 441-13034. Piano, bass, guitar, and drums.

Me and My Shadow—Jolson and Dreyer, arr. Ades. Shawnee Press No. A-0512. Piano accompaniment. Medium.

Mercy, Mercy, Mercy—Zawinul, arr. Sechler. Shawnee Press No. A-1153. Piano with optional guitar, drums, and bass. Moderately easy.

Michelle—Lennon and McCartney, arr. Puerling. Shawnee Press No. A-1344. *A cappella*. Soprano and tenor solos. Difficult.

Mood Indigo—Ellington, arr. Simeone. Shawnee Press No. A-0800. Piano and optional guitar, string bass, and drums. Medium.

My Funny Valentine—arr. K. Shaw. Hal Leonard No. 08658800. *A cappella*. Medium.

My Romance—Rogers, arr. K. Shaw. Jenson No. 441-13014. *A cappella*. Moderately difficult.

Mystery—Temperton, arr. Zegree. Hal Leonard No. 07357770. Piano and optional instrumental accompaniment. Moderately difficult.

New York Afternoon—Cole, arr. Mattson. Jenson No. 463-14024. Piano, bass, guitar, and drums. Moderately difficult.

New York City Rhythm—Manilow and Panzer, arr. Hyde. Big 3 No. 4027. Piano with optional guitar, percussion, and bass. Medium.

Paddlin' Madelin' Home—Woods, arr. Grusin. Shapiro, Bernstein & Co. No. sb 7006. Piano accompaniment. Moderately easy.

People—Styne, arr. Puerling. Hal Leonard No. 07359307. *A cappella*. Baritone solo. Moderately difficult.

Pippin (choral medley)—Schwartz, arr. Casey. Belwin Mills No. SB 00939. Piano with optional bass, guitar, and drums. Medium.

Powerhouse—Emerson. Jenson No. 403-16074. Piano accompaniment. Medium.

Reach for the Stars—G. Fry. Belwin Mills No. OCT 02427. Piano with optional guitar, bass, and drums. Medium.

Save the Bones for Henry Jones—Barker, Lee, and Jones, arr. K. Shaw. Hal Leonard No. 07248725. Piano, electric bass, and drums. Moderately easy.

Shadow of Your Smile, The—Mandel, arr. Strommen. Shawnee Press No. A-1764. Piano with optional guitar, bass, and drums. Medium.

Side by Side—Woods, arr. Coates. Shawnee Press No. A-1389. Piano accompaniment. Moderately easy.

Silent Night—Gruber, arr. Puerling. Shawnee Press No. A-1315. *A cappella.* Optional soprano and tenor solos. Moderately difficult.

Smile—Chaplin, arr. Zegree. Hal Leonard No. 08603699. *A cappella.* Medium.

Smiles (a choral montage of songs, 1900–1920)—arr. H. Ades. Shawnee Press No. A-1322. Piano accompaniment. Moderately easy.

Sound of the Singers Unlimited, The (We've Only Just Begun, Try to Remember, On a Clear Day, Emily, My Ship, Where Is Love)—arr. Puerling. Shawnee Press No. A-1412. Instrumental accompaniment available. Medium.

Star Dust—Carmichael, arr. Ringwald. Shawnee Press No. A-0689. Piano accompaniment. Medium.

Streets A-fire!—Brymer. Hal Leonard No. 08639211. Piano with optional instrumental accompaniment. Moderately difficult.

Summer Nights (from *Grease*)—Casey and Jacobs, arr. Lojeski. Hal Leonard No. 08264480. Piano with electric guitar, percussion, and electric bass. Moderately easy.

Summertime—Gershwin, arr. K. Shaw. Hal Leonard No. 08664217. Piano, electric bass, and drums. Medium.

Sweet Georgia Brown—Bernie, Pinkard, and Casey, arr. K. Shaw. Warner Bros. No. 441-19064. Piano accompaniment. Moderately difficult.

Their Hearts Are Full of Spring—Troup, arr. K. Shaw. Hal Leonard No. 08664515. *A cappella.* Medium.

There's No Business Like Show Business—Berlin, arr. Ades. Shawnee Press No. A-0637. Piano accompaniment. Medium.

They're Playing Our Song (choral medley)—Hamlisch, arr. Lojeski. Hal Leonard No. 08240600. Piano, electric guitar, electric bass, and percussion. Medium.

Twentiana (a choral montage of songs of the 1920s)—arr. Ades. Shawnee Press No. A-1261. Piano with optional string bass and drums. Moderately easy to medium.

Varsity Drag, The—DeSylva, Brown, and Henderson, arr. K. Shaw. Hal Leonard No. 08665421. Piano with optional dixieland combo. Medium.

We—Mancini, arr. Frederickson. Kendor Music No. 4277A. Piano accompaniment. Medium.

When I Fall in Love—Young, arr. Azelton. Hal Leonard No. 07259001. *A cappella.* Medium.

When Sunny Gets Blue—Fisher, arr. Emerson. Jenson No. 403-23304. *A cappella.* Solo (male or female). Moderately difficult.

When the Saints Go Marchin' In—arr. K. Shaw. Hal Leonard No. 08665921. Piano with optional bass, drums, and dixieland combo. Medium.

Woodchoppers' Ball—Merman and Bishop, arr. H. Brooks. Hal Leonard No. 07259075. Piano, bass, and drums. Medium.

You Made Me Love You—Monaco, arr. Puerling. Hal Leonard No. 07359465. Piano, bass, and drums. Moderately difficult.

You're Never Fully Dressed without a Smile—Strouse, arr. Metis. Columbia Pictures Publications No. T6540YC1. Piano, with optional guitar, percussion, and bass. Moderately easy.

CHORAL COLLECTIONS

Whether or not to use choral collections has been a subject of some concern to conductors. One's criterion in arriving at a decision should simply be: Is it possible to use the majority of the selections in the collection? If so, the use of a collection may be a saving to the budget. When it is not feasible to use most of the selections, then it is a better practice to utilize separate octavo publications. Following are particular collections that the author has found useful and that the conductor will want to examine to see if they meet the particular needs of his groups.

Collections for Mixed Voices (SATB, SAB)[3]

A Cappella Singer, The—edited by H. Clough-Leighter.   E. C. Schirmer 1682.   A collection of 30 secular selections, primarily madrigals, from the choral literature of the sixteenth and early seventeenth centuries.   An excellent basic book for madrigal groups.

Carols for Choirs—edited and arranged by Reginald Jacques and David Willcocks.   Oxford University Press.   A collection of 50 Christmas carols, arranged mostly for mixed voices.

Choral Perspective—compiled by Don Malin.   Marks Music Corp.   A cross-section of choral music from the Renaissance to the twentieth century, with compositions representing 18 composers.

Concord Anthem Book, The—compiled and edited by Archibald T. Davison and Henry Wilder Foote.   E. C. Schirmer No. 13 (clothbound).   Contains 40 anthems selected from the choral literature of the sixteenth through the nineteenth centuries.   Music varies in difficulty from easy to moderately difficult.

First Motet Book, A—compiled and edited by Paul Thomas.   Concordia Publishing House.   Contains 17 motets in a variety of styles from the Renaissance to the twentieth century.

Five Centuries of Choral Music—compiled by a committee of teachers in the Los Angeles City High Schools.   William C. Hartshorn, Supervisor in charge.   G. Schirmer, Inc.   A collection of 30 compositions representing various types and styles from the Renaissance to the present.

Golden Age of the Madrigal, The—edited by Alfred Einstein.   G. Schirmer, Inc.   Twelve Italian madrigals for five-part chorus of mixed voices.

Madrigals and Motets of Four Centuries.   Associated Music Publishers.   A Choral songbook of 18 European classics.

Rediscovered Madrigals—edited by Don Malin.   Marks Music Corp.   A collection of sixteenth-century Italian madrigals and French chansons representing seven composers.

Renaissance Choral Music—edited by Don Malin.   Edward B. Marks Music Corp.   A collection of 14 secular choral works from the sixteenth century.   Music is by French, English, German, and Italian composers, with notes on the background of each.

Renaissance to Baroque—edited by Lehman Engel.   Harold Flammer.   A collection, in seven volumes, of choral music from the Renaissance and Baroque periods.   Volume I, French-Netherland Music; Volume II, Italian Music; Volume III, English Music; Volume IV, German Music; Volume V, Spanish Music; Volume VI, English Music; Volume VII, French Music.

Second Concord Anthem Book, The—compiled and edited by Archibald T. Davison and Henry Wilder Foote.   E. C. Schirmer No. 1200 (clothbound).   Contains 40 additional anthems selected from the choral literature of the sixteenth through the nineteenth centuries.   Music varies in difficulty from easy to moderately difficult.

3 to Make Music—Hawley Ades, and edited by Lara Hoggard.   Shawnee Press.   "Three-part songs for girls and boys."   A collection of 32 songs—folk songs, spirituals, patriotic, faith and brotherhood, Christmas and general secular.   Difficulty: easy to medium.

Collections for Treble Voices (SA, SSA, SSAA)

Christmas Carols for Treble Choirs—arranged and edited by Florence M. Martin.   Schmitt, Hall & McCreary, Auditorium Series No. 56 (SA and SSA).   A collection of 15 Christmas carols.   Difficulty: easy to medium.

Glenn Glee Club Book for Girls—edited by Mabelle Glenn and Virginia French.   Oliver Ditson.   A collection of 42 songs for use in junior and senior high schools.

Presser Choral Collection; Sacred and Secular Literature—Past and Present—general editors, Geraldine Healy and William C. Hartshorn.   Theodore Presser Company.   A collection of 40 compositions for treble voices, representing various types and styles of

[3]All collections are for SATB unless otherwise indicated.

choral music, compiled by a committee of choral music teachers in the Los Angeles City Public Schools.

Collections for Male Voices (TB, TTB, TTBB)

Gentlemen Songsters—Livingston Gearhart, edited by Lara Hoggard. Shawnee Press. A collection of 42 songs for boys' glee clubs in two, three, and four parts (TB, TTB, and TTBB). Sea chanties, songs of the American Revolution, ballads, folk songs, classics, songs for Christmas and other special occasions, college songs and novelties, songs of faith and brotherhood, spirituals, and patriotic songs. Difficulty: easy to medium.

EXTENDED CHORAL WORKS

All choral conductors should familiarize themselves with the extended choral works of various composers, for if a conductor is not familiar with major choral works, which in certain instances represent the crowning achievement of a composer, he has only an incomplete picture or concept of choral literature. Although the advanced high school choir could perform some of these works in their entirety, even an advanced choir could not perform certain others because of their overall difficulty. Conductors of college, university, and adult community choruses should examine all these works for possible use by their groups.

AHLE, JOHANN RUDOLF
  Be Not Afraid — Concordia
ANTHEIL, GEORGE
  Cabeza de Vaca — Templeton Pub. Co.
BACH, JOHANN CHRISTOPH
  Childhood of Christ, The — J. Fischer
BACH, JOHANN SEBASTIAN
  Beautify Thyself, My Spirit (Cantata No. 180) — G. Schirmer
  Be Not Afraid (Motet IV) — C. F. Peters
  Christ Lay in Death's Dark Prison (Cantata No. 4) — Breitkopf & Härtel; G. Schirmer
  Christmas Oratorio — G. Schirmer
  Coffee Cantata, The (3-part chorus) — G. Schirmer
  Come, Jesus, Come (Motet V) — H. W. Gray; C. F. Peters
  Come, My Spirit, Come Exalt (Cantata No. 189) — Breitkopf & Härtel
  Come, Thou Lovely Hour (Cantata No. 161) — E. C. Schirmer
  Deck Thyself, My Soul, with Gladness (Cantata No. 180) — E. C. Schirmer
  For As the Rain and Snow from Heaven Fall (Cantata No. 18) — G. Schirmer
  For the Righteous, Wedding Cantata (No. 195) — Breitkopf & Härtel
  For Us a Child Is Born (Cantata No. 142) — Galaxy; Mark Foster
  From Depths of Woe (Cantata No. 38) — E. C. Schirmer
  Gerechten muss das Licht, Dem (Cantata No. 195) — Breitkopf & Härtel
  Gloria in excelsis Deo (Cantata No. 191) — G. Schirmer
  God, the Lord Is Sun and Shield (Cantata No. 79) — G. Schirmer
  God Is My King (Cantata No. 71) — Breitkopf & Härtel
  God's Time Is the Best (Cantata No. 106) — G. Schirmer
  Great David's Lord and Greater Son (Cantata No. 23) — E. C. Schirmer
  Heavens Declare the Glory of God, The (Cantata No. 76) — Breitkopf & Härtel
  Heavens Laugh, the Earth Exults, The (Cantata No. 31) — G. Schirmer

How Brightly Shines Yon Morning Star (Cantata No. 1)	E. C. Schirmer
If Thou Wilt Suffer God To Guide Thee (Cantata No. 93)	G. Schirmer
In God I Place My Faith and Trust (Cantata No. 188)	G. Schirmer
I Suffered with Great Heaviness (Cantata No. 21)	G. Schirmer
It Is Enough (Cantata No. 82)	Breitkopf & Härtel
Jesus, My Great Pleasure (Motet III)	C. F. Peters
Jesus, Thou My Constant Gladness (Cantata No. 147)	H. W. Gray
Jesus, Thou My Wearied Spirit (Cantata No. 78)	G. Schirmer
Kantate	Breitkopf & Härtel
King of Heaven, Come in Triumph (Cantata No. 182)	E. C. Schirmer
Kyrie in D Minor	G. Schirmer
Let Songs of Rejoicing Be Raised (Cantata No. 149)	H. W. Gray
Lord, Enter Not into Wrath (Cantata No. 105)	E. C. Schirmer
Magnificat	Breitkopf & Härtel; C. F. Peters; G. Schirmer
Mass in B Minor	G. Schirmer
Messe No. 4 in G Major	C. F. Peters
Missa Brevis in G	H. W. Gray
My Soul Doth Magnify the Lord (Cantata No. 10)	G. Schirmer
My Soul Exalts the Lord (Cantata No. 10)	E. C. Schirmer
New-Born Babe, The (Cantata No. 122)	G. Schirmer
Now Thank We All Our God (Cantata No. 192)	G. Schirmer
Nun ist das Heil und die Kraft (Cantata No. 50)	Breitkopf & Härtel
O Christ, My All in Living (Cantata No. 95)	Novello
Ode of Mourning (Cantata No. 198)	G. Schirmer
O God, How Grievous (Cantata No. 3)	E. C. Schirmer
O Jesus Christ, My Life and Light (Cantata No. 118)	G. Schirmer
O Light Everlasting (Cantata No. 34)	E. C. Schirmer
O Lord, Relent, I Pray (Cantata No. 135)	E. C. Schirmer
O Lord, This Grieving Spirit (Cantata No. 135)	G. Schirmer
O Praise the Lord for All His Mercies (Cantata No. 28)	H. W. Gray
Out of Darkness Call I Lord to Thee (Cantata No. 131)	Breitkopf & Härtel
Passion According to St. John, The	Breitkopf & Härtel; G. Schirmer
Passion According to St. Mark, The	Chantry Music Press
Passion According to St. Matthew, The	Breitkopf & Härtel; G. Schirmer
Peasant Cantata, The	Paterson's Pub. Ltd.
Praise Him, the Lord, the Almighty King (Cantata No. 137)	Breitkopf & Härtel
Praise Our God in All His Splendor (Cantata No. 11)	G. Schirmer
Praise the Lord, All Ye Nations (Motet VI)	C. F. Peters
Sheep May Safely Graze (Cantata No. 208)	G. Schirmer
Sing Ye to the Lord (Motet I)	C. F. Peters
Sleepers, Wake! (Cantata No. 140)	H. W. Gray
Spirit Also Helpeth Us, The (Motet II)	H. W. Gray; C. F. Peters
Stronghold Sure, A (Cantata No. 80)	G. Schirmer
There Uprose a Great Strife (Cantata No. 19)	G. Schirmer
Thou Guide of Israel (Cantata No. 104)	H. W. Gray
Thou Very God and David's Son (Cantata No. 23)	G. Schirmer
To Us a Child Is Given (Cantata No. 142)	G. Schirmer
Weeping, Crying, Sorrow, Sighing (Cantata No. 12)	G. Schirmer
We Must through Great Tribulations (Cantata No. 146)	G. Schirmer
When Will God Recall My Spirit? (Cantata No. 8)	E. C. Schirmer
BACH, KARL PHILIPP EMANUEL	
Holy Is God	Concordia
Magnificat	G. Schirmer
BARBER, SAMUEL	
Prayers of Kirkegaard	G. Schirmer

BARTÓK, BÉLA
  Cantata Profana   Boosey & Hawkes
  Shepherd's Christmas Songs   Boosey & Hawkes
BEETHOVEN, LUDWIG VAN
  Cantata on the Death of Emperor Joseph II   G. Schirmer
  Choral Fantasia   Edwin F. Kalmus
  Choral Finale to the Ninth Symphony   H. W. Gray; G. Schirmer
  Christ on the Mount of Olives   Edwin F. Kalmus
  Mass in C Major   Edwin F. Kalmus
  Mass in D   Novello
  Missa Solemnis, Op. 123   G. Schirmer
BERGER, JEAN
  Brazilian Psalm   G. Schirmer
  Fiery Furnace, The   G. Schirmer
  Psalm 57   Presser
  Vision of Peace   Broude Bros.
BERLIOZ, HECTOR
  Childhood of Christ   G. Schirmer
  Childhood of Christ (abridged version)   H. W. Gray
  Choral Suite from Benvenuto Cellini   Oxford
  Grand Death Mass, Op. 5   Breitkopf & Härtel
  Requiem   G. Schirmer
  Te Deum   G. Schirmer
BERNSTEIN, LEONARD
  Chichester Psalms   G. Schirmer
  Choruses from The Lark   G. Schirmer
  Kaddish   G. Schirmer
BLITZSTEIN, MARC
  Airborne, The (cantata)   Chappell
BLOCH, ERNEST
  Sacred Service   Broude Bros.
BOITO, ARRIGO
  Prologue in Heaven (from Mefistofele*)*   G. Schirmer
BORODIN, ALEX
  Polovetzian Dance and Chorus (from Prince Igor*)*   G. Schirmer
BRAHMS, JOHANNES
  Love-Song Waltzes (Liebeslieder Walzer)   Associated
  Marienlieder   Breitkopf & Härtel; C. F.
                                                                           Peters; E. C. Schirmer
  Motet from Psalm LI, Op. 29, No. 2   G. Schirmer
  Nänie   G. Schirmer; E. C.
                                                                           Schirmer
  Neue Liebeslieder   Lawson-Gould
  Requiem, Op. 45   Edwin F. Kalmus;
                                                                           G. Schirmer
  Schicksalslied (Song of Destiny)   H. W. Gray; E. C.
                                                                           Schirmer; Belwin Mills
  Triumphal Hymn, Op. 55   G. Schirmer; Kalmus
BRITTEN, BENJAMIN
  Ballad of Heroes   Boosey & Hawkes
  Cantata Misericordium   Boosey & Hawkes
  Ceremony of Carols, A (SATB; SSA)   Boosey & Hawkes
  Festival Te Deum   Boosey & Hawkes
  Hymn to St. Cecilia   Boosey & Hawkes
  Rejoice in the Lamb   Boosey & Hawkes
  Saint Nicolas   Boosey & Hawkes
  Spring Symphony   Boosey & Hawkes
  Voices for Today   G. Schirmer

War Requiem	Boosey & Hawkes
Wedding Anthem, A (Amo, ergo sum)	Boosey & Hawkes
BRUCKNER, ANTON	
Mass in E minor	Broude Bros.
Mass No. 1 in D minor	C. F. Peters
Mass No. 3 in F minor	C. F. Peters
Te Deum laudamus	G. Schirmer; C. F. Peters
BUXTEHUDE, DIETRICH	
Aperite mihi portas justitiae (Open to Me Gates of Justice)	C. F. Peters
Good Christian Men, with Joy Draw Near	Concordia
Jesu, Joy and Treasure	C. F. Peters
Laudia Sion Salvatorem	Chantry Music Press
Missa Brevis	Mercury
Open to Me Gates of Justice	C. F. Peters
Rejoice, Earth and Heaven	C. F. Peters
Sing to God the Lord	Concordia
What Is the World to Me	Concordia
BYRD, WILLIAM	
Magnificat and Nunc dimittis	Oxford
Mass for 5 Voices	Galaxy: Stainer & Bell
Mass for 4 Voices	Galaxy: Stainer & Bell
CALDARA, ANTONIO	
Credo	E. C. Schirmer
CARISSIMI, GIACOMO	
Jephte	Ricordi
CHARPENTIER, MARC-ANTOINE	
Midnight Mass for Christmas	Elkan-Vogel
Venite ad me	G. Schirmer
CHERUBINI, LUIGI	
Requiem in D Minor	C. F. Peters
Requiem Mass in C Minor	G. Schirmer
COLERIDGE-TAYLOR, SAMUEL	
Hiawatha's Wedding Feast	G. Schirmer
COMES, JUAN BAUTISTA	
Beatus vir	G. Schirmer
Lamentación	G. Schirmer
Magnificat	G. Schirmer
COPLAND, AARON	
Canticle of Freedom	Boosey & Hawkes
In the Beginning	Boosey & Hawkes
CRESTON, PAUL	
Celestial Vision, The	Shawnee Press
Isaiah's Prophecy	Franco Colombo
Missa Solemnis, Op. 44	Belwin Mills
DEBUSSY, CLAUDE	
Blessed Damoiselle, The	G. Schirmer
L'Enfant Prodigue	Elkan-Vogel
Ode à la France	Elkan-Vogel
DELIUS, FREDERICK	
Appalachia	Boosey & Hawkes
Mass of Life, A	Universal
Sea Drift	Boosey & Hawkes
Songs of Farewell	Boosey & Hawkes
DELLO JOIO, NORMAN	
Mystic Trumpeter, The	G. Schirmer
Psalm of David, A	Carl Fischer
Psalm of Peace	Edw. B. Marks
Song of Affirmation	Carl Fischer

Song of the Open Road	Carl Fischer
To St. Cecilia	Carl Fischer
Years of the Modern	Edw. B. Marks
DIAMOND, DAVID	
This Sacred Ground	Southern Music
DORATI, ANTAL	
Missa Brevis	Belwin Mills
DUBOIS, THEODORE	
Seven Last Words of Christ, The	G. Schirmer
DURUFLÉ, MAURICE	
Requiem	Durand
DVOŘÁK, ANTON	
Stabat Mater, Op. 58	G. Schirmer
EFFINGER, CECIL	
Invisible Fire, The	H. W. Gray
St. Luke Christmas Story, The	G. Schirmer
Set of Three	Elkan-Vogel
ELGAR, EDWARD	
Dream of Gerontius	Novello
48th Psalm	Novello
29th Psalm	Novello
ETLER, ALVIN	
Ode to Pothos	Associated
FAURÉ, GABRIEL	
Requiem	H. T. Fitzsimons
FETLER, PAUL	
Now This Is the Story (SSA)	Carl Fischer
Te Deum	Augsburg
FOSS, LUKAS	
Parable of Death, A	Carl Fischer
Prairie, The	G. Schirmer
Psalms	Carl Fischer
FRANCK, CÉSAR	
Beatitudes, The (oratorio)	G. Schirmer
Communion Service in A Major, Op. 12.	E. C. Schirmer
GABRIELI, GIOVANNI	
Jubilate Deo	Bourne; G. Schirmer
Timor et tremor	Annie Banks
GALUPPI, BALDASSARE	
Kyrie	Lawson-Gould
GESUALDO, CARLO	
Illumina nos	Boosey & Hawkes
Tres sacrae cantiones	Boosey & Hawkes
GINASTERA, ALBERTO	
Lamentations of Jeremiah, The	Mercury
GOUDIMEL, CLAUDE	
Messe audi filia	Éditions Salabert
GOUNOD, CHARLES	
Gallia	G. Schirmer
Mass in C	G. Schirmer
Messe Solennelle (St. Cecilia)	G. Schirmer
Missa Choralis	E. C. Schirmer
Missa Paschalis	E. C. Schirmer
GRIEG, EDVARD	
Choral Suite	Hinrichsen & Peters
Psalms for Mixed Chorus	C. F. Peters
HAMMERSCHMIDT, ANDREAS	
Holy Is the Lord	Concordia

How Then Shall We Find Bread?   Concordia
Now Death Is Devoured   Concordia
HANDEL, GEORGE FRIDERIC
   Acis and Galatea   Novello
   Alceste   Novello
   Autumn Day, An   Oxford
   Belshazzar   Associated
   Canticle of Praise   G. Schirmer
   Dettingen Te Deum   H. W. Gray
   Foundling Hospital Anthem   C. F. Peters
   Funeral Anthem for Queen Caroline   G. Schirmer
   Israel in Egypt   G. Schirmer
   Joshua   Novello
   Judas Maccabaeus   G. Schirmer
   King Shall Rejoice, The   Novello
   Laudate pueri Dominum (Psalm 112)   C. F. Peters
   Messiah   G. Schirmer
   O Sing unto the Lord (Psalm 96)   G. Schirmer
   Samson   G. Schirmer
   Saul   H. W. Gray
   Sixth Chandos Anthem   G. Schirmer
   Solomon   Breitkopf & Härtel;
        H. W. Gray
   Te Deum laudamus   Verlag Merseburger
   Utrecht Jubilate, The   Breitkopf & Härtel
   Utrecht Te Deum, The   G. Schirmer
HANSON, HOWARD
   Beat! Beat! Drums!   J. Fischer
   Cherubic Hymn, The   Carl Fischer
   Song of Democracy   Carl Fischer
   Song of Human Rights   Carl Fischer
   Songs from Drum Taps   J. Fischer
HARRIS, ROY
   Mass in C (for Male Voices and Organ)   Carl Fischer
HASSLER, HANS LEO
   Mass No. 5   Concordia
   Missa Super "Dixit Maria"   Arista
HAYDN, JOSEPH
   Creation, The   G. Schirmer
   Der Sturm (La Tempesta)   Belwin Mills
   Mass in Time of War   G. Schirmer
   Missa Brevis in F   Doblinger
   Missa Sancti Nicolai   Arista
   Missa Solemnis   C. F. Peters
   Seasons, The   G. Schirmer
   Seven Last Words of Christ, The   G. Schirmer
   Sixteenth Mass   H. W. Gray
   Stabat Mater   G. Schirmer
   Third Mass (The Imperial or Lord Nelson)   G. Schirmer
HAYDN, MICHAEL
   Laudate populi   Breitkopf & Härtel
   Timete Dominum (O Fear the Lord)   G. Schirmer
HINDEMITH, PAUL
   Apparebit repentina dies   Schott
   Four Songs   Schott
   Messe   Schott
   When Lilacs Last in the Door-Yard Bloom'd   Schott

HOLST, GUSTAV
  Coming of Christ, The   G. Schirmer
HONEGGER, ARTHUR
  Cantate de Noël   Éditions Salabert
  Danse des morts, La   Éditions Salabert
  King David   E. C. Schirmer
  Nicholas de Flue   E. C. Schirmer
HOVHANESS, ALAN
  Glory to God   C. F. Peters
  In the Beginning Was the Word   C. F. Peters
  Look toward the Sea   C. F. Peters
  Make a Joyful Noise   C. F. Peters
  30th Ode of Solomon   C. F. Peters
JANEQUIN, CLEMENT
  Messe La Bataille   Éditions Salabert
KODÁLY, ZOLTÁN
  Missa Brevis   Boosey & Hawkes
  Psalmus Hungaricus   Universal
  Te Deum   Universal
KUBIK, GAIL
  Litany and Prayer (TTBB)   Southern Music
  Record of Our Time, A   MCA Music
LASSO, ORLANDI DI
  Missa Puisque j'ay perdu   J. Fischer
LISZT, FRANZ
  Hymn to the Virgin Mary   Lawson-Gould
  XIIIth Psalm, The   G. Schirmer
LOCKWOOD, NORMAND
  Ballad of the North and South, A   Associated
  Carol Fantasy   Associated
  Holy Birth, The   Choral Services
LOTTI, ANTONIO
  Mass VII in the Doric Mode   E. C. Schirmer
LULLY, JEAN BAPTISTE
  Te Deum   Schott
MCDONALD, HARL
  Pioneers, O Pioneers   Elkan-Vogel
  Songs of Conquest   Elkan-Vogel
MACHAUT, GUILLAUME
  Messe Notre-Dame   Éditions Salabert
MCKAY, GEORGE F.
  Choral Rhapsody   J. Fischer
MAHLER, GUSTAV
  VIII. Symphonie   Universal
  Waldmärchen (Forest Legend)   Belwin Mills
MARTIRANO, SALVATORE
  O O O O That Shakespearian Rag   Schott
MENDELSSOHN, FELIX
  As the Hart Pants (42nd Psalm)   G. Schirmer
  Christus   G. Schirmer
  Come Let Us Sing (95th Psalm)   G. Schirmer
  Elijah (oratorio)   G. Schirmer
  First Walpurgis Night, The, Op. 60   G. Schirmer
  Hear My Prayer   Mark Foster; G. Schirmer
  Hymn of Praise   G. Schirmer
  Kyrie   Oxford
  Magnificat   Augsburg

114th Psalm	Novello
St. Paul (oratorio)	G. Schirmer
MENNIN, PETER	
Christmas Story, The	Carl Fischer
Cycle, The (Symphony No. 4)	Carl Fischer
MENOTTI, GIAN CARLO	
Death of the Bishop of Brindisi, The	G. Schirmer
MILHAUD, DARIUS	
Cantate pour louer le Seigneur	Universal
Cantique du Rhône	Elkan-Vogel
Château du Feu, Le	Associated
Miracles of Faith	G. Schirmer
Naissance de Vénus	Heugel
Pan et Syrinx	Éditions Salabert
Three Psalms of David	Associated
MONTEVERDI, CLAUDIO	
Laetatus sum	Mark Foster
Lagrime d'Amante al Sepolcro dill'Amata	Lawson-Gould
Magnificat Primo	Lawson-Gould
MOZART, WOLFGANG A.	
Davidde penitente (K. 459)	Broude Bros.
Glory, Praise and Power	H. W. Gray
Grand Mass in C Minor	G. Schirmer
Litania in E Flat (K. 243)	Edwin F. Kalmus
Mass in C (K. 317, "Coronation")	Breitkopf & Härtel;
	G. Schirmer
Misericordias offertorium de tempore	G. Schirmer
Missa Brevis in C (K. 220)	Associated
Missa Brevis in D (K. 194)	Edw. B. Marks
Missa Brevis in F Major (K. 192)	G. Schirmer
Regina coeli	Lawson-Gould
Requiem Mass	H. W. Gray; C. F. Peters;
	G. Schirmer
Vesperae Solennes de Dominica (K. 321)	E. C. Schirmer
ORFF, CARL	
Carmina Burana	Schott
Catulli Carmina	Schott
Trionfo di Afrodite	Schott
PACHELBEL, JOHANN	
Deus in adjutorium	Edw. B. Marks
Herr ist König, Der	Concordia
Jauchzet dem Herrn (Shout Forth to the Lord)	Concordia
Magnificat in C	Summy-Birchard
PALESTRINA, GIOVANNI	
Assumpta est Maria	Breitkopf & Härtel
Leichte Chore	Breitkopf & Härtel
Missa Aeterna Christi Munera	Arista
Missa Brevis	Breitkopf & Härtel;
	G. Schirmer
Missa Iste Confessor	Breitkopf & Härtel; Edw.
	B. Marks
Missa Papae Marcelli	J. Fischer; G. Schirmer
Missa Tu es Petrus	Breitkopf & Härtel
Pater Noster	Breitkopf & Härtel
Stabat Mater	Belwin Mills; G. Schirmer
PENDERECKI, KRZYSZTOF	
Canticum Canticorum Salomonis (Song of Songs)	Schott
Kosmogonia	Schott

Passion According to St. Luke	Belwin Mills
Utrenja	
Entombment of Christ, The	Schott
Resurrection of Christ, The	
PERGOLESI, GIOVANNI	
Magnificat, The	Walton Music
PERSICHETTI, VINCENT	
Celebrations	Elkan-Vogel
Mass	Elkan-Vogel
Stabat Mater	Elkan-Vogel
PIERNÉ, GABRIEL	
Children at Bethlehem, The	G. Schirmer
PINKHAM, DANIEL	
Ascension Cantata	E. C. Schirmer
Canticle of Praise	E. C. Schirmer
Christmas Cantata	E. C. Schirmer
Daniel in the Lions' Den	E. C. Schirmer
Easter Cantata	C. F. Peters
Emily Dickinson Mosaic, An (SSAA)	C. F. Peters
Fanfares	E. C. Schirmer
Jonah	E. C. Schirmer
Jubilate Deo	E. C. Schirmer
Mass of the Word of God	E. C. Schirmer
Requiem	C. F. Peters
Saint Mark Passion	C. F. Peters
Wedding Cantata	C. F. Peters
POULENC, FRANCIS	
Gloria	Éditions Salabert
Messe en sol majeur	Éditions Salabert
Stabat Mater	Éditions Salabert
PRAETORIUS, MICHAEL	
Canticum trium puerorum	Sam Fox
PROKOFIEFF, SERGE	
Alexander Nevsky	Leeds Music
PUCCINI, GIACOMO	
Gloria (from Messa di Gloria*)*	Lawson-Gould
Messa di Gloria	Belwin Mills
PURCELL, HENRY	
Te Deum laudamus and Jubilate Deo	G. Schirmer
RACHMANINOFF, SERGEI	
The Bells, Op. 35	Kalmus; Boosey & Hawkes (rental)
Springtide	G. Schirmer
RAMíREZ, ARIEL	
Misa Criolla	G. Schirmer
Navidad Nuestra (The Nativity)	G. Schirmer
REIZENSTEIN, FRANZ	
Voices of Night	H. W. Gray
RESPIGHI, OTTORINO	
Laud to the Nativity	Franco Colombo
RIMSKY-KORSAKOV, NIKOLAI	
Polonaise with Chorus	Boosey & Hawkes
ROGERS, BERNARD	
Letter from Pete, A	Southern Music
Prophet Isaiah, The	Southern Music
ROREM, NED	
From an Unknown Past	Southern Music
Two Psalms and a Proverb	E. C. Schirmer

ROSSINI, GIOACCHINO
   Stabat Mater   G. Schirmer
ROZSA, MIKLOS
   To Everything There Is a Season   Broude Bros; Breitkopf
                                             & Härtel

SAINT-SAËNS, CAMILLE
   Christmas Oratorio   G. Schirmer
SCARLATTI, ALESSANDRO
   Salve Regina   Walton
   Te Deum laudamus   Presser
SCHOENBERG, ARNOLD
   De profundis (Psalm 130)   MCA Music
   Gurre-Lieder   Universal
   Kol Nidre   Boelke-Bomart
   Ode to Napoleon (for speaker and string orchestra)   G. Schirmer
   Peace on Earth   Schott
   Survivor of Warsaw, A   Boelke-Bomart
SCHUBERT, FRANZ
   Gesang der Geister über den Wassern (for male voices)   Carl Fischer
   Mass in A-flat   Breitkopf & Härtel;
                                             Novello
   Mass in F   G. Schirmer
   Mass in G   H. W. Gray; G. Schirmer
   Mass No. 3 in B-flat   Arista
   Miriam's Song of Triumph   G. Schirmer
   Rosamunde   G. Schirmer
SCHUMAN, WILLIAM
   Free Song, A   G. Schirmer
   This Is Our Time   Boosey & Hawkes
SCHÜTZ, HEINRICH
   Annunciation According to St. Luke, The   J. Fischer; G. Schirmer
   Christmas Story, The   G. Schirmer
   Deutsches Magnificat   Bärenreiter-Ausgabe
   84th Psalm   G. Schirmer
   German Requiem, A   G. Schirmer
   Magnificat   Breitkopf & Härtel
   Mein Sohn, warum hast du uns das getan?   Oxford
   Nativity   Bärenreiter
   Passion According to St. John, The   Oxford
   St. Luke Passion, The   Oxford
   St. Matthew Passion, The   Augsburg; Breitkopf &
                                             Härtel; Oxford
   Seven Last Words, The   Oxford; G. Schirmer;
                                             E. C. Schirmer
   Symphonia Sacra No. 4   Oxford
SENFL, LUDWIG
   Ave Maria, gratia plena   Associated
   Ich stund an einem Morgen   Lawson-Gould
SHOSTAKOVICH, DIMITRI
   Song of the Forests (cantata)   Leeds
SOWERBY, LEO
   Ark of the Covenant, The   H. W. Gray
   Canticle of the Sun, The   H. W. Gray
   Christ Reborn   H. W. Gray
   Forsaken of Man   H. W. Gray
   Great Is the Lord   H. W. Gray
   Throne of God, The   H. W. Gray

SPOHR, LOUIS
  Mass, Op. 54 — Arista
STAINER, JOHN
  Crucifixion, The — G. Schirmer
  Daughter of Jairus, The (cantata) — G. Schirmer
STEVENS, HALSEY
  Magnificat — Mark Foster
STRAVINSKY, IGOR
  Cantata — Boosey & Hawkes
  Canticum Sacrum — Boosey & Hawkes
  Flood, The — Boosey & Hawkes
  Mass — Boosey & Hawkes
  Noces, Les — Boosey & Hawkes
  Oedipus Rex — Boosey & Hawkes
  Perséphone (ballet with chorus) — Boosey & Hawkes
  Symphony of Psalms — Boosey & Hawkes
  Threni — Boosey & Hawkes
SURINACH, CARLOS
  Cantata of St. John — Associated
SWEELINCK, JAN PIETERSZOON
  Psalm 150 — E. C. Schirmer
TALLIS, THOMAS
  Lamentations (Parts I and II) — Oxford
TELEMANN, GEORG PHILIPP
  Jesu, Joyous Treasure — Augsburg
THOMPSON, RANDALL
  Americana — E. C. Schirmer
  Concord Cantata, A — E. C. Schirmer
  Feast of Praise, A — E. C. Schirmer
  Mass of the Holy Spirit — E. C. Schirmer
  Nativity According to St. Luke — E. C. Schirmer
  Ode to the Virginian Voyage — E. C. Schirmer
  Passion According to St. Luke — E. C. Schirmer
  Peaceable Kingdom, The — E. C. Schirmer
  Place of the Best, The — E. C. Schirmer
  Psalm of Thanksgiving, A — E. C. Schirmer
  Requiem — E. C. Schirmer
  Testament of Freedom — E. C. Schirmer
THOMSON, VIRGIL
  Mass (unison) — G. Schirmer
  Missa pro defunctis — H. W. Gray
VAUGHAN WILLIAMS, RALPH
  Dona nobis pacem — Oxford
  Epithalamion — Oxford
  First Nowell, The — Oxford
  Five Tudor Portraits — Oxford
  Four Songs of the Four Seasons — Oxford
  Hodie — Oxford
  Mass in G Minor — G. Schirmer
  Pilgrim's Journey — Oxford
  Sancta civitas — Oxford; G. Schirmer
  Sea Symphony, A — Galaxy; Oxford; Stainer & Bell
  Serenade to Music — Oxford
  Song of Thanksgiving, A — Oxford
  Thanksgiving for Victory — Oxford
  This Day — Oxford
  Vision of Aeroplanes, A (Motet) — Oxford

VERDI, GIUSEPPE
   Four Sacred Pieces   Franco Colombo
   Requiem   G. Schirmer
   Te Deum   C. F. Peters
VICTORIA, TOMAS LUIS DE
   O magnum mysterium   Associated; J. Fischer &
                                     Bros.
   Missa "O Quam Gloriosum"   Arista
VIERNE, LOUIS
   Solemn Mass   Mark Foster
VIVALDI, ANTONIO
   Chamber Mass   Lawson-Gould
   Gloria   Ricordi
WALTON, WILLIAM
   Belshazzar's Feast   Oxford
   Coronation Te Deum   Oxford
   Gloria   Oxford
   In Honor of the City of London   Oxford
WEBER, CARL MARIA VON
   Mass No. 1 in G   Lawson-Gould
WEBERN, ANTON
   Das Augenlicht, Op. 26   Universal
   Kantate, Op. 29   Universal

MUSIC PUBLISHERS/DISTRIBUTORS[4]

Addington Press (order from Hinshaw Music, Inc.)
Agape (order from Hope Publishing Co.)
Alexandria House, P.O. Box 300, Alexandria, IN 46001
Alfred Publishing Co., 15335 Morrison St., P.O. Box 5964, Sherman Oaks, CA 91413
American Composers Alliance, 170 W. 74th St., New York, NY 10023
Arista Music Co., Box 1596, Brooklyn, NY 11201
Art Masters Studios, Inc., 2614 Nicollet Ave., Minneapolis, MN 55408-1696
Associated Music Publishers, Inc., 24 E. 22nd St., New York, NY 10010 (order from Hal
    Leonard Publishing Corp.)
Augsburg Publishing House, 426 S. Fifth St., Box 1209, Minneapolis, MN 55440
Bärenreiter Music Publishers (order from Foreign Music Distributors)
Beckenhorst Press, P.O. Box 14273, Columbus, OH 43214
Belmont Music Publishers, P.O. Box 231, Pacific Palisades, CA 90272
Belwin Mills Publishing Corp., 15800 N.W. 48th Ave., P.O. Box 4340, Miami, FL
    33014-9969
Irving Berlin Music Corp., 1290 Avenue of the Americas, New York, NY 10104
Big 3 Music Corp. (order from Belwin Mills Publishing Corp.)
Birch Tree Group, Ltd., P.O. Box 2072, Princeton, NJ 08540
Boelke-Bomart, Inc., and Mobart Music Publications (order from Jerona Music Corp.)
Boosey & Hawkes, Inc., 200 Smith St., Farmingdale, NY 11735
Boston Music Company, 116 Boylston St., Boston, MA 02116

---

    [4]As in any business, publishers may change addresses or make new arrangements for the sales and distribution of their music. Generally, music dealers are aware of these changes; however, choral directors desiring reasonably up-to-date information may request a copy of the latest *Music Publishers Sales Agency List*, available from the Music Publishers' Association of the United States, 130 W. 57th Street, New York, NY 10019.

Bote & Bock Musikverlag (order from Hal Leonard Publishing Corp.)
Bourne Company, 5 W. 37th St., New York, NY 10018
Breitkopf & Härtel (order from Associated Music Publishers)
Broadman Press, 127 Ninth Ave. N., Nashville, TN 37234
Broude Brothers, Ltd., 141 White Oaks Rd., Williamstown, MA 01267
Cambiata Press, P.O. Box 1151, Conway, AR 72032 (order from The Kendale Company)
Carus-Verlag, Stuttgart (order from Mark Foster Music Co.)
Chantry Music Press, 32 N. Center St., P.O. Box 1101, Springfield, OH 45501
Chappell Music Co. (order from Hal Leonard Publishing Corp.)
Charter Publications, P.O. Box 850, Valley Forge, PA 19482
Cherry Lane Music Co., Inc., 110 Midland Ave., Port Chester, NY 10573 (order from
   Alfred Publishing Co.)
John Church Company (order from Theodore Presser Co.)
Franco Colombo Publications (order from Belwin Mills Publishing Corp.)
Columbia Pictures Publications, 15800 N.W. 48th Ave., P.O. Box 4340, Miami, FL
   33014-9969
Concordia Publishing House, 3558 S. Jefferson Ave., St. Louis, MO 63118
Consolidated Music Publishers, Inc. (order from Music Sales Corp.)
Continuo Music Press (see Tetra/Continuo Music Group)
Coronet Press (order from Theodore Presser Co.)
Creative World Music Publications (order from Jenson Publications)
Curtis Music Press (order from Neil A. Kjos Music Co.)
J. Curwen & Sons (order from Hal Leonard Publishing Corp.)
Dartmouth Collegium Musicum (order from Shawnee Press, Inc.)
Roger Dean Publishing Company (order from The Lorenz Corporation)
Oliver Ditson (order from Theodore Presser Co.)
Editio Musica, Budapest, Hungary (order from Boosey & Hawkes, Inc.)
Edition Musicus, P.O. Box 1341, Stamford, CT 06904
Éditions Salabert (order from Hal Leonard Publishing Corp.)
Edizione Suvini Zerboni, Milan, Italy (order from Boosey & Hawkes, Inc.)
Elkan-Vogel, Inc. (order from Theodore Presser Co.)
European American Music Distributors Corp., P.O. Box 850, Valley Forge, PA 19482
The Evangel Press (order from Art Masters Studios, Inc.)
Fine Arts Music Press (order from Alexandria House)
Carl Fischer, Inc., 62 Cooper Sq., New York, NY 10003
J. Fischer & Bros. (order from Belwin Mills Publishing Corp.)
H. T. Fitzsimons Co., Box 333, Tarzana, CA 91356 (order from Alexandria House)
Harold Flammer, Inc. (order from Shawnee Press, Inc.)
Foreign Music Distributors, 305 Bloomfield Ave., Nutley, NJ 07110
Fortress Press, 2900 Queen Lane, Philadelphia, PA 19129
Mark Foster Music Company, Box 4012, Champaign, IL 61820
Sam Fox Music Sales Corp. (order from Plymouth Music Co., Inc.)
Frank Music Corp. (order from Hal Leonard Publishing Corp.)
Galaxy Music Corporation (order from E. C. Schirmer Music Co.)
Galleon Press (order from Plymouth Music Co., Inc.)
Gene Gabriel Publications, Ltd., P.O. Box 1959, Cathedral Station, New York, NY 10025
Genesis III Music Corp. (order from Plymouth Music Company, Inc.)
Gentry Publications, 18345 Ventura Blvd., P.O. Box 333, Tarzana, CA 91356
G.I.A. Publications, 7404 S. Mason Ave., Chicago, IL 60638
Glory-Sound (order from Shawnee Press, Inc.)
H. W. Gray Company, Inc. (order from Belwin Mills Publishing Corp.)
Dick Grove Publications (order from Alfred Publishing Co.)
Hansen House, 1870 West Avenue, Miami Beach, FL 33139
T. B. Harms Co. (order from Cherry Lane Music Co., Inc.)
The Frederick Harris Music Co., Ltd., 529 Speers Blvd., Oakville, Ontario, Canada
   L6K 2G4 (in the U.S. order from Carl Fischer, Inc.)
Heritage Music Press (order from The Lorenz Corporation)

Heugel and Cie (order from Theodore Presser Co.)
Hinrichsen Edition (order from C. F. Peters Corp.)
Hinshaw Music, Inc., P.O. Box 470, Chapel Hill, NC 27514-0470
The Raymond A. Hoffman Co. (order from Alexandria House)
Charles W. Homeyer & Co. (order from Carl Fischer, Inc.)
Hope Publishing Co., 380 S. Main Place, Carol Stream, IL 60188
Ione Press (order from E. C. Schirmer Music Co.)
Jenson Publications, Inc., 2770 South 171st St., P.O. Box 278, New Berlin, WI 53151-0248
Jerona Music Corp., P.O. Box 5010, Hackensack, NJ 07606-4210
Kalmus Music (order from Belwin Mills Publishing Corp.)
Kenbridge Music (order from Jerona Music Corp.)
The Kendale Company, 6595 South Dayton, Englewood, CO 80111
Kendor Music, Inc., P.O. Box 278, Delevan, NY 14042
E. C. Kerby, Ltd., P.O. Box 5010, Hackensack, NJ 07606-4210
Neil A. Kjos Music Co., 4382 Jutland Cr., P.O. Box 178270, San Diego, CA
    92117-0894
Laurel Press (order from The Lorenz Corp.)
Lawson-Gould Music Publishers, Inc., 250 W. 57th Street, Suite 932, New York, NY 10107
    (order from Alfred Publishing Co.)
Hal Leonard Publishing Corp., 8112 W. Bluemound Rd., Milwaukee, WI 53213
The Lorenz Corporation, 501 E. Third St., Dayton, OH 45401
Don McAfee (order from Belwin Mills Publishing Corp.)
McLaughlin & Reilly Company (order from Birch Tree Group, Ltd.)
Manna Music, Inc. (order from Alexandria House)
Margun Music, Inc., 168 Dudley Rd., Newton Centre, MA 01259
Edward B. Marks Music Company (order from Hal Leonard Publishing Corp.)
MCA Music, Universal City Plaza, Universal City, CA 91608 (order from Hal Leonard
    Publishing Corp.)
Mercury Music Corp. (order from Theodore Presser Co.)
Merion Music Corp. (order from Theodore Presser Co.)
Edwin H. Morris & Co., Inc. (order from Hal Leonard Publishing Corp.)
Mosaic Music Co. (order from Boston Music Co.)
Musical Comedy Productions, Inc. (order from Plymouth Music Co., Inc.)
Music Press (order from Theodore Presser Co.)
Music Sales Corp., 5 Bellvale Rd., Box 572, Chester, NY 10918
Music 70 Publishers, 170 N.E. 33rd St., Ft. Lauderdale, FL 33334
National Music Publishers, 1326 Santa Ana, P.O. Box 8279, Anaheim, CA 92802
Nova Editions (order from E. C. Schirmer Music Co.)
Novello Publications (order from Theodore Presser Co.)
Orpheus Music Co. (order from Plymouth Music Co., Inc.)
Oxford University Press, 200 Madison Ave., New York, NY 10016
Patterson's Pub., Ltd. (order from Carl Fischer, Inc.)
Paull Pioneer Publications (order from Shawnee Press, Inc.)
J. W. Pepper & Son, Inc., P.O. Box 850, Valley Forge, PA 19482
C. F. Peters Corp., 373 Park Ave. South, New York, NY 10016
Hal Peterson Music Publications, 3250 Keller St., No. 10, Santa Clara, CA 95054
Plymouth Music Co., Inc., 170 NE 33rd St., P.O. Box 24330, Ft. Lauderdale, FL 33307
Theodore Presser Co., Presser Place, Bryn Mawr, PA 19010
Pro-Art Publications (order from Belwin Mills Publishing Corp.)
The Richmond Organization, 11 W. 19th St., New York, NY 10011 (order from Plymouth
    Music Co., Inc.)
G. Ricordi & Co. (order from Hal Leonard Publishing Corp.)
Robbins Music (order from Columbia Pictures Publications)
Rongwen Music (order from Broude Brothers, Ltd.)
R. D. Row Music Co. (order from Carl Fisher, Inc.)
Sacred Music Press (order from The Lorenz Corp.)
E. C. Schirmer Music Co., 138 Ipswich St., Boston, MA 02215

G. Schirmer, Inc., 24 E. 22nd St., New York, NY 10010 (order from Hal Leonard Publishing Corp.)
Arthur P. Schmidt Co. (order from Birch Tree Group, Ltd.)
Schmitt, Hall & McCreary (order from Belwin Mills Publishing Corp.)
Schott & Company (order from European American Music Distributors Corp.)
Scott Music Publications (order from Alfred Publishing Co.)
The Shapiro, Bernstein Organization (order from Plymouth Music Co., Inc.)
Shawnee Press, Inc., Waring Drive, Delaware Water Gap, PA 18327-1099
John Sheppard Music Press, P.O. Box 6784, Denver, CO 80206
Somerset Press (order from Hope Publishing Co.)
Southern Music Co., 1100 Broadway, P.O. Box 329, San Antonio, TX 78292
Spratt Music Publishers (order from Plymouth Music Co., Inc.)
Staff Music Publishing Co., Inc. (order from Plymouth Music Co., Inc.)
Stainer & Bell, Ltd. (order from E. C. Schirmer Music Co.)
Studio 4 (order from Alfred Publishing Co.)
Studio P/R, Inc. (order from Belwin Mills Publishing Corp.)
Summa Productions (order from Art Masters Studio, Inc.)
Summy-Birchard Co. (order from Birch Tree Group, Ltd.)
Templeton Publications (order from Shawnee Press, Inc.)
Tetra/Continuo Music Group (order from Plymouth Music Co., Inc.)
Thomas House Publications, P.O. Box 6023, Concord, CA 94524
Gordon V. Thompson Music, 29 Birch Ave., Toronto, Ontario, Canada M4V 1E2 (order from Hal Leonard Publishing Corp.)
Transcontinental Music Publications, 838 Fifth Ave., New York, NY 10021
Triune Music, Inc. (order from The Lorenz Corp.)
Tuskegee Music Press (order from Neil A. Kjos Music Co.)
UNC Jazz Press, College of Performing and Visual Arts, School of Music, Jazz Studies Division, Greeley, CO 80639
Universal Edition (order from European American Music Distributors Corp.)
Walton Music Corp. (order from Plymouth Music Co., Inc.)
Warner Bros. Publications, 265 Secaucus Road, Secaucus, NJ 07094 (order from Jenson Publications, Inc.)
Joseph Weinberger, Ltd., London (order from Boosey & Hawkes, Inc.)
Williamson Music (order from Hal Leonard Publishing Corp.)
Willis Music Co., 7380 Industrial Rd., Florence, KY 41042
M. Witmark (see Warner Bros. Publications)
Word, Inc., P.O. Box 1790, Waco, TX 76710
World Library Publications, 3815 N. Willow Rd., P.O. Box 2701, Schiller Park, IL 60176
The Zondervan Music Group, 365 Great Circle Rd., Nashville, TN 37228

MANUFACTURERS OF MUSIC EQUIPMENT

In general, choral directors will find that local dealers can meet their particular music equipment needs, especially as they pertain to audiovisual equipment, pianos, and storage cabinets. In the event that certain equipment is not available through local firms, directors should contact the manufacturer directly for general information, including exact specifications and prices, as well as the name and address of the nearest dealer or company representative. Upon request, most companies will send catalogs as well as other pertinent information. The names of various companies and their addresses follow.

AUDIOVISUAL EQUIPMENT[5]

Microphones

AKG Acoustics, Inc., 77 Selleck St., Stamford, CT 06902
Electro-Voice, Inc., 600 Cecil St., Buchanan, MI 49107
Gotham Audio Corp., 1790 Broadway, New York, NY 10019-1412
Peavey Electronics Corp., P.O. Box 2898, Meridian, MS 39301
Shure Brothers, Inc., 222 Hartrey Ave., Evanston, IL 60204-3696
Telex Communications, Inc., 9600 Aldrich Ave., S., Minneapolis, MN 55420

Motion Picture Projectors (16 mm)

Atlantic Audio-Visual Corp., 630 Ninth Ave., New York, NY 10036
Eastman Kodak Co., 343 State St., Rochester, NY 14650
Eiki International, Inc., 27882 Camino Capistrano, Laguna Niguel, CA 92677
Elmo Mfg. Corp., 70 New Hyde Park Rd., New Hyde Park, NY 11040
Hokushin Rangertone, 115 Roosevelt Ave., Belleville, NJ 07109
International Audio-Visual, P.O. Box 1096, Coquitlam, British Columbia, Canada V3J6Z4
International Cinema Equipment Co., 6750 NE Fourth Court, Miami, FL 33138
Kalart Victor Corp., Hultenius St., Plainville, CT 06062
Lafayette Instrument Co., P.O. Box 5729, Lafayette, IN 47903
Radmar, Inc., 1263B Rand Rd., Des Plaines, IL 60016
Telex Communications, Inc., 9600 Aldrich Ave. S., Minneapolis, MN 55420
Visual Instrumentation Corp., 903 N. Victory Blvd., Burbank, CA 91502

Record Players

Audiotronics Corp., P.O. Box 3997, 7428 Bellaire Ave., North Hollywood, CA 91609
Audio-Visual Devices, 99 Washington St., East Orange, NJ 07017
AVAS Corporation, 196 Holt St., Hackensack, NJ 07602
Califone International, Inc., 21300 Superior St., Los Angeles, CA 91311-4312
Dealers Audio-Visual Supply Corp., 1 Madison St., P.O. Box 105, East Rutherford, NJ
    07072
Hamilton Electronics Corp., 2003 W. Fulton St., Chicago, IL 60612
Radio-Matic of America, P.O. Box 250, Maplewood, NJ 07040

Tape Recorders

Gotham Audio Corp., 1790 Broadway, New York, NY 10019-1412
Otari Corp., 2 Davis Drive, Belmont, CA 94002
Studer Revox America, Inc., 1426 Elm Hill Pike, Nashville, TN 37210
Tandberg of America, Inc., Labriola Court, Armonk, NY 10504
TEAC Corp. of America, P.O. Box 750, 7733 Telegraph Rd., Montebello, CA 90640
Telex Communications, Inc., 9600 Aldrich Ave. S, Minneapolis, MN 55420

Video Equipment

JVC Industries, 41 Slater Dr., Elmwood Park, NJ 07407
Olympus Corporation, 32A Kinderkamack Rd., Oradell, NJ 07639
Panasonic Industrial Co., Video Systems Division, Matsushita Electric Corp. of America,
    One Panasonic Way, Secaucus, NJ 07094
Sharp Electronics Corp., 10 Sharp Plaza, P.O. Box 588, Paramus, NJ 07652
Sony Corp. of America, Sony Dr., Park Ridge, NJ 07656

---

[5]For descriptions and prices of audiovisual equipment, see *The Equipment Directory of Audio-Visual, Computer, and Video Products,* published by NAVA, the International Communications Industries Association, 3150 Spring St., Fairfax, Virginia 22031, and available in many school audiovisual departments.

ACOUSTICAL SHELLS

Stage Engineering International Ltd., 325 Karen La., Colorado Springs, CO 80907
Wenger Corp., 555 Park Dr., Owatonna, MN 55060

CHOIR APPAREL

Ascot Formal Wear, 7807 South Main, Houston, TX 77030
Bettina Uniform Co., 715 E. Armour Rd., 3rd. Flr., North Kansas City, MO 64116
Collegiate Cap & Gown Co., 1000 N. Market St., Champaign, IL 61820
Colorifics, P.O. Box 329, Worthington, OH 43085
Formal Fashions, Inc., 1500 W. Drake, Tempe, AZ 85283
Ireland Needlecraft, 4216 San Fernando Rd., Glendale, CA 91204
Lyric Choir Gown Co., P.O. Box 16954-AZ, Jacksonville, FL 32216
Masters Professional Performers Service, 315 Federal Plaza, W., Youngstown, OH 44503
E. R. Moore Co., 5555 W. Howard, Skokie, IL 60017
Oak Hall Choir Robe Company, 840 Union St., Salem, VA 24153
Regency Cap & Gown Co., P.O. Box 10557CJ, Jacksonville, FL 32207
Southeastern Apparel, Inc., P.O. Box 6942, 142 Woodburn Dr., Dothan, AL 36302
Tuxedo Wholesaler, 7750 E. Redfield Rd., Scottsdale, AZ 85260
Uniformals, 940 West 19th St., Hialeah, FL 33010

CHOIR RISERS

Humes & Berg Mfg. Co., Inc., 4801 Railroad Ave., East Chicago, IN 46312
Mitchell Mfg. Co., 2740 S. 34th St., Milwaukee, WI 53215
Peery Products Co., P.O. Box 22434, Portland, OR 97222
Wenger Corp., 555 Park Dr., Owatonna, MN 55060

MUSIC STANDS

King Musical Instruments Corp., 33999 Curtis Blvd., Eastlake, OH 44094
Selmer Company, The, P.O. Box 310, Elkhart, IN 46515
Wenger Corp., 555 Park Dr., Owatonna, MN 55060

PIANOS

Baldwin Piano & Organ Co., 422 Wards Corner Rd., Loveland, OH 45140-8390
Everett Piano Co., 6600 Orangethorpe Ave., Buena Park, CA 90622
Steinway & Sons, Steinway Pl., Long Island City, NY 11105
Story & Clark Piano Co., 825 E. 26th St., La Grange Park, IL 60525
Walter Piano Co., 700 W. Beardsly Ave., Elkhart, IN 46514
Wurlitzer Co., 403 East Gurler Rd., DeKalb, IL 60115
Yamaha International Corp., 6600 Orangethorpe Ave., Buena Park, CA 90622
Young Chang America, Inc., 13336 Alondra Blvd., Cerritos, CA 90701

SAFETY CANDLES (Battery Operated)

Gamble Music Co., 312 South Wabash Ave., Chicago, IL 60604
Strayline Products Co., 336 Putnam Ave., P.O. Box 4124, Hamden, CT 06514

STORAGE CABINETS

All-Steel, Inc., P.O. Box 871, Aurora, IL 60507
Gamble Music Co., 312 South Wabash Ave., Chicago, IL 60604
Humes and Berg Mfg. Co., Inc., 4801 Railroad Ave., East Chicago, IN 46312
Lyon Metal Products, Inc., Box 671, Aurora, IL 60507
Norren Mfg. Inc., 778 N. Georgia Ave., Azusa, CA 91702
Wenger Corp., 555 Park Dr., Owatonna, MN 55060

HAND SIGNALS FOR TELEVISION

Stand by. *Arm bent. Hand up and open.*

Cue for "on the air." *Arm bent. Full arm motion with forefinger pointing to speaker.*

Time signals: 1. One minute. *Upright extended forefinger.*

2. One-half minute. *Crooked forefinger.*

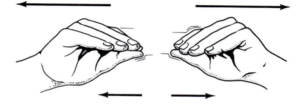

3. Stretch. *Motion like pulling taffy (with finger-tips close together).*

4. Speed up. *Extended fore-finger, spun around . . . slow or fast, accordingly.*

5. Time is up. *Clenched fist. Given at 10 seconds, to allow speaker to complete thought.*

Cut. *Slashing motion of hand across throat.*

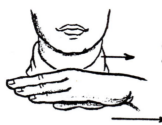

"On the air" camera. *Arm fully extended, forefinger pointing to camera.*

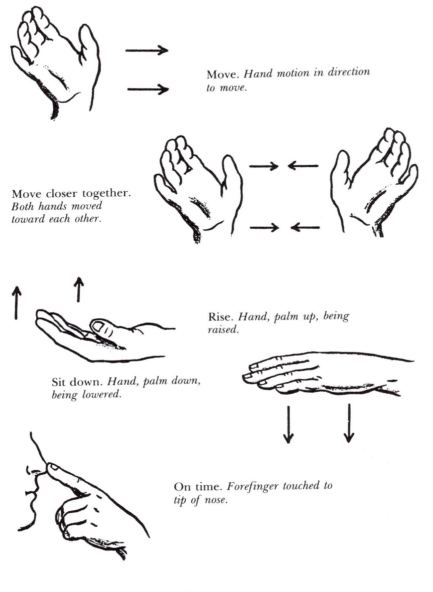

Move. *Hand motion in direction to move.*

Move closer together. *Both hands moved toward each other.*

Rise. *Hand, palm up, being raised.*

Sit down. *Hand, palm down, being lowered.*

On time. *Forefinger touched to tip of nose.*

Spot signal. *Forefinger pointed to palm of other hand.*

Station break. *Both hands clenched, with breaking motion.*

Repeat. *Windmill movement of entire arm. Used only for musical numbers.*

(*Note:* All time signals are indicated with the right hand. All other movements, etc., are indicated with the left hand.)

Index